MW01248914

Guide To

LIMITED
LIABILITY
COMPANIES

Ninth Edition

CCH Editorial Staff Publication

Editorial Staff

Editors . . . . Tom Cody, J.D., LL.M., M.B.A., Dem A. Hopkins, J.D. and
Lawrence A. Perlman, C.P.A., J.D., LL.M.

Production . . . . Linda L. Kalteux

ISBN 978-0-8080-1784-4

Printed in the United States of America

Preface

Business and tax planners have long sought an entity that delivers the key advantages of passthrough taxation for the business and limited liability for its owners. Traditionally, the S corporation and the limited partnership have been used to obtain these important benefits, but both possess significant drawbacks. The S corporation is subject to several eligibility requirements and the limited partnership leaves the general partner personally liable. With limited liability company (LLC) statutes now in place in all 50 states and in the District of Columbia, and with the 1996 release of the federal entity classification rules (the "check-the-box" regulations), entrepreneurs and their business and tax advisers have relatively easy access to a business entity that provides the best attributes of both corporations and partnerships, with few of their disadvantages.

The *Guide to Limited Liability Companies*, currently in its ninth edition, addresses numerous questions faced by business and tax professionals regarding the formation, operation and termination of an LLC. In this invaluable resource, readers will find insightful explanations and key practice tools (for example, a model articles of organization and a model operating agreement) for organizing, operating, and dissolving an LLC.

The *Guide* first compares and contrasts the LLC with the more traditional business structures and suggests certain strategic uses for this novel entity. Subsequently, the *Guide* looks at the assorted issues surrounding the formation, operation, and termination of an LLC, answering questions when answers are available. Currently, some questions cannot be answered until the applicable administrative, legislative, and judicial authorities squarely confront them. The *Guide* then explores the sometimes complex and uncertain tax ramifications of operating as an LLC, analyzing, among other important topics, the impact of the check-the-box regulations, single-member entities, entity reclassifications due to numerical membership changes, application of the at-risk rules and the controversial self-employment tax regulations. The *Guide* further examines the use of an LLC in family estate planning and addresses the role of foreign LLCs, professional LLCs and even limited liability partnerships. Finally, the *Guide* discusses the latest state developments and provides a synopsis of every state's LLC act (including the District of Columbia).

The widespread availability of the LLC as an entity choice is perhaps the most significant development in many years for those planning to form and operate a small or medium-sized business, as well as for those business and tax professionals who must advise these entrepreneurs. With this book, CCH customers have a clear, concise, practical and up-to-date guide that will enable them to prudently take advantage of the numerous benefits attributable to the LLC.

October 2007

Table of Contents

viii

Appendices

Chapter 1

LLCs: The Emerging Business Entity

¶ 101
LLCs as a Business Alternative

Business and tax planners have long sought a business entity that delivers the key advantages of passthrough taxation for the business and limited liability for its owners. Until the late 1980s, S corporations and limited partnerships were drawn upon in order to obtain these beneficial characteristics for a business or investment.

However, both S corporations and limited partnerships have some drawbacks. Even though restrictions were relaxed with the Small Business Job Protection Act of 1996,[1] and the American Jobs Creation Act of 2004,[2] S corporations, a creature of the federal tax law, still have relatively restrictive and inflexible requirements on the number of owners and types of ownership. Limited partnerships do not provide 100-percent limited liability since at least one general partner must be responsible for entity obligations under state law (although this drawback can be avoided somewhat by using a corporate general partner). In addition, the management participation of limited partners is generally prohibited or severely restricted.

Against this backdrop, another alternative emerged—the limited liability company (LLC). An LLC is a hybrid entity that combines the most favorable features of both partnerships and corporations. It allows:

(1) complete passthrough tax advantages and the operational flexibility of a partnership;

(2) corporation-style limited liability under state law; and

(3) management participation by all members, if desired.

Many of the concerns regarding LLCs are diminishing as businesses and tax planners become more familiar with this entity form. Nonetheless, some practitioners are still apprehensive about organizing

---

[1] P.L. 104-188.   [2] P.L. 108-357.

LLCs, primarily due to the fact that there is not a great deal of case law on this relatively new arrival. However, the Internal Revenue Service (IRS) and the Treasury Department paved the way for wider acceptance of the LLC with federal entity classification regulations.[3] A detailed discussion of these regulations, commonly known as the check-the-box regulations, appears in Chapter 9. Additionally, all 50 states, plus the District of Columbia, now have laws providing for the formation and operation of LLCs.

¶ 102
LLCs in a Nutshell

An LLC is a legal entity created under state law. The LLC is an entity separate from its owners. It may own property, incur debts, enter into contracts, and sue or be sued. Members are shielded from the entity's liabilities. In professional LLCs, members are shielded from the negligent acts and omissions of their fellow members; they are not, however, relieved of liability for their own misdeeds or negligence. Professional LLCs are discussed in greater detail in Chapter 8.

To form an LLC, articles of organization are filed with the state. To do business outside of the state of formation, LLCs generally must apply with the host state for a certificate of authority to transact business as a foreign LLC. An operating agreement generally governs the LLC's operations and the rights and duties of its members.

Since the IRS issued its check-the-box regulations,[4] many states have modified their LLC statutes to permit more flexibility.

LLC members are usually vested with management authority under state law. This authority is similar to that of a general partner. The management function may be delegated by the members to a select group of managers, who may or may not be members.

Although restrictions are often placed on the transfer of LLC membership interests, transferability rules have also relaxed in the time since the check-the-box regulations were issued. State statutes typically require either unanimous or majority consent for a transferee to become a member, unless otherwise provided. Many states allow the individual LLC to determine its own rules for the transfer of membership interests, either in the articles of organization or in the operating agreement. This characteristic meets the needs of small businesses which are most likely to use the LLC form.

In the wake of check-the-box, more and more states permit LLCs to have perpetual lifespans. Previously, in order to avoid the unfavorable corporation classification for federal tax purposes, state LLC statutes required that LLCs dissolve after a given time period or after a

[3] T.D. 8697. Reg. §§301.7701-1, 301.7701-2 and 301.7701-3.

[4] T.D. 8697. Reg. §§301.7701-1, 301.7701-2 and 301.7701-3.

member's interest terminated. Many state laws and LLC operating agreements provide that remaining members may continue the business after a member withdraws or a member's interest is otherwise terminated.

Since most LLCs want to be classified as partnerships for federal tax purposes, they will file IRS Form 1065, *U.S. Partnership Return of Income,* for federal tax purposes and the corresponding partnership form in most states. Similarly, LLC members generally are treated as partners for tax purposes. Single-member LLCs may **not** file a partnership return. If an LLC wants to file as a corporation Form 8832 must be files, see Chapter 9 for details.

¶ 103

Explosion in LLC Statutes

Until 1990, only two states, Wyoming and Florida, allowed the formation of an LLC. The major obstacle to further expansion of the LLC as a business entity was uncertainty about the tax treatment. Clearly, each state could control how LLCs would be treated for state tax purposes, but would LLCs be treated by the IRS as partnerships or corporations?

In late 1988, the IRS ruled that any Wyoming LLC would be treated as a partnership.[5] This opened the door for other states to begin considering LLC legislation. Taxing LLCs as partnerships is *the* key reason for the rush among states to enact LLC legislation. This is evidenced by the growth in LLC states since the IRS's 1988 ruling.

LLC Growth (1989—present)

1989	2 states
1990	4 states
1991	8 states
1992	18 states
1993	36 states
1994	46 states & District of Columbia
1995	48 states & District of Columbia
1996	49 states & District of Columbia
1997	50 states & District of Columbia

[5] Rev. Rul. 88-76, 1988-2 CB 360, obsoleted by Rev. Rul. 98-37, 1998-1 CB 1269.

All U.S. jurisdictions have now enacted LLC legislation, as Hawaii's LLC Act became the last state LLC statute to take effect. A state-by-state treatment of LLCs is presented in Chapter 10.

Another indication of growing LLC popularity is that federal agencies in addition to the IRS have found it necessary to formalize their treatment of these entities, see ¶ 106. The Federal Trade Commission (FTC), the Federal Election Commission (FEC), the Department of Agriculture (USDA) and the Small Business Administration (SBA) have all taken action on this matter.

¶ 104

LLCs Are an International Entity

LLCs are a relatively new phenomenon in the United States, but many foreign countries have had entities with the essential LLC characteristics for decades: the *GmbH* in Germany, the *SARL* in France and the *limitada* throughout Central and South America. The LLC entity now being embraced in the United States is modeled on these predecessors.

¶ 105

Model Acts

As states adopted LLC statutes and LLCs became more common, the need for uniform legislation became apparent. In response to this need, the Uniform Limited Liability Company Act (ULLCA) was adopted by the National Conference of Commissioners on Uniform State Laws at its annual meeting in August 1994. ULLCA was subsequently amended to conform to relevant and consequential IRS announcements.[6] Many states have looked at ULLCA to make amendments to existing statutes. Some states have adopted ULLCA with few moderations, while other states have relied less on ULLCA.

ULLCA is flexible. A majority of its provisions may be modified by LLC members in a private agreement, such as the LLC's operating agreement. The Act is designed with default rules, however, so that small entrepreneurs may operate LLCs without complex agreements. These default provisions allow at-will dissolution, rather than a term of years. Additionally, unless otherwise provided, LLCs organized according to ULLCA are member-managed.[7] ULLCA also permits single-member LLCs.[8]

---

[6] Uniform Limited Liability Company Act (1996), prefatory note.

[7] Uniform Limited Liability Company Act (1996), prefatory note.

[8] Uniform Limited Liability Company Act (1996), § 202(a).

¶ 106

Federal Agency Guidelines

As LLCs gained popularity, federal agencies other than the IRS have found it necessary to formalize their treatment of these entities. Agencies that have specifically set policy in this regard are the Federal Trade Commission (FTC), the Federal Election Commission (FEC), the Department of Agriculture (USDA), the Small Business Administration (SBA) and the Federal Deposit Insurance Corporation (FDIC). See ¶ 402 for a discussion of FTC guidelines and ¶ 411 for FEC guidelines.

Chapter 2

Choice of Entity Considerations

¶ 201

Choice of Entity—Overview

No single form of business entity is ideal for all businesses in all situations. Instead, entrepreneurs and their business and tax professionals must evaluate any number of important factors, both financial and personal, when determining the most appropriate entity through which to conduct a business. However, despite the many variables that can come into play, generally, the two most significant factors remain: (1) the owner's liability for business obligations; and (2) the impact of the federal, state, and local income tax laws.

In the United States, there are a number of business entity choices available to an entrepreneur:

(1) the sole proprietorship;

(2) the general partnership;

(3) the limited partnership;

(4) the limited liability partnership (LLP);

(5) the limited liability limited partnership (LLLP);

(6) the C corporation;

(7) the S corporation; and

(8) the limited liability company (LLC).

Oftentimes, certain business and tax considerations might suggest that a combination of these entities may be most desirable for a particular enterprise. Accordingly, an awareness and an understanding of these entities and their various business and tax characteristics are essential when selecting the most appropriate business vehicle for a specific commercial pursuit.

Liability Concerns

Almost every business operation is exposed to both contractual and tort liability. Accordingly, any business owner with any amount of wealth outside of the business will understandably try to protect his or her personal assets from any potential creditors of the business. Consequently, those business formats that provide the business owner with "limited liability" are held in high regard. With the attribute of limited liability, an entrepreneur can lose no more than the amount that he or she has invested (or has promised to invest) in the business. The corporate entities, the limited partnership entities and the LLC, all provide this beneficial protection to varying degrees.[1]

Tax Concerns

"Passthrough" vehicles often afford the most favorable tax outcomes for business owners. With entities like the sole proprietorship, all of the partnership entities, the S corporation and the LLC, any income, loss, deduction and credit attributable to the business pass through the business and are recorded on the income tax return of the business owner. Consequently, there is but a single level of taxation, and any business loss can possibly offset the owner's other income. In contrast, the C corporation may be subject to two levels of taxation: first, at the corporate level, when the corporation receives the income; and, second, at the shareholder level, if the C corporation distributes its remaining income as dividends to the shareholder-owners. Further, since a C corporation may only use its losses against its own income, such corporate losses are unavailable to offset the income of the shareholders.

Best of Both Worlds

Historically, the limited partnership and the S corporation have been the entity of choice for those seeking both limited liability and passthrough taxation. Entrepreneurs and their advisers have always recognized, however, that these traditional choices were imperfect in operation. Increasingly, the LLC, providing both limited liability and passthrough taxation without the operational drawbacks, has become the entity of choice for many new entrepreneurs and their advisers. Efforts by the IRS and the state legislatures to further refine the taxation and operation of this evolving entity have contributed to the LLC's growth.

In the next few sections, we briefly examine the aforementioned entity choices, paying particular attention to their ease of formation and operation, the extent of owner liability and the availability of pass-

---

[1] If a business operation is relatively risk-free and its owners have few personal assets, the sole proprietorship or the general partnership may remain a feasible option.

through taxation. We follow up with an analysis of those business ventures to which the LLC is most particularly suited. The chapter concludes with a chart comparing the LLC with its natural rivals, the S corporation and the limited partnership.

¶ 202

Sole Proprietorship

In a sole proprietorship, a popular business format due to its organizational and operational simplicity, one owner controls all of the business assets, pockets all of the profits, and makes all of the management decisions. However, along with these obvious benefits comes at least one serious drawback—the sole proprietor's personal liability for all of the business's contractual and tortious debts. Business creditors can attach *all* of the proprietor's assets, both business and personal. While sole proprietors attempt to avert such unlimited liability through careful contractual negotiations, astute money management, and sufficient tort liability insurance, some are more successful than others at this variation of Russian roulette.

The sole proprietorship, which is not a taxable entity separate from its owner, enjoys the benefits of "passthrough" taxation. That is, all of the income, loss, deduction, and credit generated by the business are reflected and reported on Schedule C of the individual owner's personal income tax return (Form 1040). This passthrough can be a significant advantage if the business initially operates at a loss because such losses can help offset the sole proprietor's income from other sources.

¶ 203

General Partnership

A successful business initially begun as a sole proprietorship is often reorganized into another entity as the business progresses and begins to make money. One possible choice is the formation of a "general partnership." To form such a partnership, all that is really required is an agreement between two or more persons to operate a business together. Although an oral agreement is binding, a well-drafted, comprehensive written agreement settling the rights and duties of the partners among themselves can eliminate much future misunderstanding. While no other particular formalities need be satisfied and, in general, nothing need be filed with any government agency, a general partnership is more complex, from an organizational and operational perspective, than a sole proprietorship.

For business purposes, a partnership is generally governed by a state's Uniform Partnership Act, which defines a partnership as "an association of two or more persons to carry on as co-owners a business for profit." In a general partnership, the self-directed autonomy inherent in the sole proprietorship is lost. Every partner in a general partnership is an agent of the partnership, capable of contractually binding the partnership by his or her acts, even if none of the other partners are aware of, or consent to, such a contract, so long as the activity falls within the normal scope of the partnership's business.

Further, each partner in a general partnership is personally liable, jointly and severally, for all of the partnership's contractual and tortious liabilities. If the assets of the partnership are insufficient to pay the entity's debts, creditors of the partnership can pursue the individual personal assets of the general partners to satisfy any unpaid partnership obligations. Since a creditor need not collect a portion of the obligation from each partner, but may instead collect the entire amount from a single partner, that unfortunate partner may be left with the unenviable, perhaps unfruitful, task of seeking contribution from the others.

For federal tax purposes, the Internal Revenue Code defines a partnership as a syndicate, group, pool, joint venture, or other unincorporated organization through or by means of which any business, financial operation, or venture is carried on and which is not . . . a corporation or a trust or estate.[2] A general partnership, like a sole proprietorship, is not a separate taxable entity. Rather, the partnership serves as a conduit to the individual partners; *i.e.,* any income, loss, deduction or credit is first computed at the partnership level (using Form 1065 and Schedule K-1) and then passed through to the partners according to their "distributive share." A partner's distributive share is generally determined by the partnership agreement. These amounts are then included on the partners' individual income tax returns.

Since the general partnership format directly passes the relevant tax items through to the partners, the double taxation of income that burdens the C corporation (see below) is avoided. Additionally, like the sole proprietorship, any tax loss attributable to the general partnership's business that is passed on to the partners may be used, subject to some limitations, to offset any of the partners' taxable income from other sources. (For more information on the taxation of partnerships, see Chapter 9.)

¶ 204

C Corporation

Unlike a sole proprietorship or a general partnership, the corporation is a statutory entity separate and distinct from its owners (*i.e.,* the shareholders). The formation and operation of a corporation requires proper documentation and adherence to statutory formalities, often at a significant cost far above that attributable to organizing a sole proprietorship or a general partnership. But many entrepreneurs and their advisers are willing to accept the paperwork and the additional costs of organizing a corporation in order to obtain limited liability for the corporation's shareholders. Unlike sole proprietors or general partners,

---

[2] Code Sec. 7701(a)(2).

shareholders are not personally liable for the debts and obligations of the business.[3] A corporate shareholder is at risk only for the amount of the shareholder's investment in the entity.

If the proper documentation is provided (*i.e.,* articles of incorporation and annual reports are appropriately filed with the secretary of state along with the requisite filing fees) and the organizational formalities are followed (*i.e.,* board of directors' meetings and annual shareholders' meetings are timely held, bylaws are adopted, officers are elected, and evidentiary minutes are kept), the courts will generally recognize the limited liability of the corporation's shareholders.[4] However, failure to abide by these rules may subject the corporate shareholders to personal liability for the debts of their corporation beyond the shareholders' investment in the enterprise.[5]

From the tax perspective, the C corporation (that is, a corporation falling under Subchapter C of the Internal Revenue Code) is a separate tax-paying entity whose profits are subject to the applicable corporate income tax rates. As a separate taxable entity, there is no passthrough of corporate tax items to the shareholders. If the corporation subsequently distributes dividend income to its shareholders, the shareholders are subject to another layer of tax when the distribution is included on their individual tax returns. This "double taxation" of the same income is the primary tax disadvantage attributable to the C corporation. Further, the absence of the flow-through of corporate losses to the shareholders makes the C corporation an inferior business format, from a tax viewpoint, for the first years of an operation's existence if losses are expected. Note that certain types of corporations have been given favorable tax treatment. For example, a loss from the sale of "small business stock" is an ordinary loss, not a capital loss.[6] Also, a 50-percent capital gains exclusion is available for gain generated from stock ("qualified small business stock") held by noncorporate taxpayers for more than five years in qualified small business corporations.[7]

¶ 205
Limited Partnership

To a certain extent, the limited partnership combines the characteristics of a general partnership with that of a corporation. A limited partnership consists of one or more general partners, who manage the business and are personally responsible for all of the debts of the business, and one or more limited partners, who contribute capital and

---

[3] Admittedly, the advantage of limited liability in the contractual and tort sense is more apparent than real in many small corporations.

[4] The courts also consider such factors as whether the corporation's business operations are properly capitalized, whether the corporation is used for an illegal or fraudulent purpose, or whether there is a commingling of personal and business assets.

[5] Many states have adopted statutes based on the Model Statutory Close Corporation Act that are applicable to "small" corporations. Under such a statute, if the articles of incorporation contain the appropriate provisions, the small corporation can dispense with a board of directors entirely and can be managed, formally and practically, by all of its shareholders or by a committee of shareholders.

[6] Code Sec. 1244.

[7] Code Sec. 1202.

share in the profits of the business, but who neither take part in actually running the business nor incur liability with respect to obligations of the limited partnership beyond the amount of their original contributions. In this respect, limited partners are like the shareholders in a corporation who are not personally liable for the debts of the enterprise.

Unlike a general partnership, a limited partnership is a creature of statute, recognized as a form of business entity only because state legislatures have authorized their creation and defined their operation. Usually, in order to form a limited partnership, a "certificate of limited partnership" must be executed and publicly filed with the applicable secretary of state's office, containing such information as the names of all general and limited partners and the amount of each partner's investment. Additionally, the limited partnership's name must include either the words "Limited Partnership" or the abbreviation "L.P." Although the filing of a properly executed certificate of limited partnership is sufficient for statutory purposes, in most cases the parties to the limited partnership also execute a private written partnership agreement, an often complex document delineating the rights and duties of the participants.

The primary advantage of the limited partnership over the general partnership, from a nontax perspective, is that while a limited partner's management participation rights are somewhat more circumscribed than that of a general partner, the limited partner possesses limited liability.[8] A limited partner is only liable for business debts and obligations to the extent of his or her capital contribution.

Although a properly formed limited partnership provides protection to the limited partners from the debts and obligations of the business, a limited partnership must have at least one general partner who has unlimited personal liability for the business debts and obligations. One well-known strategy to address this liability concern is to utilize a corporation as the general partner of the limited partnership since the shareholders of the corporate general partner are not liable for any of the corporation's debts. However, this combination-entity arrangement increases the business and tax complexity of this operating format.

From a tax perspective, everything stated above regarding the general partnership applies equally to the limited partnership. That is, the limited partnership is not a separate taxable entity but rather a conduit through which the items of income, loss, deduction, and credit from the partnership's business operations pass through to the general and limited partners. There is no double taxation. Although, like the general partnership, a limited partnership must file its federal informa-

---

[8] In fact, under many jurisdictions, a limited partner who takes too active a role in managing the business risks being held liable as a general partner for the limited partnership's debts.

tion return (Form 1065), the partnership is not required to pay any income tax. Instead, all of the profits, losses, etc., are allocated among the partners, subject to their agreement, and included on the partners' individual returns.

¶ 206

Limited Liability Partnership

All 50 states and the District of Columbia have modified their partnership acts to authorize the formation, registration and operation of certain general partnerships as "registered limited liability partnerships" (LLPs). As stated above, the general partners of a general partnership are usually jointly and severally liable for all of the debts and obligations of the partnership. However, upon the proper registration of an eligible general partnership (for the most part, a professional partnership) as an LLP, each general partner becomes immune to the tortious, negligent, and wrongful conduct of the other general partners and of the employees, agents, and representatives of the partnership not under the partner's direct supervision and control. Although the traditional vicarious liability of general partners is thus limited, a general partner remains liable for his or her own tortious, negligent, and wrongful conduct and that of those employees, agents, and representatives under the partner's direct supervision and control. An increasing number of states even permit the general partners in an LLP to shield themselves from the contractual debts and obligations of the LLP as well. Aside from this statutory protection from vicarious, and sometimes contractual, liability, an LLP and its general partners operate, are liable, and are taxed like any other general partnership and its partners. Registration as an LLP does not require the partnership to change its partnership agreement or the way that it conducts its business.

To register as an LLP, a general partnership need only file an application with the appropriate state authority, usually the secretary of state, and pay a designated fee.[9] In most states, the application simply includes the name of the partnership,[10] its address and principal office, the name and address of a registered agent if the principal office is in another state, the number of partners, a brief description of the business, and a statement as to whether the partnership is applying for or renewing LLP status.[11] The application must be signed by general partners representing a majority in interest or by a partner authorized to sign the application. For more information on LLPs, see ¶ 804.

---

[9] A minority of jurisdictions require that an LLP maintain insurance against liabilities arising from the type of conduct, the liability of which is limited under the LLP act. Alternatively, LLPs can set aside or segregate in escrow funds equal to the amount of insurance required.

[10] A partnership that registers as an LLP must adopt a name that signifies its status as an LLP. In most jurisdictions, the name of an LLP must include the words "registered limited liability partnership" or the initials "L.L.P." at the end of the name to alert third parties that the partners of the LLP are not personally liable for many of the debts and obligations normally associated with a general partnership.

[11] An LLP registration is usually effective for one year, and may be renewed for successive one-year periods by filing a renewal application or submitting an annual report with the proper state authority, along with the requisite fee. Failure to renew an application will cause a registration to lapse, exposing the partners to liability to the same extent as general partners.

Unlike LLC members, general partners in LLPs or limited partners, the general partner in a limited partnership was unable to acquire limited liability protection. Thus, a limited partnership's general partner position gained the distinction of being the least desirable business role. Limited liability is now provided by states that have passed *limited liability limited partnership* (LLLP) statutes or recognize LLLPs as business entities. For more information on LLLPs, see ¶ 805.

Although for federal tax purposes an LLP is a passthrough entity, some states may impose entity level taxes.[12]

¶ 207

S Corporation

The designation "S corporation" only has relevance from a tax perspective. In all other areas, such as separate identity, and the presence of limited liability, this entity has all of the attributes of any other state corporation. That said, the rest of this brief explanation will concentrate upon defining the term for tax purposes and upon delineating some of the perceived complexities in forming an S corporation.

Recognizing that the feature of "double taxation"[13] present with corporations subject to Subchapter C of the Internal Revenue Code was often a severe financial disadvantage to the owners and operators of small corporate businesses, Congress added Subchapter S to the Code and made it available to specifically designated corporations and shareholders. Subchapter S thus provides certain small businesses with all of the advantages of the corporate form of organization without the detrimental attribute of double taxation. Upon a proper election by an eligible entity with certain shareholder characteristics, the income of an S corporation passes through the corporate-level free of taxation and is only taxed at the personal rates of the recipient shareholders.

In order to be eligible for the passthrough tax benefits of S corporation status, certain qualifications must be met and applicable procedures must be followed. To qualify, a domestic corporation, other than certain financial institutions, insurance companies, and DISCs, etc., must meet several requirements. Among others, the corporation must:

(1) have no more than 100 shareholders;

(2) have as shareholders only U.S. citizens or resident aliens, estates or certain trusts and exempt organizations (partnerships and corporations are shareholders);

(3) not have a nonresident alien as a shareholder; and

(4) not have more than one class of stock.[15]

---

[12] For example, Kentucky subjects LLPs to the corporate income tax and its requirements, Ky. Rev. Stat. Ann. § 141.010(24).

[13] That is, the income of the corporation is taxed at corporate rates at the entity level and again, at personal rates, when distributed to the shareholders.

[15] Code Sec. 1361(b).

Family members may elect to be treated as one shareholder.[16]

LLC shareholders' ownership of S corporation would not end the S election provided none of the LLCs elected treatment as an association taxable as a corporation.[17] Similarly, a single-member LLC that is a disregarded entity for federal tax purposes is eligible to be an S corporation shareholder because the sole owner would be treated as directly owning the stock.[18]

The statutory conversion of a state-law business corporation taxable as an S corporation to an LLC followed by an election to be treated as an association taxable as a corporation will qualify as an F reorganization and will have no effect on the converting entity's S corporation status.[19]

Procedurally, such an eligible corporation must elect S corporation status by filing with the IRS Form 2553, as signed by all of the shareholders. In order to take effect during the corporation's first tax year, the election must be made within the first 2½ months after the beginning of the corporation's first tax year. Even if it does not elect to be taxed as an S corporation during its first tax year, an otherwise eligible corporation may in later years elect to be taxed as an S corporation.

Although it must file an informational tax return with the IRS (Form 1120S), the S corporation itself is generally not taxed separately on its income.[20] Rather, the S corporation's net income or loss is allocated among the shareholders in proportion to each shareholder's percentage of stock ownership. These shareholders must then include their share of the net corporate income or loss on their personal income tax returns.

Any losses that flow through to the shareholders are deductible, subject to some qualification, on the shareholders' individual returns. Since a shareholder can derive an immediate tax benefit from the losses of a start-up S corporation, at the time of inception, an entrepreneur and his or her tax advisers should seriously consider the election of S corporation status.

Despite the increased flexibility granted to S corporations by recent tax legislation, several significant drawbacks to S corporation status remain unchanged. For example, despite the expansion of permissible S corporation shareholders, restrictions regarding who or what may own S corporation stock continue. Corporations, partnerships, LLCs, nonresident alien individuals, and trusts with beneficiaries that are not eligible shareholders still cannot hold stock in an S corporation. Thus, many investor combinations looking for an amena-

---

[16] Code Sec. 1361(c)(1).

[17] IRS Letter Ruling 200107025 (November 17, 2000).

[18] IRS Letter Ruling 200008015 (November 18, 1999).

[19] IRS Letter Ruling 200528021 (April 8, 2005).

[20] While there is generally no corporate-level of taxation when operating as an S corporation, an S corporation is subject to tax in three instances: (1) if it realizes "built-in gains"; (2) if it has "excess passive investment income"; or (3) if it has investment credit recapture.

ble entity for the private placement of equity capital may continue to look elsewhere. In addition, an S corporation is still only permitted to have one class of stock. Thus, items of income, gain, loss, deduction, or credit of an S corporation cannot be separately allocated to a particular shareholder.

Additionally, shareholder debt may be reclassified as equity and treated as a second class of stock unless it comes under the straight debt safe harbor rules.[21] Note that the IRS has privately ruled that the use of an LLC to hold S corporation assets under an indemnity arrangement did not constitute the creation of a second class of stock. The LLC was used for a discrete business purpose and did not truly create a second set of general rights to the S corporation assets.[22]

Many entrepreneurs and their business and tax advisers, however, are not ready to dispose of the S corporation option entirely. While for many the LLC is still an untested and unfamiliar entity, entrepreneurs and their advisers are familiar and comfortable with the rules for setting up and maintaining an S corporation. In the S corporation area, there is a wealth of case law and IRS guidance. Further, many trades and businesses are required by regulators to have a corporate charter and the LLC may not meet those regulatory requirements. In some states, certain professions are even barred from organizing as an LLC. Thus, in order to establish a liability shield, a professional association must often incorporate.

The attractiveness of S corporation status can fluctuate along with comparable individual and corporate tax rates. For 2006, the maximum tax rate of 35 percent for individuals is the same as the maximum corporate rate of 35 percent, making the S corporation appear a desirable choice, considering that the S corporation earnings will not be subject to a second layer of tax. Note that current S corporation earnings passed through to shareholders are not considered dividends and are not taxed at the lower 15-percent tax rate for dividends.

Subchapter S also provides eligible current C corporations with the ability to convert from C to S corporation status subject to certain rules, generally without adverse tax consequences. The conversion of a C corporation into a partnership or LLC, however, is treated as a liquidation of the corporate entity, taxable to both the corporation and its shareholders. Additionally, if there is a chance that an entity may go public at some time in the future, a business may want to organize as an S corporation, at least until LLC interests are as easily issued in capital markets as traditional corporate stock.

The bottom line is that the S corporation will likely remain a viable entity choice for many businesses, especially smaller enterprises.

---

[21] Code Sec. 1361(c)(5)(B).   [22] IRS Letter Ruling 9330009 (April 26, 1993).

¶207

¶ 208

Limited Liability Company

The limited liability company (LLC), a statutory creation with its own separate legal identity, is a hybrid business entity providing its owners, called "members," with both the limited liability characteristic of the corporation and the operational flexibility and passthrough tax treatment of the partnership. The LLC generally begins its existence upon the filing of "Articles of Organization" with the appropriate secretary of state, along with the requisite filing fee. These articles usually set forth such basic information as:

(1) the LLC's name (which often must include the words "Limited Liability Company" or the abbreviation "L.L.C." or some variation thereof);

(2) the LLC's period of duration (although many states are now removing this requirement in light of the federal entity classification regulations (see Chapter 9));

(3) the name and address of its registered agent;

(4) the address of its principal office; and

(5) its business purpose.

Many states also require that the LLC subsequently file an annual report.[23]

Although often not legally required, the members of an LLC, like the owners of any other significant business enterprise, usually draft a written "operating agreement" specifically establishing and regulating the affairs of the LLC, the conduct of its business, and the rights, duties and relations of the members.

The most obvious nontax advantage of an LLC is that *none* of its members are personally liable for the debts and obligations of the business beyond their actual or promised investment in the LLC. Thus, the members of an LLC enjoy the same protections from personal liability for business obligations as shareholders in a corporation or limited partners in a limited partnership. But unlike the limited partnership form, which requires that there be at least one general partner who is personally liable for all of the debts and obligations of the business, no such requirement exists for an LLC. Further, the members of an LLC may participate in the LLC's business affairs and management to a greater extent, without exposing themselves to possible personal liability, than may limited partners with respect to a limited partnership.[24]

---

[23] In addition, many states' LLC acts provide that certain businesses, such as banks and insurance companies, cannot form as an LLC.

[24] The divergence between limited partnerships and LLCs varies somewhat from state to state because some states (those conforming to the Revised Uniform Limited Partnership Act) allow a greater participation in management by the limited partners.

From a tax perspective, a domestic LLC will generally qualify as either a partnership or will be disregarded as an entity for federal tax purposes. (See Chapter 9 for a more thorough explanation of the federal entity classification rules.)[25] Either way, however, all of the LLC's income, loss, deductions, and credits pass through the entity and are reflected on the returns of the members. Like a partnership, the LLC must file federal information Form 1065 and each member of the LLC must report his or her share of the LLC's income or loss on his or her personal income tax return.

Further, an LLC is free from the ownership restrictions faced by a corporation desiring S corporation status. For an LLC, there is no limit on the number of owners, or on the persons permitted to be owners, or on the permissible types of ownership interests. For example, while an S corporation is confined to a single class of stock, the LLC is able to structure different and multiple types of ownership interests, with varying rights to distributions and liquidation proceeds. This overall flexibility that is inherent in the LLC helps attract a wider array of business investors than is possible in the S corporation format. This LLC flexibility can be especially advantageous to family businesses that want to employ "estate freezes," and also to businesses that require a pliable vehicle for employee incentive plans and private placements of capital.

In order to protect the assets of one division from the claims of creditors of another division, an S corporation may wish to place the assets and liabilities of a division into an entity that is disregarded for federal tax purposes. The S corporation may choose to place that division into either a single-member LLC or into a qualified Subchapter S subsidiary (QSub). A QSub is a domestic corporation that would be eligible to be an S corporation if the stock of the corporation were held directly by the shareholders of its parent S corporation, and if: (1) 100 percent of the stock of the subsidiary is held by its S corporation parent; and (2) the parent elects to treat the subsidiary as a QSub. Depending on the facts and circumstances, the single-member LLC format may be the preferred choice, rather than the QSub.

The S corporation is less likely to recognize gain if it forms a single-member LLC. Further, passthrough taxation will continue after the addition of another member to a single-member LLC if that multi-member LLC is treated as a partnership. Note, however, that the passthrough taxation from the subsidiary to the parent is lost if a QSub is not 100 percent owned by the parent. Finally, the termination of a QSub election (transforming an S corporation into a C corporation) is likely to trigger more gain recognition than the conversion of a single-

---

[25] Note that the states continue to react to the federal taxing authorities' entity classification guidance. For specific state information as of the date of publication, see the state synopses beginning at ¶ 1001.

member LLC disregarded as an entity separate from its owner into a multi-member LLC taxed as a partnership.

Despite the many apparent benefits of operating within the LLC format, several concerns must also be addressed. The preparation of a comprehensive LLC operating agreement, as is true for a partnership, usually requires the consideration of more issues than is required in organizing a corporation, leading to an increased formation cost. Moreover, the LLC is still a relatively new business form and there is not much legal precedent on how certain issues would be resolved if they were adjudicated. The LLC acts are so new that courts have not accumulated a body of precedents upon which counsel can rely in predicting the outcome of possible litigation. Finally, notwithstanding the increased number of states now allowing the formation of single-member LLCs in response to the federal entity classification regulations, many analysts and practitioners still have doubts about the acceptance of this "entity" by the judiciary. While some commentators argue that single-member LLCs will be treated in the same way as single-shareholder corporations, others express concern that single-member LLCs are more vulnerable to veil-piercing.

¶ 209

Strategic Uses of the LLC

With its operational flexibility, its limited liability protection and its passthrough tax treatment, the LLC is quickly becoming an attractive alternative to the traditional partnership and corporate business structures. The LLC may be particularly useful for closely held businesses, for venture capitalists and for international transactions. Professional groups and exempt organizations may also find the LLC format to be beneficial. We briefly address these uses in the following paragraphs.

Closely Held Businesses

The closely held business where ownership is limited to a small number of investors will significantly benefit from using an LLC. The LLC can provide such an enterprise not only with limited liability protection and passthrough tax treatment, but also with a simplified management structure and more operational flexibility. With an LLC, a managerial team, unfettered by the formalities attendant a corporate board of directors, can more efficiently oversee and operate the business, and respond to the changing commercial environment.

Additionally, since an LLC has no restriction upon the types of ownership interests that it can offer, the founding or controlling members of the LLC can provide newer members or managerial teams with equity incentives without giving up their voting control, and without sacrificing any passthrough tax treatment (as would happen to an S corporation that issued ownership interests constituting a second class of stock).

Further, a venture capitalist interested in investing in a start-up or an early-stage business will find the LLC format more appealing than the traditional choices. As a passthrough entity for tax purposes, the LLC helps the capitalist maximize the profit from the investment. As stated above, the LLC's ability to offer the venture capitalist a complex array of financial inducements to invest in the company is often critical. While the limited partnership format discourages such investors from active intervention in the management of the business in order to avoid personal liability, the LLC permits the investor to participate in management without exposure to such expansive liability.

International Transactions

Business entities similar to the LLC have been generally available in many foreign countries for a number of years.[26] Accordingly, while the same cannot be said of U.S. corporations and partnerships, foreign investors should be quite comfortable investing in a domestic LLC. Moreover, unlike with an S corporation, there is no limitation on the ownership of a domestic LLC by a nonresident alien. In addition, an international LLC can now do business in the United States since the provisions of most state LLC acts permit an LLC from another jurisdiction to register to do business in the state even if the LLC were formed in a foreign country (but often subject to the rights and obligations that a domestic LLC in the applicable state could possess). For more information, see Chapter 7.

Professional LLCs

A professional limited liability company (PLLC) is an obvious alternative to partnerships and professional corporations because the PLLC affords the professional practitioner with both a shield from liability as well as with passthrough tax treatment. However, each jurisdiction has its own statutory answer in regards to the question, "Will the state permit a designated professional to utilize the LLC?" Some states specifically authorize all "professionals," as defined, to use a PLLC. Other states permit only certain professionals to operate as a PLLC. Accordingly, when the question arises, specific reference to the applicable state statute must be made.

With respect to lawyers, the mere statutory availability of a PLLC may not be enough. The state's bar association or its highest court must often rule whether such an entity is an ethical means through which a lawyer may provide professional services to the public.

With respect to accountants, the American Institute of Certified Public Accountants has amended its organizational rules to permit an accountant to practice within a PLLC if the laws of the particular state so permit. For more information on PLLCs, see Chapter 8.

---

[26] Countries that recognize LLCs are: Argentina (1932); Belgium (1935); Brazil (1919); Chile (1923); Cuba (1929); France (1925); Germany (1892); Italy (1936); Mexico (1934); Panama (1917); Portugal (1901); Switzerland (1936); and Turkey (1926).

Exempt Organizations

The nonprofit community is also increasingly interested in using the LLC as a form of business. Allowing a nonprofit organization to be formed as an LLC would give the nonprofit flexibility in structuring company management.

In determining whether a state would allow a nonprofit organization to be an LLC, it is important to look at the state's LLC "purposes" provision. Delaware, for example, expressly permits not-for-profit as a lawful purpose. Other states either allow any lawful purpose or restrict the LLC to "business" purposes. Questions then arise as to whether "nonprofit" is a business purpose. However, there is currently a debate among commentators as to whether the LLC model is appropriate for nonprofit charitable organizations. The IRS is considering whether state attorneys general have the power to regulate LLCs that claim Code Sec. 501(c)(3) status as traditional charitable corporations and trusts.[27] A few courts have held that corporations organized under state for-profit statutes are exempt under Code Sec. 501(c)(3).[28]

The long-standing IRS position is that a partnership cannot qualify as a tax-exempt entity under Code Sec. 501(c)(3). However, an eligible entity, which may include an LLC or a partnership, that claims exemption as a separate entity is treated as an association, rather than as a partnership or disregarded entity, during the period in which it claims exemption or is determined to be exempt.[29] The IRS has announced 12 conditions that an LLC must meet in order to be a regarded entity or association. If the LLC meets these conditions, it can claim exemption as a separate entity if it otherwise qualifies under Code Sec. 501(c)(3) or Code Sec. 501(c)(4).[30]

An IRA or a Roth IRA may hold stock in a bank S corporation if the IRA held the stock on or after October 22, 2004.[31]

¶ 210
Choice of Entity Table

As indicated above, the right entity choice is often dependent on the circumstances of each client and that client's business and investment needs. The table beginning on the following page is designed to aid tax and business practitioners in identifying differences between the LLC, the S corporation and the limited partnership. The table may also help in determining the advantages of the LLC when compared to the traditional entity choices.

---

[27] Exempt Organizations: *IRS Technical Instruction Program for Fiscal Year 2000,* Topic H, "Limited Liability Companies as Exempt Organizations."

[28] *Unity School of Christianity,* Dec. 1435, 4 BTA 61; *University of Maryland Physicians, P.A.,* Dec. 37,633(M), 41 TCM 732, TC Memo. 1981-23.

[29] Reg. §301.7701-3(c)(1)(v)(A).

[30] Exempt Organizations: *IRS Technical Instruction Program for Fiscal Year 2001,* Topic B, "Limited Liability Companies as Exempt Organizations—Update."

[31] Code Sec. 1361(c)(2).

LLCs v. Other Passthrough Entities

	LLC	S Corporation	Limited Partnership
Entity name	"Limited," "Ltd.," "LC," "LLC" or some variation thereof generally must appear.	"Corporation," "Company," "Incorporated" or abbreviation must appear.	"Limited Partnership," "Limited," "Ltd." or "L.P." must appear.
Liability for entity debts and obligations	No member liable.	No shareholder liable.	General partner liable. Limited partners generally protected.
Participation in management by all members.	Yes.	Yes.	No. Participation by limited partners generally restricted to maintain limited liability.
Ownership restrictions	Majority of states allow single shareholder; no upper limit on number of members. No restrictions on types of persons who may be members.	From one to 100 shareholders. Significant restrictions on types of members. For example, no corporations, no partnerships, no nonresident aliens, no foreign entities, and only certain qualifying trusts (*e.g.*, QSSTs and ESBTs). Note recent QSub and ESOP provisions.	At least two members. No restrictions on types of persons who may be members.
Types of ownership interests	No restrictions.	Single class of stock only, but there may be differences in voting rights.	No restrictions.
Ownership of subsidiary entities	No restrictions.	Permitted to own 80% or more of a C corporation, and 100% of a QSub.	No restrictions.

	LLC	S Corporation	Limited Partnership
Dissolution events	Generally, as specified by operating agreement or upon dissociation event of member unless remaining members agree to continue.	Dissolution ordinarily does not result from changes in shareholder ownership.	Death, retirement, resignation, expulsion or bankruptcy of general partner generally results in dissolution unless remaining general partner or all remaining partners agree to continue business.
Federal entity-level income tax	No, if taxed as partnership.	Generally, no. Possible entity-level tax on excess net passive income and on built-in gains in the case of former C corporations.	No.
Contributions of appreciated or debt-encumbered property	Nontaxable, unless the contribution results in net reduction of member's liabilities in excess of member's basis in LLC.	Taxable, unless shareholder has control (80% voting power) immediately after the contribution.	Nontaxable, unless the contribution results in net reduction of partner's liabilities in excess of partner's basis.
Special allocations of income, gain, loss, etc.	Permitted.	Not permitted. Pro rata allocations only due to single-class-of-stock requirement.	Permitted.
Inclusions of entity debt in basis for interest	Yes. LLC debt is allocated among members under partnership rules and included in tax basis for LLC interests accordingly. Additional basis may be used to offset LLC deductions/losses.	No. Tax basis of a shareholder's stock does not include any share of entity debt, even if the debt is guaranteed by the shareholder.	Yes. Partnership debt is allocated among members and included in tax basis for partnership interests accordingly.

	LLC	S Corporation	Limited Partnership
Distributions of property (other than cash)	Generally, no recognition of gain or loss until member sells or disposes of the distributed property. Exception for distribution that is deemed to include member's share of Code Sec. 751 "hot assets."	Distributions of appreciated property treated as sale by the corporation and cause pro rata recognition of gain at shareholder level.	Generally, no recognition of gain or loss until partner sells or disposes of the distributed property. Exception for distribution that is deemed to include partner's share of Code Sec. 751 "hot assets."
Liquidation	Nontaxable to extent of a member's tax basis in LLC.	Generally, nontaxable at corporate level but taxable at shareholder level due to passthrough of corporate tax items.	Nontaxable to extent of a partner's tax basis in partnership.
Basis adjustment on transfer of interest	Election permitted to adjust basis of LLC assets to reflect transferee's basis in LLC interest.	Basis adjustment of S corporation assets not permitted.	Election permitted to adjust basis of partnership assets to reflect transferee's basis in partnership interest.

Chapter 3

Forming an LLC: Administrative and Procedural Matters

¶ 301

Articles of Organization

An LLC begins its formal legal existence when articles of organization have been delivered to the appropriate state official (usually the secretary of state) and filed by, or otherwise certified by, the state. The term "articles of organization," unfortunately, is not uniform across the country. Some states refer to them as the LLC's "certificate of formation," for instance.

There are a number of approaches taken by the states regarding the information that must be included in the articles. See the state-by-state analysis in Chapter 10 for a given state. Many states call for the articles to contain only a minimal amount of information in order to apprise the state of the LLC's intention to do business within the state. These states require the articles to set forth only:

(1) the LLC's name;

(2) its principal or registered office; and

(3) its registered agent.

Many states also require that the articles include either the names and addresses of any LLC managers or a statement that the LLC is managed by managers rather than by all of the members. Both serve to put potential creditors and any others contracting with the LLC on notice as to the LLC's management structure.

Two interesting exclusions from this list are statements as to the LLC's purposes and powers. To date, no state requires a listing of LLC powers in the articles, and many state statutes expressly provide that a listing of the LLC's powers is unnecessary. States are split concerning whether a statement of purpose must be included. However, where a purpose statement must be inserted into the articles, in many states generic language (e.g., "the transaction of any or all lawful business activities") will suffice.

Additional information that some states require to be disclosed in the articles includes the LLC's duration or a statement that duration will be perpetual, lists of members or managers at the time of formation, information concerning the members' capital contribution, and information concerning the members' rights to admit additional members or to transfer their interests.

For an example of how the articles of organization might appear, see Appendix A.

Amending the Articles of Organization

All state statutes contain procedures for amending the articles of organization. Typically, the "articles of amendment" must state the name of the LLC and the changes to the articles of organization that have been approved by the members.[1] Most enabling statutes provide that the articles of organization may be amended in "any and as many respects as may be desired so long as the articles of organization as amended contain only provisions that may be lawfully contained in articles of organization at the time of making the amendment."[2]

In addition, most states require amendment where key information contained in the standing articles has changed (such as the LLC's name, whether the LLC is managed by its members or by designated managers and, often, to simply provide a more accurate reflection of the agreement of the members) or where the standing articles contain false or erroneous statements. In a few states, amendments are permitted, but not formally required.[3] As with the filing of the original articles of organization, the filing of the articles of amendment will often be accompanied by a mandatory amendment fee.[4]

The process that an LLC will need to go through in amending its articles of organization will differ depending on whether or not it has accepted members or not. Before members are accepted, the organizers are generally permitted to amend the articles. However, after the LLC accepts members, the amendment process is usually accomplished in two steps. First, the amendment must be adopted by the members of the LLC, and then the amendment must be submitted for filing to the same state agency that accepted the original articles of organization. Note that, unlike the board of directors of a corporation, the managers of an LLC do not have to recommend to the members that they accept or reject the articles or otherwise approve the amendments.

---

[1] *See, e.g.,* Cal. Corp. Code § 17054(b) (also requires the Secretary of State's file number); Del. Code tit. 6, § 18-202.

[2] *See, e.g.,* Ga. Code § 14-11-210(b); 805 Ill. Comp. Stat. 180/5-10.

[3] *See, e.g.,* Iowa Code § 490A.1101; Virginia Code § 13.1-1014(A).

[4] *See, e.g.,* Ind. Code § 23-18-12-3; Me. Rev. Stat. tit. 31, § 751.

Unless the articles of organization or the operating agreement provide otherwise, the members may initiate an amendment to the articles of organization. Usually, however, it will be the managers, if any, who will first become aware in the normal course of events of the need to amend the articles of organization. When that occurs, the managers will typically propose that the members take the necessary steps.

Business Purpose

Many states have removed the requirement that the articles of organization state a business purpose. In those states that still require that a business purpose be disclosed, some allow the articles of organization to provide that the LLC exists for "any lawful purpose." In these instances, the stated purpose can be very broad, having little effect on either creditors or the managers of the LLC. The rationale for limiting the lawful use of an LLC is difficult to sustain, particularly in light of the Model Business Corporation Act and the Revised Uniform Limited Partnership Act (RULPA).[5] Further, providing that an LLC can engage in any lawful purpose does not give the reader of the articles of organization much useful information.

Certain regulated industries, such as banking and insurance, may be prohibited from operating in LLC form. Also, the use of LLCs by professional firms may be prohibited or may depend upon changes to regulations promulgated by the appropriate state regulatory body (see Chapter 8).

Then, too, there are statutes that do not expressly forbid specific types of business activity, but simply allow an LLC to engage in any purpose as long as it is not contrary to any other special regulation or control. In other words, the LLC enabling statute defers to other statutes for guidance. Another approach is for a statute to provide that the LLC may engage in any business activity in which any other corporation or partnership can lawfully engage.

Status Opinion

Some states and third parties require a legal opinion on LLCs. A status opinion basically addresses whether an LLC is duly formed and validly existing. Although in Delaware the only requirement is a certificate of formation, opinion givers are expected to provide more. Issues include whether the LLC has met the statutory conditions for maintaining its existence, are there conditions in the operating agreement that have to be satisfied, are there other contractual obligations that need to be satisfied, and has a termination occurred. The question of whether an LLC is duly formed might lead an attorney to check whether the certificate of formation was filed, the third-party, relying on the opinion,

---

[5] Model Business Corporation Act § 3.01; Revised Uniform Limited Partnership Act (2001) §§ 111 and 201.

would likely expect the opinion to mean that the LLC or LLP had the ability to operate. Attorneys answering this question need to use due diligence in order to determine that the LLC or LLP formation was proper. Similarly, the issue of whether the LLC or LLP is "validly existing" needs to be answered with the expectations of the third-party recipient of the opinion in mind.

> *Caution:* Of primary concern to lawyers is the fact that while they may not be liable for professional malpractice for a legal opinion that they issued, they may still be liable for negligent misrepresentation of fact.

¶ 302

LLC Operating Agreement

The articles of organization are not a substitute for an operating agreement by which the members govern the business of, and their economic interest in, the LLC. In almost all cases, LLC members will want to draft an operating agreement that sets forth, among other things, the sharing of profits and losses, capital account rules and distribution rights, and voting rights. This operating agreement is comparable in purpose and importance to a partnership agreement in a partnership.

The operating agreement should provide guidelines for any situation that may arise in the future. Therefore, the drafters of an operating agreement may want to:

> (1) define and distinguish different types of membership interests;

> (2) provide that assets be brought up to their fair market value prior to the admittance of a new member so that appreciation is allocated to the existing members;

> (3) provide rules regarding the withdrawal of members;

> (4) provide transfer provisions for membership interests;

> (5) provide for an exit strategy, such as transfers, disassociations, buy-sell or dissolution; and

> (6) set procedures for amending the operating agreement, including rules for voting on amendments.

Conversely, drafters of the operating agreement should be careful not to include provisions that could adversely affect the LLC in the future. For example, it is best to avoid putting investment representations, which would suggest that a membership interest is a security, in the operating agreement.

A sample operating agreement appears in Appendix A.

Because, in some states, no operating agreement is required, LLC laws are typically drafted with "default" provisions. Default provisions furnish key rules of operation that will govern the LLC in the absence of contrary operating agreement provisions.

For instance, it is common for a state's LLC law to provide that an LLC's management is vested in its members, absent a contrary agreement. Other common default rules deal with the allocation of voting rights and the sharing of LLC profits and distributions. Thus, when drafting an operating agreement, it is important to review the state's LLC statutes to ensure that all of the default provisions in the governing act are in the best interests of the LLC members. Any statutory provision that is not mandatory may be overridden in the operating agreement and tailored to meet the particular goals of the LLC members.

Fiduciary Duties

Drafters of an operating agreement may also want to address the fiduciary duties of the LLC members. In general, the principal fiduciary duties are the duty of loyalty and the duty of care. Moreover, under traditional common law, anyone who participates in LLC management is considered to have an implied contractual duty of good faith and fair dealing.

The duty of loyalty implies the related duties not to compete against the LLC, to refer business opportunities to the LLC, to transfer money and other benefits received in the course of LLC business to the LLC and to avoid self-dealing. Successful operation of an LLC requires mutual trust between members and managers. An operating agreement cannot mandate trust, but it can impose a duty of care. The duty of care may include a duty to disclose to other managers and, when appropriate, to nonmanager members any information that is material to the LLC's business and affairs, a duty to protect confidential information and a duty to act prudently and diligently.

The operating agreement may also contain provisions prohibiting managers from any form of self-dealing unless with the consent of disinterested members. If intellectual property is a significant asset of the LLC, the LLC may want to require managers and employees to sign over any intellectual property that is discovered or developed on LLC time, through the use of LLC facilities, or on the basis of existing LLC intellectual property. The operating agreement may also address the effect of a breach of fiduciary duty in terms of personal liability, defenses, and indemnification.

Courts have shown a willingness to look beyond the traditional nature of fiduciary duties and examine provisions in the operating agreement in making a determination of whether fiduciary duties have been breached. If the operating agreement allows things that would normally be a breach of fiduciary duties, courts usually respect the operating agreement.[6]

Recently, states have enacted legislation allowing LLC operating agreements to significantly limit and define fiduciary duties. Delaware has taken the lead by allowing a member's or manager's duties to be expanded, restricted or eliminated. However, the operating agreement may not eliminate the implied contractual covenant of good faith and fair dealing.[7] Delaware has a long tradition of allowing business organizations great flexibility to contract between the members or partners for the agreement they want. The underlying notion seems to be that astute businesspeople can decide for themselves how they want there business to operate.

Colorado is more typical of the trend to allow LLCs to limit fiduciary duties. In 2004, Colorado adopted statutes that provide that an LLC may not unreasonably reduce the duty of care or a manager's right to access LLC books and records. However, an LLC agreement may identify categories or types of duties that do not violate the duty of care or the obligation of good faith and fair dealing. The Colorado statutes provide that an operating agreement may eliminate other duties and determine the standard by which the performance of good faith and fair dealing is to be measured.[8]

What Not to Include in an Operating Agreement

Although state statutes provide great latitude in what may be included in an operating agreement, there are limitations. Generally, because LLCs are subject to both agency and contract law, they may not adopt provisions contrary to either. The Illinois LLC Act is typical. It provides that an LLC operating agreement may not:

(1) unreasonably restrict a right to information or access to records;

(2) vary the right to expel a member by judicial determination;

(3) vary the requirement to wind up the business when an event makes it unlawful to continue the business or upon a judicial decree;

(4) restrict rights of a person, other than a member, manager and transferee of a member's distributional interest;

(5) restrict the right of a member to dissociate, although an operating agreement may determine when a dissociation is wrongful and it may eliminate or vary the LLC's obligation to purchase the dissociated member's distributional interest;

---

[6] *See, e.g.,* McConnell v. Hunt Sports Enterprises, 725 N.E.2d 1193 (Ohio App. 1999); Gotham Partners, L.P. v. Hallwood Realty Partners, L.P., 805 A.2d 882 (Del. 2002).

[7] Delaware Code, tit. 6, § 18-1101(c).
[8] Colo. Rev. Stat. § 7-80-108.

(6) eliminate or reduce a member's fiduciary duties, but may create categories of activities that do not violate these duties, specify the number or percentage of members or disinterested managers that may authorize or ratify a specific act that would otherwise violate these duties; or

(7) eliminate or reduce the obligation of good faith and fair dealing, but the operating agreement may determine the standards by which the performance of obligation is to be measured, if the standards are not unreasonable.[9]

Single-Member LLCs

Except for the six states that require an LLC to have an operating agreement, it is not necessary for single-member or multi-member LLCs to have operating agreements. However, a single-member LLC may provide itself and its member with additional liability protection by executing an operating agreement. Single-member LLCs are more prone to having their LLC veil pierced because they have only one member. Because a single-member LLC is likely to be identified as the sole member's business, there may be an impression that there is such a unity of interest and ownership that the separate personalities of the sole member and the LLC do not exist. An operating agreement can serve as evidence that the LLC and the sole member are separate and distinct.

Several states now have provisions that outline what the operating agreement for a single-member LLC should include. Generally, these states provide some flexibility. For example, the "operating agreement" may include: (1) *any* writing, signed by the sole member, regarding the LLC's affairs; (2) any written agreement between the member and the company; or (3) an oral or written agreement between the member and the company regarding the LLC's affairs *if* the LLC is managed by a manager that is not the sole member of the LLC.[10] The operating agreement may be replaced by a "declaration"[11] or, in some states, it need only be any written or oral statement made by the sole member in good faith purporting to govern the affairs of the LLC or the conduct of business.[12]

The agreement should contain many of the same aspects as an organizational agreement between two or more persons. For example, the agreement should specify how much capital the member contributed to the LLC for their membership interest. Also, the terms for dissolution should be carefully and specifically spelled out so that the member may determine the future vitality of the LLC should they decide to leave the business, or if they should die unexpectedly (this is

---

[9] 805 Ill. Comp. Stat. 180/15-5(b).

[10] *See, e.g.,* Colo. Rev. Stat. §7-80-102(11)(b); 805 Ill. Comp. Stat. 180/15-5(c).

[11] *See, e.g.,* Ohio Rev. Code §1705.01(J); S.D. Codified Laws §47-34A-101(12).

[12] *See, e.g.,* Ariz. Rev. Stat. §29-601(12)(b); La. Rev. Stat. §12:1301(16).

particularly relevant if the owner finds the standing default provisions in their state unsatisfactory).

Conversely, if dissolution of the LLC is addressed, so too should the subject of the addition of new members. The terms of admittance and the share of any additional future ownership should be discussed in order to eliminate any confusion or ambiguity as to whether someone is or is not a member of the LLC. On the topic of additional members, the operating agreement should specify the extent of a new member's authority to contractually bind the company. The operating agreement should outline the powers of the member or manager responsible for the LLC's business operations. Lastly, an indemnification clause would be a good idea, specifically in the instance where the original member has transferred his interest to another party. This clause can help to protect the original member, as well as inform the new member, regarding liability from any conflict that should arise after the interests have been transferred.

¶ 303
Combining the Documents

Almost all of the enabling statutes allow limited liability companies broad discretion to include items in the articles of organization that are not required by the statute.[13] For example, the Michigan statute permits an LLC to include any "provision not inconsistent with this act or another statute of this state, including any provision that under this act is required or permitted to be in an operating agreement."[14] Accordingly, most LLCs could include in their articles of organization all of their working agreements, instead of executing a separate operating agreement. The drawback is that the articles of organization, unlike an operating agreement, is a public document. Therefore, the members of an LLC which used the articles of organization as a substitute for an operating agreement would surrender a great deal of privacy. Also, it may be more cumbersome in some jurisdictions to amend the articles of organization than to amend the operating agreement.[15]

¶ 304
Miscellaneous Documentation and Filing Requirements

In addition to filing the articles of organization, organizers of an LLC must address a host of other filing proprieties in order to comply with state law.

---

[13] The only exception seems to be Wisconsin, which provides that, "The articles of organization shall contain *all of and only* the following information . . ." The statute goes on to list five specific pieces of information. Wis. Stat. § 183.0202 (emphasis added).

[14] *See, e.g.,* Mich. Comp. Laws § 450.4203(2); Fla. Stat. ch. 608.407(2)(H).

[15] See ¶ 301 concerning how to amend the articles of organization and an operating agreement, respectively.

LLC Name

An LLC name must contain language or an abbreviation clearly identifying it as an LLC. Permitted abbreviations vary from state to state, but the following are common: LC, L.C., LLC, L.L.C., Ltd., or Limited. Like a corporation or partnership, the LLC name must not be too similar to names of other LLCs. One problem that naturally arises as a result of the differing requirements among the states is that a name may be acceptable in one state for an LLC, but not in another. Therefore, if an LLC anticipates doing business in more than one state, it will be necessary to choose a name that will meet the requirements of *every* state it expects to do business in. For example, in Iowa, the necessary words which must appear at the end of a limited liability company's name are "limited company," "limited liability company" or the abbreviation "L.C." or "L.L.C." In Nebraska, however, the name must contain either "Limited Liability Company" or "L.L.C." The Nebraska statute does not permit a foreign LLC to do business in the state if its name includes an abbreviation other than "L.L.C." Thus, in a situation like this, where it is possible that business dealings will cross the state border between the two states, a company should choose the name that will be accepted in both states.

Number of Persons Required

Prior to the check-the-box regulations, most states required that an LLC have at least two members at the time of formation. This element, which limits the utility of the LLC in some instances, was thought to be necessary to preserve partnership tax status under federal tax law. In most states, however, it was not required that two or more persons actually "organize" the LLC.

In the past few years, this has turned completely around, and now all states currently permit (either explicitly or implicitly) single-member LLCs. See ¶ 302 for a more detailed discussion of single-member LLCs.

Another issue frequently encountered by practitioners is whether a husband and wife together, in a community property state, may be the sole member of an LLC or whether they constitute a two-member LLC subject to the federal partnership tax rules.

The IRS recently provided guidance, for federal tax purposes, of a qualified entity, including an LLC, that is owned solely by a husband and wife as community property under the laws of a state, a foreign country or a possession of the United States. A business entity is a qualified entity if:

(1) it is wholly owned by a husband and wife as community property under the laws of a state, foreign country or U.S. possession;

(2) no person other than one or both spouses would be considered an owner for federal tax purposes; and

¶304

(3) the entity is not treated as a corporation under Reg. § 301.7701-2.

If the husband and wife, as community property owners treat the LLC as a disregarded entity for federal tax purposes, the IRS will accept that position. If the entity is treated as a partnership for federal tax purposes and the appropriate partnership tax returns are filed, the IRS will accept the position that the LLC is a partnership for federal tax purposes. This revenue procedure did not offer guidance regarding the treatment for federal tax purposes of a similarly situated husband and wife in a noncommunity property state, such as a husband and wife who own the LLC as tenants by the entirety.[17]

Another potential weakness when only a husband and wife are involved as members of an LLC is that one of the parties may have made the total contribution for the interest received. If a husband and wife are to be the sole members of an LLC, they should each contribute the money or property that is required for their interests. Moreover, the need for an operating agreement delineating each person's exact rights and obligations would appear to be even more appropriate in this sort of case. At least this will document the separate ownership of their respective interests.

Organizers

The requirements regarding organizers of the entity and their relationship to the LLC have not drastically changed. An LLC is formed when an organizer (or organizers) prepares, signs and files the articles of organization, or comparable state document, with the appropriate state agency, usually the secretary of state. Most, if not all, states (plus the District of Columbia) permit an LLC to be organized by one (or more) persons.[18] Also, some states explicitly allow the organizer(s) to not be a member of the LLC (in these instances, oftentimes the attorney for the LLC will be the organizer).

For purposes of being an LLC organizer, the term "person" can be generally understood in most states to include an individual, general partnership, limited partnership, another LLC, business trust, real estate trust, or other association.[19] A few states do, however, require organizers to be "natural persons," and some require that these persons be at least 18 years old at the time of organization.[20]

Recordkeeping

Most state statutes list the records required to be kept by an LLC at its principal or registered office. The records are generally available to members, but not assignees, for inspection.

---

[17] Rev. Proc. 2002-69, 2002-2 CB 831.

[18] Mississippi is silent regarding how many people are required to organize an LLC.

[19] See, e.g., Ark. Code §4-32-102(1); Del. Code tit. 6, §18-101(12).

[20] See, e.g., 805 Ill. Comp. Stat. 180/5-1; Tex. Rev. Civ. Stat. art. 1528n, §3.01. See also Md. Code Corps. & Ass'ns §4A-206(a)(1) and N.D. Cent. Code §10-32-05, which specify that a person, and no other entity, must organize an LLC.

Arizona contains typical recordkeeping requirements. It mandates that the following records and information be kept: [21]

- name and last known address of each current member;
- copies of articles of organization and all amendments;
- all written operating agreements, including those no longer in effect;
- copy of any written promise of a member to make a capital contribution;
- tax returns for three most recent years; and
- financial statements for three most recent years.

Some states also provide that records be maintained reflecting certain information concerning members' contributions and rights to distributions.[22]

Annual Report

More than half of the jurisdictions require the filing of an annual report[23] and a few jurisdictions require the filing of a biennial report.[24] This report may contain basic information—name and office(s) of the LLC, names and addresses of members, managers, agents, etc.—that essentially repeats and verifies information set forth in the LLC's articles of organization.

Fees

Each state has its own fee structure in place for the various documents that may need to be filed by an LLC at the time of formation or during its life. Many states also have some sort of annual registration fee. Fees for filing articles of organization typically range from $50 to $500. In Wyoming, the filing fee can be as much as $25,000 for heavily capitalized LLCs. The state-by-state analysis in Chapter 10 contains a description of some of the basic fees one might encounter in each state.

¶ 305

Registered Office and Service of Process

In order to transact business within a state, an LLC must maintain a legal presence within the state. Almost all states require that the LLC maintain a registered office, which may or may not be its principal business office, and a registered agent to receive service of process. The registered agent's office generally must be at the same address as

---

[21] Ariz. Rev. Stat. § 29-607.

[22] *See, e.g.,* Colo. Rev. Stat. § 7-80-411(f) and Va. Code § 13.1-1028A.5.

[23] California, Connecticut, D.C., Florida, Georgia, Hawaii, Idaho, Illinois, Kansas, Kentucky, Louisiana, Maine, Massachusetts, Michigan, Minnesota, Montana, Nevada, New Hampshire, New Jersey, North Carolina, North Dakota, Oregon, Rhode Island, South Dakota, Tennessee, Utah, Vermont, Washington, Wisconsin and West Virginia. Texas requires an annual public information report to be filed when an LLC pays its franchise taxes.

[24] Alaska, California, Colorado, D.C., and Indiana. New York requires a biennial statement to be filed with the Department of State.

the LLC's registered office. State treatment varies widely as to who may serve as a registered agent.

Further, the name of the registered agent and the address of the registered office must be stated in the articles of organization. This law was intended to protect the creditors of the LLC. As a public document, it will be accessible to the creditors, and will thus allow them to theoretically get in touch with some authorized agent of the LLC, if for no other reason than to serve process. Most statutes allow an individual, a domestic corporation or a foreign corporation authorized to do business in the state to act as the agent for an LLC, as long as the chosen agent and the LLC have the same registered address.[25] Some states permit a domestic or foreign LLC to be a registered agent as well,[26] and a few states even specifically authorize an LLC to be its own registered agent.[27]

---

[25] *See, e.g.,* Fla. Stat. ch. 608.415; 805 Ill. Comp. Stat. 180/1-35.

[26] *See, e.g.,* Ark. Code § 4-32-105; N.J. Rev. Stat. § 42:2B-6.

[27] *See, e.g.,* Del. Code tit. 6, § 18-104; Kan. Stat. § 17-7611(A)(2).

Chapter 4

Membership Rights and Obligations— Management of LLCs

¶ 401
Nature of an Interest in an LLC

An LLC interest is personal property. An LLC interest includes rights to share in the LLC's profits and to receive distributions or the return of capital in accordance with the LLC's operating agreement. The holder of an LLC interest has no interest in specific LLC property. Rather, LLC property is owned by the entity.

Ownership of an LLC interest should be distinguished from membership in the LLC. Owning an interest and membership are not equivalent. Generally, a membership interest provides the member with the right to manage and control the LLC and also provides the member with economic rights to the profits, losses and distributions of the LLC. An ownership interest only provides the owner with economic rights to the profits, losses, and distributions of the LLC. Merely owning an interest without being a member generally does not entitle the owner to the right to manage and control the LLC. Thus, when a member assigns an interest in the LLC, the assignee receives only the economic rights that the member possessed. The member still retains the right to manage and control the LLC.

Although most LLC statutes do not specifically address separating the management rights from the economic rights, the possibility of doing so and creating a variety of ownership interests provides added flexibility to structure various business arrangements. Also, separating the management rights from the economic rights may enable the LLC to place restrictions on the management rights while allowing the economic rights to be freely transferred.

¶ 402

Securities Law Impact on LLCs

Federal Treatment of Membership Interests

There has been some discussion among legal commentators as to whether an LLC interest should be treated as a "security" under federal and state laws.[1] LLCs seem likely to be treated on a case-by-case basis under the federal securities laws. Usually, a *Howey* investment contract analysis will be employed.[2] Under this analysis a court will determine whether:

(1) there is an investment of money in a common enterprise

(2) with an expectation of profits to come

(3) solely from others.

The amount of control the members can realistically exercise within the LLC and the extent to which they are simply passive investors is examined. Therefore, the more passive the investors are, the more investors there are, and the less knowledgeable they are, the more likely that the LLC membership interest will be seen as a security under the federal laws.

Certain provisions could be included in the articles of organization or the operating agreement to ensure that the membership interests of the LLC would not be securities. The articles could require that management of the LLC and its daily activities rest with the members. The articles could also prohibit delegation by the members of their management authority to anyone else. Finally, membership in the LLC could be limited to only those people who are sophisticated and knowledgeable about the business. The membership may also be limited to a very small number of people who would all work daily with the LLC.

If the LLC is operating on the other end of the spectrum, it is very likely that its membership interests would be securities. For example, if the operating agreement states that managers are to operate the business of the LLC and the members do not have any voting rights over any aspect of the company, an LLC membership interest would be considered a security. However, an operating agreement that provides that investing members, who are not involved in the LLC's management, retain the right to remove existing management may prevent LLC interests from being classified as securities.

Between these two extremes will fall the vast majority of the LLCs that are currently being formed in the United States. Whether or not

[1] See Marc I. Steinberg and Karen L. Conway, *The Limited Liability Company as a Security*, 19 Pepperdine L. Rev. 1105 (1992).

[2] *Securities & Exchange Commission v. W.J. Howey Co., et al.*, 328 U.S. 293 (1946).

membership interests in these LLCs will be securities may be difficult to determine in advance. LLCs may want to avoid putting investment representations in operating agreements for anything other than private placement deals so as not to concede the status of a membership interest as a security.

Federal Trade Commission

The FTC, with concurrence of the Antitrust Division of the Department of Justice (DOJ), issued a notice of amendment of Formal Interpretation 15, which involves LLCs and the Hart-Scott-Rodino Antitrust Improvements Act of 1976.[3] The Act requires those planning certain mergers, consolidations or other acquisitions to report information about the proposed transactions to the FTC and the DOJ. At first, LLCs were treated as corporations for purposes of the Act. This treatment of LLCs, however, required many unnecessary filings. Further, the FTC's pre-merger notification office found that, in most LLCs, the interest held by the members of the LLC was more like a partnership interest than a voting security interest. Consequently, in 1994, the FTC began looking at LLCs on a case-by-case basis to determine the character of the membership interest.

The FTC found that this solution was also not completely satisfactory, particularly since LLCs are often used to combine competing businesses under common control. Therefore, the treatment of LLCs by the FTC has again been revised. The FTC now treats the formation of an LLC as reportable if: (1) two or more pre-existing, separately controlled businesses will be contributed; and (2) at least one of the members will have an interest entitling the member to 50 percent or more of the profits or assets of the LLC upon dissolution. The formation of an LLC with three or more parties will not be reportable unless one member has a 50 percent or greater interest. The formation of all other LLCs will be treated similarly to the formation of a partnership (*i.e.*, not reported). An LLC formation must be reported only if the formation joins the LLC with two formerly separately controlled businesses.

The acquisition of a membership interest in an existing LLC will be a potentially reportable event if: (1) it results in the acquiring person holding a 100-percent membership interest in the LLC; and (2) that person had not previously filed for and consummated the acquisition of control of that LLC. This is similar to the treatment of acquisitions of partnership interests. Acquisitions of additional businesses by existing LLCs that result in a change in the membership interest of any member will be treated as the formation of a new LLC. Acquisitions of businesses by existing LLCs that do not result in a change in the percentage membership interest of any member will be treated as the acquisition of assets or voting securities of the business by the LLC.

---

[3] 15 U.S.C. § 18a.

State Treatment of Membership Interests

The state securities statutes, known as Blue Sky laws, are not pre-empted by the federal securities laws. Instead the two regulatory schemes operate side by side. Therefore, the same considerations with federal securities laws apply to the state laws. Although each state's definition of a security varies, the vast majority of the state statutes use a definition of security very similar to that found in the federal securities acts. Some states have passed legislation concerning the treatment of LLCs under their securities laws or judicially confront the issue of whether an LLC membership interest is a security and the availability of an exemption from registration for membership interests. Several of these states have adopted the *Howey* test for determining whether a membership interest is a security.[4]

The states take a more dogmatic, less refined approach to determining securities treatment. The various state approaches may generally be categorized into five groupings, which include:

(1) those in which the relevant statutes, court decisions and administrative rulings or informal communications establish a bright-line definition that LLC interests are securities by definition or implication;[5]

(2) those where a rebuttable presumption exists that LLC interests are securities;

(3) those taking a facts and circumstances approach with no apparent presumption;

(4) those where LLC interests are specifically defined not to be securities; and

(5) those states where no authority exists on the question.

In states that do not have bright-line definitional exclusions or inclusions, several factors have emerged. Manager-managed LLCs will result in greater scrutiny.[6] By contrast, interests in member-managed LLCs with few members usually will not constitute securities. In addition, in a facts and circumstances determination, investor reliance upon the particular skill of one member may tend to lead regulators to the conclusion that the interests constitute securities. Smaller LLCs tend to draw less attention than larger LLCs. The lowest level of scrutiny tends to be given to member-managed LLCs.

Exemptions

Federal or state exemptions from treatment as a security also may exist. There are two types of exemptions from registration that are

---

[4] *See, e.g.,* Montana, Opinion Letter, *H-I Missoula, LLC* (Mon. Sec. Dept. 6/15/95); Oklahoma, No-Action letter, *Amici Pecuniarius, L.C.* (Okla. Dept. Sec., 8/28/92); *Nutek Information Systems, Inc. v. Arizona Corporation Commission,* Ariz. Ct. App. No. CV96-20499 (11/5/98).

[5] *See, e.g.,* Ohio and Vermont, which are among the states that define securities to include LLC membership interests.

[6] States that define memberships interests in manager-managed LLCs as securities, subject to rebuttal include California and Pennsylvania.

recognized by the federal securities laws: exempt securities and exempt transactions. Section 3 of the Securities Act of 1933 ("Securities Act") lists exempt securities and some exempt transactions. If an exemption exists for the security, it is never required to be registered, but remains subject to anti-fraud provisions. Exempt securities include certain short-term promissory notes, securities issued by municipal, state or federal governments and securities issued by nonprofit organizations.

Exempt transactions are set forth in Section 4 of the Securities Act. They include transactions that are part of an intrastate offering; transactions by any person other than an issuer, underwriter, or dealer; and transactions not involving any public offering. In contrast to exempt securities, which, because of their character, are never required to be registered regardless of the form of the transaction, the availability of transaction exemptions depends on the nature of the particular transaction being undertaken. Those transaction exemptions which may have the most impact on LLCs include intrastate offering exemptions, limited offering exemptions and secondary offering exemptions.

Several states also provide exemptions from registration for membership interests. One type of exemption is for a transaction involving the offer and sale of a membership interest in a professional LLC.[7] Like the federal securities statutes, certain states provide limited offering exemptions for issuers that are LLCs.[8] A limited exemption may also be available for the offer or sale of securities by an issuer that is an LLC organized in a particular state or that has its principal place of business in a specific state.[9] Georgia's LLC act, on the other hand, contains a statement that its LLC law shall not be construed to mean that an LLC interest is not a security for Georgia state law purposes.[10]

LLC Membership Interests as Securities

If a membership interest in an LLC is deemed to be a security, then the offer and sale of the interest must comply with the registration and disclosure requirements of the Securities Act. Section 5 of the Securities Act states that unless a registration statement is in effect for a security, or the transaction is exempt from registration, it is unlawful to offer for sale or sell the security. Compliance with such registration and disclosure requirements can be complex and costly. Further, in registering, the issuer loses the confidentiality available in private transactions. Thus, most organizations prefer to avoid registration unless it is absolutely necessary.

On the other hand, if a membership interest is determined to be a security and to have been sold in violation of the securities laws, the

---

[7] Mich. Comp. Laws § 451.802 and 70 Pa. Cons. Stat. § 1-202(j).

[8] See, e.g., Me. Rev. Stat. tit. 32, § 10502 and N.H. Rev. Stat. § 421-B:17.

[9] See, e.g., Kan. Stat. § 17-1262(1) and N.M. Stat. § 58-13B-27(J).

[10] Ga. Code § 14-11-1107(n).

LLC, its organizers and its members are all exposed to civil liability and even possibly criminal prosecution. Thus, an LLC does not want to make a mistake about the current classification of interests it issues. Even if it appears that the membership interest probably will be a security, an exemption from the registration requirements for the sale of the membership may be available. If a membership interest is a security, it will be subject to the anti-fraud provisions of the federal securities laws.

¶ 403

Transfers of LLC Interests

Significant restrictions are generally placed on the transfer of an LLC interest to reflect the intent of the parties who often desire veto power or a substantial voice concerning who joins the LLC.

Generally, a state's LLC act provides that unanimous, or at least majority, consent of the other members is necessary to transfer all incidents to membership, including a financial interest in the LLC, the right to participate in management, the right to see the LLC's books and records, and the right to compel dissolution. Depending on the state, this restriction on transferability may be mandatory or it may be a statutory default provision that can be altered in an operating agreement or articles of organization. LLC members, however, are generally free to assign their economic interests without the approval of other members.

As a general rule, when an assignee becomes a member, he or she has, to the extent assigned, the rights, powers, preferences and limitations of a member under the articles of organization, the operating agreement, and the pertinent enabling legislation. At the same time, the assignee is subject to all of the restrictions and liabilities of a member.

The liability assumed by an assignee can range from only those liabilities agreed to between the assignor and assignee, to liability for promised contributions and unknown indebtedness. Typically, an assignee who becomes a member is responsible for promised contributions of the assignor and, in some states, wrongful distributions as well. Under this rule, however, an assignee who becomes a member will generally not assume liabilities that were unknown to the assignee at the time he or she became a member and that could not be discovered from the written records of the LLC.

Disadvantages of Requiring Unanimous Consent

Prohibiting the transfer of a member's interest without unanimous consent creates some real disadvantages. It gives every member veto power over transfers and the admission of new members. Also, except in LLCs with very few members, it may be cumbersome to obtain consent from all members. Particularly in LLCs with passive members, unanimous consent may be an unwanted barrier.

Pledge of LLC Interest as Security

LLC members and assignees generally can pledge their interests in an LLC as security for debt. The security interest does not extend to specific LLC property; rather, the security interest is limited to the member's or assignee's interest in LLC property. The rights of a judgment creditor generally are limited to those of an assignee—in other words, the creditor's interest is limited to the member's financial interest in the LLC.[11] Thus, creditors who accept an LLC interest as security cannot vote the member's interest or participate in management. Nor may creditors of a member compel dissolution of the LLC.

¶ 404

Management of LLC by Managers or Members

Generally, management rights are vested in all LLC members unless the operating agreement or the articles of organization provide for a more limited management group. This default provision is present in almost all state statutes.[12] The default provision reflects the management structure that will be preferred by small LLCs, which are most likely not to enter into a customized operating agreement.

A few states have modeled many of the management provisions of their LLC laws on the states' business corporation acts. In these states, management authority is vested with a board of governors similar to a corporate board of directors.[13]

Customizing Management Rights in Operating Agreement

Many LLCs will want to designate a group of persons to manage the business. Management authority can be tailored in a number of ways in the operating agreement. The following are some examples:

- A class of ownership interests could carry with it the management authority for the LLC.

- The operating agreement could establish an annually selected group analogous to a corporate board of directors.

[11] *See, e.g.,* Iowa Code § 490A.904.

[12] North Carolina is one notable exception, providing that management rights are vested in a group of designated managers. The North Carolina Act actually comes very close to vesting management in the LLC's members since there is a presumption that all members are managers. N.C. Gen. Stat. § 57C-3-20.

[13] *See, e.g.,* Minn. Stat. § 322B.606.

- Management rights relating to LLC policy-setting could remain with the members, while certain administrative powers could be executed by an LLC manager.

- The LLC could be managed by a nonmember management company.

Who May Serve as a Manager

Most states do not delineate qualifications for LLC managers, although qualifications may be prescribed in the articles of organization or operating agreement. Managers generally are not required to be members of the LLC.[14] Nor are they required to be state residents. In professional LLCs, managers generally must be eligible to practice within the state in which the LLC is organized (see Chapter 8).

In some cases, an LLC will want to restrict the manager's business activities outside the LLC. Thus, it could choose not to allow its managers to have ownership interests in businesses that are competitive with the LLC's business. The sample operating agreement in Appendix A contains a liberal provision that is suitable where anti-competition issues are not relevant.[15]

Managers are generally elected by the members. In some states, the LLC has a free hand in crafting the selection and removal process. In others, statutory provisions may more rigidly define the process. It is not uncommon, for example, for there to be a mandatory annual election of managers.[16]

Role of Officers

Corporations, by state statute, must have officers. LLCs do not generally have the same requirement, but LLC organizers may want to assign similar roles. Some states authorize officer provisions. California provides that officers may be appointed in a written operating agreement.[17] It further provides that any written action undertaken and signed by an LLC officer on behalf of the LLC is not invalidated by the officer's lack of authority unless the other person had actual knowledge that the officer had no authority to execute the document.

Iowa allows a member or manager of an LLC to delegate the member or manager's rights and powers to manage and control the business, including to agents or employees.[18] Delaware also permits such delegation *and* expressly includes officers as persons to whom management and control may be delegated.[19] Both states also give members or managers the right to delegate by management agreement or another agreement with other persons.

---

[14] *See, e.g.,* Colo. Rev. Stat. § 7-80-401(1)(b).
[15] See Article VI, .06 Other Activities.
[16] *See, e.g.,* Wyo. Stat. § 17-15-116 (annual elections unless the operating agreement provides otherwise).
[17] Cal. Corp. Code § 17154(c).
[18] Iowa Code § 490A.710.
[19] Del. Code tit. 6, § 18-407.

¶404

Some states have adopted a more elaborate approach to delegating management. North Dakota and Tennessee, for example, provide for management by or under the direction of a board of governors.[20]

The role of officers in LLCs may take different forms. A manager who believes that the title of "manager" does not adequately reflect the degree of authority that the person has in the company may prefer the title of "president" as a more corporate, better-recognized title. The second form is the manager who wishes to delegate certain duties to others. He or she might want to assume the role of a traditional "chairman of the board" and appoint others to the roles of president, vice president, secretary, and treasurer. Alternatively, in a large LLC, the manager may want to assume the role of president and delegate authority to a series of vice presidents. Generally, the statutes permit a manager to call himself or herself whatever he or she wants as long as there is authority to back up the implications of the title.

¶ 405

Duties and Authority of Managers and Managing Members

Whether an LLC is managed by its members or by certain designated managers, the "office" of manager carries with it certain duties, obligations and authority.

Management Authority

State law typically gives LLC members management authority similar to that of a general partner. They may actively participate in all management and policy-setting decisions of the LLC. This authority may be fully or partially delegated in a group of managers, depending on the terms of the LLC's operating agreement.

It is important to distinguish management authority from the ability of managers or members to bind the LLC (see ¶ 408). Limitations on a manager's rights set forth in the operating agreement will not necessarily prevent the manager from legally binding the LLC in dealings with third parties, for example, unless the third party is aware of the restriction.

Fiduciary Duties

Managers or managing members owe certain fiduciary duties to the LLC. States vary in their approach to defining these duties. Iowa and Virginia adopt as a fiduciary standard a good-faith judgment of the best interests of the LLC.[21] Delaware provides that a member or manager is not liable to the LLC or its members for actions arising out of a good-faith reliance on the LLC's operating agreement.[22]

---

[20] N.D. Cent. Code § 10-32-69 and Tenn. Code § 48-238-101.

[21] Iowa Code § 490A.706.
[22] Del. Code tit. 6, § 18-1101(d).

Many states do not directly address the scope and nature of a manager's or managing member's fiduciary duties. Presumably, in all states, the legal principles setting forth standards of conduct for business fiduciaries will apply to LLC managers and managing members as well. Most states do not allow an operating agreement to eliminate or reduce a member or manager's fiduciary duties. However, the operating agreement may determine reasonable standards by which the performance of fiduciary duties is to be measured.[23]

Under the Uniform Limited Liability Company Act, a member, manager, or their delegates owe to the company and to the other members the fiduciary duties of loyalty and care. In addition, a member is required to discharge his or her duties under the operating agreement and exercise any rights consistently with the obligation of good faith and fair dealing.[24] Other fiduciary duties include candor (*i.e.,* the duty to disclose, as appropriate, certain information to other managers or nonmanagers) and confidentiality. For a further discussion of fiduciary duties, see ¶ 302.

¶ 406

Voting Rights in an LLC

The operating agreement should clearly spell out the method for allocating voting rights among the members or managers eligible to participate in LLC decisions. The agreement should also set out any actions that require greater than a majority vote to be approved. The default provision under state law will govern in the absence of an operating agreement.

States are split about evenly in their default provisions between allocations of voting rights according to the members' relative capital contributions and per capita allocations of voting rights. Capital-based voting raises several issues: What are the voting rights of a member who has received an interest in exchange for services? Are promissory notes or other unsecured obligations taken into account in determining a member's voting rights?[25] Also, it would seem necessary to determine the member's relative book capital account each time a vote on LLC matters is taken.

Allocating voting rights among the members on a per capita basis is the default method in the Uniform Limited Liability Company Act.[26] It is also present in many state LLC statutes.[27] A slightly less popular

---

[23] *See, e.g.,* 805 Ill. Comp. Stat. 180/15-5. See, also, *Lynch Multimedia Corporation v. Carson Communications, L.L.C., et al.,* No. 99-1134-JTM (D. Kan. June 26, 2000) (members may expand or restrict their duties to each other by agreement).

[24] Uniform Limited Liability Company Act (1996) § 409.

[25] Virginia, for instance, has a capital-based voting mechanism and specifically defines a contribution to include cash

or property contributed and services rendered or a binding obligation to contribute cash, property or services. Va. Code § 13.1-1022(B). Virginia does not, however, delineate how to value the contribution of services or unsecured promises to contribute cash, property or services at a later date.

[26] Uniform Limited Liability Company Act (1996) § 404.

[27] *See, e.g.,* Ariz. Rev. Stat. § 29-681(E).

default provision utilized by some states allocates voting rights according to the members' relative profits interests.[28]

Typically, a majority vote by members or managers is sufficient to authorize most LLC actions, with the exception of some critical decisions for which a greater percentage or a unanimous vote may be required—amendments to the operating agreement, for example. In some states, the unanimity requirement for certain actions cannot be altered in an operating agreement.

¶ 407

Liabilities of Members and Managers to Third Parties

Limited liability is a hallmark of LLCs. It extends protection to members and managers from legal suits against the LLC by third parties. However, like limited partners, LLC members are at risk of losing the property they contribute to the LLC.

The Delaware limited liability provision is typical. It states:

> . . . no member or manager of a limited liability company shall be obligated personally for any such debt, obligation or liability of the limited liability company solely by reason of being a member or acting as the manager of the limited liability company.[29]

Notice that an individual is not protected from direct liabilities to third parties—*i.e.,* those that do not "pass through" the LLC by virtue of member or manager status. Thus, an LLC member may be liable to third parties for the debts and obligations of the LLC if the member has guaranteed such obligations.[30] Similarly, a member may become liable for tort claims against the LLC as the result of the member's own negligence.

Many states affirmatively provide that LLC members are not proper parties to an action against an LLC, unless it is to enforce a member's right against, or liability to, the LLC.[31]

"Piercing the LLC Veil"

Many courts have now confronted the issue of piercing the LLC veil. The doctrine of piercing the corporate veil has been applied to LLCs to determine whether LLC members are personally liable for the LLC's debts and obligations. Under this principle, a corporation's existence (and liability shield for shareholders) is disregarded. Theories for piercing the LLC veil that would be recognized in most states include undercapitalization, distributions made to members in insolvency situa-

---

[28] Del. Code tit. 6, § 18-402.

[29] Del. Code tit. 6, § 18-303(a).

[30] An LLC member also may be liable for an obligation to make an additional capital contribution. This is an obligation to the LLC, and third parties generally are not able to directly enforce the member's contribution obligation (see ¶ 501), although the LLC could compel the member to fulfill his obligation as part of a third-party proceeding against the LLC.

[31] *See, e.g.,* Kan. Stat. § 17-7688 and Nev. Rev. Stat. § 86.381.

tions, and failure to inform a third party that it was dealing with an LLC. Lack of separateness between the member(s) and the LLC and failure to follow formalities are also theories for piercing the LLC veil. Much light has been shed on this issue in some recent court decisions.

In *Ditty v. Checkrite, Ltd., Inc., et al.*,[32] the court equated members of an LLC to shareholders and, therefore, adopted the corporate alter ego doctrine outright. To pierce the LLC veil under Utah's alter ego doctrine, it must be shown that: (1) there is such a unity of interest and ownership that the separate personalities of the LLC and the individual no longer exist, but that the LLC is, instead, the alter ego of one or a few of its members; and (2) if observed, the LLC form would sanction a fraud, promote injustice or result in an inequity. Although the court held that there was insufficient evidence to pierce the protective veil of the LLC and hold the member personally liable for the LLC's unlawful practices, it did hold the member personally liable for the same conduct under common law tort theories.

Similarly, a bankruptcy court in Florida applied corporate standards to determine that two related LLCs were not alter egos in the case of *In re Multimedia Communications Group Wireless Associates of Liberty County*.[33] The LLCs had common management, a common business location, common personnel, and a common computer network. Moreover, the entities lacked company formalities. However, the LLCs kept separate books and accounts for each entity, and each entity was engaged in its own distinct business practices. The LLCs were not set up to engage in a fraudulent or improper purpose. Thus, the principal managers were not personally liable for the LLCs' debts.

Although allegations of fraud often accompany creditor's actions to pierce the LLC veil, such an allegation is not required. In *Hollowell v. Orleans Regional Hospital, LLC, et al.*, the court held that the veil of an LLC could be pierced in the same manner as a corporation.[34] A finding of fraud was not necessary to pierce the LLC veil. Instead, the totality of the circumstances determined that the LLC was the alter ego of its owners. Evidence that the LLC owners received a $1.5 million distribution on the eve of the LLC shutdown, used the company for nonbusiness purposes and profited at the expense of LLC employees was sufficient to find that an alter ego relationship existed. The court also found that where LLC owners formed a new LLC to defraud creditors or as a continuation of the old LLC, the newly organized LLC was liable for the debts of the old one.

One state court that has looked at the veil-piercing issue is the Colorado Supreme Court. In *Water, Waste & Land, Inc., d/b/a Westec v.*

---

[32] *Ditty v. Checkrite, Ltd., Inc., et al.*, Civ. No. 2:95-CV-430C (D. Utah, August 11, 1997).

[33] *In re Multimedia Communications Group Wireless Associates of Liberty County*, Bankr. M.D. Fla., No. 95-5528-BKC-3F7, Adv. No. 96-349 (August 28, 1997).

[34] *Hollowell v. Orleans Regional Hospital, LLC, et al.*, No. 98-31105 and No. 99-30123 (5th Cir. July 18, 2000) affirming the U.S. District Court, Eastern District of Louisiana.

Lanham,[35] an LLC's member-managers were not protected from liability when they failed to disclose their agency relationship. The court found that the Colorado LLC Act provision that shields LLC members or managers from liability applies only where a third party seeks to impose liability on members or managers strictly due to their status as members or managers. It does not, the court said, protect members or managers in situations involving a partially disclosed agent.

Some states address the issue in their LLC enabling statutes. Two of these states mandate that courts apply corporate case law to LLCs when determining the circumstances under which the liability veil of an LLC will be pierced.[36] Others have specifically provided that state laws allowing the piercing of the corporate veil apply to LLCs.[37] Still other states apply the principles of common law that are similar to those applicable to business corporations and shareholders.[38] The failure of an LLC to observe the usual company formalities or requirements relating to the exercise of its company powers or management of its business will usually not be a ground for imposing personal liability on the members or managers of the LLC.[39] However, LLC operating agreements should not require formalities, such as annual meetings, unless the LLC members will strictly adhere to the requirements.

Two Connecticut cases highlight the importance of paying attention to formalities. In *Bastan et al. v. RJM and Associates, LLC et al.*, a sole member of an LLC argued that the LLC veil could not be pierced because the LLC was member-operated and the state statutes allowed members to act as individuals.[40] The court reasoned that it would only serve to defeat justice and equity if the LLC's single member was permitted to disregard the structure required in the formation and operation of the LLC but still benefit from personal liability protection. Similarly, in *Rodale Press, Inc. v. Harold Salm et al.*, the court imposed personal liability on an LLC member who failed to properly comply with the statutory requirements for registering the LLC with a fictitious business name.[41]

Most LLC statutes provide that a judgment creditor of an LLC member may apply to a court for a charging order against a membership interest for payment of the unsatisfied judgment with interest. A creditor receives no greater rights than that of an assignee of the membership interest. A charging order is typically the exclusive remedy for a judgment creditor of an LLC member. Most creditors do not find a charging order to be a very satisfactory solution to collecting a

---

[35] *Water, Waste, & Land, Inc., d/b/a Westec v. Lanham,* Colo. S. Ct., No. 97SC199 (March 9, 1998).

[36] N.D. Cent. Code § 10-32-29(3) and Wash. Rev. Code § 25.15.060.

[37] *See, e.g.,* Cal. Corp. Code § 17101(b); Minn. Stat. § 322B.303.

[38] *See, e.g.,* Me. Rev. Stat. tit. 31, § 645(3); Wis. Stat. § 183.0304(2).

[39] *See, e.g.,* Cal. Corp. Code § 17101(b); Mont. Code § 35-8-304(2).

[40] *Bastan et al. v. RJM and Associates, LLC, et al.,* Conn. Super. Ct., No. CV990593189S (June 4, 2001).

[41] *Rodale Press, Inc. v. Harold Salm et al.,* Conn. Super. Ct., No. CV000374938S (April 23, 2001).

judgment because it provides no interest in the LLC except economic. As a result, creditors have sought to reach the LLC's assets to satisfy the judgment against the individual member. This has become known as "reverse veil piercing."[42]

Single-Member LLC Tax Liability

When a single-member LLC elects to be a disregarded entity, the IRS treats the activities of the LLC in the same manner as a sole proprietorship. Thus, a single member is responsible for the LLC's tax liabilities. In a 1999 ruling, the IRS issued its policy regarding the IRS's ability to place a lien against the assets of a single-member LLC to satisfy the tax obligations of the single member.[43] The IRS ruled that the mere fact that the LLC is disregarded for federal tax purposes does not mean that the IRS will disregard the entity for purposes of collection. Code Secs. 6321 and 6331 authorize the IRS to create a lien against all assets belonging to an individual owing taxes. However, under state law, LLCs are separate entities from their members and individual members do not have property interests in LLC property. As a result, the IRS could not serve a levy against the LLC property because it does not belong to the member. The IRS reasoned that if the taxpayer had a transferable distributional in the LLC (under state statute), the IRS could place a lien on that interest. In addition, the IRS was entitled to pursue the same veil piercing grounds as any other third party.

Indemnification of Members and Managers by the LLC

Many states grant LLCs the power to indemnify a member or manager from costs, judgments, settlements, and penalties incurred in the capacity as an LLC member or manager. The indemnification provisions vary from state to state. Many are simple grants of power.[44]

In other states, the power may be restricted. Some states have even enacted indemnification provisions for managers, employees, and agents that attempt to specifically address a number of scenarios. Minnesota, for example, requires an LLC to make advances to a manager or member who is made or threatened to be made party to a proceeding upon a written request to the LLC for payment or reimbursement of reasonable expenses including attorney's fees and disbursements incurred prior to the final disposition of the proceeding. The LLC is entitled to receive written assurances from the member or manager that the member or manager's believe, in good faith, that they are entitled to reimbursement. In addition, the members or managers must promise to repay the amount advanced in the event they do not

---

[42] *Litchfield Asset Management v. Howell*, 806 A.2d 49 (Conn. App. July 17, 2002) (based upon the alter ego, instrumentality and identity theories, the court reverse pierced the veils of two LLCs to reach the LLC assets in satisfaction of a judgment against the individual who controlled and owned a vast majority of the LLC interests).

[43] Chief Counsel Advice 199930013 (April 18, 1999).

[44] *See, e.g.,* Del. Code tit. 6, § 18-108.

meet the reimbursement criteria. Many state indemnification statutes also expressly permit the purchase of liability insurance.[45]

Compromise of Member's Contribution Obligation

Generally, state LLC law provides that a member's obligation to make a contribution to an LLC may be reduced (*i.e.,* "compromised") by unanimous consent of the members. The unanimity rule can be altered in the operating agreement. Notwithstanding the compromise, an LLC creditor who extends credit or otherwise relies on the contribution obligation before the compromise may enforce the original obligation against the LLC.[46]

¶ 408

Ability of Members or Managers to Bind the LLC

The rules of agency will generally govern in determining whether the acts or omissions of an LLC manager or member bind the LLC and are enforceable against the LLC. Many state LLC acts provide little or no guidance on the issue, preferring to rely upon the state's judicial developments regarding agency law. Because LLC statutes are influenced by both partnership and corporation law, agency law relating to either entity will likely have a strong influence on developing LLC law.

Under agency law, the authority of general partners versus the authority of corporate directors and officers is not always identical. It remains to be seen how the law of agency will be applied to an LLC's managers or managing members. In the Uniform Limited Liability Company Act, members of a member-managed LLC and managers of a manager-managed LLC, as agents of the firm, have the apparent authority to bind the LLC to third parties.[47]

Management Authority Distinguished

There is an important distinction between the management authority granted to a member or manager in the LLC's operating agreement and the authority of a member or manager to bind the LLC. Whether the LLC is managed by members or designated managers, the *apparent authority* to act, from the viewpoint of a third party, will govern in determining whether the member's or manager's actions bind the LLC. Restrictions on actual authority, defined in the operating agreement, will be irrelevant unless the third party has knowledge or should know of the restriction.

Member-Managed LLCs

If the LLC is member-managed, this "apparent authority" standard will likely be the governing principle. In most states, any member can bind the LLC with respect to acts that are within the ordinary course of

---

[45] *See, e.g.,* Tex. Rev. Civ. Stat. art. 1528n, § 2.20(A).

[46] *See, e.g.,* Mich. Comp. Laws § 450.4302(4).

[47] Uniform Limited Liability Company Act (1996) § 301.

business. Some states provide that any member can contract debts on behalf of the LLC.[48] The Arizona statute expressly states the apparent authority standard as follows:

> The act of each member, including the execution in the name of the LLC of any instrument, for apparently carrying on in the usual way the business of the LLC of which he is a member binds the LLC unless the acting member has in fact no authority to act for the LLC in the particular matter and the person with whom he is dealing has knowledge of the fact that the member has no such authority.[49]

LLC members (and managers) bind the LLC for all actions for which they possess actual authority, even if the act is not within the ordinary course of carrying on the LLC's business.

Manager-Managed LLCs

If a designated group of managers is managing an LLC, most states require that the articles of organization contain some information concerning the managers. Common requirements are that the articles either list the names and addresses of managers or contain a statement indicating that the LLC is managed by managers and not the LLC members.

Like members in member-managed LLCs, managers bind the LLC for acts for which they have either apparent or actual authority. In some states, the LLC statute affirmatively states that a member is not an agent of a manager-managed LLC and, therefore, cannot bind the LLC unless specifically authorized to act as its agent.[50] Also, some states specifically reserve for LLC managers, and not members, the authority to contract debts on behalf of the LLC if the LLC is not member-managed.[51] In all states, creditors should determine whether the LLC is manager-managed or member-managed before dealing directly with members.

Restrictions on Authority in the Articles of Organization

An LLC's articles of organization may, in most states, express restrictions on a manager's or member's authority. Also, as noted above, states often require the articles to include information regarding an LLC's managers. In these situations, creditors may be found to be on notice of these restrictions. Creditors must protect their interests accordingly.

---

[48] *See, e.g.,* Wyo. Stat. § 17-15-117.
[49] Ariz. Rev. Stat. § 29-654(A)(2).

[50] *See, e.g.,* Ariz. Rev. Stat. § 29-654B.1.
[51] *See, e.g.,* Wyo. Stat. § 17-15-117.

¶ 409

Transactions Between LLCs and Members or Managers

LLC acts generally are quite open to members and managers transacting business with the LLC. Most state statutes, particularly the more recent enactments, put members and managers on the same footing as unrelated third parties. The following language from Virginia law is typical:

> Except as provided in the articles of organization or an operating agreement, a member or manager may lend money to and transact other business with the limited liability company and, subject to other applicable law, has the same rights and obligations with respect thereto as a person who is not a member or manager.[52]

Clearly, LLCs may restrict member or manager transactions in the operating agreement. Most states do not legislatively address the issue of self-dealing and potential conflicts of interest, but there are exceptions. For instance, Iowa has delineated certain standards for LLC transactions with its managers. In Iowa, an LLC cannot void a business transaction with an LLC manager if: (1) the facts of the transaction and the manager's interest are disclosed to the managers or members who authorized or ratified the transaction; or (2) the transaction was, in fact, "fair" to the LLC.[53]

¶ 410

Inspection of Books and Records

Members of an LLC have the right to inspect the LLC's books and records. A list of the records typically required to be maintained by the LLC and made available for inspection is found in Chapter 3.

Until recently, a member's right to inspect books was restricted only as to a reasonable time and place. In 2002, Delaware took the lead in placing further restrictions on a member's right to access an LLC's books and records. The amended Delaware LLC statutes allow the LLC, itself, or the LLC's manager to limit the documents that are to be available to the members. A manager, acting in good faith, may keep confidential information that involves trade secrets or other information that the manager believes, in good faith, is not in the best interest of the LLC to disclose. The amended statute also provides a judicial remedy for a member who believes that information is being wrongfully withheld.[54]

---

[52] Va. Code § 13.1-1026.
[53] Iowa Code § 490A.708(1).

[54] Del. Code tit. 6, § 18-305.

¶ 411

Federal Election Commission

The Federal Campaign Act[55] sets forth the rules for contributions to federal campaigns. Corporations and labor organizations are prohibited from making any contribution or expenditure in connection with a federal election, although they may establish "separate segregated funds" (SSFs) and solicit contributions from their restricted class to the SSF. Other "persons," including partnerships, may make contributions to federal elections, but they are subject to the limits of the Act. Partnership contributions are attributed proportionately against each contributing partner's limit for the same candidate and election.

The FEC has announced that it will follow the "check-the-box" approach with regard to LLCs. The FEC determined that LLCs that elect corporate status for IRS purposes were more akin to corporations than to partnerships. Thus, the agency said that it could most effectively follow the intent of the law by classifying LLCs according to their federal tax status, which reflects the LLC's structure and function.

Another factor in the decision to follow "check-the-box" was single-member LLCs. Since these entities are not eligible for partnership treatment, it would not be practical to treat them as partnerships for federal election purposes. Thus, contributions made by a single-member LLC will be attributed to the member.

It is possible that the recipient of contributions could unintentionally accept an illegal contribution, because the recipient would have no way of knowing whether the LLC had opted for corporate tax treatment and was prohibited from making contributions to federal campaigns. Moreover, the recipient would have no way of knowing how to attribute an LLC contribution, unless that information was provided. Therefore, an LLC making a contribution must provide information to the recipient as to how the contribution is to be attributed and affirm that the LLC is eligible to make a contribution.

---

[55] 2 U.S.C. §431.

Chapter 5

Contributions and Distributions

¶ 501

Contributions to Capital and Admission of Members

In every state, a membership interest in an LLC may be obtained through a contribution of cash, property, or services rendered, or by providing a promissory note or other binding obligation to contribute cash, property or services.[1] As a general rule, no gain or loss is recognized by an LLC or its members when the contribution is made by a member in exchange for a membership interest in the LLC.[2]

Members are generally admitted to an LLC according to the terms of the entity's operating agreement, which should be in writing. In the absence of an agreement, the unanimous consent of the other members is usually required to admit a person, whether that interest is acquired from a member or from the LLC directly.[3]

A member is liable to the LLC for any enforceable promise to contribute cash or property, or to perform services. Generally, only a written promise to contribute is enforceable. Note that, in most states, a member remains obligated even if that member is subsequently unable to perform due to death, disability, or for any other reason.[4] If a contributing member assigns the member's interest to another party, the assignee does not ordinarily become liable for any promised contributions of the assignor.[5] However, if an assignee becomes a member of the LLC, the assignee may be liable for the known obligations of the assignor.[6]

---

[1] *See, e.g.,* Del. Code tit. 6, § 18-501.

[2] Code Sec. 721(a), assuming that the LLC is treated as a partnership for federal income tax purposes. Note that, with the exception of personal services, "property" is broadly defined (Reg. § 1.721-1(b)). For further discussion of the federal income tax consequences of contributions to capital, see Chapter 9.

[3] *But see, e.g.,* N.Y. LLC Law § 602(b)(1) (majority in interest of the members required to admit members).

[4] *See, e.g.,* Del. Code tit. 6, § 18-502(a).

[5] *See e.g.,* N.Y. LLC Law § 603.

[6] *See e.g.,* Utah Code § 48-2c-1104(3).

A member's obligation to make a contribution may be altered in most states only by the unanimous consent of the other members, absent an agreement to the contrary.

While many state LLC acts have no specific provision for creditors' rights in the event that a member's contribution obligation is released or compromised, some state LLC acts do contain language permitting creditors to directly enforce a member's contribution obligation if the creditors extended credit or otherwise acted in reliance on that obligation.[7]

¶ 502

Sharing of Profits, Losses, and Distributions

The members' LLC operating agreement should control the sharing of profits, losses, and distributions. However, if there is no operating agreement, or if the operating agreement does not address this issue, the most popular statutory default provision provides for the sharing of profits, losses, and distributions in accordance with the value of the members' relative capital contributions, as adjusted to reflect any returns of capital.[8] Colorado and Oklahoma are capital-based, but do not specifically mention any adjustments for returns.[9] Arizona law provides for capital-based allocations until capital contributions have been repaid and per capita sharing thereafter.[10] South Carolina provides for straight per capita sharing as a default provision.[11]

There are a variety of ways in which the state LLC statutes have expressed and defined capital-based allocations. Some state statutes refer to the "book value" of member contributions. Other state statutes refer to "capital interests." At least one state statute refers to "capital value." Note that these semantic and definitional differences may have some impact in actual operation even though the capital-based principle is the same.

The profit and loss sharing default provisions primarily refer to tax allocations of income, gain, loss, deduction, and credit.[12] Real economic consequences are governed by the members' rights to interim and liquidating distributions.

---

[7] *See, e.g.,* Del. Code, tit. 6, § 18-502(b). Arizona permits enforcement by a third-party creditor only if the member has so agreed or the LLC has assigned its interest in the member's obligation to the creditor. Ariz. Rev. Stat. § 29-702(C).

[8] *See, e.g.,* Del. Code tit. 6, §§ 18-503 and 18-504 and Iowa Code §§ 490A.802 and 490A.803.

[9] Colo. Rev. Stat. §§ 7-80-503 and 7-80-504 and Okla. Stat., tit. 18, § 2025.

[10] Ariz. Rev. Stat. §§ 29-703 and 29-709.

[11] S.C. Code § 33-44-405.

[12] Some states refer specifically to these items, as opposed to addressing the sharing of profits and losses generally. *See, e.g.,* N.C. Gen. Stat. § 57C-4-03.

¶ 503

Drafting Considerations Concerning Distributions and Tax Allocations

The members of an LLC will want a profit and loss sharing and distribution scheme that matches the economic agreement of the members. For that reason, the assorted statutory default provisions will be too simplistic in many cases. LLC members desiring more complex economic interests, such as preferred returns of profits or capital and special tax allocations, will need a customized sharing and distribution scheme based on the members' capital accounts.

Partnership agreements commonly set out a complex tax allocation scheme that satisfies the safe harbor provisions of the regulations under Code Sec. 704(b). Drafters of LLC operating agreements will need to decide whether to include these complex provisions. (See the sample LLC operating agreement in Appendix A, which contains an example of a capital-based allocation provision.)

¶ 504

Form of Distribution

All states that limit the form of distribution permit the parties to establish their own rules for the distribution of cash and noncash assets. Therefore, after considering the issues involving noncash distributions, the members should include a provision in the operating agreement which determines to what extent, if any, noncash distributions will be permitted.

Generally, most members will welcome cash distributions from the LLC. However, there may be instances when an alternate form of distribution is desired. For example, there is generally no recognition of gain for federal income tax purposes on noncash distributions.[13] If a piece of property owned by an LLC is no longer needed by the company, instead of selling the property and distributing the cash proceeds, which would be taxable to the extent that the cash distribution exceeds a member's ownership basis, one or more members could accept a distribution of the property and defer the gain recognition until the property is sold by the members. Additionally, upon winding up the LLC, the members of the LLC may want to retain some of the originally contributed property instead of liquidating all of its assets.

Many state LLC statutes provide that the members of an LLC have no right to demand noncash distributions and no obligation to accept noncash distributions greater than the member's percentage share in distributions.[14]

---

[13] See Code Sec. 731 and Chapter 9.

[14] *See, e.g.,* Del. Code tit. 6, § 18-605.

¶ 505

Wrongful Distribution

A distribution to a member is considered wrongful if the LLC is insolvent or the distribution, if made, would render the LLC insolvent. There are two types of tests for determining whether a distribution is wrongful: (1) the balance sheet test; and (2) the equity test. Under the balance sheet test, assets are compared to liabilities. If an LLC's liabilities, except for its liabilities for members' contributions, are greater than its assets, the distribution is wrongful.[15] The equity test, on the other hand, considers a distribution to be wrongful if it would render the LLC unable to pay its debts as they come due, or if the LLC's assets would be less than the sum of its liabilities (including the amount that would be needed to satisfy the superior preferential rights of members upon dissolution).[16]

Liability to Creditors for Wrongful Distribution

An LLC is liable to third parties for damages caused by a wrongful distribution. The creditors can force the LLC to retrieve the wrongful distributions. While the members and managers will not be directly liable to the creditors, they are liable to the LLC to the extent of the wrongful distribution.

Liability to the LLC for Wrongful Distribution

Most LLC statutes permit an LLC to recover a wrongful distribution. The member who accepts the distribution will sometimes be liable for repayment only if the member accepted the distribution knowing that it was wrongful.[17] Some statutes even hold a member liable whether or not that member knew the distribution was wrongful.[18] Managers or members who voted for, or assented to, the distribution may also be held responsible.[19] Several states, however, have no provision regarding the liability for a wrongful distribution.

When found personally liable, members and managers who voted for the distribution usually are allowed to seek contribution from other members and managers who voted for the distribution and from the members who received the distribution.[20] Many statutes limit the time in which an LLC may recover from a member who received, or voted for, a wrongful distribution to two or three years from the time that the distribution was made.[21]

---

[15] *See, e.g.,* Del. Code tit. 6, § 18-607 and N.J. Rev. Stat. § 42:2B-42.

[16] *See, e.g.,* Nev. Rev. Stat. § 86.343 and Utah Code § 48-2c-1005.

[17] *See, e.g.,* Del. Code tit. 6, § 18-607(b).

[18] *See, e.g.,* Utah Code § 48-2c-1006 (a member who receives a distribution by mistake is obligated to return it and remains liable to the LLC for the amount wrongfully received for five years).

[19] *See, e.g.,* 805 Ill. Comp. Stat. 180/25-35.

[20] *See, e.g.,* N.C. Gen. Stat. § 57C-4-07(b).

[21] *See, e.g.,* R.I. Gen. Laws § 7-16-32(c) (two years); Del. Code tit. 6, § 18-607(c) (three years); Utah Code § 48-2c-1006 (five years).

¶ 506

Distributions upon Liquidation of Member's Interest

Whether it is called resignation, retirement, or withdrawal, most LLC statutes address a member's right to withdraw from an LLC (see ¶ 603). In most states, upon a member's withdrawal that does not cause the LLC to dissolve,[22] the withdrawing or retiring member is entitled to the fair market value of the member's LLC interest.[23] These default rules may be altered by the members in their operating agreement. Some states, such as Maryland, are silent on the issue.

¶ 507

Distributions upon Dissolution of the LLC

Upon any event that causes an LLC to dissolve, a familiar hierarchy of priorities applies in distributing the LLC's assets. Most states have modeled their distribution scheme on Revised Uniform Limited Partnership Act (2001) § 812 and provide for distributions in the following order:

(1) to creditors, including LLC members who are creditors, in satisfaction of the LLC's liabilities;

(2) to members and former members in respect of their accrued share of interim or liquidating distributions; and

(3) to members in respect of their capital contributions, with any remainder shared according to the LLC's or state's distribution-sharing mechanism.[24]

All state LLC laws mandate that creditors are given the first priority. However, many LLC statutes permit the operating agreement to alter the default rule for those distributions described in priorities (2) and (3).

---

[22] As of January 1, 1997, the federal check-the-box regulations permit an LLC to have perpetual existence and still be taxed as a partnership. Consequently, most states have eliminated the requirement that the LLC dissolve upon the dissociation of a member.

[23] *See, e.g.,* La. Rev. Stat. § 12:1325(c).

[24] *See, e.g.,* Ariz. Rev. Stat. § 29-708 and Del. Code, tit. 6, § 18-804.

Chapter 6

Dissolution, Bankruptcy, Mergers, and Consolidations

¶ 601

Dissolution of the LLC—Overview

An LLC's operating agreement should include provisions on dissolution and liquidation of the LLC. As a default, all LLC state statutes describe events that can cause an LLC to dissolve. Once dissolution occurs, the LLC's business must be wound up and the entity terminated. Generally, an LLC will be dissolved upon:

(1) the occurrence of events specified in the articles of organization or in the operating agreement;

(2) the written consent of a percentage of members specified in the operating agreement;

(3) the entry of a judicial decree of dissolution; or

(4) an administrative dissolution.

The reason for exiting or breaking up a business (for example, member desire, dispute, or failure of the business) often will determine the exit strategy. Common exit strategies include transfer, disassociation, buy-sell and dissolution.

The statutory judicial dissolution mechanism is initiated by a member if the LLC is unable to carry on its business.[1] An administrative dissolution procedure would be implemented against those LLCs that fail to pay the required fees or penalties, file the required documents, or maintain a registered agent or office.[2]

A member's dissociation (*i.e.,* by death, withdrawal, resignation, expulsion, bankruptcy, or dissolution) can also trigger dissolution of

---

[1] Mich. Comp. Laws §450.4802; N.Y. LLC Law §702. Maryland provides for judicial dissolution when it is not "reasonably practicable" for the LLC to carry on business "in conformity with" the articles or operating agreement. Md. Code Corps. & Ass'ns §4A-903.

[2] *See, e.g.,* Fla. Stat. ch. 608.448; Ind. Code §23-18-10-1; Ky. Rev. Stat. §275.295.

the LLC. While the check-the-box entity classification regulations[3] permit LLCs to have perpetual existence and still receive passthrough treatment for federal income tax purposes, several states still provide that the dissociation of a member will dissolve the LLC, unless there is an agreement to continue the business. However, because of the regulations, many states dropped the list of triggering events that would cause the dissolution of an LLC. Thus, in those states, LLCs have shifted from a fragile entity that could be dissolved for any number of reasons to a much more durable entity.

¶ 602

Effects of Dissolution

Discontinuation and Winding Up of Business

The most obvious results of dissolution are that the entity must be discontinued and that the process of winding up begins. However, most LLCs will want the ability to continue the LLC's business if the remaining members choose to do so. For instance, when a member withdraws, the LLC's remaining members should be able to continue the business with the consent of the remaining members. While the withdrawing member may be entitled to fair value for his or her interest in the LLC, the remaining members can weigh the need for dissolution against the considerable costs that may be entailed in liquidating all or a portion of the LLC's assets.

If the business is not continued, the managing members or managers are vested with the authority to wind up the LLC's affairs. This may simply mean the sale of the business to the remaining members or to third parties, but it also includes:

- the gathering and disposition of assets;
- the discharge of liabilities;
- the prosecution and defense of suits on behalf of the LLC; and
- the closing of any LLC transactions.

The cancellation or discharge of debt generally qualifies as taxable income to members.

Articles of Dissolution and Claims of Creditors

Most states either mandate or permit the filing of articles of dissolution. The primary benefit of filing these articles is to provide creditors with notice of the LLC's dissolution. Not all states have a provision that will presumptively put creditors on notice.

Upon dissolution, the LLC can begin to dispose of any claims against it. Notice should be sent to known creditors, who will then have

---

[3] See Chapter 9.

a certain time period in which to press their claims against the LLC. Claims of unknown creditors are generally handled by placing notice of dissolution in a newspaper of general publication. The time period in which a creditor must make a claim after the notice of dissolution has been executed varies from state to state. Under the Uniform Limited Liability Company Act, claims of unknown creditors will be barred if the claimant does not file suit to enforce the claim within five years after the date that the LLC published the notice.

¶ 603

Retirement or Withdrawal of a Member

As with any business enterprise, it is crucial that LLC members plan for the eventual withdrawal or retirement of members from the LLC. Most LLC acts either state or imply that a member may withdraw from the LLC at any time, absent contrary terms in the operating agreement. However, it is fairly common for state law to condition the right to withdraw on written notice anywhere from 30 days to six months prior to withdrawal, unless otherwise provided in the LLC's operating agreement.[4] Some acts specifically permit the LLC to recover damages from a member whose withdrawal violates the operating agreement and to offset these damages against any amounts distributable to the withdrawing member.[5]

States have generally not addressed what happens when an LLC loses the minimum number of members or a limited partnership loses the last remaining limited partner. However, some states provide that an LLC does not dissolve upon its last remaining member if a new member is admitted within 90 days.[6]

The issue to be addressed by persons forming an LLC is whether there should be any restrictions on the right to withdraw. For instance, it would not be uncommon for a minimum term of membership to be included in the operating agreement. Also, the parties may want to specify withdrawal and other events that will and will not cause dissolution of the LLC (see ¶ 601). State LLC statutes have moved away from the position that an individual member's bankruptcy triggers the LLC's dissolution.

Expulsion

Expulsion is another type of exit that is provided in some state statutes. Typically, an operating agreement provides for the expulsion of a member who fails to meet his or her capital contribution obligations. In this situation, an operating agreement may provide for the buyout of the member.

---

[4] *See, e.g.,* Ga. Code § 14-11-601 and Md. Code Corps. & Ass'ns § 4A-605.

[5] Ariz. Rev. Stat. § 29-734.

[6] Ind. Code § 23-18-9-1.1(c); N.C. Gen. Stat. § 57C-6-01(4).

¶ 604

LLC Bankruptcy

The federal Bankruptcy Code, like most other laws, was enacted before LLCs were widespread as an alternative business form. Even though the Bankruptcy Code was reformed in 1994, after many states had already enacted LLC statutes, the Bankruptcy Reform Act of 1994 does not even mention LLCs.[7] Nonetheless, it is important to consider the Bankruptcy Code's probable treatment of LLCs, their managers and their members.

Only Chapter 7 (Liquidation) and Chapter 11 (Reorganization) procedures of the Bankruptcy Code are likely to apply to LLCs. The definition of eligible debtors contained in Section 109 of the Bankruptcy Code is very expansive. According to its terms, an entity may be a debtor under Chapter 7 as long as the entity is a "person" according to the Bankruptcy Code. Chapter 11 reorganization is generally available to any entity that may be a debtor under Chapter 7.

The Bankruptcy Code defines "person" to include individuals, partnerships, and corporations.[8] Although this definition does not specifically mention LLCs, the use of the nonexclusive term "includes" indicates that other businesses that are not listed may be entitled to seek relief under the Bankruptcy Code. Since an LLC should fit within the definition of "person" and is not excluded by Section 109, it is eligible for relief under Chapter 7 of the Bankruptcy Code. Further, since an LLC can be a debtor under Chapter 7, it is also eligible for relief under Chapter 11.

Commencement of an LLC Bankruptcy Case

An LLC bankruptcy proceeding commences when the debtor files a voluntary petition or a creditor files an involuntary petition. Who has the authority to file bankruptcy on behalf of an LLC is not clear. With a general partnership, the Bankruptcy Code provides that a general partner has the authority to file a bankruptcy petition. However, the Bankruptcy Code does not address who has this authority within an LLC. The authority to file bankruptcy should be put in an LLC operating agreement.

Before an LLC can file for protection from its creditors under the Bankruptcy Code, it will need to determine whether the rules regarding partnerships or corporations will apply. All general partners must consent to a voluntary petition for bankruptcy relief by a general partnership, whereas only the managing partners in a limited partnership must agree to commence a case. Authority for a corporation to commence a

---

[7] Note that the National Bankruptcy Review Commission, after conducting a two-year congressionally mandated study, made several recommendations to specifically address LLCs in the Bankruptcy Code, including: the treatment of LLC members and managers; the treatment of LLC management rights; and *ipso facto* provisions rendered unenforceable under the Bankruptcy Code.

[8] 11 U.S.C. § 101(41).

bankruptcy action, on the other hand, is usually delegated to the corporation's officers or board of directors.

Although an LLC meets the Bankruptcy Code Section 101(9) definition of the term "corporation," a determination of who must consent to a voluntary petition for bankruptcy may turn more upon the management structure of the LLC itself than whether an LLC may be considered a corporation for bankruptcy purposes. Because a member-managed LLC more closely resembles a general partnership, the Bankruptcy Court may require that all of the members consent to a voluntary petition. A manager-managed LLC, however, bears a greater similarity to a corporation and, thus, the managers would vote for a voluntary petition.

The Bankruptcy Estate

The estate created by the filing of a bankruptcy petition by or on behalf of an LLC generally includes only the assets of the LLC, including obligations of the members to the LLC, and not the assets of the LLC members. Most LLC statutes provide that property that the LLC acquires is property of the LLC and that members do not have an interest in specific LLC property.

Since the applicable property is owned by the LLC and not by the members, this property will be part of the bankruptcy estate and, therefore, will be protected by an automatic stay (*i.e.*, all claims against the debtor LLC that arose before the bankruptcy case commenced are halted upon the filing of the bankruptcy petition). Conversely, the property of an individual member is not owned by the LLC and, thus, is not protected by the stay.

The trustee in an LLC *Chapter 7* bankruptcy will be required to administer any claims that the LLC may have against its members and any claims that the members may have against the LLC. As owners of the LLC, members are accorded the lowest priority in the order of claims payment. Further, because the LLC is not an individual, it does not receive a discharge of claims outstanding on the date that the bankruptcy proceedings were filed. Therefore, if an LLC is not dissolved after a Chapter 7 bankruptcy, it will be responsible for any debts not paid through the bankruptcy petition.

In a *Chapter 11* bankruptcy proceeding, the managers or members who were operating the LLC prior to the bankruptcy will remain in control of the business while undergoing the reorganization. The claims and interests of the LLC members will, in most cases, be treated as a separate class of claims and, like Chapter 7 bankruptcies, will be accorded the lowest priority in the order of claims payment. The members' primary goal is to retain their equity interests in the reorganized LLC. To do so, the LLC's plan of reorganization must comply with the plan confirmation criteria set forth in the Bankruptcy Code.

Single-Member LLC

One court has held that the members of single-member LLCs who incur debts in their personal capacity may not invoke the charging order provisions of the governing LLC act to protect these assets from transfer to bankruptcy trustees under Chapter 7 of the Bankruptcy Code.[9] Charging orders, granted by a court, assure a creditor of distributions made by an LLC while preserving the right to management of the LLC to its members.

Bankruptcy of an LLC Member

With the implementation of the federal check-the-box regulations, some states have eliminated the bankruptcy of a member as a dissolution event for the LLC. However, there is a potential adverse consequence that can flow from the continuation of the business after the bankruptcy of one of its members. If the debtor's status as a member is not automatically terminated and a corresponding dissolution fails to occur, the debtor-in-possession or the trustee could step into the shoes of the debtor as a member of the LLC. This ability to assume the bankrupt member's membership interest in the LLC would result in the remaining members dealing with a new member whose interest in the conduct of the LLC's affairs is not necessarily in accord with their own interests.

Aiding and Abetting Breach of Fiduciary Duties

Lawyers who work with financially insolvent or troubled businesses may be involved with claims from creditors of these businesses or a trustee in bankruptcy of the business alleging a cause of action against an attorney under the theory of aiding and abetting a breach of fiduciary duty. In order to establish such a claim, the plaintiff/creditor/trustee must establish that (1) it has a claim against the business, (2) the managers of the business breached a fiduciary duty owed to the plaintiff, and (3) the lawyer aided and abetted the managers' breach of fiduciary duty to the plaintiff.

¶ 605

Mergers, Consolidations or Conversions Involving LLCs

The two statutory ways of changing an entity into another entity entail the formation of a new entity through a merger or the change of form of the existing entity through a conversion. When using the statutory method of converting or merging entities, careful attention must be paid to state law. It is important to look at the state statutes that govern both the disappearing entity and the surviving entity.

All of the state LLC statutes have provisions governing a combination of an LLC with other business entities. Statutory conversions allow

---

[9] *In re: Ashley Albright, Debtor,* 291 BR 538 (Bnkr. D. Colo. 2003). Charging orders, granted by a court, assure a creditor of distributions made by an LLC while preserving the right to management of the LLC to its members.

a business to change its tax form with a minimum of legal disruption. If entities enter into a statutory merger or consolidation transaction, the business entity surviving the merger generally must deliver articles of merger or consolidation to the secretary of state or other governing official.

The trend among the states is to authorize the conversion of a *corporation into an LLC*, although many states still do not allow this type of merger or conversion. Currently, most states provide for the statutory merger of a general or limited partnership into an LLC. Fewer, but a growing number of states authorize the merger of a corporation into an LLC. There are no Internal Revenue Code sections describing the treatment of statutory mergers or conversions.

Conversion of a *sole proprietorship into an LLC* is generally accomplished by filing a certificate of formation with the state along with appropriate fees, and operating the business under the new entity. Transfer all identification numbers, licenses and permits to the new entity.

Taxpayers may wish to convert a corporation to an LLC or limited partnership for many reasons (see ¶ 201), including the savings of state franchise taxes or federal estate and gift taxes. A statutory merger or conversion might be useful if the acquired entity has contracts or licenses that would be difficult to transfer. In some states, franchise taxes are not imposed on LLCs. In addition, deeper discounts, due to lack of marketability, may be available on transfers of LLC or limited partnership interests, thus saving estate or gift taxes.

The information required to be included in the articles of merger or consolidation may vary from state to state. The Uniform Limited Liability Company Act (ULLCA) includes the following information:[10]

- Name and the jurisdiction of formation or organization for all business entities that are party to the transaction;

- For each LLC that is to merge, the date that its articles of organization were filed with the respective secretary of state;

- Statement that all of the parties agree to the merger or consolidation;

- Name of the surviving or the resulting business entity;

- Effective date of the merger or consolidation;

- If an LLC is the surviving entity, a statement setting forth the changes that must be made to the LLC's articles of organization by reason of the merger;

- Jurisdiction and the date of the filing of the initial articles of organization of any foreign LLC that is party to the merger and the date when its application for authority was filed with the respective

---

[10] Uniform Limited Liability Company Act (1996) § 905.

secretary of state or, if applicable, a statement that such application has not been filed; and

  • Statement that a foreign surviving entity will be subject to service of process in the state in which the merger occurs.

The ULLCA further requires that the surviving entity must furnish a copy of the plan of merger or consolidation, on request and without cost, to any person holding an interest in an entity that is party to the transaction. Note that a foreign LLC that is the surviving entity may not do business in the state until an application for authority has been filed.

Some states, anticipating a number of entity conversions to LLCs, have enacted statutory provisions dealing specifically with this situation.[11]

The ULLCA lists the following effects of entering into a merger or consolidation:

  • All parties to the transaction are merged or consolidated into a single surviving or new entity, and the parties cease to exist as separate entities;

  • The surviving or new entity, if an LLC, possesses all of the rights, privileges, immunities, and powers inherent in an LLC and is subject to the restrictions, disabilities, and duties of an LLC;

  • All of the property, debts, and interests belonging to the constituent entities are vested in the surviving or new entity;

  • The surviving or new entity becomes liable for all of the obligations of the constituent entities, and creditors and claimants can proceed against the surviving or new entity as if no merger or consolidation has occurred; and

  • The conversion or exchange of shares, interests, cash, securities, or other obligations under the terms of the transaction takes effect.

One interesting issue involves the merger or conversion of a partnership into an LLC. Note that the personal liability of any general partner is not extinguished by the merger or conversion, even though the general partner becomes a member of an LLC.

The IRS has issued two revenue rulings on the tax consequences of converting a domestic LLC to, and from, a multi-owner entity classified as a partnership for federal tax purposes. One ruling examines the conversion of a single-member LLC, disregarded as a separate entity for tax purposes, into a multi-owner entity classified as a partnership.[12] The second ruling, in contrast, discusses the tax consequences of converting a multi-member LLC classified as a partnership into a single-member LLC.[13] A comprehensive discussion of these two rulings, as

---

[11] Ga. Code § 14-11-212 (corporation or partnership into LLC); Va. Code § 13.1-1010.1 (partnership into LLC).

[12] Rev. Rul. 99-5, 1999-1 CB 434.
[13] Rev. Rul. 99-6, 1999-1 CB 432.

well as an examination of the federal tax treatment of the merger or conversion of a partnership or a corporation into an LLC, can be found in Chapter 9.

The IRS has also issued regulations governing the tax consequences of partnership mergers and divisions. These regulations also apply to LLC mergers and divisions. For more information, see Chapter 9.

¶ 606
Spin-Offs, Split-Offs and Split-Ups

Spin-offs, split-offs and split-ups can be useful if members want to divide their control over operations of one or more businesses.

A spin-off is a distribution of the stock of a controlled subsidiary (the controlled corporation) by its parent corporation (the distributing corporation). A split-off is a distribution of stock of a pre-existing or newly created controlled subsidiary by the distributing corporation. However, unlike a spin-off, stock of the distributing corporation of equivalent value is redeemed. In a split-up, the distributing corporation distributes its stock in two or more controlled corporations (pre-existing or newly created) in complete liquidation.

The IRS has issued a revenue ruling that applies the five-year active conduct of a trade or business requirement of Code Sec. 355(b) to a spin-off transaction involving a corporation holding a membership interest in a member managed LLC. The requirement is satisfied when, immediately after the spin-off distribution of the newly formed corporation's stock to the original corporation's shareholders, each company is engaged in the active conduct of a trade or business that is treated as having been actively conducted throughout the five-year period ending on the date of the distribution and that was not acquired during that period in a transaction prohibited by Code Sec. 355(b)(2)(C).[14]

---

[14] Rev. Rul. 2002-49, 2002-32 CB 288.

Chapter 7

Foreign LLCs

¶ 701

Status of Foreign LLCs and Key Concerns

Almost all state LLC statutes contain a section that outlines the treatment of foreign LLCs, which refers to both LLCs formed in other states and entities resembling LLCs from other countries. This regulation of the terms and conditions under which a foreign LLC may do business in the particular state is accomplished by requiring each foreign LLC doing business in the state to register with the secretary of state, or other appropriate official, and to maintain a registered office and registered agent in the state. LLCs that transact business in a foreign state without registering as a foreign LLC will find that some of the benefits of a registration are withheld from them (see ¶ 703, below). These LLCs may also be subject to a court-ordered injunction against doing business in the state.

At some point, almost every LLC will have some contact with another state that may be incidental to the conduct of business in the home state, or merely a temporary event or single transaction (thereby making that LLC a "foreign LLC" in the other state). Often, the LLC may not consider the contact sufficient to warrant registration in the foreign jurisdiction. To alleviate some of the resultant concern, several LLC statutes provide a nonexclusive list of those activities that do not constitute doing business in the state.

As a general rule, the organization and internal affairs of foreign LLCs, and the liability of its members and managers, are governed by the laws of the state or country of formation. In fact, in their treatment of foreign LLCs, the LLC statutes in all 50 states and the District of Columbia provide that the laws of the jurisdiction where an LLC is formed will govern the organization and internal affairs of that LLC.

However, foreign LLCs typically are not entitled to any greater rights or privileges than in-state LLCs with respect to transactions with third parties, the exercise of powers, and the types of business that may be engaged in by the LLC.[1] This can create conflict of law problems, as is further discussed in ¶ 702. State LLC statutes generally provide that the admission of foreign LLCs cannot be denied by reason of differences between state or country laws.

Although all 50 states and the District of Columbia have LLC statutes on their books, this does not eliminate some of the same fears of multi-state LLCs that existed when some states did not have LLC statutes. This is due to the fact that the 51 domestic statutes are not all the same, and difficulties can arise in situations where an LLC is conducting business in more than one state.

As a result, LLC members will want to know the following before transacting business in other states with differing LLC statutes in order to fully understand the laws and rules that will be governing their dealings in those states:

- to what extent their limited liability will be recognized by the other LLC state, and how that differs from their own state;

- the filing requirements and fees for registering the entity in the foreign state; and

- the taxation of the LLC and tax filing requirements in the foreign state.

Tax and business advisers should proceed conservatively and with caution due to the uncertainty in this area. Even though a state may have an LLC statute, there may be administrative rulings that attempt to provide guidance on the three key questions listed above and interpret the patent differences in the laws. As more states adopt model LLC statutes, however, the differences in the application and enforcement of these issues, as well as these concerns, will obviously diminish. For more specific state information, see Chapter 10.

¶ 702

Liability Protection for Foreign LLCs

The states do not wield unlimited authority in determining whether to recognize the limited liability of a foreign LLC. Two clauses of the U.S. Constitution—the Full Faith and Credit Clause[2] and the Commerce Clause[3]—both strongly support the enforcement of formation state law in limiting the liability of LLC members.

Assuming that limited liability exists outside of the state of formation, open questions remain as to the exact application of the limited liability privilege.

---

[1] *See, e.g.,* Ariz. Rev. Stat. § 29-801; Va. Code § 13.1-1051.

[2] "Full Faith and Credit shall be given in each State to the public Acts, Records, and Judicial Proceedings of every other State." U.S. Const., Art. IV, § 1.

[3] "The Congress shall have the power . . . To regulate Commerce with foreign Nations, and among the several States, and with the Indian Tribes . . ." U.S. Const., Art. I, § 8, cl. 3.

Example: The Starline LLC formed in State A engages in business in State B. Both states have LLC statutes, but while State A limits the liability of both members and managers, State B offers liability protection only to members and not to managers. State B's choice-of-laws provision is typical. It states that:

"Subject to the Constitution of this State, the laws of the state or other jurisdiction under which a foreign limited liability company is organized shall govern its organization, internal affairs and the liability of its members."

State B's LLC act also provides:

"The managers and members of a foreign limited liability company shall have no greater rights and privileges than those granted to the managers and members of a domestic limited liability company."

Under these circumstances, will the courts in State B extend liability protection to the managers of the Starline LLC, even though managers of LLCs formed in State B would not enjoy that privilege? Would State B be obligated to extend that protection by the U.S. Constitution? These questions remain unanswered.

¶ 703

Registration of Foreign LLCs

An LLC seeking to do business in other states generally must register in those states, file the requisite documents, and pay the requisite fees. All U.S. LLC acts provide for the registration of foreign LLCs. The information contained in the registration is generally minimal, although there are variations from state to state. Information typically required includes:

- the name of the LLC;
- the date and the jurisdiction of organization;
- a description of the business to be transacted within the state;
- the address of the registered office and the name of the registered agent within the state;
- a statement that the foreign LLC validly exists in the jurisdiction of organization; and
- the address of the office in the state of organization or, if different, the principal office.

If the appropriate official, such as the secretary of state, finds that the application for foreign registration is complete, and that the document conforms with the applicable LLC act, a certificate of registration will be issued. Upon issuance of the certificate, the foreign LLC is authorized to transact business in that state.

careless business owners, without creating a windfall for the other party to the action.

¶ 704

Entities Formed in Foreign Countries

All state LLC statutes anticipate the business of LLCs both from other states and from foreign countries or other sovereigns. Entities organized in foreign countries that have the characteristics of an LLC should be treated in the same manner as foreign LLCs from another state. These LLCs should derive comfort from state law provisions stating that admission cannot be denied by reason of differences in governing laws.

A company that is formed in another country that is seeking LLC status in the United States should, of course, be sure to adhere to the relevant laws of the country where it is organized so as to not disqualify itself from its original domestic status.

Chapter 8

Other Types of Limited Liability Entities

¶ 801
Availability of LLC Form for Professional Firms

LLCs are an attractive entity choice for professional firms because they offer member participation in management, passthrough tax benefits, and a measure of limited liability. While many professional practices are organized as general partnerships, others are professional corporations or partnerships comprised of professional corporations. Like professional corporations and these combination entities, professional LLCs (PLLCs) generally insulate a member from liability for the misdeeds, malpractice, or negligence of colleagues, but do not offer any protection from liability for the member's own actions.

Once a professional company decides that a PLLC is its chosen form for doing business, the company must ascertain that the relevant state law allows such an entity. In most states, LLC statutes expressly permit professionals to operate their practice in LLC form. See the state-by-state analysis in Chapter 10 for the treatment in any particular state.

It would appear that professionals (such as lawyers, accountants, physicians, architects, etc.) may use an LLC absent an express prohibition. However, if state law is silent, tax and business advisers should seek the approval of the appropriate regulatory bodies—state government authorities and professional societies or commissions—before establishing a client's professional practice as an LLC.[1]

Even in states having LLC acts permitting PLLCs, regulatory changes may be necessary before LLCs can be properly utilized for

---

[1] In Virginia, for instance, accounting and law firms must obtain a registration certificate before the PLLC can practice either of those professions (Va. Code §§ 13.1-1112 and 13.1-1113). Iowa, on the other hand, specifically states that a PLLC is not required to register with a "regulating board," although its members are not exempted from registration simply by virtue of practicing through the PLLC (Iowa Code § 490A.1506). Note that the AICPA has expressly approved the use of LLCs by accountants if the LLC form is available under state law. AICPA Code of Professional Conduct, Rule 505.

professional practices in these states. Specifically, before practicing law in LLC form, the highest state court, bar association, or other regulating body may need to amend its rules. For example, with respect to the legal profession, the Colorado LLC act does not specifically authorize lawyers to practice as LLCs, but the Colorado Supreme Court has amended its rules to allow it.[2] Moreover, there may be difficult questions concerning practice by a professional LLC outside of the state of formation. Other professions should consult their respective governing bodies for further guidance before committing to this decision (such as the American Medical Association (AMA) or the American Institute of Certified Public Accountants (AICPA)).

Finally, note that the use of the LLC form by a professional practice does not alter any laws applicable to the relationship between the professional service provider and the client.

¶ 802

Synopsis of State Statutes Permitting PLLCs

Professional limited liability company (PLLC) statutes characteristically resemble state professional corporation laws. The following is a summary of some notable provisions typically found in most state statutes that expressly approve of the use of an LLC for the practice of a professional business.

Membership and Management Restrictions

PLLC members and managers generally must be licensed to practice the profession that the PLLC is authorized to practice. It is also common for a state to require that a professional who is licensed, such as an attorney, remain in good standing.[3] For multi-state PLLCs that are authorized to practice in several states, members generally may practice only in those states in which they are licensed.

Transfers of Membership Interests

A corollary to the membership restrictions is that membership interests may be transferred only to persons eligible to practice the PLLC profession or to the PLLC itself. This is logical since, without such a provision, the owners of a PLLC could conceivably not have any working knowledge of the profession. Ownership of a law firm by a nonlawyer, for example, is in direct violation of almost every state bar's legal ethics code.

Where an event triggers the transfer of a PLLC membership interest to a noneligible member, states generally require the PLLC to either dissolve or purchase the membership interest. In Iowa, the PLLC must either dissolve within 60 days or purchase the interest of any member who dies, is disqualified from practice, or whose interest is

---

[2] Change #1991 (17) amending Colo. R. Civ. P. 265 (effective 11/1/91).

[3] *See, e.g.,* Wyo. Stat. § 17-15-103.

transferred involuntarily (for example, as the result of bankruptcy proceedings).[4] In Virginia, the buy-out by the PLLC must occur within one year of the event that terminates a membership interest.[5] In Arizona, the interest must be liquidated by the PLLC within 180 days.[6]

Some state PLLC laws contain default buy-out provisions to govern these involuntary transfers. Of the three states listed in the paragraph above, both the Iowa and Virginia statutes include such language, and the Iowa provision is particularly detailed. These provisions may be overridden by a buy-sell or cross-purchase agreement among the PLLC members.

Limits on Purposes and Powers

Unlike the purpose statement in regular LLCs, which is seldom even mandatory, purpose is more important in PLLCs. This is due to the fact that PLLCs generally may only engage in the business(es) of rendering professional services that the entity was authorized to practice.

Name

States that explicitly approve the use of LLCs for professional businesses may require that the name include the initials "P.L.C." or "P.L.L.C.," the words "Professional Limited Liability Company" or some similar designation.

¶ 803

Federal Tax Treatment of PLLCs

PLLCs are generally taxed as partnerships. This is especially true in light of the check-the-box regulations, which basically give unincorporated organizations the ability to be taxed as a partnership by simply making an election. By contrast, most incorporated professional entities are categorized as personal service corporations (PSCs) for federal tax purposes. All PSC income is taxed at a flat rate of 35 percent. Although PSCs that are C corporations may be able to eliminate entity-level income through payments of salary and bonuses and other year-end maneuvering, this potential entity-level tax is not a concern for PLLCs. PSCs that are S corporations do not have entity-level tax problems, but they do have other drawbacks when compared to PLLCs (see Chapter 2).

Conversions of PSCs into PLLCs can usually be accomplished without adverse tax consequences. The tax disadvantages often inherent in the conversions of corporations into LLCs are not normally present in the conversion of a PSC, which typically does not possess a

---

[4] Iowa Code § 490A.1512.
[5] Va. Code § 13.1-1117(C).
[6] Ariz. Rev. Stat. § 29-847.

significant amount of appreciated property that can trigger gain in an LLC conversion.

For more information on the taxation of LLCs, see Chapter 9.

¶ 804

Limited Liability Partnerships

In every state and the District of Columbia, another entity may be an option for general partnerships and professional firms: the limited liability partnership (LLP). These LLPs are essentially general partnerships, except that each partner is able to insulate himself or herself from the negligence of the other partners. Thus, LLPs have the same combination of: (1) partnership tax status; and (2) protection from the malpractice liabilities of colleagues that make LLCs so attractive to professionals. Some states, such as Iowa,[7] permit all general partnerships to register as LLPs. Other states, New York for example, limit LLPs to professional organizations.

LLPs have become the entity form of choice for many professions, including law firms. Liability protection becomes especially critical when a professional firm fails. One area of particular concern involves liability for wrongful distributions. Look to state statutes regarding distributions when forming an LLP and include a "compensation for services" provision in the LLP operating agreement section covering distributions. As an addition benefit, most LLP statutes do not impose a limit on distributions.

In a number of states, the general LLP statute requires the entity, at least for all professionals, to carry or maintain professional liability insurance.[8]

Liability

As mentioned above, LLPs afford the general partner more protection than general partnerships. Specifically, a partner is not liable for the debts and obligations of the registered LLP to the extent that the debts and obligations arise from the negligence, wrongful acts or misconduct of another partner, or an employee, agent or representative of the partnership in the course of the partnership's business.[9] Partners still may be liable for those liabilities arising out of the actions of other partners, employees, agents, etc. if the partners either supervised or were directly involved in the activity.[10] However, under a no-fault statute, it is not necessary for a claimant to establish negligence in supervision. In addition, partners remain liable for their personal misconduct.

While many LLP statutes do not limit the partners' liability for the general debts of the partnership, a growing number of states have what

---

[7] Iowa Code § 486.15.
[8] *See, e.g.,* Cal. Corp. Code § 16956(a)(2)(c); Conn. Gen. Stat. § 34-327(e).

[9] *See, e.g.,* Del. Code tit. 6, § 1515; 805 Ill. Comp. Stat. 205/15(b).
[10] *See, e.g.,* N.C. Gen. Stat. § 59-45(b).

are called "full shield" LLP statutes.[11] Full shield protection for an LLP essentially means that a partner in an LLP is not liable for the debts or obligations of the LLP arising in tort, contract, or otherwise.

Some states afford only a "partial shield." That means that the general LLP statute protects against claims arising only from "omissions, negligence, wrongful acts, misconduct or malpractice."[12] That leaves vicarious liability for general business obligations.

Due to the differing language in the various state LLP statutes, different conduct is protected from liability from state to state. For example, in some states a partner is not liable for the negligence, wrongful acts or misconduct of others.[13] But Kentucky and Virginia add malpractice to the list of tortious conduct.[14] Idaho, Illinois, and Michigan include malpractice and omissions.[15] Maryland substitutes omissions for misconduct.[16] Lastly, this liability shield only protects against conduct that arises while the partnership is registered as an LLP, and does not apply to past acts. There are no cases on whether veil piercing would apply to an LLP, an issue that arises because an LLP does not have a general partner who is liable for the debts and obligations of the partnership.

Filing Requirements

Converting an existing professional general partnership into an LLP is a rather simple undertaking. A document must be filed with the secretary of state, or other appropriate official, that typically includes:[17]

- partnership name
- address of principal office
- name of registered agent for service of process
- number of partners
- brief statement of partnership's business

In Louisiana and North Carolina, the change must typically be approved by a majority in interest of the partners. Generally, formation of or conversion to an LLP involves a fee, and the LLP's registration must be renewed annually. If the registration is allowed to lapse, the partners will once again be exposed to liability as if they were general partners. Further, the name of an LLP generally must contain the words "registered limited liability partnership" or the abbreviation "L.L.P."[18]

---

[11] *See, e.g.,* Del. Code tit. 6, §§ 1502, 1515 and 1544 through 1553; N.Y. Partnership Law § 121-1500.

[12] *See, e.g.,* Tenn. Code Ann. § 61-1-306(c).

[13] *See, e.g.,* Conn. Gen. Stat. § 34-53(2); Del. Code tit. 6, § 1515.

[14] Ky. Rev. Stat. § 362.220(2); Va. Code § 50-15(B).

[15] Idaho Code § 53-315(3); 805 Ill. Comp. Stat. 205/15(b); Mich. Comp. Laws § 449.46(1).

[16] Md. Code Corps. & Ass'ns § 9-307(B).

[17] La. Rev. Stat. § 9:3432; N.C. Gen. Stat. § 59-84.2.

[18] La. Rev. Stat. § 9:3432; N.C. Gen. Stat. § 59-84.2.

Foreign LLPs

In the past, a major drawback to LLPs, similar to that experienced by LLCs until recently, was that not all of the states had enacted LLP legislation. LLPs operating in a foreign state that did not have an LLP statute may not have been entitled to the limited liability protection granted by their own state's statute. Currently, although all states now have LLP statutes enacted, confusion still results when an LLP from one state does business in another state with a slightly different set of LLP laws. For instance, a number of states specifically provide that a foreign LLP does not have to register to do business in the state.[19] In these states, the laws of the state of organization will be applied.[20] In other states, foreign LLPs must register to do business in the state.[21] Finally, there are those states that do not contemplate the registration of foreign LLPs or expressly provide that they do (or do not) have to register.[22]

In those states that require registration, the process is not unlike the registration of a foreign LLC. The application for registration will typically require the name of the LLP, the address of its principal office, the number of partners, a general description of its business and, if not in the state, the name and address of a registered agent. Similar to the rules governing domestic LLPs, the registration will usually be valid for one year, and must be renewed by filing a renewal application or annual report. Some states impose a penalty for the failure to file, and also restrict the rights of an unregistered foreign LLP.[23]

One state, Illinois, does not allow a foreign LLP (or LLC) to use a name to intentionally misrepresent the geographic origin or location of the company.[24]

¶ 805

Limited Liability Limited Partnerships

Since 1977, when Wyoming passed the first LLC statute, states have responded to the business community's desire for entities that provided limited liability and passthrough taxation without the imposed structure and formalities required to operate a corporation. Today, all states and the District of Columbia have adopted LLC and limited liability partnership statutes. While LLP statutes shield general partners from the debts, obligations, and liabilities of the partnership, general partners in limited partnerships additionally have received no such protection unless the limited partnership changed its business form to a general partnership that then registered as an LLP or set up an LLC and transferred its assets into it. In both situations, the fundamental

---

[19] Iowa Code § 486.46(4); Utah Code § 48-1-44(1).

[20] Iowa Code § 486.46(5); Utah Code § 48-1-44(2).

[21] *See, e.g.,* Ariz. Rev. Stat. § 29-247; Conn. Gen. Stat. § 34-14.

[22] For example, Delaware, Louisiana, Minnesota, Ohio and Texas.

[23] *See, e.g.,* S.C. Code § 33-41-1200; Va. Code § 50-43.9.

[24] 805 Ill. Comp. Stat. 180/1-20(i).

structure of the limited partnership was changed and the cost associated with setting up a new business entity was incurred. A limited partnership's general partner position gained the distinction of being the least desirable business role. Unlike LLC members, general partners in LLPs or limited partners, the general partner in a limited partnership was unable to acquire limited liability protection. Limited liability is now provided by states that have passed limited liability limited partnership (LLLP) statutes or recognize LLLPs as business entities.[25]

State Overview

In states that have not expressly authorized business entities to use the LLLP form, there is some confusion as to whether LLLPs are a recognized business entity. This confusion is exacerbated by the interaction of the Revised Uniform Limited Partnership Act (RULPA) and the Uniform Partnership Act (UPA). RULPA § 1105 acts as a default provision for limited partnerships and directs that situations not covered in RULPA are governed by UPA. Although logic should dictate that a limited partnership be allowed to elect LLLP status in every state that allows LLPs, this is not the case.

Currently, 22 states and the District of Columbia have adopted LLLP statutes. New York and California specifically exclude limited partnerships from electing to become LLLPs. In the states where the statutes are silent, it is often unclear, even to attorneys within the state's government, whether these states recognize and register LLLPs. Inquiries to each of these states resulted in only one response that referred to the provisions of RULPA. The Illinois Secretary of State's office explained that a limited partnership may elect LLLP status under RULPA by adopting an assumed name that complied with RULPA at the time of registration as an LLLP. In contrast to Illinois' position that it recognizes LLLPs in spite of the fact that the Illinois statute is silent, New Jersey is unclear whether or not it recognizes and registers LLLPs.

If the rapid enactment of state LLP statutes is any indication, most, if not all, states should have LLLP statutes in the next few years. In the meantime, practitioners should know whether their home state recognizes and registers LLLPs and whether the states where their clients do business recognize LLLPs. Until all states adopt LLLP statutes or implement substantially similar LLLP registration provisions, this confusion will not subside. In addition, it may not be a good idea to use an LLLP for a multi-state business because many states still have not enacted LLLP statutes.

---

[25] *See, e.g.,* Ark. Code § 4-42-706; Colo. Rev. Stat. § 7-60-144.

Impact of Electing LLLP Status

The primary reason for a limited partnership to elect LLLP status is to provide individual liability protection to the limited partnership's general partner. This liability protection shields the general partner from partnership debts, obligations, and liabilities unless they result from the general partner's own wrongful acts, misconduct, or negligence. Still, the general partner remains individually liable for all liabilities incurred before the limited partnership elected LLLP status and for any obligations arising from the contractual obligations resulting from the limited partnership agreement. Electing LLLP status provides a limited partnership with a simple and cost-efficient way to achieve the goal of protecting the general partner from personal liability, but electing LLLP status may also result in other changes within the limited partnership that may or may not be desirable. Most state LLLP statutes make it clear that a limited partnership that elects LLLP status remains a limited partnership under state law and continues to be governed by the state limited partnership law and the limited partnership agreement. However, the limited partnership has potentially undergone changes other than the acquisition of limited liability for the general partner.

Under RULPA § 303, a limited partner is liable for the obligations of the limited partnership when he or she participates in the control of the business to the extent that others who transact business with the limited partnership believe, based upon the limited partner's conduct, that the limited partner is a general partner. RULPA also denies a limited partnership the right to use the name of a limited partner in the partnership name (with exceptions) without running the risk that the limited partner could be held individually liable as if the limited partner were a general partner.[26] Arguably, a limited partner in a limited partnership that has elected LLLP status is able to exert as much control and participate as actively as the LLLP's general partner without running any risk of individual liability.

If a major factor in choosing the limited partnership entity is to limit the participation of limited partners, electing to become an LLLP may defeat that purpose. Although electing LLLP status may result in a limited partner being able to take an active role in the partnership, the limited partnership agreement is still controlling. If the only goal of the limited partnership is to protect its general partner from individual liability, the limited partnership agreement should expressly define the role of the limited partners in partnership operations.

In some cases a limited partnership may desire to have its limited partners play a larger role in the business. Electing LLLP status allows a limited partner to assume a greater business role without the limited

---

[26] RULPA § § 102 (2) and 303 (b) (8) (d).

partnership having to restructure itself as an LLC, S corporation, or a general partnership. At the same time, the limited partnership may continue to restrict the voting rights of limited partners, remain flexible in the distribution of its assets, and avoid the costs involved in changing the limited partnership into another entity. Remaining a limited partnership also allows the limited partnership to keep its operating agreement in place (although some amendments may be necessary) and the limited partnership may continue to rely upon the body of law that governs limited partnerships. This is an advantage over converting to an LLC because LLC case law is sparse and statutes are not uniform. Limited partnership case law is fully developed and virtually all states have adopted some form of RULPA.

Liability Protection

Prior to the enactment of LLC and LLP statutes, the limited partnership was the only noncorporate entity that could achieve almost complete liability protection. This was often done by forming an S corporation to serve as the general partner and having limited partners operate the limited partnership through the S corporation. The limited partnership had general partner liability only to the extent that the S corporation had assets. Although it may seem more practical to avoid the creation of two entities and just operate as an S corporation, S corporations are restricted in the number and type of shareholders they may have. A limited partnership is not restricted in this regard. With the enactment of LLLP statutes, limited partnerships have the opportunity to simplify this structure and provide even greater liability protection to the general partner. An LLLP election eliminates the need for the S corporation to serve as general partner.

Along with eliminating the S corporation as general partner, the limited partnership eliminates the need to keep separate sets of records, comply with separate statutory requirements and can avoid filing two sets of tax documents. As important, having an undercapitalized entity as the general partner increases the risk that creditors will seek to pierce the veil of the limited partnership. Although a limited partnership with a corporate general partner has less of a need to elect LLLP status than a limited partnership that has a truly liable general partner, for the sake of structural simplicity it may still be desirable to elect LLLP status.

Family Limited Partnerships

One situation where a limited partnership would nearly always elect LLLP status rather than convert to an LLC or LLP is in the case of family limited partnerships. Family limited partnerships are often used to transfer assets to family members and reduce the consequences of estate and gift transfer taxes.

In a family limited partnership, a family member, usually a parent, contributes assets to the partnership and serves as the general partner. Over time, the parent transfers limited partnership interests to family members that are discounted in value because of the lack of control and marketability of the limited partnership interest. This reduces the amount of taxes due on the gift, and as the general partner, the parent keeps control of the limited partnership assets. Electing LLLP status in this situation does not create the risk that a limited partner will participate in the control of the business because the family limited partnership is not an active business. Instead, this is a situation where a limited partnership may elect LLLP status and receive exactly what the LLLP statute intended—liability protection for the general partner.

Making the LLLP Election

LLLP statutes vary in their approaches to electing LLLP status. Some statutes allow a limited partnership to elect LLLP status according to its partnership agreement LLLP conversion clause. Of course, the probability is low that more than a few limited partnership agreements contain an LLLP conversion clause. Therefore, limited partnerships will need to conform to the LLLP election requirements contained in their state LLLP statute. Most common are provisions that require a limited partnership to elect LLLP status by the same vote that is required to amend the partnership agreement. The exception to this provision is in situations where the partnership agreement expressly considers contribution obligations. In this case, an LLLP election requires the same vote as it would take to amend those provisions.[27]

Almost as common are LLLP statutes that require the approval of all general and limited partners. The exception to this rule is applied to situations where the limited partnership has more than one class or group of limited partners. In this case, a vote of all the general partners and the limited partners who own more than 50 percent of the limited partner's interest in the limited partnership is required.[28] Other state LLLP statutes require a simple majority interest vote[29] or a unanimous vote of all partners subject to a contrary limited partnership agreement.[30]

¶ 806

Series LLCs

Series LLCs are those that have two or more series of members, managers or assets, each of which is immune from third-party claims against any other series of the same LLC. A primary use for a Series LLC is for each series to hold specific property as an alternative to

---

[27] *See, e.g.,* Ariz. Stat. §29-367(A)(1); Fla. Stat. ch. 620.187(1)(a).

[28] Ark. Code §4-43-1110(1)(a) and Tex. Rev. Civ. Stat. art. 6132a-1, §2.14(a)(1).

[29] Mo. Stat. §359.172.1(1).

[30] Ga. Code §14-8-62(g).

multiple LLCs holding the property. Treating each LLC itself, and not the series, as a legal entity is a goal in establishing a series.

Although Series LLCs can be useful in, among other things, simplifying the management structure of complex multi-asset enterprises, it is questionable whether the insulation of each series of the LLC from each other series will be respected in non-Delaware or Illinois courts. A Series LLC could also be set up by a business with many lines of business so that each has its own equity compensation plan.

There are two significant reasons for using a Series LLC. First, a Series LLC provides ease of administration. Second, by using a Series LLC, franchise taxes might be avoided on each separate LLC. Forming a Series LLC to avoid paying the franchise tax for each LLC could very well be found to violate a state's public policy.

There are currently many unknowns with regard to Series LLCs, including how they will be treated in interstate transaction and whether a distribution may be made from a financially sound series if it hurts an LLC that includes a financially unhealthy series. Further, there is no certainty as to how the IRS will treat a Series LLC. If the IRS treats a Series LLC as a single entity it would permit taxpayers to avoid tax they would otherwise pay. Thus it may be more likely that the IRS will treat each series as a separate entity. Although there are many sound business reasons for using a Series LLC, this uncertainty has put a damper on their usage.

Chapter 9

Federal Tax Treatment of LLCs

¶ 901
Introduction

To the extent that an LLC is treated as a partnership for federal tax purposes, the federal tax rules applicable to a partnership apply equally to an LLC. Further, with the popular check-the-box regulations now firmly in place, and with the release of several revenue rulings and numerous private letter rulings, the majority of the questions regarding the application of the federal partnership tax rules to an LLC have been answered. Nonetheless, several questions remain unanswered, primarily because an LLC and a partnership, though similar, have one significant structural difference—the LLC does not differentiate its members, as does the partnership with its "general" and "limited" partner distinctions.

In this chapter, we first address the issue of entity classification, analyzing the check-the-box regulations and reviewing two federal revenue rulings addressing entity conversions attributable to numerical membership changes. We examine the inventive use of the "disregarded entity" provisions in the check-the-box regulations to facilitate certain real estate like-kind exchanges. We then discuss the application of some of the more important aspects of the federal taxation of partnerships to the LLC, noting where the distinction between the partnership and the LLC requires further administrative guidance or legislative resolution. Finally, we explore some of the benefits and pitfalls of using the LLC in estate planning.

¶ 902

Entity Classification

Since its inception in 1977, the classification of an LLC for federal tax purposes involved a complex technical determination. Many entrepreneurs who could otherwise have benefited from the LLC format dismissed it as an entity choice due to their inability to ascertain the LLC's status for federal tax purposes. However, with the release of the check-the-box regulations in 1997, the entity-classification process significantly improved[1] and the future of the LLC brightened considerably as the access of entrepreneurs to the simultaneous benefits of limited liability and passthrough taxation was simplified.

Several classification questions that the check-the-box regulations left open have been addressed by later regulations,[2] and by two revenue rulings, which we explore in some detail, addressing the federal income tax consequences of converting a domestic LLC to and from a multi-owner entity classified as a partnership for federal tax purposes.

We conclude our discussion of entity classification by examining one use of the check-the-box regulations' disregarded entity provisions to facilitate certain real estate like-kind exchanges.

Check-the-Box Regulations

The check-the-box regulations set forth a step-by-step analysis for determining the appropriate federal tax classification of an entity (see the flowchart at the end of this section).[3] The following paragraphs will walk through this analysis, separately examining each of the applicable three regulations. We also address the actual classification election process and the regulations' effective date and related transitional rules.

Determine Whether a Separate Entity Exists

Determining an organization's federal tax classification is a two-step process. The first step in the analysis is to determine whether there is an "entity" that is separate and apart from its owners for *federal* tax purposes.[4] Generally, a joint venture or other contractual arrangement where the participants carry on a trade, business, financial operation or other venture for profit is a separate entity. The mere co-ownership of property, or a joint undertaking simply to share expenses, however, does not create a separate entity for federal tax purposes. Note that a joint undertaking that is not an entity under local law may

---

[1] Under the former *Kintner* entity classification regulations, the IRS, taxpayers, and their tax advisers were required to look for, and to balance, four "corporate characteristics" in determining the tax status of an entity: limited liability; continuity of life; centralized management; and the free transferability of interests.

[2] T.D. 9202 (May 20, 2005); T.D. 9139 (July 19, 2004); T.D. 9093 (October 21, 2003); T.D. 8970 (December 14, 2001); and T.D. 8844 (November 28, 1999).

[3] Reg. §§ 301.7701-1 through 301.7701-3.

[4] Reg. § 301.7701-1.

very well be a separate entity for federal tax purposes, and that an entity recognized under local law may not constitute a separate entity for federal tax purposes. Further, specific Internal Revenue Code sections may provide special classification treatment for certain organizations.[5]

Once an organization is recognized as a separate entity for federal tax purposes, the second step is to determine whether that entity is either a "trust" or a "business entity." A trust is distinguishable from a business entity in that the trust lacks associates and an objective to carry on a business for profit. The definition of a business entity, however, is more complex.

Distinguish Between Certain Business Entities

A business entity is any entity recognized for federal tax purposes that is not more properly classified as a trust or subject to special treatment under the Code. Such a business entity with two or more members can be classified as either a "corporation" or as an "eligible entity." A business entity with only one owner can be classified as a corporation, or it can be disregarded as an entity separate from its owner. If a one-owner entity is disregarded for federal tax purposes, the entity's activities are treated as if it were a sole proprietorship, if the owner is an individual, or as a branch or a division, if the single owner is a bank or a corporation.[6]

Certain business entities must be classified as "corporations" for federal tax purposes. These *per se* corporate entities include not only corporations denominated as such under applicable federal or state law, but also associations, joint-stock companies, insurance companies, certain banking organizations, certain state organizations, organizations that are taxable as corporations under a provision of the Code other than Code Sec. 7701(a)(3), and certain organizations formed under the laws of a foreign jurisdiction (including a U.S. possession, territory, or commonwealth).[7]

Use of the Elective Regime

Any business entity not required to be treated as a corporation for federal tax purposes may elect its classification under Reg. § 301.7701-3. An eligible entity with at least two members can elect to be classified as either a partnership or as a corporation. An eligible entity with only a single owner can elect to be classified as a corporation or it can be disregarded as an entity separate from its owner.

In order to provide most eligible entities with the tax classification that they would likely choose without requiring them to actually file an election form (Form 8832, *Entity Classification Election* (see below)), the entity classification regulations provide certain default classification rules that attempt to match the taxpayers' expectations (thus reducing

---

[5] For example, see the real estate mortgage investment conduit rules under Code Secs. 860A—860G.

[6] Reg. § 301.7701-2(a).

[7] Reg. § 301.7701-2(b).

the number of elections that need be filed). These entity default classifications are effective until the entity affirmatively elects to change its classification.

Under the passthrough default rule for "domestic" entities, a newly formed eligible entity will be classified as a partnership if it has at least two members, or will be disregarded as an entity separate from its owner if it has a single owner. An entity is a "domestic" entity if it is created or organized in the United States, under the laws of the United States, or under that of any state or the District of Columbia.

The default rules for foreign entities are generally based on whether the members of the foreign entity possess limited liability. A member does not have limited liability if the member, by virtue of being a member, has personal liability for all or any portion of the debts of the entity. Generally, only the statute or law of a particular country providing for limited or unlimited liability is relevant. However, where the underlying statute allows the entity to specify in its organizational documents whether the members will have limited liability, the organizational documents may be relevant.[8]

Thus, a foreign eligible entity will be classified as a corporate entity if all of the members have limited liability. A foreign eligible entity will be classified as a partnership if it has two or more members and at least one member does not have limited liability. The entity will be disregarded as an entity separate from its owner if it has a single owner and that owner does not have limited liability.

For both domestic and foreign entities, the default classification for an entity in existence prior to January 1, 1997, is the classification that the entity claimed immediately prior to that date, unless the entity elects otherwise. However, if an eligible entity with a single owner claimed to be a partnership, the entity is now disregarded as an entity separate from its owner.

Making a Classification Election

If the default rules do not provide the desired tax classification, an eligible entity may elect to be classified differently. As indicated by its euphemistic name, the election is as simple as checking a box on Form 8832, *Entity Classification Election* (see below). Although the election is generally effective on the date filed, taxpayers can specify another date, provided that date is not more than 75 days prior to the date on which the election is filed and not more than 12 months after the date on which the election is filed.[9]

Generally, the election is effective at the start of the day of the election. Any transactions that are deemed to occur because of a change in classification are treated as occurring the day before.[10] If a

---

[8] Reg. § 301.7701-3(b).

[9] Reg. § 301.7701-3(c)(1)(iii).

[10] Reg. § 301.7701-3(g)(3)(i).

taxpayer elects to treat a stock purchase as an asset purchase, under Code Sec. 338, an election to convert the target corporation's classification cannot be effective before the day after the acquisition date of the target corporation.[11]

A copy of Form 8832 must also be attached to the entity's federal tax or information return for the year in which the election is to be effective. If the entity is not required to file a return for that year, a copy of Form 8832 must be attached to any direct or indirect owner's federal income tax return or information return for the owner's tax year in which the election is effective. Although the failure of the entity or an owner to attach a copy of Form 8832 to the applicable return will not void an otherwise valid election, such a failure may give rise to penalties against the nonfiling party. Other applicable penalties may also apply to parties who file federal tax or information returns inconsistent with their entity's election.

To ensure that the taxpayers who recognize the tax consequences of a conversion election approve of the election, the election must be signed by every owner on the date of the deemed conversion transactions.[12]

The ability of an entity to make multiple classification elections is limited by prohibiting an eligible entity from changing its classification more than once during any 60-month period. However, the IRS is permitted to waive this 60-month limitation when there has been a more than 50-percent change in the ownership of the entity.[13]

[11] Reg. § 301.7701-3(g)(3)(ii).
[12] Reg. § 301.7701-3(c)(2)(iii).
[13] Reg. § 301.7701-3(c)(1)(iv).

Check-the-Box Entity Classification Flowchart

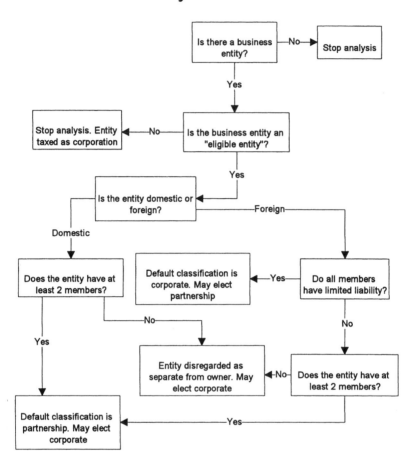

Form **8832**
(Rev. March 2007)
Department of the Treasury
Internal Revenue Service

Entity Classification Election

OMB No. 1545-1516

Type or Print	Name of eligible entity making election

Employer identification number

Number, street, and room or suite no. If a P.O. box, see instructions.

City or town, state, and ZIP code. If a foreign address, enter city, province or state, postal code and country. Follow the country's practice for entering the postal code.

▶ Check if: ☐ Address change

1 Type of election (see instructions):

a ☐ Initial classification by a newly-formed entity. Skip lines 2a and 2b and go to line 3.
b ☐ Change in current classification. Go to line 2a.

2a Has the eligible entity previously filed an entity election that had an effective date within the last 60 months?

☐ **Yes.** Go to line 2b.
☐ **No.** Skip line 2b and go to line 3.

2b Was the eligible entity's prior election for initial classification by a newly formed entity effective on the date of formation?

☐ **Yes.** Go to line 3.
☐ **No.** Stop here. You generally are not currently eligible to make the election (see instructions).

3 Does the eligible entity have more than one owner?

☐ **Yes.** You can elect to be classified as a partnership or an association taxable as a corporation. Skip line 4 and go to line 5.
☐ **No.** You can elect to be classified as an association taxable as a corporation or disregarded as a separate entity. Go to line 4.

4 If the eligible entity has only one owner, provide the following information:

a Name of owner ▶ ....
b Identifying number of owner ▶ ....

5 If the eligible entity is owned by one or more affiliated corporations that file a consolidated return, provide the name and employer identification number of the parent corporation:

a Name of parent corporation ▶ ....
b Employer identification number ▶ ....

For Paperwork Reduction Act Notice, see instructions.   Cat. No. 22598R   Form **8832** (Rev. 3-2007)

Reclassification Due to Numerical Membership Changes

¶3

An entity's classification may change as a result of a change in the number of its members. Specifically, an eligible entity classified as a partnership will become a disregarded entity when the entity's membership is reduced to one member, and a disregarded entity will be classified as a partnership when the entity has more than one member.[14] Guidance on the federal income tax consequences of converting a domestic LLC to and from a multi-owner entity classified as a partnership has been addressed in two related revenue rulings. Rev. Rul. 99-5 discusses the conversion of a single-member LLC, disregarded as a separate entity for federal tax purposes, to a multi-owner entity classified as a partnership.[15] Rev. Rul. 99-6 addresses the converse, that is, the federal tax consequences of converting a multi-member LLC classified as a partnership into a single-member LLC.[16] In the following discussion of these two revenue rulings, assume that the usual check-the-box default rules apply.

Rev. Rul. 99-5

Rev. Rul. 99-5 analyzes:

(1) the sale by the sole member of a 50-percent interest in the member's LLC; and

(2) the exchange of a 50-percent interest in the LLC for a capital contribution made directly to the LLC.

This ruling specifically addresses the recognition of gains and losses on the sale and conversion, the basis and holding periods of the members in their membership interests, and the basis and holding periods of both the members and the LLC in the assets deemed contributed to the LLC.

In the first factual situation, Beth purchased 50 percent of Art's ownership interest in an LLC, but none of the purchase price was contributed to the LLC. According to the IRS, the LLC is converted from a disregarded entity into a partnership. Beth's purchase is treated as the purchase of a 50-percent interest in each of the LLC's assets, which are treated as held directly by Art. Immediately thereafter, Art and Beth are treated as contributing their respective interests in those assets to a partnership in exchange for ownership interests in that partnership. In the final analysis, Art recognizes any gain or loss from the deemed sale of 50 percent of each asset.

In the second factual situation, Beth contributed money to the LLC in exchange for a 50-percent ownership interest. According to the IRS, the LLC is again converted from a disregarded entity into a partnership. Beth's contribution is treated as a contribution to a partnership in

---

[14] Reg. §301.7701-3(f)(2).
[15] Rev. Rul. 99-5, 1999-1 CB 434.
[16] Rev. Rul. 99-6, 1999-1 CB 432.

¶902

exchange for an ownership interest. Art is treated as contributing all of the assets of the LLC to the partnership in exchange for an ownership interest. In the final analysis, no gain or loss is recognized by the parties as a result of this conversion.

Tax Tip. In order to avoid the recognition of gain, any purchase money should be contributed directly to the LLC.

Rev. Rul. 99-6

In Rev. Rul. 99-6, the IRS analyzes the tax consequences of converting a multi-owner LLC classified as a partnership into a single-member LLC, specifically:

(1) the sale of one member's interest in a two-member LLC to the other member; and

(2) the sale of the entire interests of both members of a two-member LLC to an unrelated third person, who continues the business as a single-member LLC.

In each case, the partnership is terminated upon completion of the transaction[17] and a liquidating distribution of the partnership assets is deemed to have been made. In addition to addressing the recognition of any gains and losses, the revenue ruling addresses certain holding period issues.

In the first scenario, Art and Beth are equal partners in AB, an LLC. Art sells its entire interest in AB to Beth. According to the IRS, the AB partnership terminates, and Art must treat the transaction as the sale of a partnership interest and report any gain or loss. The AB partnership is deemed to make a liquidating distribution of all of its assets to Art and Beth and, following this distribution, Beth is treated as acquiring the assets deemed to have been distributed to Art in liquidation of Art's partnership interest. Upon termination of AB, Beth is also considered to receive a distribution of those assets attributable to Beth's former interest in AB, and must recognize any gain or loss on the deemed distribution.[18]

---

[17] See Code Sec. 708(b)(1) for the statutory partnership termination rules.

[18] In the first scenario analyzed in Rev. Rul. 99-6, the IRS treats the buyer and the seller of the LLC interest differently in that the applicable termination of the LLC's partnership status is deemed to occur at *different* times for the two parties to the transaction. For Art, the seller, the termination occurs after the interest is sold. For Beth, the buyer, the termination is deemed to occur *before* the sale. With this recharacterization the LLC terminates, distributes its assets to its members in liquidation of their interests, and the buyer is deemed to purchase these distributed assets from the departing member. While the sale of Art's interest in the LLC is treated as a sale of an LLC *interest*, this *same* transaction is treated as a sale of LLC *assets* with respect to Beth, the buyer.

Under this analysis, Beth is subject to at least two adverse income tax consequences. First, the timing of the termination with respect to Beth results in her obtaining the LLC's assets with a split holding period. Beth obtains the portion of the LLC's assets that is attributable to her own LLC interest with a carryover holding period. However, Beth's holding period in regard the assets attributable to Art's LLC interest begins on the day after the date of sale. Should the resulting single-member LLC sell any of the former LLC's capital assets within one year of Art's sale of his LLC interest, Beth may be faced with short-term capital gain. Second, Rev. Rul. 99-6's timing provisions may prevent Beth from amortizing that portion of the purchase price that is attributable to the former LLC's goodwill (see the "anti-churning" rules of Code Sec. 197).

While the administrative conclusion in Rev. Rul. 99-6 conforms with both case law and other administrative guidance (see the *McCauslen* case, 45 TC 588 (1966) and Rev. Rul. 67-65, 1967-1 CB 168), several commentators have suggested that the timing of the entity's termination in regard to the buyer may be based upon a misinterpretation of the Code Sec. 708 partnership termination regulations.

In the second scenario, Cal and Daria are equal partners in CD, an LLC. Cal and Daria sell their entire interests in CD to Ed. The CD partnership terminates and Cal and Daria must report gain or loss, if any, from the sale. The CD partnership is deemed to make a liquidating distribution of its assets to Cal and Daria. Immediately following this distribution, Ed is deemed to acquire, by purchase, all of the former partnership's assets.

One Application of the "Disregarded Entity" Provisions

The check-the-box regulations expressly provide that taxpayers may disregard, for federal tax purposes, certain single-member entities. Accordingly, a single-member LLC may be treated as a sole proprietorship, if it is owned by an individual, or as a branch or division, if it is owned by a corporation. Practitioners looking for inventive solutions to their assorted tax planning problems have discovered intriguing tax planning opportunities by applying this section of the check-the-box regulations. A review of the periodical tax literature and of the numerous private letter rulings over the past few years indicates that taxpayers and their tax planning advisers have utilized the availability of a disregarded entity to resolve any number of corporate, partnership and compensatory tax planning issues. Disregarded entities have been used to facilitate corporate reorganizations, the filing of consolidated returns and Code Sec. 1031 like-kind exchanges. While the use of disregarded entities may be limited only by the imagination of creative tax planners, the use of single-member LLCs in real estate acquisitions and to facilitate Code Sec. 1031 like-kind exchanges is particularly noteworthy.

Real estate acquisitions. The use of numerous single-member LLCs to hold individual real estate assets has become increasingly common in the last few years because such an arrangement can reduce the real estate investor's administrative costs[19] and, more importantly, permits the investor to segregate his or her property assets, and their applicable liabilities, from one another and from the rest of his or her investment portfolio. This single-member LLC structure limits the owner's financial exposure to the fallout from nonperforming properties and to properties that encounter unforeseen liability issues, such as environmental contamination and the resultant requisite clean-up costs. When real estate owners hold their multiple real estate assets in separate, distinct single-member LLCs, their other assets receive some measure of liability protection in the event of litigation involving one of the investor's holdings.[20]

---

[19] Since a single-member LLC is a disregarded entity, it is not required to file a separate federal income tax return, as would a partnership or a corporate entity. The disregarded entity's tax consequences flow through to the underlying owner and are reflected on that owner's federal income tax return. See also, Chief Counsel Advice 199930013 (April 19, 1999).

[20] Further, many financial institutions require that borrowers who hold real estate as security for a loan hold that real estate, and nothing else, in a "bankruptcy-remote" entity, such as a single-member LLC. Lenders do not want other assets held in the same entity to subject their security interest in the asset to a risk of forfeiture by another party.

In IRS Letter Ruling 199911033 (December 18, 1998) the IRS ruled that a two-member LLC set up as a bankruptcy-remote entity to protect the principal lender could still be treated as a single-member LLC because one of the members, the lender, held no economic interest. A business

Like-kind exchanges. In regard to a Code Sec. 1031 like-kind exchange, one of the critical requirements for deferring any gain recognition is that the owner of the relinquished property must acquire the replacement property in the exchange. A number of private letter rulings have held that the receipt of replacement property by a taxpayer's 100-percent owned single-member LLC will be treated as the receipt of real property by the taxpayer itself for the purposes of qualifying for the nonrecognition of gain under Code Sec. 1031.[21] The reasoning appears to be that since, under Reg. §301.7701-2(c)(2), a business entity that has a single owner and is not a corporation is disregarded as an entity separate from its owner for federal tax purposes, the assets of the single-member LLC are treated as the assets of the taxpayer. Such rulings indicate that the single-member LLC may be a valuable tool in structuring real estate like-kind exchanges in the partnership context. Accordingly, taxpayers and their tax and financial advisers must give single-member LLCs appropriate consideration during the acquisition and disposition of real estate.[22]

¶903

Contributions of Property and Services to an LLC

As a partner in a partnership, a member in an LLC generally receives a capital interest in the LLC upon the contribution of cash, property, services rendered, or a promissory note or other binding obligation to contribute cash or property. Also, as a partner in a partnership, a member in an LLC can receive a profits interest upon the contribution of services to the LLC. However, the payment by an LLC to a member in exchange for property is treated as a sale or exchange under Code Sec. 707, allowing the LLC a cost basis in the assets considered purchased.[23]

Property

Pursuant to Code Sec. 721(a), the contribution of cash or property by a member to an LLC in exchange for a membership interest is generally a nontaxable event for both the member and the LLC.[24]

(Footnote Continued)

entity with only one owner is disregarded as an entity separate from its owner unless it elects to be treated as a corporation (Reg. §301.7701-3(c)). Since no corporate election was made, the LLC was disregarded for federal tax purposes rather than being treated as a partnership (Reg. §301.7701-3(b)(1)(i)). Consequently, the LLC's acquisition of replacement property in a like-kind exchange was treated as a direct acquisition by the applicable taxpayer.

[21] See, for example, IRS Letter Ruling 9807013 (November 13, 1997). In this ruling, the receipt of replacement properties by single-member LLCs created and wholly owned by a limited partnership qualified for the nonrecognition of gain even though it was the limited partnership that had actually relinquished the exchanged property to a qualified intermediary. The IRS determined that since a single-member LLC is disregarded as an entity separate from its owner under the check-the-box regulations, the assets of the single-member LLCs were treated as the assets of the lim-

ited partnership. The IRS concluded that the receipt of replacement properties by the single-member LLCs was the receipt of real property directly by the limited partnership for purposes of qualifying as a tax-free, like-kind exchange.

See also Rev. Proc. 2000-37, 2000-2 CB 308; Rev. Proc. 2004-51, IRB 2004-33, July 20, 2004.

[22] See also IRS Letter Ruling 200118023 (January 31, 2001).

[23] See Field Service Advice 199936011 (June 3, 1999). The anti-abuse regulations promulgated under Code Sec. 701 did not apply to the transaction.

[24] While Code Sec. 721(a) may defer the recognition of gain or loss on the contribution of property by a partner or LLC member to a partnership or LLC, Code Secs. 704(c)(1)(B), 707 and 737(b)(1) prevent the transfer of this gain or loss to another partner or member. A discussion of these statutes, however, is beyond the scope of this product.

"Property" is broadly defined to include money, tangible property, and intangible property, such as accounts receivable, goodwill, and patents. The member takes a basis in the member's LLC interest equal to the cash and/or the value of the property contributed to the LLC.[25] After the initial contributions capitalizing the LLC, subsequent contributions of cash and property to the LLC by a member are also likely to be tax free.[26] The member's basis in the LLC is simply increased by the amount contributed.

The application of the partnership tax rules to the LLC presents several advantages that would not be available to an alternatively structured entity, such as an S corporation. In regard to the contribution of appreciated property, for example, the partnership tax scheme provides a more accurate allocation of a property's built-in gain than would be available under the S corporation rules. Since property contributions to an LLC are initially tax free, any gain reflecting the property's built-in appreciation will not be taken into account until some later point in time, generally when the property is sold or cost recovery deductions are claimed with respect to the property. However, when an LLC member contributes appreciated property, subsequent tax allocations take the variation between the property's basis and its fair market value into account in an effort to reduce the variation.[27] Consequently, a member of an LLC can obtain a more accurate allocation of the tax attributes inherent in appreciated property contributed to the entity.

Services

While the contribution of services in exchange for an LLC interest is acceptable, the federal taxation of such an exchange requires some analysis. Clearly, an LLC member who contributes services in exchange for an interest in the entity recognizes ordinary Code Sec. 61 compensation for services, unless that interest is subject to a forfeiture.[28] With the transfer of a capital interest, the amount of the member's taxable compensation income is basically determined by ascertaining the fair market value of the membership interest in capital transferred to the member. But what about where a venture capitalist provides the cash for an enterprise and another individual provides the "sweat equity"? In such a case, a profits interest, rather than a capital interest, is offered to those involved in the day-to-day operation and

(Footnote Continued)

For more information on any and all aspects of partnership taxation, see the CCH PARTNERSHIP TAX PLANNING and PRACTICE GUIDE.

[25] However, the contribution of property that is subject to a debt can trigger gain recognition by the contributing member if the contributing member's basis in the LLC is less than the contributing member's decreased share of liabilities with respect to the property. See Code Sec. 752.

[26] While, *at the time of formation*, investors forming an S corporation generally can obtain tax-free treatment, the *post-formation* contribution of property to an S corporation is a fully taxable event unless the shareholder has 80-percent control over the corporation immediately after the transfer. See Code Sec. 351.

[27] Code Sec. 704(c). The S corporation allocation rules do not take this appreciation into account. The contribution of appreciated property to an S corporation tends to shift these tax attributes. However, where the parties wish to shift a property's built-in gain, the S corporation allocation mechanism may present a tax opportunity not available to an LLC classified as a partnership.

[28] Code Secs. 83 and 721.

management of the business. How should this type of profits interest be valued?

After much litigation regarding the definition and taxation of such a profits interest, the IRS has ruled that, with three exceptions, it will not treat the receipt of a profits interest as a taxable event for the member or the LLC if the interest is received in exchange for services to, or for the benefit of, a partnership (or similarly treated LLC) by a person acting in a partner (or member) capacity or in anticipation of becoming a partner (or member). In the LLC context, these exceptions are:

(1) if the profits interest relates to a substantially certain and predictable stream of income from LLC assets, such as income from high-quality debt securities or a high-quality net lease;

(2) if within two years of receipt, the member disposes of the profits interest; or

(3) if the profits interest resembles a limited partnership interest in a "publicly traded partnership" within the meaning of Code Sec. 7704(b).[29]

Options

In a variety of situations, partnerships issue options or convertible instruments that allow the holder to acquire by purchase or conversion an equity interest in the partnership. There are three major types of options: compensatory options (options and other instruments that are issued by partnerships in connection with the performance of services), noncompensatory options and convertible debt.

Noncompensatory options. The IRS issued proposed regulations in January 2003, that generally provide that the exercise of a noncompensatory option does not cause recognition of gain or loss to either the issuing partnership or the option holder. In addition, the proposed regulations would modify the regulations under Code Sec. 704(b) regarding the maintenance of the partners' capital accounts and the determination of the partners' distributive shares of partnership items.[30]

Compensatory options. On May 23, 2005, the IRS issued proposed regulations under Code Sec. 83 describing the tax consequences of transferring partnership interests in exchange for services, and providing rules for coordinating Code Sec. 83 with partnership taxation principles. The proposed regulations provide that the amount includible in income by the transferee of the partnership interest, and the amount of the corresponding compensation deduction to the partnership, generally is equal to the fair market value of the transferred interest. The proposed regulations also provide that no gain or loss is recognized by

---

[29] Rev. Proc. 93-27, 1993-2 CB 343. Rev. Proc. 2001-43, 2001-2 CB 191, clarifies Rev. Proc. 93-27, with respect to situations where a partnership grants an interest in the partnership that is substantially nonvested to a service provider.

[30] NPRM REG-103580-02.

a partnership on the transfer or vesting of an interest in the transferring partnership in connection with the performance of services for the transferring partnership.[31]

Convertible debt. Although the proposed regulations, discussed above, treat convertible partnership debt as stock for purposes of the original discount rules, it appears the IRS has not yet decided whether it is appropriate to require a partnership to recognize accrued but unpaid interest as gain upon the exercise of convertible debt.

¶ 904

Computation of Basis

The computation of tax basis in the LLC context mirrors the computation of tax basis for the partnership. Accordingly, the initial basis of a membership interest in an LLC is the amount of cash contributed plus the member's adjusted basis in any other property contributed by the member in exchange for the membership interest.[32] The basis is subsequently increased by the member's share of taxable income (as determined under Code Sec. 703(a)) and by LLC income that is exempt from tax, etc. This basis is decreased (but not below zero) by the member's share of distributions (as provided in Code Sec. 733), by the member's distributive share of current and prior tax year losses of the LLC, and by LLC expenditures not deductible in computing its taxable income and, therefore, not properly chargeable to the capital account.

The tax basis of property contributed to an LLC by a member is equal to the adjusted basis of the property to the member at the time of the contribution. The LLC's holding period for the contributed property includes the member's holding period since the basis is a carryover basis.[33]

Beneficial Use of Code Sec. 752

Like a partner in a partnership, each member's basis in an LLC is also increased by the member's allocable share of the LLC's liabilities. Since, by definition, no LLC member is personally obligated for an entity liability that becomes due and payable, all LLC indebtedness will generally be considered a "nonrecourse liability." These nonrecourse liabilities are allocated to the basis of all LLC members pursuant to a complex regulatory formula. (For more information on this liability topic, see ¶ 907.)

Since members of an LLC qualifying as a partnership can include their allocable shares of the LLC's liabilities in the bases of their own LLC membership interests, the basis increase resulting from this inclu-

---

[31] NPRM REG-105346-03.

[32] Code Sec. 722.

[33] Code Sec. 723.

sion affords an LLC member with two distinct tax advantages not otherwise available to, for example, an S corporation shareholder:[34]

(1) tax losses may be claimed in excess of the LLC member's capital investment; and

(2) a greater amount of money and property may be distributed tax-free to the LLC member.

Conversely, if a member is relieved of personal liability, such as when the member contributes property subject to an indebtedness to an LLC and the LLC assumes that liability, the contributing member's tax basis is reduced by the portion of the liability assumed by the LLC. In effect, the member transferring the encumbered property is deemed to have received a distribution of cash from the LLC equal to the amount of the liability assumed.[35]

Beneficial Use of Code Sec. 754

An LLC member may also receive the flexibility (and the resulting tax advantages) associated with the partnership tax rules allowing the LLC to elect a basis adjustment of its assets at the time that an interest in the entity is sold, exchanged, or inherited.[36] An adjustment to the basis of LLC assets is also permitted to reflect gain recognized by a member upon the receipt of a property distribution.[37]

There are at least two tax advantages to electing to adjust the basis of LLC assets:

(1) increased cost recovery deductions for the incoming LLC member to reflect the extent to which the fair market value of LLC assets exceeds their tax basis; and

(2) avoiding excess capital gain allocated to the incoming LLC member when appreciated LLC assets are sold.

¶ 905

Allocation of LLC Tax Items

As with a partner in a partnership, a member's distributive share of each item of the LLC's income, gain, loss, deduction, and credit is generally determined in accordance with a written agreement (*i.e.,* the operating agreement). If the LLC does not have such an agreement or the LLC fails to provide for an allocation or the provided allocations do not have "substantial economic effect,"[38] then the member's distributive

---

[34] An S corporation shareholder is not able to use the corporation's debt to increase the basis for his or her stock even if the shareholder guarantees the debt.

[35] Code Sec. 752. If that deemed cash distribution exceeds the contributing member's basis in his or her membership interest, the recognition of gain is possible.

[36] Code Secs. 743(b) and 754.

[37] Code Sec. 734(b).

[38] The determination of whether an allocation of income, gain, loss, or deduction to a partner (or LLC member) has

"substantial economic effect" involves a two-part analysis that is made at the end of the tax year to which the allocation relates. First, the allocation must have economic effect and, second, the effect must be substantial. In order for an allocation to have economic effect, there must be an economic benefit or economic burden that corresponds to the allocation. The economic effect of an allocation is substantial if there is a reasonable possibility that the allocation will affect substantially the dollar amounts to be received by the partners (or members) from the partnership (or LLC), independent of tax consequences. See Code Sec. 704(b).

share of each LLC item is determined in accordance with the member's interest in the LLC. In determining the extent of such an interest, all of the applicable facts and circumstances are considered, including:

(1) relative contributions;

(2) interests in profit and losses;

(3) interests in cash flow and other nonliquidating distributions; and

(4) rights to distributions of capital upon liquidation.

¶ 906

Accounting Periods/Methods of an LLC

Accounting Periods

An LLC taxed as a partnership is generally required to conform its tax year to that of its partners. Since a partner's income includes the income for the partnership's tax year that ends with or within the partner's tax year, the requirement of tax year conformity between partners and the partnership restricts the opportunity for partners to choose a tax year for the partnership that defers the partners' recognition of partnership income. The tax year for a partnership that conforms to the tax year of its partners is determined under one of the following rules:

(1) the majority interest rule;

(2) the principal partner rule; or

(3) the least aggregate deferral rule.[39]

Under the majority interest rule, the required tax year for a partnership is the common tax year of any group of partners that holds a majority interest in the partnership. If no tax year can be established under the majority interest rule, then the required tax year for a partnership is the common tax year of all of its principal partners. If no tax year can be established under either of these rules, then the required tax year is the tax year that results in the least aggregate deferral of income.[40]

Accounting Methods

At first blush, it appears that an LLC may choose any accounting method that it desires (cash basis, accrual basis or a combination of the two) as long as that method clearly reflects income and is regularly used in keeping the LLC's books.[41] There are, however, certain restrictions on when a partnership (and thus an LLC classified for tax purposes as a partnership) can utilize the cash method of accounting.[42]

---

[39] Code Sec. 706.
[40] Reg. § 1.706-1.
[41] Code Sec. 446.
[42] Code Sec. 448.

Briefly, an accrual method taxpayer is entitled to a deduction in the year in which all of the events have occurred that establish the fact of the liability, and the amount of the deduction is determinable with reasonable accuracy. Similarly, an accrual method taxpayer recognizes income when all events have occurred which fix the taxpayer's right to receive income, and the amount of income is determinable with reasonable accuracy. Cash method taxpayers generally recognize income in the year in which the income is actually or constructively received. Similarly, these taxpayers recognize expenditures in the year in which the payments are actually made.

For LLC purposes, the most interesting accounting method restriction applies to entities characterized as "tax shelters."[43] An analysis of this term leads to the surprising conclusion that nearly every LLC that reports losses may be precluded from using the cash method of accounting.

The term "tax shelter" includes a "syndicate." An LLC with a substantial number of passive investors (*i.e.,* members who do not actively participate in management) can likely be characterized as a syndicate and thus find the cash method of accounting to be unavailable. A syndicate is any entity (except a C corporation) where more than 35 percent of the losses of the entity are allocable to limited partners or limited entrepreneurs. A "limited entrepreneur" is a person who has an interest in an enterprise other than as a limited partner and who does not actively participate in the management of the enterprise. While the term "active participation," for purposes of determining whether a member is a limited entrepreneur, is not clearly defined, applicable treasury regulations indicate that having limited liability for losses indicates a lack of active participation. Thus, if a member may be characterized as a limited entrepreneur, the logical conclusion is that the cash method of accounting is off-limits to many LLCs.

Organization and Syndication Fees

An LLC or any member is not allowed a deduction for any amounts paid or incurred, directly or indirectly, to organize an LLC or to promote the sale of, or to sell, an interest in the LLC.[44] However, an LLC may elect to amortize organization expenses.

An LLC may elect to deduct, on a straight-line basis, over a period of not less than 60 months, all amounts paid or incurred in organizing the LLC, beginning with the month that the LLC first starts its business.[45] An LLC using the cash method of accounting, however, may not take an amortization deduction in excess of the amount of organization expenses actually paid by the end of the tax year. Amortization deductions denied by virtue of this accounting rule are deductible in a later

---

[43] See Code Secs. 448(a)(3) and 461(i)(3).
[44] Code Sec. 709; Reg. § 1.709-1.

[45] Reg. §§ 1.709-1(b)(1) and 1.709-2(c).

year when the expenses are actually paid. If the LLC is terminated before the end of the requisite 60-month period, any undeducted balance of the organization expenses may be deducted as a loss to the extent permitted under Code Sec. 165.

¶ 907

Sharing of Liabilities

While most of the federal tax partnership rules apply without much problem to an LLC classified as a partnership, the partnership debt allocation regulations[46] appear to operate differently for an LLC. This difference is primarily attributable to the fact that, in an LLC, no member is liable for entity debts while, in a general or limited partnership, at least the general partner is personally liable for the partnership's obligations.

These regulations distinguish between "recourse" and "nonrecourse" debt according to whether any partner ultimately bears the "economic risk of loss" with respect to the entity debt. In general, a partnership liability is a recourse liability to the extent that any partner bears the economic risk of loss. A partner bears the economic risk of loss for a partnership liability to the extent that, if the partnership is constructively liquidated, the partner would be immediately obligated to make a payment to any person or to make a contribution to the partnership without the right to any reimbursement from any other party.

Since the liability of all LLC members is limited under state law to the members' capital contributions, it appears that all LLC debt is nonrecourse for purposes of the allocation rules, absent a guarantee of entity debt by an LLC member. Note that, in a limited partnership, debt secured by the partnership's general assets is typically allocated to the general partners who do not have limited liability and who bear ultimate responsibility for repayment of the debt. Thus, the general partners, and not the limited partners, enjoy the basis increase associated with the allocation of the liability. However, since a similar debt of an LLC is treated as nonrecourse because all of the members have limited liability, the debt (and the accompanying basis increase) is allocated among *all of the members* according to their interests in the LLC, as provided in the LLC operating agreement.

While this appears to be the correct analysis, confirmation from the IRS is still needed because the partnership debt allocation rules were not designed with LLCs in mind.

---

[46] Reg. §§ 1.752-1 through 1.752-5.

¶ 908

Distributions and Dispositions of LLC Interests

Taxation of Distributions

As with a partner in a partnership, when money is distributed by an LLC to a member, no gain is recognized by the member except to the extent that the amount of money distributed exceeds the adjusted basis of the member's interest in the LLC immediately prior to the distribution.[47] This is true with respect to both current distributions and to distributions in liquidation of a member's interest in the LLC. Further, no gain is recognized by a member with respect to a distribution of property (other than money), except to the extent otherwise provided by Code Sec. 736 (relating to payments to retiring or deceased partners), Code Sec. 751 (relating to unrealized receivables and inventory items), and Code Sec. 737 (relating to recognition of precontribution gain in case of certain distributions).

Loss is recognized by a member only upon the liquidation of the member's entire interest in the LLC and only if the property distributed to the member consists solely of money, unrealized receivables, and inventory items.[48] In such a case, loss is recognized to the extent that the member's adjusted basis in his or her membership interest exceeds the sum of (i) any money distributed to the member and (ii) the basis to the distributee member (as determined under Code Sec. 732) of any unrealized receivables and inventory items that are distributed to the member. Any loss recognized under this rule is a capital loss.

The basis of property (other than money) received by a member in a distribution from an LLC, other than in liquidation of the member's entire interest, is its adjusted basis to the LLC immediately prior to the distribution; however, the basis cannot exceed the adjusted basis of the member's interest in the LLC reduced by the amount of money distributed to the member in the same transaction.[49]

Taxation of Dispositions of LLC Interests

Sale or Exchange of an LLC Interest

The sale or exchange of an LLC membership interest generally triggers the recognition of gain or loss.[50] Except with respect to unrealized receivables and inventory, the character of this gain or loss is capital. The existence of unrealized receivables or inventory in the LLC generally requires a special computation to determine what portion of the gain or loss is ordinary in nature.[51]

---

[47] Code Sec. 731(a)(1).
[48] Code Sec. 731(a)(2).
[49] Code Sec. 732(a).

[50] Code Sec. 741.
[51] Code Sec. 751. In regard to a sale or exchange of an interest in a passthrough entity that holds "collectibles," see Reg. §§ 1.1(h)-1 and 1.741-1.

Liquidation of an LLC Interest

Code Sec. 736 characterizes the payments made by an LLC to a retiring member or to a deceased member's successor-in-interest in liquidation of the member's *entire* LLC property interest. When an LLC makes payments to retire the withdrawing member's entire interest in the LLC, the payments must be allocated and characterized as payments made pursuant to Code Sec. 736(a) and (b).

Code Sec. 736(a) provides that, unless otherwise provided in Code Sec. 736(b), payments made in liquidation of a member's interest will be considered (i) a distributive share of the LLC's income if the amount of the payment is determined with regard to the income of the LLC *or* (ii) as a guaranteed payment under Code Sec. 707(c) if the payment is determined without regard to the income.

Code Sec. 736(b) provides that payments made in liquidation of a membership interest, to the extent these payments are considered to be made in exchange for the member's interest in LLC property, are to be treated as a distribution by the LLC that is not a distributive share of LLC income or a guaranteed payment.

Most interesting from the LLC viewpoint, however, again pointing out the structural difference between a partnership and an LLC, is the provision that generally provides that "partnership property," for purposes of Code Sec. 736(b), includes unrealized receivables and goodwill if (i) the withdrawing partner is other than a general partner (e.g., a limited partner) or (ii) capital is a material income-producing factor for the partnership. In other words, only when the withdrawing partner is a *general partner* and capital is not a material income-producing factor for the partnership do unrealized receivables and goodwill (unless the partnership agreement otherwise provides) become categorized as Code Sec. 736(a) property.

The logical question presented by Code Sec. 736(b)(3)(B) in the context of an LLC is whether members are more appropriately characterized as either general partners or as limited partners. Unfortunately, the underlying treasury regulations are dated and of little help with this question. However, by strict definitional standards, an LLC does not have general partners and limited partners, but rather "members." Consequently, administrative guidance is sorely needed in this area.

Transactions Between Member and LLC

Transactions between an LLC and a member who is not acting as a member are taxed as if between the LLC and a third party.[52] Payments to a member acting as a member is treated as a distribution of his or her share of LLC income if the amount is determined from LLC income; if not, payment is included in his or her ordinary income and

---

[52] Code Sec. 707(a)(1).

deducted or capitalized by the LLC.[53] A distribution or allocation related to a member's contribution of property or performance of services may be recharacterized as a transaction with a nonmember.[54] On a property sale between an LLC and a controlling person, no loss is recognized and gain is ordinary income.[55]

The IRS can recharacterize member-LLC transactions as if they occurred between the LLC and a nonmember.[56] Whether a member is acting in a member or nonmember capacity is determined from the facts surrounding the transaction, including pertinent provisions of the LLC agreement.[57] A member who renders services required by the LLC agreement is likely to be considered to act in his or her capacity as a member. Other factors that bear on this issue include the nature, scope and continuity of the member's services for the LLC and whether the payments he or she receives depend on the LLC's income.

When a member receives a cash distribution from the LLC that is related to a property contribution he or she makes, the transaction may be recast as a sale of the property to the LLC. When an allocation of income to a member is related to his or her performance of services or contribution of property, the transaction may be treated as a disguised payment for the services or property. If a member is not acting as a member of the LLC, the transaction is treated as if it involves the LLC and an unrelated person.[58] An allocation to a member acting in a member capacity for his or her services or for the use of his or her capital or property is included in his or her distributive share if the amount is determined with regard to the LLC's income. The actual payment to the member is treated as a cash distribution.[59]

If an LLC makes payments to a member acting in a member capacity for services rendered to, or use of his or her property by the LLC, and the amount is determined without regard to LLC income (a guaranteed payment), the member includes the entire payment in his or her ordinary income. Depending on the nature of the services or loan, the LLC either deducts the payment as an ordinary and necessary business expense or capitalizes it. The member reports the guaranteed payment in his or her tax year in which or with which the LLC's tax year for taking the deduction ends or in the year he or she receives it if capitalized by the LLC.[60]

The gains or losses from sales or exchanges of property between a member and LLC are further restricted if the member owns, directly or indirectly, more than 50 percent of the LLC's capital or profits interest. Neither the member nor the LLC may recognize a loss from the sale or exchange, and any gain recognized is treated as ordinary income.

---

[53] Reg. § 1.707-1(c); Code Secs. 162 and 163.

[54] Code Sec. 707(a)(2)(A).

[55] Code Sec. 707(b)(2).

[56] Reg. § 1.707-1(c).

[57] Reg. § 1.707-1(a).

[58] Reg. § 1.707-6(a).

[59] Code Sec. 707(a)(2).

[60] Code Sec. 707(c).

Similar rules apply to transactions between two LLCs controlled by the same person. In these cases, the member includes any payment in his or her income and the LLC deducts or capitalizes it.[61]

Special rules for the treatment of payments to members for services performed or property transferred to a LLC that are aimed at eliminating disguised payments for services or property and disguised sales are provided.[62]

¶ 909

Termination of an LLC

For tax purposes, an LLC classified as a partnership continues to be treated and taxed as a partnership unless it is terminated in either one of two ways:

(1) when no part of the business, financial operation, or venture continues within the LLC format; or

(2) when 50 percent or more of the total interests in LLC capital and profits are sold or exchanged within a 12-month period.[63]

Cessation of Business within LLC/Partnership Form

An LLC terminates for tax purposes when (1) no part of the business, financial operation, or venture continues (2) within the LLC/partnership format. Thus, to terminate under this provision, both parts of the test must be satisfied.

First, an LLC classified as a partnership terminates only when the LLC's business ceases *completely*. Even the mere collection of interest on LLC notes, or minor purchases, is sufficient to prevent termination.

Second, subject to two exceptions, an LLC classified as a partnership terminates for tax purposes where, as a result of a sale or liquidation, only one member remains. However, such an LLC can continue to be treated as a partnership with only one member after the death of the other member if the estate or other successor-in-interest of the deceased member continues to share in the entity's profits and losses. One member may also continue the LLC classification as a partnership for the period of time in which liquidating payments are made to a retiring member under Code Sec. 736 (see above).

Sale or Exchange of 50 Percent or More Interest

An LLC classified as a partnership for federal tax purposes also terminates when 50 percent or more of the LLC's interests in both capital *and* profits are sold or exchanged within any consecutive 12-month period. For example, the sale or exchange of a cumulative 52-percent capital interest and a cumulative 60-percent profits interest

---

[61] Code Sec. 707(b).

[62] Code Sec. 707(a)(2)(B).

[63] Code Sec. 708(b)(1).

between March 5, 2001 and March 4, 2002, will cause a termination. Note that a "sale or exchange" does not apply to gifts or bequests, consecutive sales of the same membership interest, or to a contribution of property.

For tax purposes, if an LLC classified as a partnership is terminated by the sale or exchange of 50 percent or more of the LLC's interests in both capital and profits, the following is deemed to occur:

(1) the LLC contributes all of its assets and liabilities to a new LLC in exchange for an interest in the new LLC; and

(2) immediately thereafter, the terminated LLC distributes interests in the new LLC to the purchasing member and to the other remaining members in liquidation of the terminated LLC, either for continuation of the business by the new LLC, or for its dissolution and winding up.[64]

¶ 910

Application of the At-Risk Rules

The tax losses of individual members of an LLC may be claimed only to the extent that a member's investment is "at risk."[65] The at-risk rules do not permanently deny a deduction with respect to the losses but merely suspend these losses until more of the member's investment becomes at risk or the member disposes of the entire activity.[66] Under these rules, capital investments are clearly at risk, as are economic obligations for which a member is "ultimately liable." Since no LLC member is ultimately liable for the repayment of the LLC's liabilities, the liabilities of an LLC generally are nonrecourse and do not increase any member's amount at risk, even if the members have been allocated these liabilities under the partnership allocation rules.

An LLC member is considered to be at risk to the extent of the amount of money and the adjusted basis of any *unencumbered* property contributed to the LLC, plus any amounts borrowed by the member for use in the LLC to the extent that the member is personally liable for their repayment. Any money borrowed without recourse to the member that is subsequently contributed to the LLC will not increase the member's at-risk amount. Further, an LLC member who contributes encumbered property to the LLC increases his or her at-risk amount by the adjusted basis of the property, only to the extent that the member remains personally liable on the loan creating the encumbrance or pledges other property as security for the loan creating the encumbrance. Finally, the mere guarantee of an LLC liability by a member will not increase the member's at-risk amount since, in most cases, the

---

[64] Reg. § 1.708-1(b)(4). If a Code Sec. 754 election is in effect, the election applies to the incoming member, Reg. § 1.708-1(b)(5).

[65] Code Sec. 465.
[66] Code Sec. 465(b)(5).

member will have a common law right of subrogation against the LLC, and thus the member is not the "obligor of last resort."

There is, however, an exception to the general rule that a taxpayer is not at risk with respect to amounts borrowed without recourse to the taxpayer. A taxpayer is considered to be at risk with respect to the amount of "qualified nonrecourse financing" that is secured by real property used in the activity of holding real estate.[67] Code Sec. 465(b)(6) provides that, where an activity involves the holding of real property, the taxpayer's share of any qualified nonrecourse financing that is secured by real property used in the activity of holding realty is includable as an amount at risk, even if the taxpayer is not personally liable for the repayment of the financing. This financing must be from a bank, credit union, insurance company, or related person (if the terms are commercially reasonable) and must not be convertible.[68] Further, no *person* may be personally liable on the obligation, except to the extent provided in the regulations.[69]

Under the regulations a three-part test is adopted, providing that the personal liability of any partnership (or LLC treated as a partnership) will be disregarded and, providing that certain other requirements are satisfied, the financing will be treated as qualified nonrecourse financing secured by real property if:

(1) the only persons personally liable for repayment are partnerships;

(2) each partnership with personal liability holds only property that is permitted as security for qualified nonrecourse financing; and

(3) in exercising its remedies to collect on the financing in a default or default-like situation, the lender may proceed only against property that is permitted as security for qualified nonrecourse financing and that is held by the partnership or partnerships.[70]

The regulations also clarify that entities that are disregarded as entities separate from their owners under Reg. § 301.7701-3 are disregarded as well under Code Sec. 465(b)(6).[71]

---

[67] Code Sec. 465(b)(6)(A). Note that Reg. § 1.465-27(b)(2)(i), addressing the fact that real estate partnerships and LLCs often hold assets in addition to real property, permits qualified nonrecourse financing to be secured not only by real property, but also by property that is "incidental" to the activity of holding real property. In general, if the incidental property remains below a prescribed percentage of the fair market value of the property securing the financing, the incidental property will be ignored in determining whether the financing satisfies the "secured-by-real-property" requirement.

[68] Reg. § 1.465-27(b)(1) provides that financing secured by real property can be characterized as "qualified nonrecourse financing" if four conditions are met: (1) it is borrowed by a taxpayer with respect to the activity of holding real property; (2) it is borrowed from a qualified person or represents a loan from any federal, state or local government or instrumentality thereof, or is guaranteed by any government; (3) no person is personally liable for repayment; and (4) it is not convertible debt.

[69] Code Sec. 465(b)(6)(B)(iii).

[70] Reg. § 1.465-27(b)(4).

[71] Reg. § 1.465-27(b)(5).

¶ 911

Application of the PAL Rules

An LLC classified as a partnership for federal tax purposes is indirectly subject to Code Sec. 469 since its members must report the activities of the LLC as either active or passive.[72] These passive activity limitation (PAL) rules generally apply (i) to most rental activities and (ii) to all trade or business activities in which the taxpayer does not "materially participate."[73] The PAL rules provide that deductions from passive activities may only offset the income from passive activities and that any credits from passive activities are limited to the tax attributable to the income from passive activities. Any excess passive activity losses and credits are not permanently disallowed, but rather deferred until the time that the taxpayer has offsetting passive activity income or the taxpayer disposes of the passive activity to an unrelated party in a fully taxable transaction.[74]

At present, it remains unclear as to whether an LLC member can materially participate in an LLC trade or business activity. The structural differences between the LLC and the partnership again come into play and cause some question (*i.e.,* the LLC has no distinction among its members similar to the general partner and the limited partner, and an LLC member may actively participate in management while most limited partners are prohibited by state law from materially participating in the management of the limited partnership). Although the applicable treasury regulations do not specifically address whether a member in an LLC is a limited partner for purposes of the material participation tests, the regulations do provide that no interest in a limited partnership as a limited partner will be treated as an interest with respect to which a taxpayer materially participates, except under more limited circumstances.[75]

Should the PAL regulations be interpreted to include an LLC member within the definition of a limited partner, thus subjecting the LLC member to the more stringent material participation tests? Classification as a limited partner would be disadvantageous to an LLC member since a limited partner has a much more difficult task to show material participation in an activity than a taxpayer who is not a limited partner.

In *S.A Gregg,*[76] a district court held that a member of an LLC was a general partner for purposes of the material participation requirement

---

[72] Reg. § 1.469-4(a).

[73] Code Sec. 469(c). A taxpayer materially participates in an activity only if the taxpayer is involved in the operations of the activity on a basis which is regular, continuous and substantial (Code Sec. 469(h)(1)). In general, an individual is considered to materially participate in an activity if he or she can satisfy any one of the seven regulatory tests.

[74] Code Sec. 469(g). The taxpayer may defer unused passive activity losses indefinitely into the future until the disposition of the passive activity. All unused passive activity losses at the time of the disposition may be used to offset other nonpassive income. Passive activity losses may not be carried back.

[75] Code Sec. 469(h)(2).

[76] *S.A. Gregg,* DC Ore., 2001-1 USTC ¶ 50,169.

of the passive activity loss rules. To date, no other court has decided the issue of whether an LLC member should be treated as a general or limited partner for federal tax purposes. While *Gregg* seems to provide welcome news to taxpayers, the decision is of questionable value. The results in *Gregg* were not dependent on whether the taxpayer should be treated as a general or limited partner. Instead, the court allowed the taxpayer to use his share of the LLC's losses to offset active income because the court determined that the LLC's business activity should be grouped with the activities of a corporation in which the taxpayer materially participated.[77]

¶ 912

Application of the Self-Employment Tax Rules

The Internal Revenue Code imposes a self-employment tax on a general partner's distributive share of income from the partnership's trade or business.[78] In contrast, the distributive share of a *limited* partner is generally *excluded* from the self-employment tax, except to the extent that this share is a "guaranteed payment."[79] Limited partners are excepted from the self-employment tax rule under the theory that they are more like passive investors than true partners.

When Congress first enacted this limited partner exclusion, many state's laws did not permit a limited partner to actively participate in the partnership's trade or business. However, today, under the Uniform Limited Partnership Act and other state laws, a limited partner may more freely participate in his or her partnership without being recharacterized as a general partner for liability purposes. Further, LLCs, for which there is generally no distinction between general and limited members as a matter of state law, and which were unknown at the time of the enactment of the statutory limited partner exception, are now viable business entities in all 50 states and in the District of Columbia. Finally, LLCs can now generally be treated as partnerships for federal income tax purposes.[80] It thus became clear to the IRS that the traditional definitions of "general partner" and "limited partner," as used in the currently applicable treasury regulations, do not adequately account for the new ways in which partnerships and LLCs are operated.

In an effort to more satisfactorily address the limited partner exclusion and to resolve mounting questions involving the self-employment tax status of limited partners and LLC members, the IRS pro-

---

[77] See, Susan Kalinka, *S.A. Gregg: Is an LLC Member a General Partner or a Limited Partner for Purposes of the PAL Rules?*, Taxes—The Tax Magazine, March 2001, at 22.

[78] Code Secs. 1401 and 1402. The self-employment tax consists of two components, the Old Age Survivors and Disability Insurance fund (OASDI), comprising 12.4 percent of the first $97,500 (2007) of net earnings from self-employment, and the Hospital Insurance fund (HI) or Medicare, comprising 2.9 percent of self-employment earnings without limit.

[79] Code Sec. 1402(a)(13). Pursuant to Code Sec. 707(c), a "guaranteed payment," an amount paid to a partner for services actually rendered to or on behalf of the partnership without regard to the income of the partnership, is considered as made to one who is not a member of the partnership, and is thus subject to the self-employment tax.

[80] Reg. §§ 301.7701-1 through 301.7701-3, the check-the-box regulations.

posed amendments to current Reg. § 1.1402(a)-2. According to the IRS, the proposals were an attempt to establish a single set of "functional" rules that applied identical standards to all entities classified as partnerships for federal tax purposes. The proposed amendments would have allegedly resolved the issue by classifying general and limited partners on the basis of functional tests, rather than on historic state law definitions.[81]

Numerous critics maintained that the proposed self-employment tax regulations would impose new taxes on partners and require more recordkeeping, urged the IRS to withdraw its proposed regulation defining "limited partner" for self-employment tax purposes. Congress, in the Taxpayer Relief Act of 1997 (P.L. 105-34), asserted that it, and not the IRS, should determine the tax law governing self-employment income for such individuals. Accordingly, the Act provided that no temporary or final regulation with respect to the definition of a "limited partner" under Code Sec. 1402(a)(13) could be issued or made effective before July 1, 1998.[82] No new regulations have been issued.

The general rule that members of an LLC are not personally liable for the entity's employment taxes does not apply to single-member LLCs, unless the LLC selects association status under the check-the-box regulations. Absent such an election, the LLC entity will be disregarded for federal tax purposes, and the single member will be treated as the statutory employer liable for employment taxes.[83]

Employer Identification Number.

With respect to employees of a disregarded entity reporting and payment of employment taxes can be done in either of two ways:

- under the owner's name and taxpayer identification number

or

- by each state law entity with respect to its employees under its own name and taxpayer identification number.[84]

¶ 913

Designation or Selection of an LLC's TMP

An LLC classified as a partnership for federal tax purposes is also subject to the unified partnership audit and litigation procedures, which are designed to handle tax disputes and issues common to all members in a single entity-level process.

Thus, a TEFRA proceeding is the exclusive forum for judicial review of assessments involving so-called "partnership items." Administrative and judicial procedures for determining the tax treatment of

---

[81] Proposed Reg. § 1.1402(a)-2, REG-209824-96, January 13, 1997.

[82] Act Sec. 935 of the Taxpayer Relief Act of 1997 (P.L. 105-34).

[83] Notice 99-6, 1999-1 CB 321.

[84] Field Service Advice 200114006 (December 18, 2000).

partnership items (*i.e.*, income, deductions, gains, losses and credits that are determined by regulation to be more properly determined at the partnership level by partnerships and their partners) differ from those determining nonpartnership items. Separate procedures for partnership and nonpartnership items help to ensure that consistent treatment of all partnership items is determined in a single, partnership-wide proceeding, rather than in multiple, partner-by-partner proceedings.[85]

These rules require certain larger partnerships to choose a tax matters partner (TMP) either by designation or on the partnership tax return.[86] If no partner is so designated, the statute provides that the general partner having the largest profits interest in the partnership will automatically be deemed the TMP.[87]

The TMP, as the representative of the partnership in tax proceedings, receives certain notices and information from the IRS and is obligated to keep the other partners informed of all tax matters, such as audits and other tax disputes. In addition, the TMP is required to provide the IRS with information regarding the partners' identities, addresses, and profits interests. The TMP is specifically authorized to act on behalf of the partnership for certain tax matters, such as extending the partnership's statute of limitations, selecting the forum for litigation of the partnership's tax disputes, and even settling the partnership's tax adjustments for all of the other partners.

An LLC "member-manager" is treated as a general partner for purposes of the TMP rules. Thus, a member-manager can be designated as a TMP. A member-manager is a member of the LLC who, alone or together with others, is vested with the continuing and exclusive authority to make the management decisions necessary to conduct the business for which the LLC was formed. Any member of an LLC who is not a member-manager is treated as a partner other than a general partner. However, where an LLC is formed in such a manner that all of the members have management authority and no member-managers are elected or designated, each LLC member is considered to be a member-manager and, thus, is eligible to serve as the TMP.[88]

When no TMP designation is made by the LLC and the first option—the largest-profits-interest rule—is inapplicable or impractical to apply, the IRS may consider several factors when selecting a member to serve as the TMP, including:

---

[85] Thus the Tax Court lacked jurisdiction to rule on claims raised in a partnership-level proceeding by the TMP of a limited liability company regarding the partners' entitlement to a refund of the overpayment that would result if an increased casualty loss deduction were determined. Those claims had to be resolved in a partner-level proceeding following the conclusion of the partnership-level proceeding. *Jaco L.C.*, Dec. 54,014(M), 80 TCM 270, TC Memo. 2000-265.

[86] Code Sec. 6231(a)(7).

[87] If such a general partner is not determinable, the IRS is authorized to appoint a TMP of its own choosing. However, within 30 days of selecting a TMP for an LLC, the IRS must notify all of the members entitled to receive notice under Code Sec. 6223(a) of the selected TMP's name and address. See Code Sec. 6231(a)(7).

[88] Reg. § 301.6231(a)(7)-2.

(1) the general knowledge of the member in tax matters and the administrative operation of the LLC;

(2) the member's access to the books and records of the LLC;

(3) the profits interest held by the member;

(4) the views of the members having a majority interest in the LLC regarding the selection;

(5) whether the member is a member of the LLC at the time that the TMP selection is made; and

(6) whether the member is a U.S. person within the meaning of Code Sec. 7701(a)(30).[89]

Rather than have the IRS, or perhaps a court, designate an LLC's TMP, an LLC would be well-advised to designate its own TMP in the manner required by the regulations.[90]

¶ 914

Converting an Existing Entity into an LLC

With all of the excitement generated by the business and tax planning literature on the limited liability and passthrough tax benefits of the LLC, many entrepreneurs and their business and financial advisers wonder whether they should convert an existing business entity into an LLC. While this explanation concentrates on the federal tax ramifications of a conversion, note that when converting from any business entity into an LLC, one must also be aware of any applicable state or local tax consequences.

Partnership-to-LLC

To convert a partnership (*i.e.,* a general partnership, limited partnership, or limited liability partnership) into an LLC, the organizers must follow the formalities required by both the state of organization and the states in which the LLC is going to do business. Failure to follow formalities imposed by a state LLC statute could expose the members of the LLC to personal liability for the debts and obligations of the business.

A partnership will usually convert into an LLC using one of the following processes:

(1) the partners exchange their partnership interests for LLC membership interests, and the partnership is dissolved immediately thereafter;

(2) the partnership's assets and liabilities are exchanged for LLC membership interests, which are then distributed to the part-

---

[89] Reg. §§ 301.6231(a)(7)-1 and 301.6231(a)(7)-2.

[90] Although the Tax Court is permitted to appoint a TMP, it is not obligated to do so. *Cinema '84*, CA-2, 2005-2 USTC ¶ 50,439.

ners when the partnership is dissolved immediately after the exchange; or

(3) the partnership is liquidated, and the partners contribute their liquidation distributions to the newly formed LLC in exchange for LLC membership interests.

An IRS revenue ruling,[91] regarding the tax consequences of converting a general partnership into a limited partnership, provides that:

(1) no gain or loss is recognized by the partners under Code Sec. 741 or Code Sec. 1001 as a result of the conversion;

(2) the partnership does not terminate under Code Sec. 708 because the business of the partnership continues after the conversion;

(3) each partner's adjusted basis in the partner's partnership interest remains unchanged if no change in each partner's share of liabilities results from the conversion;

(4) there is a change in the partner's adjusted basis if there is a change in a partner's share of liabilities, and the change is deemed to be a contribution or distribution by or to a partner;[92] and

(5) there is no change in the holding period of a partner's interest.

In a subsequent revenue ruling,[93] the IRS ruled that the federal income tax consequences discussed above generally apply as well to the conversion of a domestic partnership into a domestic LLC that is classified as a partnership for federal tax purposes. (The same holds true for a conversion from a domestic LLC classified as a partnership into a domestic partnership.[94]) This later ruling provides that the federal tax consequences of converting a partnership interest into a membership interest in an LLC are the same, whether the resulting LLC is formed in the same state or in a different state from that of the converting partnership.

Upon a conversion, the basis of a partner-member's interest in the new LLC will generally be the same as the partner's basis in the former partnership, assuming that the partner's share of partnership liabilities does not change. If the share of liabilities does change, then the partner-member's basis in the new LLC must be adjusted accordingly and, under the terms of Code Sec. 752, the recognition of gain is possible. Further, upon a partnership-to-LLC conversion, the tax year of the converting partnership and of any partner of the partnership does

---

[91] Rev. Rul. 84-52, 1984-1 CB 157. See also IRS Letter Ruling 9841030 (July 14, 1998).

[92] Note that it would not be uncommon for the conversion of a partnership into an LLC to trigger changes in the member's shares of entity liabilities because no LLC member is personally liable for LLC debts while a general partner is personally liable for the recourse liabilities of a limited partnership.

[93] Rev. Rul. 95-37, 1995-1 CB 130.

[94] In IRS Letter Ruling 199935065 (May 28, 1999) the conversion of two LLCs into limited partnerships did not result in termination of either LLC under Code Sec. 708, and each limited partnership was considered to be a continuation of the respective LLC.

not close as a result of the conversion, and the resulting LLC is not required to obtain a new taxpayer identification number.

Corporation-to-LLC

To convert a corporation (*i.e.,* a C corporation or an S corporation) into an LLC, the organizers must follow the formalities required by both the state of organization and the states in which the LLC is going to do business. Failure to follow formalities imposed by a state LLC statute could expose the members of the LLC to personal liability for the debts and obligations of the business.

The conversion process generally begins with the board of directors adopting, and the required shareholders approving, a proposal to convert. Articles of dissolution are filed with the appropriate state authority, and the corporation liquidates using one of the following processes:

(1) *a merger*—the shareholders exchange their stock interests for LLC membership interests, with the corporation dissolving immediately;

(2) *an asset exchange*—the corporate assets and liabilities are exchanged for LLC membership interests, which are distributed to the shareholders in liquidation; or

(3) *a liquidation*—the corporation liquidates, and the shareholders contribute their distributions to the newly formed LLC for LLC membership interests.

Each of the above processes, however, will usually be treated as a taxable liquidation. However, the conversion of an S corporation to an LLC followed by an election to be treated as an association taxable as a corporation qualified as a nontaxable F reorganization.[95]

C Corporation-to-LLC. The conversion of an existing C corporation into an LLC is generally a liquidation of the corporation and thus a taxable event for both the corporation and its shareholders. Gain will be recognized by the C corporation on the disposition of any appreciated assets, including goodwill and going-concern value.[96] The shareholders will recognize a shareholder-level gain when they exchange their stock for LLC interests if the amount realized exceeds their basis in the stock.[97] Obviously, then, the possible tax hit diminishes the attractiveness of an LLC for existing corporate entities. This is especially true if the corporation holds appreciated property. Only a corporation with little or no net worth and shareholders with bases exceeding the amount of any distribution can escape this tax scheme.[98]

---

[95] IRS Letter Ruling 200528021 (April 8, 2005).
[96] Code Sec. 336.
[97] Code Sec. 331.

[98] However, the conversion of a closely held corporation to an LLC did not result in a transfer of an interest subject to Code Sec. 2701, when the shareholders exchanged their shares in the corporation for identical membership interests in the LLC (IRS Letter Ruling 199947034 (August 26, 1999)).

S Corporation-to-LLC. Unlike a C corporation, when an S corporation distributes appreciated assets to its shareholders in exchange for their stock, there is no double tax. Because the S corporation is a flow-through entity, the gain incurred at the corporate level passes through to the shareholders and is generally included in income on the shareholder's individual tax return. Any gain recognized by the shareholder as a result of the gain attributable to the liquidating distribution increases the shareholder's stock basis. The shareholder's increased basis then reduces the amount of gain recognized or increases the amount of loss recognized.

Thus, with one exception, there is but a single level of taxation to contend with here, and this tax occurs at the shareholder level. (The exception relates to any possible Code Sec. 1374 built-in gains tax, which is an entity-level tax.) Although, with an S corporation, there is usually only this one level of taxation, rather than the two levels of taxation inherent with the C corporation, this single level of taxation may still be enough to impede an S corporation's wish to convert to an LLC.[99]

Professional Corporation-to-LLC. The conversion of an existing professional corporation into an LLC can usually be accomplished without any adverse tax consequences. The tax disadvantages often inherent in a conversion of a corporation into an LLC are not normally present in the conversion of a professional corporation, which typically does not possess a significant amount of appreciated property that can trigger gain in an LLC conversion.

¶ 915

Using the LLC in Estate Planning

One goal of estate planning is certainly to pass the wealth of a more senior generation to a younger generation while incurring as little tax on the wealth transfer as possible. Understandably, the senior generation often wishes to pass on the economic benefits of the family's business and investments to that younger generation without relinquishing all of their managerial control of the family's assets. To accomplish this dual goal, various estate planning techniques and methods may be utilized. One popular and successful method is to set up a family entity to manage the family's assets and to facilitate the transfer of those assets among family members. An LLC taxed as a partnership is an excellent vehicle for such an estate planning strategy.

Further, an LLC taxed as a partnership can achieve certain step-ups in the basis of the entity's assets that cannot be obtained in, for example, the corporate context.[100] This ability to step up the "inside

---

[99] Note that the IRS has privately ruled that a company's conversion under state law to a state limited partnership did not terminate its pre-existing S corporation status (IRS Letter Ruling 199942009 (July 16, 1999)).

[100] See Code Sec. 754 and Reg. § 1.754-1.

basis" upon a member's death is a significant estate planning advantage of the LLC taxed as a partnership over the corporate form. In addition, an LLC may be better able to use buy-sell agreements to preserve control and to prevent disruption than a corporation because the LLC membership interests can be bifurcated between management and economic rights.

Family LLC

A family LLC can serve as a valuable tax planning vehicle to pass a family's business and investments to succeeding generations in much the same way as a family limited partnership (FLP) has been used in recent years.[101] The owners of a closely held business may want their children to succeed them in the business. And even if the children are not going to succeed to, or participate in, the family business, the parents may still want those children to own a share of that business. At the same time, however, the parents may not be willing to turn over complete control of the business to their children, especially if the parents want or need to receive income from that business. A family LLC can be used to address both of these issues.

A business and investment vehicle organized as an LLC permits the parent members to: (1) pass on their accumulated assets to their children; (2) reduce their potential estate tax; and (3) maintain adequate control of those assets. To do so, the parents first contribute their business and investment assets to an LLC in exchange for interests in that LLC. The parents can then transfer fractional parts of those LLC interests to their children by gift in increments calculated to take advantage of the applicable dollar amount of the annual gift tax exclusion.[102] These gifts immediately reduce the current value of the parents' estates and also transfer any potential appreciation in those interests to the younger generation, thus removing that future appreciation from the parents' estates. Note that, for gift tax purposes, the value of the interests transferred is determined immediately after the transfer and does not take into account any future appreciation.

Further, by organizing their LLC with perhaps two types of membership interests, such as a preferred interest and a common interest, the parents can retain the preferred interests so as to maintain control of the family's assets and part of any income generated by the transferred assets. In transferring the common interests to their children, the parents may take advantage of any available valuation discounts.[103]

---

[101] In fact, an LLC generally provides greater personal liability protection and more flexible management structures than a partnership or another entity form.

[102] If the LLC interests are given away, rather than sold or exchanged, the parents may be subject to a gift tax on the value of the interest transferred (see Code Sec. 2501). However, the parents are entitled to an annual gift exclusion under Code Sec. 2503(b) before a gift tax is assessed. The Economic Growth and Tax Relief Reconciliation Act of 2001

(P.L. 107-16) reduced the rate, but did not eliminate the gift tax.

[103] Minority and marketability discounts are often used to reduce the value of the transferred interests. A "minority discount" is a discount of the value of a transferred business interest due to the transferred interest being a minority interest in the entity. A minority interest in an entity is usually worth less than a majority interest in an entity because the holder of the minority interest does not have control of the entity, cannot direct the payment of distribu-

For the senior generation, the net result is the transfer of assets to the next generation while still retaining control and incurring little or no tax on the transfer.

Comparison of the Family LLC to the FLP

There are several advantages to using a family LLC, rather than an FLP, for estate planning purposes. First, no member of a family LLC is personally liable for the debts and obligations of the entity, while, in an FLP, at least one partner (the general partner) is personally liable for the entity's debts and obligations. Second, because there is no distinction among LLC members similar to that between limited and general partners, an LLC member does not risk personal liability by actively participating in LLC management. This active participation allows the member to treat any income or loss arising from the investments or activities of the LLC as active, and not passive, income or loss for income tax purposes. A limited partner, who cannot by definition be an active participant in the FLP's business, must treat his or her income and loss from the FLP as passive income and loss. While the limited partner can only use passive activity losses to offset any passive activity income (see above), the ordinary loss taken by the member of the family LLC can be deducted from the gross income of the member, thereby offsetting any other income that the member might be receiving from other sources.

There are, however, certain drawbacks to using the family LLC for estate planning purposes. First, entrepreneurs and their advisers who are averse to risk may wish to wait until there is more definitive resolution of some of the uncertainty attributable to the operation and treatment of the LLC. Second, there is some concern over whether a family LLC membership interest is eligible for the valuation discounts enjoyed by the partners of an FLP. Since, in some states, any member can force the dissolution of the LLC and thereby receive the value for his or her LLC interest, valuation discounts would appear to be inappropriate.

The IRS has expressed an unwillingness to recognize the validity of either a family LLC or an FLP.

With regard to a family LLC, an IRS Field Service Advice advanced several arguments to support the issuance of deficiency notices for gift

---

(Footnote Continued)

tions and cannot compel a liquidation of the entity. Note that the amount of a minority discount is based on each individual case, and one must consider all of the relevant facts and circumstances of that case. Discounts applied in other cases are generally inapplicable.

"Marketability discounts" can be applied in addition to minority discounts and refer to the fact that interests in family entities generally have no market outside of the family. Unlike minority discounts, marketability discounts can be applied to transfers of interests that exceed 50 percent of the total closely held business interests.

If a valuation discount is used in determining the value of a transferred interest, any reports or other data used in valuing the interest should be submitted with the tax return (see Reg. § § 25.2512-2(f) and 25.2512-3(a)).

Further, the valuation of the interest can result in the imposition of a penalty if the value is ultimately determined to be substantially understated (see Code Sec. 6662).

Finally, tax practitioners must be aware of the important valuation limitations imposed by Code Sec. 2704. See also Reg. § § 1.2704-2 and 25.2704-1.

taxes and estate taxes in connection with transfers to a family LLC. A decedent had established a family LLC in which he and his three children were members. The transfers upon the formation of the family LLC were deemed transfers of cash and securities, rather than transfers of LLC interests. No further capital contributions were required of the members and none of the children had contributed funds upon formation. Therefore, a portion of the decedent's contribution was, in substance, a transfer to his children, followed by the children's contribution of the assets in exchange for their membership interests. Applying the economic substance doctrine, the family LLC and/or the transfers to the entity could be disregarded if it could be shown that the primary purpose for the transaction was the reduction of federal transfer taxes.[104]

The IRS has made similar attacks on FLPs.[105] However, in 2000, taxpayers in two cases, *Strangi Est.*[106] and *I.F. Knight,*[107] prevailed against the IRS and obtained FLP discounts that the IRS sought to disallow. (Although the amount of the FLP discounts were significantly less than the amounts asserted by the taxpayers.[108]) On remand, the Tax Court in *Strangi,* found that the value of the transferred property was includible in the decedent's gross estate because the documents governing the FLP and the corporate general partner contained no restrictions that prevented the decedent himself from being designated as a recipient of income from the FLP and the corporation.[109] The Fifth Circuit affirmed the Tax Court.[110]

Based on these cases it would appear that a family LLC or an FLP should be recognized for tax purposes, provided the proper formalities are followed provided and there are credible non-tax business reasons for the entity's formation.

---

[104] Field Service Advice 200049003 (September 1, 2000). The FSA advanced other issues. Code Sec. 2703(a) could apply to disregard the restriction on the right to sell or use an family LLC interest contained in the family LLC agreement in valuing the transferred interests. Further, Code Sec. 2704 applied to invalidate valuation discounts that were claimed with respect to liquidation restrictions contained in the family LLC agreement. Moreover, the transferred interests retained their character as family LLC interests; they did not become merely assignee interests lacking liquidation rights under the agreement or under state law. The suggestion that the interests were assignee interests conflicted with the legislative purpose of Code Sec. 2704. In addition, Code Sec. 2036 applied to the formation of the family LLC, if the decedent retained the economic benefits of the assets transferred pursuant to an implied understanding between the decedent and the children. As a result, the transferred assets could be included in the decedent's gross estate.

[105] In IRS Letter Ruling 9725002 (March 3, 1997) the IRS disregarded the creation of a FLP, followed by the transfer of assets held in a decedent's revocable trust, for purposes of valuing the property includable in the decedent's gross estate. Two months before his incompetent father died, the decedent's son formed the FLP and transferred cash and securities to the FLP in exchange for a limited partner interest. On the estate tax return filed following the decedent's death, the son valued the trust's limited partnership interest with a 38-percent discount.

[106] *Strangi Est.*, Dec. 54,135, 115 TC 478.

[107] *I.F. Knight,* Dec. 54,136, 115 TC 506.

[108] For example, in *Knight,* the Tax Court allowed a 15-percent discount for minority interest and lack of marketability, rejecting the taxpayer's assertion of a 44-percent valuation discount.

[109] *Strangi Est.*, Dec. 55,160(M), 85 TCM 1331, TC Memo. 2003-145, on remand from CA-5, 2002-2 USTC ¶ 60,441; 293 F3d 279 (*Gulig, Rosalie*).

[110] *Strangi Est.*, *Albert*, CA-5, 2005-2 USTC ¶ 60,506.

Chapter 10

State-by-State Synopsis of LLC Acts

¶ 1001

Overview

This section presents an analysis of the progress of LLCs in all 50 states and the District of Columbia. The section also summarizes the key statutory provisions in all 51 jurisdictions.

The state summaries do not purport to describe each state's LLC law in detail. Rather, they focus primarily on procedural and substantive considerations that practitioners will encounter immediately when organizing an LLC for clients:

• What information needs to be included in the Articles of Organization?

• What fees are involved?

• What records need to be maintained by the LLC?

• Are professional limited liability companies (PLLCs) expressly permitted and, if so, which professions may or may not organize as LLCs?

• How will the entity be classified for federal and state tax purposes?

• What are the general state law rules concerning key issues, such as LLC management, member contributions, distribution rights, and assignments of member interests?

If a state's law relating to LLCs varies notably from the norm in a particular area, that information is generally included in the state-by-state summaries. Where state law, as summarized, is subject to alteration in the LLC's articles of organization or operating agreement, the words "unless otherwise provided" will follow the explanation of the state's operative provision.

State Taxation of LLCs

Generally, an LLC is subject to tax under the jurisdiction of the state in which it does business to the same extent as a partnership doing business in the state. In addition, most states will follow the federal income tax classification of an LLC for state tax purposes. Accordingly, an LLC with two or more members will be treated as a "partnership" and an LLC with only a single member will be disregarded as an entity separate from its owner (see Chapter 9). Two states, Texas and Kentucky, tax all LLCs as corporations.

The members of an LLC doing business in more than one state will usually be taxable in each state in which the LLC does business. Whether the members of an LLC are subject to an income tax on LLC income in a state is determined by the same rules of nexus that are generally applicable to corporations.

Although LLCs with two or more members may be classified as partnerships for state income tax purposes, they may be subject to other taxes as well, such as franchise taxes.

Michigan has long had a "single business tax" that LLCs and other entities were required to pay. Under legislation passed in 1999, Michigan will phase out the single business tax over a 23-year period, provided that certain revenue targets are met.[1]

Tennessee expanded its franchise and excise tax to apply to all organizations or entities engaged in business, including LLCs and PLLCs. Only general partnerships and sole proprietorships are not subject to the tax.[2] Alabama enacted a privilege tax imposed on corporations, LLCs, LLPs, and disregarded entities after its franchise tax was held to be unconstitutional.[3] This tax is based upon the net worth of the entity.[4]

In addition, many states have increased their LLC formation and annual reporting fees. For example, starting in tax year 2005, New York increased its LLC filing fees from $50 to $100 per member, with a minimum fee of $500 (previously, $325) and a maximum fee of $25,000 (previously, $10,000). The $500 minimum does not apply to single-member LLCs that are disregarded entities for federal income tax purposes.[5]

States have continued to show great concern with collecting individual taxes from nonresident LLC members. Many states now require nonresident LLC members to file an agreement to pay their individual state taxes. If an agreement is not received, these states have placed the burden on the LLC to pay the taxes of the nonresident members. These statutes provide that the LLC is entitled to recover payments made on a nonresident member's behalf, plus any interest or penalties.[6] To facilitate tax collection from LLCs, other states have established rules that bar LLCs from filing any forms with the government unless

[1] Mich. H.B. 4745.
[2] Tenn. Code § 67-4-2004.
[3] *South Central Bell*, 119 S. Ct. 1180 (1999).
[4] Alabama, Act 665 (H.B. 1), Laws 1999.
[5] New York LLC Law § 1101.
[6] *See, e.g.,* Rules 710:50-3-54, 710:90-3-11 and 710:90-7-3, Oklahoma Tax Commission, effective June 25, 2004.

all taxes are paid.[7] Finally, more states are holding LLC and LLP members or partners with the responsibility of paying the LLC or LLP's taxes personally liable for delinquencies.[8]

State Response to Federal LLC Developments

The event that triggered the most state legislation was the finalization of the federal entity classification regulations, the "check-the-box" regulations.[9] With the IRS no longer looking at an entity's corporate characteristics to determine its federal tax status, states were free to give LLCs more organizational options. Provisions in many state LLC acts affecting the transferability of LLC membership interests, management, and dissolution events have since been amended.

Probably the most notable, and perhaps the most common, change was a move to allow single-member LLCs. Some states changed language in their statutes to specifically permit single-member LLCs, others simply dropped their two-member requirement.

Another aspect of LLC formation that has seen a great deal of change is the duration requirement. Traditionally, in order to avoid a corporate tax classification, an LLC was required to lack continuity of life. Many states limited an LLC's duration to a period of 30 years. With the check-the-box regulations now in place, LLCs are no longer required to dissolve on a fixed date, and many states have responded by allowing LLCs to have perpetual duration.

¶ 1002

State Legislation and Recent Developments

Piercing the LLC Veil

Although many state LLC statutes do not address the application of traditional corporate veil piercing to LLCs, the courts have made it clear that the principles of piercing the corporate veil will be applied to LLCs. Veil piercing theories that most states would likely recognize include undercapitalization, lack of separateness, and failure to follow formalities. However, some state statutes specifically provide that an LLC's failure to follow formalities will not result in the LLC's veil being pierced. After a long period of uncertainty, it appears that the risk of an LLC's veil being pierced is no greater than that of a corporation.

Securities Laws

Only a handful of states have defined LLC membership interests as securities. Courts that have addressed this issue uniformly apply the *W.J. Howey* test and look at the amount of control the member has to

---

[7] *See, e.g.,* Rhode Island (H.B. 5911), effective August 1, 2007.

[8] Ga. Code §§ 14-11-303 and 14-8-15.

[9] T.D. 8697. Reg. §§ 301.7701-1, 301.7701-2 and 301.7701-3.

affect the LLC and whether the member is fundamentally reliant upon the skill of others to affect the investment.[10]

Fiduciary Duties

Most states have allowed LLCs some latitude in defining fiduciary duties without eliminating their existence. Usually fiduciary duties are not imposed on LLC members unless the members take on management responsibilities. In late 2004, Delaware went a step further and enacted legislation that allows an LLC's operating agreement to eliminate fiduciary duties, but not the contractual duty of good faith and fair dealing. Colorado also adopted statutes that provide LLCs with great latitude to limit or eliminate fiduciary duties. The Colorado provisions are becoming more typical of other state's LLC fiduciary duties statutes. It provides that an LLC may not unreasonably reduce the duty of care or a manager's right to access LLC books and records. However, an LLC agreement may identify categories or types of activities that do not violate duties such as the duty of care or the obligation of good faith and fair dealing. In addition, an operating agreement may eliminate fiduciary and other duties other than the obligation of good faith and fair dealing. By agreement, LLC members may determine the standards by which the performance of good faith and fair dealing is to be measured.[11] Operating agreements need to clearly address this issue.

Cross Entity Conversions and Mergers

Most state statutes authorize conversions and mergers. Every state permits LLCs to merge into another LLC. State conversion and merger statutes are frequently placed throughout various entity statutes. This makes it difficult to determine whether certain types of conversions or mergers are allowed. Alabama, Colorado, and Nevada are among a handful of states that have enacted "junction box" statutes that govern the procedure and authority for implementing a conversion or merger. However, Alabama and Colorado did not repeal the existing conversion and merger statutes and, as a result, any inconsistencies and conflicts will lead to confusion. Currently, most states provide for the statutory merger of a general or limited partnership into an LLC. In addition, a growing number of states now authorize the merger of a corporation into an LLC.

Other legislation

In 2003, Massachusetts followed 49 other states and the District of Columbia and amended its LLC Act to permit single-member LLCs. Prior to passing this legislation, Massachusetts recognized foreign single-member LLCs only. The legislation also gave LLCs the power to make guarantees of the obligations of another person or entity.

---

[10] *Securities & Exchange Commission v. W.J. Howey Co., et al.*, 328 U.S. 293 (1946).

[11] *See* Del. Code tit. 6, § 18-1101(c) and Colo. Rev. Stat. § 7-80-108.

¶1002

In the past few years, states that had previously restricted the types of businesses that could organize as an LLC began relaxing those restrictions. Oregon now allows banks and trust companies to organize as an LLC. West Virginia amended its statutes to allow a state-chartered bank to organize as an LLC. Louisiana also allows financial institutions to be organized as LLCs and Illinois now permits attorneys to form LLCs.[12] Recently Nevada and Oklahoma have joined Delaware, Illinois, Kansas, Kentucky, Tennessee and Vermont in adopting statutes that permit the creation of separate series within an LLC. The Illinois statutes provide that an LLC operating agreement may establish designated series of members, managers or LLC interests having separate rights, powers and duties with respect to specified property or obligations of the LLC or profits and losses associated with specified profits or obligations. In addition, any series may have a separate purpose or investment objective.[13]. The Illinois LLC statutes make it clear that each series within an LLC is a separate legal entity; the LLC statutes in other states that allow series LLCs have not specifically stated this.

Over half of the states and the District of Columbia have statutes recognizing limited liability limited partnerships (LLLP) as entities. Other states continue to consider LLLP statutes. Although New Mexico has recently enacted LLLP legislation, the legislation will not be effective until 2009 in order to give the secretary of state time to develop necessary filing forms and procedures. The primary reason for a limited partnership to elect LLLP status is to provide individual limited liability protection to the limited partnership's general partner. Electing LLLP status is a simple and cost-efficient way for a limited partnership to obtain liability protection for the general partner because usually a limited partnership is required to do nothing more than submit a form to the secretary of state. However, until all states recognize LLLPs, there is a risk that a limited partnership's general partner will not receive personal liability protection in states that do not authorize the use of LLLPs.

[12] *See, e.g.,* La. Rev. Stat.§ § 12:1302 and 12:1306; 805 Ill. Comp. Stat.180/110.

[13] § 805 Ill. Comp. Stat. 180.37-40, effective July 1, 2005.

State Summaries

¶ 1003

Alabama

Name of act:	• Alabama Limited Liability Company Act, Ala. Code § 10-12-1 to § 10-12-61.
Federal tax classification:	• The LLC statute is flexible. Any "business entity" not required to be treated as a "corporation" for federal tax purposes under Reg. § 301.7701-2 may choose its classification under Reg. § 301.7701-3.
State tax treatment:	• All LLCs, including both single-member LLCs and multiple member LLCs, , will be classified as they are classified for federal income tax purposes under the federal "check-the-box" regulations. With respect to LLCs organized before January 1, 1997, the Alabama Department of Revenue will conform to the LLC's classification under the IRS's "check-the-box" regulations for tax years preceding January 1, 1997.
Securities treatment:	• The Alabama LLC Act indicates that the terms "partnership" and "limited partnership" used anywhere other than the Alabama LLC Act, Alabama Partnership Act or the Alabama Limited Partnership Act generally include an LLC. Thus, LLC interests are not defined as "securities." (Ala. Code § 10-12-8)
Limited liability partnerships:	• Limited Liability Partnerships are expressly authorized. (Ala. Code § 10-8A-1001)
Professional LLCs:	• Professional LLCs are expressly permitted by statute, subject to compliance with other state regulatory provisions. (Ala. Code § 10-12-45)
Foreign LLCs:	• Foreign LLCs are expressly permitted by statute. The laws of the formation jurisdiction govern the LLC's organization, internal affairs, and liability of its members. Foreign LLCs may only carry on businesses that may be carried on by Alabama LLCs. (Ala. Code § 10-12-46)
Formation:	• An Alabama LLC must be formed by one or more persons. One or more members are required. (Ala. Code § § 10-12-9 and Ala. Code 10-12-37)
Naming requirements:	• The name of each LLC must have the words "Limited Liability Company" or "L.L.C.", or the abbreviations of those words as the last words of the name. (Ala. Code § 10-12-5)
Effective date of organization:	• An LLC's existence begins upon the filing of articles of organization with the probate judge. (Ala. Code § 10-12-14)

Filing requirements:	• The articles of organization must include: (1) the LLC's name; (2) its duration, if not perpetual; (3) its purpose; (4) the address of the registered office and the name of the initial registered agent; (5) the names and addresses of the initial member or members; (6) the right, if any, of the member or members to admit additional members, and the terms and conditions of that right; (7) the circumstances under which the cessation of membership of one or more members will result in dissolution of the LLC; (8) a statement indicating that the LLC is managed by managers, if applicable, and the names and addresses of initial managers; and (9) any other provision which the members elect to include in the articles of organization for the regulation of the internal affairs of the LLC. (Ala. Code § 10-12-10)
Fees—Organization and Annual:	• The fee for filing articles of organization is $40 and a minimum probate judge fee of $35. The filing fee for a foreign LLC registration application is $75. There is no annual registration fee. (Ala. Code § 10-12-60)
Recordkeeping:	• The LLC must compile and maintain: (1) a list of the members' and managers' names and addresses; (2) federal, state and local tax returns and information for the last three years; (3) copies of articles, including any amendments; (4) the written operating agreement (if any), including any amendments; and (5) financial statements for the last three years. (Ala. Code § 10-12-16)
Annual reporting:	• An annual report is not required.
Management:	• Management is vested in the members, unless otherwise provided. (Ala. Code § 10-12-22)
Membership rights and obligations:	• A member is not liable under a judgment, decree, or order of a court for a debt, obligation or liability of the LLC. If a member fails to make a promised contribution, the member is obligated at the option of the LLC to pay cash equal to the amount or value of the portion of the unpaid contribution. (Ala. Code §§ 10-12-20 and 10-12-27)
Piercing the corporate veil:	• The Act has no express provision that concerns piercing the corporate veil.
Contributions:	• Contributions may consist of cash, property, or services, or a promise to contribute the same. (Ala. Code § 10-12-26)
Distributions:	• Profits, losses and distributions are allocated based on the pro rata value of the members' capital contributions to the extent they have been made and not returned, unless otherwise provided. (Ala. Code § 10-12-28)

Resignation of member:	• Thirty days' written notice is required prior to resignation, unless otherwise provided. (Ala. Code § 10-12-36)
Transfer of LLC interest:	• A member's LLC interest is assignable in whole or in part, unless otherwise provided. Unanimous consent is required for assignee to become a member, unless otherwise provided. (Ala. Code § § 10-12-32 and 10-12-33)
Dissolution:	• An LLC will be dissolved when: (1) events specified in the articles of organization or operating agreement occur; (2) there is unanimous written consent of the members to dissolve the LLC; (3) there is no remaining member, unless the holders of the financial rights agree in writing within 90 days to continue legal existence of the LLC and to appoint one or more new members, or the legal existence is continued and one or more new members are appointed; (4) the LLC is not the successor in a merger or consolidation; or (5) a decree of judicial dissolution is entered. (Ala. Code § § 10-12-37 and 10-12-38)
Mergers and consolidations:	• Mergers or consolidations are permitted expressly by statute. (Ala. Code § 10-12-54)

¶ 1004

Alaska

Name of act:	• Alaska Limited Liability Company Act, Alaska Stat. § 10.50.010 to Alaska Stat. § 10.50.995.
Federal tax classification:	• The LLC statute is flexible. Any "business entity" not required to be treated as a "corporation" for federal tax purposes under Reg. § 301.7701-2 may choose its classification under Reg. § 301.7701-3.
State tax treatment:	• State tax classification follows federal. Thus, Alaska LLCs and foreign LLCs doing business in Alaska are treated as partnerships or disregarded as entities, unless classified as corporations for federal tax purposes.
Securities treatment:	• An LLC is defined as a security in the Alaska Securities Act. (Alaska Stat. § 45.55.990)
Limited liability partnerships:	• Limited Liability Partnerships are expressly authorized. (Alaska Stat. § 32.05.500)
Professional LLCs:	• Permitted impliedly. No prohibition is set forth in the statutory provision concerning lawful business. Subject to compliance with other regulatory provisions. (Alaska Stat. § 10.50.010)
Foreign LLCs:	• Foreign LLCs are expressly permitted by statute. Laws of formation jurisdiction govern the LLC's organization and internal affairs. (Alaska Stat. § 10.50.600)

Formation:	• One or more persons may organize an LLC. The persons who organize need not be members of the LLC. (Alaska Stat. § 10.50.070)
Naming requirements:	• The name of each LLC must contain the words "limited liability company" or the abbreviation "L.L.C." or "LLC." The word "limited" may be abbreviated as "Ltd.", and the word "company" may be abbreviated as "Co." (Alaska Stat. § 10.50.020)
Effective date of organization:	• An LLC is organized when the articles of organization are filed. (Alaska Stat. § 10.50.080)
Filing requirements:	• The articles of organization must include: (1) the LLC's name; (2) its purpose; (3) its duration, if specified; (4) the mailing address of the registered office and the name of the registered agent; (5) a statement indicating that the LLC is managed by managers, if applicable; and (6) any other provisions the members decide to include. (Alaska Stat. § 10.50.075)
Fees—Organization and Annual:	• The fee for filing articles of organization is $250. The filing fee for a foreign LLC registration application is $350. The fee for biennial registration is $100 for domestic LLCs and $200 for foreign LLCs.
Recordkeeping:	• Unless otherwise provided, an LLC must keep at its main office: (1) a list of members' and managers' names and addresses, both past and present; (2) a copy of the articles of organization, including any amendments and powers of attorney; (3) a copy of its federal, state and local tax returns or financial statements for the three most recent years; (4) copies of all operating agreements, including any amendments; and (5) a document providing information about members' capital contributions, agreements to contribute capital, events triggering additional contributions, events causing dissolution, and any other documents required by the operating agreement. (Alaska Stat. § 10.50.860)
Annual reporting:	• A biennial report is required and is due before January 2 of the filing year. (Alaska Stat. §§ 10.50.750 and 10.50.760)
Management:	• Management is vested in the members, unless otherwise provided. (Alaska Stat. § 10.50.110)

Membership rights and obligations:	• A member is not liable under a judgment, decree, or order of a court, or in another manner, for a liability of the LLC, whether that liability arises in contract, tort, or another form, or for the acts or omissions of another member, manager, agent, or employee of the LLC. If a member fails to make a promised contribution, even in the event of death, disability or other reason, the member is obligated at the option of the LLC to pay cash equal to the amount or value of the portion of the unpaid contribution. A member who knowingly receives a wrongful distribution is liable to the LLC for the amount of the distribution wrongfully made, including interest. (Alaska Stat. § § 10.50.265, 10.50.280 and 10.50.320)
Piercing the corporate veil:	• The Act has no express provision that concerns piercing the corporate veil.
Contributions:	• Contributions may consist of property, services rendered or a promise to contribute the same. (Alaska Stat. § 10.50.275)
Distributions:	• Distributions, profits and losses are to be shared equally by each member, unless otherwise provided. (Alaska Stat. § 10.50.290)
Resignation of member:	• A member may not resign from an LLC except upon the happening of events specified in the operating agreement. (Alaska Stat. § 10.50.185)
Transfer of LLC interest:	• A member's LLC interest is assignable in whole or in part, unless otherwise provided. Unanimous consent is required for an assignee to become a member. (Alaska Stat. § § 10.50.165 and 10.50.375)
Dissolution:	• Unless an LLC elects otherwise, dissolution will occur: (1) upon the happening of a specified event; (2) if all members consent in writing; or (3) if the superior court enters a decree for judicial dissolution. An LLC may be dissolved involuntarily by the Commissioner under certain circumstances. (Alaska Stat. § § 10.50.400, 10.50.405 and 10.50.408)
Mergers and acquisitions:	• Mergers or consolidations are permitted expressly by statute. (Alaska Stat. § 10.50.500)

¶ 1005

Arizona

Name of act:	• Arizona Limited Liability Company Act, Ariz. Rev. Stat. § 29-601 to Ariz. Rev. Stat. § 29-857.
Federal tax classification:	• The LLC statute is flexible. Any "business entity" not required to be treated as a "corporation" for federal tax purposes under Reg. § 301.7701-2 may choose its classification under Reg. § 301.7701-3.
State tax treatment:	• State tax classification follows federal. Thus, Arizona LLCs and foreign LLCs doing business in Arizona are treated as partnerships or disregarded as entities in applying the Arizona Income Tax, unless classified as corporations for federal tax purposes. (Ariz. Rev. Stat. § 29-857)
Securities treatment:	• The Arizona Act does not expressly provide for the treatment of an LLC interest as a security.
Limited liability partnerships:	• Limited liability partnerships and foreign limited liability partnerships are expressly authorized by statute. (Ariz. Rev. Stat. § 29-1001)
Limited liability limited partnerships:	• Limited liability limited partnerships are expressly authorized by statute. (Ariz. Rev. Stat. § 29-367)
Professional LLCs:	• Professional LLCs are expressly permitted by statute, subject to compliance with other state regulatory provisions. Banking and insurance LLCs are expressly prohibited. (Ariz. Rev. Stat. § § 29-609 and 29-841)
Foreign LLCs:	• Foreign LLCs are expressly permitted by statute. Laws of formation jurisdiction govern the LLC's organization, internal affairs, and the liability of members, except that rights and privileges are limited to those of Arizona LLCs. (Ariz. Rev. Stat. § 29-801)
Formation:	• An Arizona LLC may be formed by one or more persons. The organizers need not be members of the LLC. An Arizona LLC must have one or more members. (Ariz. Rev. Stat. § § 29-631 and 29-632)
Naming requirements:	• An LLC's name must contain the words "limited liability company" or "limited company" or the abbreviations "L.L.C.," "L.C.," "LLC" or "LC." The name may not contain the words "association," "corporation," or "incorporated," or an abbreviation of these words. (Ariz. Rev. Stat. § 29-602).
Effective date of organization:	• An Arizona LLC is formed when the articles of organization are delivered to the commission for filing. (Ariz. Rev. Stat. § § 29-634 and 29-635)

Filing requirements:	• The articles of organization must include: (1) the LLC's name; (2) its duration, if any is specified; (3) the address of its registered office and the name and address of its agent; and (4) a statement indicating whether the LLC will be managed by members or managers and, correspondingly, either the members' or managers' names and addresses. (Ariz. Rev. Stat. § 29-632)
Fees—Organization and Annual:	• The fee for filing articles of organization is $50. The fee for filing a foreign LLC registration application is $150. There is no annual registration fee. (Ariz. Rev. Stat. § 29-851)
Recordkeeping:	• The LLC must compile and maintain: (1) a list of the current members' names and last known addresses; (2) copies of the articles of organization, including any amendments; (3) copies of all effective and prior written operating agreements, including any amendments; (4) copies of federal, state and local tax returns and reports for the three most recent years; (5) copies of financial statements for the three most recent years; and (6) any writings that set forth a member's promise to make a capital contribution. (Ariz. Rev. Stat. § 29-607)
Annual reporting:	• No annual report is required.
Management:	• Management is vested in the members, unless otherwise provided. (Ariz. Rev. Stat. § 29-681)
Membership rights and obligations:	• A member is not liable for a debt, obligation or liability of the LLC whether arising in contract, tort or otherwise. Unless otherwise provided, a member is obligated to perform any promised capital contribution, even if the member is unable to perform because of death, disability or other reason. If a member fails to make the promised capital contribution, the member is obligated, at the option of the LLC, to contribute cash equal to that portion of value of the stated contribution that has not been made. If a member receives a wrongful distribution, that member is liable to the LLC for a period of six years thereafter for the amount of the wrongful distribution. (Ariz. Rev. Stat. §§ 29-651, 29-702 and 29-706).
Piercing the corporate veil:	• The Act has no express provision that concerns piercing the corporate veil.
Contributions:	• Contributions may consist of cash, property, the use of property, services rendered, or any other valuable consideration, or a promise to contribute the same. (Ariz. Rev. Stat. §§ 29-601 and 29-701)

Distributions:	• Unless otherwise provided, distributions are allocated based on the value of capital contributions, as adjusted for any withdrawals, until all capital is repaid. After that, they are shared equally. Unless otherwise provided, profits are allocated on a per capita basis, and losses are allocated according to the members' relative capital contributions, both made and promised. (Ariz. Rev. Stat. § § 29-703 and 29-709)
Resignation of member:	• Members may resign at any time, upon written notice. (Ariz. Rev. Stat. § 29-734)
Transfer of LLC interest:	• Unless otherwise provided, a member's LLC interest is assignable in whole or in part. Unanimous consent is required for an assignee to become a member, unless otherwise provided. (Ariz. Rev. Stat. § § 29-731 and 29-732)
Dissolution:	• An LLC is dissolved upon: (1) the happening of events specified in the articles of organization or operating agreement; (2) unless otherwise provided, the written consent of more than one-half of the members and by one or more members who would be entitled to receive more than one-half the value of all assets distributed upon dissolution or liquidation; (3) the entry of a judgment of dissolution or administrative dissolution; or (4) an event of withdrawal by the last remaining member unless within 90 days all assignees consent to admit at least one member to continue LLC's business. (Ariz. Rev. Stat. § § 29-781 and 29-785).
Mergers and consolidations:	• Mergers or consolidations are expressly permitted by statute. (Ariz. Rev. Stat. § 29-752)

¶ 1006

Arkansas

Name of act:	• Small Business Entity Tax Pass Through Act, Ark. Code § 4-32-101 to Ark. Code § 4-32-1401.
Federal tax classification:	• The LLC statute is flexible. Any "business entity" not required to be treated as a "corporation" for federal tax purposes under Reg. § 301.7701-2 may choose its classification under Reg. § 301.7701-3.
State tax treatment:	• State tax classification follows federal. Thus, Arkansas LLCs and foreign LLCs doing business in Arkansas are treated as partnerships or disregarded as entities, unless classified as corporations for federal tax purposes. (Ark. Code § 4-32-1313)

Securities treatment:	• The Arkansas Act does not expressly provide for the treatment of an LLC interest as a security.
Limited liability partnerships:	• Limited liability partnerships are expressly authorized. (Ark. Code § 4-46-1001)
Limited liability limited partnerships:	• Limited liability limited partnerships are expressly authorized. (Ark. Code § 4-43-1110)
Professional LLCs:	• Professional LLCs are expressly permitted by statute, subject to compliance with other state regulatory provisions. (Ark. Code § 4-32-306)
Foreign LLCs:	• Foreign LLCs are expressly permitted by statute. Laws of the formation jurisdiction govern the LLC's organization and internal affairs, and the liability and authority of its members and managers. (Ark. Code § 4-32-1001)
Formation:	• One or more persons may form an LLC. The organizers do not have to be members. One or more members are required. (Ark. Code § 4-32-201)
Naming requirements:	• The name of an LLC must contain the words "Limited Liability Company" or "Limited Company" or the abbreviations "L.L.C.," "LLC," "L.C.," or "LC". The word "limited" may be abbreviated as "Ltd." and the word "company" may be abbreviated as "Co." (Ark. Code § 4-32-103)
Effective date of organization:	• An LLC is formed when the articles of organization are delivered to the secretary of state for filing, unless a delayed effective date is stated. (Ark. Code § 4-32-206)
Filing requirements:	• The articles of organization must include: (1) the LLC's name; (2) its duration; (3) the address of the registered office and the name and business or mailing address of the registered agent; and (4) a statement indicating that the LLC is managed by managers, if applicable. (Ark. Code § 4-32-202)
Fees—Organization and Annual:	• The fee for filing articles of organization is $40 plus a $5 processing fee. The filing fee for a foreign LLC's application for a certificate of authority is $258 plus a $12 processing fee. There is no annual registration fee. (Ark. Code § 4-32-1301)

Recordkeeping:	• Unless otherwise provided, an LLC must keep at its principal place of business: (1) a list of members' and managers' names and addresses, past and present; (2) copies of the articles of organization, including any amendments and powers of attorney; (3) tax returns and financial statements for the last three years or, if unavailable, copies of the information and statements provided to members to enable them to prepare their tax returns; (4) copies of any effective written operating agreement, including any amendments and copies of any written agreements no longer in effect; and (5) writings that set forth the members' capital contributions, agreements to contribute capital, and dissolution events, if not set forth in a written operating agreement, and any other writings as required by the operating agreement. (Ark. Code § 4-32-405)
Annual reporting:	• No annual report is required.
Management:	• Management is vested in the members, unless otherwise provided. (Ark. Code § 4-32-401)
Membership rights and obligations:	• A member is not liable for a debt, obligation or liability of the LLC whether arising in contract, tort or otherwise. Unless otherwise provided, a member is obligated to perform any promised contribution, even if the member is unable to perform because of death, disability or other reason. If a member fails to make the promised contribution, the member is obligated, at the option of the LLC, to contribute cash equal to that portion of value of the stated contribution that has not been made. The statute is silent as to a member's liability for receiving wrongful distributions. (Ark. Code § § 4-32-304 and 4-32-502)
Piercing the corporate veil:	• The Act has no express provision that concerns piercing the corporate veil.
Contributions:	• Contributions may consist of property, services rendered, or a promissory note or other obligation to contribute cash or property or to perform services. (Ark. Code § 4-32-501)
Distributions:	• Distributions and profits are allocated equally among the members, unless otherwise provided. No provision is made in the Act for the allocation of losses. (Ark. Code § § 4-32-503 and 4-32-601)

Resignation of member:	• A member may withdraw from an LLC only at the time or upon the happening of an event specified in the articles of organization or operating agreement. Unless the articles of organization or an operating agreement provide otherwise, a member may not withdraw from an LLC prior to the dissolution and winding up of the LLC. (Ark. Code § 4-32-802)
Transfer of LLC interest:	• A member's interest in an LLC is assignable in whole or in part, unless otherwise provided. Unanimous consent is required for assignee to become a member, unless otherwise provided. (Ark. Code § § 4-32-704 and 4-32-706)
Dissolution:	• An LLC is dissolved: (1) at the time or upon the occurrence of events specified in writing in the articles of organization or the operating agreement, but if no such time is set forth, then the LLC shall have perpetual existence; (2) upon the written consent of all of the members; (3) at any time there are no members unless the personal representative of the last remaining member agrees in writing to continue the LLC and the representative or the representative's nominee is admitted as a member; or (4) upon entry of a decree of judicial dissolution. (Ark. Code § § 4-32-901 and 4-32-902)
Mergers and consolidations:	• Mergers or consolidations are permitted expressly by statute. (Ark. Code § 4-32-1201)

¶ 1007
California

Name of act:	• Beverly-Killea Limited Liability Company Act, Cal. Corp. Code § 17000 to Cal. Corp. Code § 17705.
Federal tax classification:	• The LLC statute is flexible. Any "business entity" not required to be treated as a "corporation" for federal tax purposes under Reg. § 301-7701-2 may choose its classification under Reg. § 301.7701-3.
State tax treatment:	• State tax classification follows federal. Thus, California LLCs and foreign LLCs doing business in California are treated as partnerships or disregarded as entities, unless classified as corporations for federal tax purposes. (1997 S.B. 1234)

Securities treatment:	• "Security" includes an interest in an LLC and any class or series of such interests (including any fractional or other interest in such interest), except a membership interest in an LLC in which the person claiming this exception can prove that all of the members are actively engaged in the management of the LLC; provided that evidence that members vote or have the right to vote, or the right to information concerning the business and affairs of the LLC, or the right to participate in management, shall not establish, without more, that all members are actively engaged in the management of the LLC. (Cal. Corp. Code § 25019)
Limited liability partnerships:	• Limited liability partnerships are expressly authorized by statute. (Cal. Corp. Code § 16101)
Professional LLCs:	• An LLC may engage in any lawful business activity, except banking, insurance or trust company business, subject to compliance with any other applicable laws. (Cal. Corp. Code § 17002)
Foreign LLCs:	• Foreign LLCs are expressly permitted by statute. Laws of the formation jurisdiction govern the LLC's organization, internal affairs and liability of its members. (Cal. Corp. Code § 17450)
Formation:	• A California LLC may be formed by one or more persons. The persons who organize the LLC need not be members of the LLC. One or more members are required. (Cal. Corp. Code § 17050)
Naming requirements:	• An LLC's name must contain, as the last words of the name, either the words "limited liability company" or the abbreviation "LLC." The words "limited" and "company" may be abbreviated to "Ltd." and "Co." (Cal. Corp. Code § 17052)
Effective date of organization:	• An LLC's existence begins upon the filing of the articles of organization. (Cal. Corp. Code § 17050)

Filing requirements:

- The articles of organization must include: (1) the LLC's name; (2) the following statement— "The purpose of the limited liability company is to engage in any lawful act or activity for which a limited liability company may be organized under the Beverly-Killea Limited Liability Company Act;" (3) the name and address of the LLC's initial agent for service of process; (4) a statement indicating whether the LLC is managed by managers or its members; and (5) any other provision not inconsistent with the law, including restrictions on the type of business, admission of members, duration, events that will cause dissolution, limitations on member or management authority or the names of managers. (Cal. Corp. Code §§ 17051 and 17151)

Fees—Organization and Annual:

- The filing fee for articles of organization is $70. The fee for filing an application for foreign LLC registration is $70. The fee for filing a biennial statement is $20. In addition, an annual fee is imposed on certain LLCs if they are classified as partnerships and if their total income from all sources reportable to California for the tax year is $250,000 or more. There is an $800 annual nondeductible minimum tax. (Cal. Gov. Code § 12190) Note: A California Superior court has ruled that California's LLC fee scheme amounts to an unfairly apportioned tax (Northwest Energetic Services, LLC v. California Franchise Tax Board, California Superior Court for San Francisco, No. CGC-05-437721, March 3, 2006). The FTB has appealed this decision. The FTB has provided protective claim procedures that taxpayers who previously paid the fee, and taxpayers who must continue to pay the fee, should follow.

Recordkeeping:

- The LLC must compile and maintain: (1) a list of the names and addresses of each member and of each holder of an economic interest in the LLC set forth in alphabetical order, together with the contribution and the share in profits and losses of each member and holder of an economic interest; (2) a list of the names and addresses of each manager, if the LLC is managed by managers; (3) a copy of the articles of organization and all amendments, together with any executed powers of attorney; (4) copies of the LLC's federal, state, and local income tax or information returns and reports, if any, for the six most recent taxable years; (5) a copy of the LLC's operating agreement, if in writing, and any amendments together with any executed powers of attorney; (6) copies of the financial statements of the LLC, if any, for the six most recent fiscal years; and (7) the books and records of the LLC as they relate to the internal affairs of the LLC for at least the current and past four fiscal years. (Cal. Corp. Code § 17058)

Annual reporting:

- A biennial report is required. The initial report must be filed within 90 days after filing of the original articles of organization and biennially thereafter during the applicable filing period in each year. (Cal. Corp. Code § 17060)

Management:

- Management is vested in members, unless otherwise provided. (Cal. Corp. Code § 17150)

Membership rights and obligations:

- LLC members will not be personally liable under any judgment of a court, or in any other manner, for any debt, obligation, or liability of the LLC, whether that liability or obligation arises in contract, tort, or otherwise, solely by reason of being a member of the LLC. If a member fails to make a required contribution, even in the event of death, disability or other reason, the member is obligated, at the option of the LLC, to contribute cash equal to that portion of the fair market value of the stated contribution that has not been made. A member or manager who assents to a wrongful distribution is personally liable to the LLC for the amount of the distribution that was wrongfully made. Each member or manager held liable is entitled to contribution from each member who knowingly received a wrongful distribution. (Cal. Corp. Code §§ 17101, 17201 and 17255)

Piercing the corporate veil:	• An LLC member is subject to liability under the common law governing alter ego liability, and is personally liable under a judgment of a court, under the same circumstances and to the same extent as a shareholder of a corporation may be personally liable, except that the failure to hold meetings of members or managers or the failure to observe formalities is not a factor tending to establish that the members have personal liability where the articles of organization or operating agreement do not expressly require such meetings. (Cal. Corp. Code § 17101)
Contributions:	• Contributions may consist of cash, property, or services, or a promise to contribute the same. (Cal. Corp. Code § 17200)
Distributions:	• Distributions, profits and losses are allocated in proportion to the contributions of each member, unless otherwise provided. (Cal. Corp. Code § § 17202 and 17250)
Resignation of member:	• A member may withdraw from an LLC at any time by giving written notice, unless otherwise provided. (Cal. Corp. Code § 17252)
Transfer of LLC interest:	• A member's LLC interest is assignable in whole or in part, unless otherwise provided. Consent of a majority in interest is required for an interest to be assigned. (Cal. Corp. Code § 17301)
Dissolution:	• An LLC will be dissolved: (1) on the date for dissolution stated in the articles of organization, if any, or upon the happening of events, if any, specified in the articles of organization or written operating agreement; (2) by a vote of a majority in interest, or greater, of the members; (3) upon entry of a decree of judicial dissolution. (Cal. Corp. Code § § 17350 and 17351)
Mergers and consolidations:	• Mergers or consolidations are permitted expressly by statute. (Cal. Corp. Code § 17550)

¶ 1008
Colorado

Name of act:	• Colorado Limited Liability Company Act, Colo. Rev. Stat. § 7-80-101 to Colo. Rev. Stat. § 7-80-1101.
Federal tax classification:	• The Colorado LLC Act is flexible. Any "business entity" not required to be treated as a "corporation" for federal tax purposes under Reg. § 301.7701-2 may choose its classification under Reg. § 301.7701-3.

State tax treatment:	• State tax classification follows federal classification. Thus, Colorado LLCs and foreign LLCs doing business in Colorado are treated as partnerships or disregarded as entities, unless classified as corporations for federal tax purposes.
Securities treatment:	• The Colorado Act does not expressly provide for the treatment of an LLC interest as a security.
Limited liability partnerships:	• Limited liability partnerships and foreign limited liability partnerships are expressly authorized by statute. (Colo. Rev. Stat. § 7-60-144)
Limited liability limited partnerships:	• Limited liability limited partnerships are expressly authorized by statute. (Colo. Rev. Stat. § 7-60-144)
Professional LLCs:	• Professional LLCs are permitted impliedly by statute. An LLC may be organized for any lawful purpose, subject to compliance with other state regulatory provisions. (Colo. Rev. Stat. § 7-80-103)
Foreign LLCs:	• Foreign LLCs are expressly permitted by statute. Laws of the formation jurisdiction govern organization, internal affairs and the liability of members and managers. (Colo. Rev. Stat. § 7-80-901)
Formation:	• A Colorado LLC may be formed by one or more persons. Colorado permits an LLC to have a single member. (Colo. Rev. Stat. § 7-80-203)
Naming requirements:	• A Colorado LLC's name must have the words "limited liability company," or the abbreviation "LLC." If "LLC" is not used, the word "Limited" may be abbreviated as "Ltd." and the word "Company" may be abbreviated as "Co." (Colo. Rev. Stat. § 7-80-201)
Effective date of organization:	• An LLC's existence begins when the articles of organization are filed, or as specified in the articles but not more than 90 days after filing the articles. (Colo. Rev. Stat. § 7-80-207)
Filing requirements:	• The articles of organization must include: (1) the LLC's name; (2) its principal place of business; (3) the name and address of the agent for service of process; (4) if the company is to be managed by a manager or managers, the names and business addresses of the initial manager or managers; (5) if the management of an LLC is reserved to the members, a statement to that effect and the names and addresses of the initial member or members. (Colo. Rev. Stat. § 7-80-204)

146

Limited Liability Companies

Fees—Organization and Annual:

- The fee for filing the original articles of organization is $50, if filed electronically and $125, if filed on paper. The fee for registration of a foreign LLC is $50, if filed electronically and $125, if filed on paper. The annual registration fee is $10 for an electronically filed report and $100 for a report filed on paper. (Colo. Rev. Stat. § 7-80-307)

Recordkeeping:

- The LLC must compile and maintain: (1) a current list of the members' and managers' full names and last known business, resident, or mailing addresses, both past and present; (2) a copy of the filed articles of organization, all amendments thereto, together with executed copies of any powers of attorney; (3) copies of the limited liability company's federal, state, and local tax returns and financial statements for the last three years, if any; (4) copies of any currently effective written operating agreement and of any financial statements of the company for the three most recent years; (5) minutes of every annual and special meeting; (6) unless contained in the articles of organization, a writing setting out the amount of cash and a description and statement of the agreed value of any other property or services contributed by each member and which each member has agreed to contribute, the times at which or events on the happening of which any additional contributions agreed to be made by each member are to be made, the manner in which a member may terminate his or her membership and the amount of or method of determining the distribution to which he or she may be entitled, any right of a member to receive a distribution including a return of the member's contribution; and (7) any written consents obtained from members regarding the LLC's actions. (Colo. Rev. Stat. § 7-80-411)

Annual reporting:

- An annual report is required. A report form is issued by the secretary of state to each LLC. (Colo. Rev. Stat. § 7-80-303)

Management:

- Management of an LLC may be by member or manager, as provided in the operating agreement. (Colo. Rev. Stat. § 7-80-401)

¶1008

Membership rights and obligations:	• Members and managers are not liable for any debt, obligation, or liability of the LLC, whether under a judgment, decree, or order of a court, or in any other manner. If a member fails to make a required contribution, even in the event of death, disability or other reason, the member is obligated at the option of the LLC to contribute cash equal to that portion of the value of the stated contribution that has not been made. Members are liable for distributions that exceed their membership interests if the distribution exceeds the fair value of the LLC and for the amount received as a return of contribution in violation of the operating agreement. (Colo. Rev. Stat. §§ 7-80-502, 7-80-606, 7-80-607 and 7-80-705)
Piercing the corporate veil:	• The Act provides that the case law regarding piercing the corporate veil applies to members of LLCs operating in Colorado. (Colo. Rev. Stat. § 7-80-107)
Contributions:	• Contributions may consist of cash, property, services rendered, a promissory note or other obligation to contribute the same. (Colo. Rev. Stat. § 7-80-501)
Distributions:	• Distributions, profits and losses are allocated on the basis of the value of the contributions of each member. (Colo. Rev. Stat. §§ 7-80-503 and 7-80-504)
Resignation of member:	• A member may resign at any time by giving written notice, unless otherwise provided; however, the LLC may recover damages from the member if such resignation is in violation of the operating agreement. (Colo. Rev. Stat. § 7-80-602)
Transfer of LLC interest:	• A member's LLC interest is transferable and assignable, unless otherwise provided. Unanimous written consent is required for an assignee to become a member of the LLC. (Colo. Rev. Stat. § 7-80-702)
Dissolution:	• An LLC is dissolved: (1) upon the unanimous written agreement of all members; (2) when an event of dissociation occurs to a member, unless the business of the company is continued by the consent of all the remaining members under a right to do so stated in the articles of organization of the company; or (3) when the period fixed for the duration of the LLC expires. (Colo. Rev. Stat. § 7-80-801)
Mergers and consolidations:	• Mergers and conversions of LLCs are expressly provided for by statute. (Colo. Rev. Stat. § 7-80-1001)

¶1008

¶ 1009
Connecticut

Name of act:	• Connecticut Limited Liability Company Act, Conn. Gen. Stat. § 34-100 to Conn. Gen. Stat. § 34-242.
Federal tax classification:	• The LLC statute is flexible. Any "business entity" not required to be treated as a "corporation" for federal tax purposes under Reg. § 301.7701-2 may choose its classification under Reg. § 301.7701-3.
State tax treatment:	• State tax classification follows federal. Thus, Connecticut LLCs and foreign LLCs doing business in Connecticut are treated as partnerships or disregarded as entities, unless classified as corporations for federal tax purposes. (Conn. Gen. Stat. § 34-113)
Securities treatment:	• The Connecticut Act does not expressly provide for the treatment of an LLC interest as a security.
Limited liability partnerships:	• The Connecticut Act expressly provides for the formation of limited liability partnerships. (Conn. Gen. Stat. § 34-406)
Professional LLCs:	• Professional service LLCs are expressly permitted by statute, with certain restrictions. (Conn. Gen. Stat. § 34-119)
Foreign LLCs:	• Foreign LLCs are expressly permitted by statute. The laws of the formation jurisdiction govern the LLC's organization, internal affairs, and liability of its members and managers. (Conn. Gen. Stat. § 34-222)
Formation:	• One or more organizers may form an LLC. The persons who organize need not be members of the LLC. One or more members are required. (Conn. Gen. Stat. §§ 34-101 and 34-120)
Naming requirements:	• The name of each limited liability company must contain the words "Limited Liability Company" or the abbreviations "L.L.C." or "LLC". The word "Limited" may be abbreviated as "Ltd." and the word "Company" may be abbreviated as "Co." (Conn. Gen. Stat. § 34-102)
Effective date of organization:	• An LLC is formed when the articles of organization are delivered to the secretary of state for filing and endorsed by the secretary of state. (Conn. Gen. Stat. § 34-123)

Filing requirements:	• The articles of organization must include: (1) the LLC's name; (2) a statement that the LLC is managed by managers, if applicable; (3) a description of the nature of business; (4) the address of the LLC's principal office; (5) an appointment of a statutory agent for service of process; and (6) any other matter the organizer(s) determines to include. In addition to the articles of organization, the LLC organizer must file a writing containing the name and respective business and residence address of a manager or member. (Conn. Gen. Stat. § 34-121)
Fees—Organization and Annual:	• The fee for filing articles of organization is $60. The fee for filing an application for certificate of registration as a foreign LLC is $60. The fee for filing the annual report is $10 plus a $250 annual tax. (Conn. Gen. Stat. § 34-112)
Recordkeeping:	• An LLC must compile and maintain: (1) a list of current and past members' and managers' names and addresses; (2) copies of the articles of organization, including any amendments, together with executed copies of any powers of attorney; (3) copies of federal, state and local tax returns and financial statements for the last three years or, if such returns and statements were not prepared for any reason, copies of the information and statements provided to, or which should have been provided to, the members to enable them to prepare such returns; (4) copies of any past (if any) and current written operating agreements including any amendments; and (5) any other writings prepared pursuant to the operating agreement. (Conn. Gen. Stat. § 34-144)
Annual reporting:	• Each LLC must file an annual report with the secretary of state on the anniversary of the filing of the LLC's articles of organization. (Conn. Gen. Stat. § § 34-106 and 34-229)
Management:	• Management is vested in members unless otherwise provided. (Conn. Gen. Stat. § 34-140)

Membership rights and obligations:	• Except for professional service LLCs, a member is not liable under judgment, decree or order of a court, for a debt, obligation or liability of the LLC, whether arising in contract, tort or otherwise. Members of a professional LLC will be personally liable and accountable only for negligent or wrongful acts or misconduct committed by the member, or by any person under the direct supervision and control of the member. Unless otherwise provided, a member is obligated to perform any promised contribution, even if the member is unable to perform because of death, disability or other reason. If a member fails to make the promised contribution, the member is obligated, at the option of the LLC, to contribute cash equal to that portion of value of the stated contribution that has not been made. The statute is silent as to a member's liability for receiving wrongful distributions. (Conn. Gen. Stat. §§ 34-133 and 34-151)
Piercing the corporate veil:	• The Connecticut Act has no express provision that concerns piercing of the corporate veil.
Contributions:	• Contributions may consist of property, services rendered, promissory notes or other obligations to contribute cash or to perform services. (Conn. Gen. Stat. § 34-150)
Distributions:	• Distributions, profits and losses are allocated on the basis of the value of each member's contribution made to the LLC and not yet returned, unless otherwise provided. (Conn. Gen. Stat. §§ 34-152 and 34-158)
Resignation of member:	• Thirty days' written notice is required, unless otherwise provided. (Conn. Gen. Stat. § 34-180)
Transfer of LLC interest:	• A member's LLC interest is assignable in whole or in part, unless otherwise provided. Consent of a majority in interest is required for an assignee to become a member, unless otherwise provided. If the LLC has only one member, the assignor may give the assignee the right to become a member. (Conn. Gen. Stat. §§ 34-170 and 34-172)
Dissolution:	• An LLC will be dissolved: (1) at the time or upon the happening of events specified in the articles of organization or the operating agreement; (2) upon the affirmative vote, approval or consent of at least a majority in interest of the members, unless otherwise provided; or (3) upon entry of a decree of judicial dissolution. (Conn. Gen. Stat. §§ 34-206 and 34-207)
Mergers and acquisitions:	• Mergers or consolidations are permitted expressly by statute. (Conn. Gen. Stat. § 34-193)

¶1009

¶ 1010

Delaware

Name of act:	• Delaware Limited Liability Company Act, Del. Code tit. 6, §§ 18-101 to 18-1109.
Federal tax classification:	• The LLC statute is flexible. Any "business entity" not required to be treated as a "corporation" for federal tax purposes under Reg. § 301.7701-2 may choose its classification under Reg. § 301.7701-3.
State tax treatment:	• LLCs are classified as partnerships for state and local purposes, unless classified otherwise for federal income tax purposes. (Del. Code tit. 6, § 18-1107)
Securities treatment:	• The Delaware Act does not expressly provide for the treatment of an LLC interest as a security.
Limited liability partnerships:	• Limited Liability Partnerships are expressly authorized by statute. (Del. Code tit. 6, § 15-1001)
Limited liability limited partnerships:	• Limited Liability Limited Partnerships are expressly authorized by statute. (Del. Code tit. 6, § 17-214)
Professional LLCs:	• Professional LLCs are permitted impliedly, subject to compliance with other state regulatory provisions. Banking LLCs are expressly prohibited. (Del. Code tit. 6, § 18-106)
Foreign LLCs:	• Foreign LLCs are expressly permitted by statute. Laws of the formation jurisdiction govern the organization, internal affairs and the liability of the members and managers. (Del. Code tit. 6, § 18-901)
Formation:	• A Delaware LLC may be formed by one or more authorized persons. At least one member is required. (Del. Code tit. 6, §§ 18-101 and 18-201)
Naming requirements:	• The name of each LLC must contain the words "limited liability company," the abbreviation "L.L.C." or the designation "LLC." (Del. Code tit. 6, § 18-102)
Effective date of organization:	• A Delaware LLC is formed when the initial certificate of formation is filed with the office of the Secretary of State, unless a delayed effective date is stated. (Del. Code tit. 6, § 18-201)
Filing requirements:	• The certificate of formation must include: (1) the LLC's name; (2) the address of the registered office and the name and address of the registered agent for service of process required to be maintained by § 18-104; and (3) any other matters that the members decide to include. (Del. Code tit. 6, § 18-201)

Fees—Organization and Annual:	• The fee for filing the certificate of formation is $70 plus a $20 courthouse municipality fee. The fee for filing the application for registration as a foreign LLC is $100. An annual tax of $200 is imposed. (Del. Code tit. 6, §§ 18-1105 and 18-1107)
Recordkeeping:	• The LLC must compile and maintain: (1) true and full information regarding the status of the business and financial condition of the LLC; (2) a copy of the LLC's federal, state and local income tax returns for each year; (3) a current list of the members' and managers' names and addresses; (4) a copy of any written LLC agreement and certificate of formation, including all amendments and any powers of attorney; (5) true and full information regarding the amount of cash and a description and statement of the agreed value of any other property or services contributed, or promised to be contributed in the future, and the date on which each member became a member; and (6) other information regarding the affairs of the LLC as is just and reasonable. (Del. Code tit. 6, § 18-305)
Annual reporting:	• Annual reporting is not required.
Management:	• Management is vested in the members, unless otherwise provided. An LLC may have more than one manager. (Del. Code tit. 6, § 18-402)
Membership rights and obligations:	• A member is not liable for a debt, obligation or liability of the LLC whether arising in contract, tort or otherwise, unless otherwise provided. A member is obligated to perform any promised capital contribution, even if the member is unable to perform because of death, disability or other reason, unless otherwise provided. If a member fails to make the promised capital contribution, the member is obligated, at the option of the LLC, to contribute cash equal to that portion of value of the stated contribution that has not been made. If a member knowingly receives a wrongful distribution, that member is liable to the LLC for the amount of the wrongful distribution. If a member unknowingly receives a wrongful distribution, that member is not liable to the LLC for the amount of the wrongful distribution. (Del. Code tit. 6, §§ 18-303, 18-502 and 18-607)
Piercing the corporate veil:	• The Act has no express provision that concerns piercing the corporate veil.

Contributions:	• Contributions may consist of anything of value including cash, property, services rendered, a promissory note or other obligation to contribute cash, property or services. (Del. Code tit. 6, § 18-501)
Distributions:	• Profits, losses and distributions are allocated on the basis of the agreed value of each member's contribution, unless otherwise provided. (Del. Code tit. 6, § § 18-503 and 18-504)
Resignation of member:	• A member may not resign from a LLC prior to the dissolution and winding up of the LLC, unless otherwise provided. (Del. Code tit. 6, § 18-603)
Transfer of LLC interest:	• A member's LLC interest is assignable in whole or in part, unless otherwise provided. Unanimous consent is required for the assignee to become a member, unless otherwise provided. (Del. Code tit. 6, § 18-702)
Dissolution:	• An LLC will be dissolved: (1) at the time specified in the LLC agreement, but if not specified, the duration is perpetual; (2) upon the happening of events specified in the LLC agreement; (3) upon the written consent of the members, unless otherwise provided; (4) at any time there are no members, unless, within 90 days, the personal representative of the last remaining member agrees in writing to continue the LLC and to the admission of the personal representative or its nominee or designee to the LLC as a member, unless otherwise provided; or (5) upon the entry of a judicial dissolution. An event of dissociation shall not cause the LLC to be dissolved, unless within 90 days following the occurrence of such event, the LLC members agree in writing to dissolve the LLC. An LLC's certificate of formation may be canceled upon a continuing failure to pay the annual state tax. (Del. Code tit. 6, § § 18-801, 18-802 and 18-1108)
Mergers and consolidations:	• Mergers and consolidations are permitted expressly by statute. (Del. Code tit. 6, § 18-209)

¶ 1011

District of Columbia

Name of act:	• Limited Liability Company Act of 1994, D.C. Code, § 29-1001 to D.C. Code, § 29-1075.
Federal tax classification:	• The LLC statute is flexible. Any "business entity" not required to be treated as a "corporation" for federal tax purposes under Reg. § 301.7701-2 may choose its classification under Reg. § 301.7701-3.

State tax treatment:	• Jurisdictional tax classification follows federal. Thus, District of Columbia LLCs and foreign LLCs doing business in the District of Columbia are treated as partnerships, unless classified as corporations for federal tax purposes. (D.C. Code § 29-1074)
Securities treatment:	• The District of Columbia Act does not expressly provide for the treatment of an LLC interest as a security.
Limited liability partnerships:	• The District of Columbia Act expressly provides for the formation of Limited Liability Partnerships. (D.C. Code § 33-110.01)
Limited liability limited partnerships:	• The District of Columbia Act expressly provides for the formation of Limited Liability Limited Partnerships. (D.C. Code § 33-211.07)
Professional LLCs:	• Professional LLCs are expressly permitted by statute. (D.C. Code § 29-1001)
Foreign LLCs:	• Foreign LLCs are expressly permitted by statute. Laws of the formation jurisdiction govern the LLC's formation, internal affairs, and liability of its members and managers. (D.C. Code § 29-1052)
Formation:	• One or more persons may form an LLC. One or more members are required. (D.C. Code §§ 29-1001 and 29-1002)
Naming requirements:	• An LLC must contain the word "limited liability company" or the abbreviation "L.L.C." or "LLC." A professional limited liability company must contain the words "professional limited liability company" or the abbreviation "P.L.L.C." or "PLLC."(D.C. Code § 29-1004)
Effective date of organization:	• An LLC is formed, unless a delayed effective date is stated, when the articles of organization are delivered to the Mayor for filing. (D.C. Code § 29-1006)
Filing requirements:	• The articles of organization must include: (1) the LLC's name; (2) the address of the LLC's initial registered office; and (3) the name of the initial registered agent and evidence of the agent's consent. (D.C. Code § 29-1006)
Fees—Organization and Annual:	• The fee for filing articles of organization is $150. The fee for the application for registration as a foreign LLC is $200. The fee for filing the biennial report is $150. (D.C. Code §§ 29-1063 and 29-1065)

Recordkeeping:	• The LLC must keep: (1) a current, alphabetical list of the members' names and addresses; (2) a copy of the articles of organization and the certificate of organization, including amendments and certificates of amendment; (3) copies of federal, state and local tax returns and reports for the last three years; (4) copies of any effective operating agreement; and (5) writings that set forth the members' capital contributions, agreements to contribute and receive capital, and dissolution events, if not set forth in a written operating agreement. (D.C. Code § 29-1022)
Annual reporting:	• Each LLC must file an biennial report with the Mayor before June 16 of each second year. (D.C. Code § 29-1064)
Management:	• Management is vested in members, unless otherwise provided. (D.C. Code § 29-1017)
Membership rights and obligations:	• A member is not personally liable for any debts, obligations, or liabilities of an LLC, whether arising in contract, tort or otherwise. Unless otherwise provided, a member is obligated to perform any promised capital contribution. If a member fails to make the promised capital contribution, the member is obligated, at the option of the LLC, to contribute cash equal to that portion of value of the stated contribution that has not been made. If the member is unable to perform because of death, disability or other reason, the member may forfeit his interest in the LLC. If a member receives a wrongful distribution, such member is liable to the LLC for 2 years thereafter for the amount of the distribution wrongfully made. (D.C. Code § § 29-1014, 29-1023 and 29-1030)
Piercing the corporate veil:	• The Act has no express provision that concerns piercing the corporate veil.
Contributions:	• Contributions may consist of anything of value, including cash, property, and services rendered, or a written promissory note or other written binding obligation to contribute the same. (D.C. Code § 29-1023)
Distributions:	• Distributions, profits and losses are allocated on the basis of the value of the contributions made by each member that have been received by the LLC and not yet returned, unless otherwise provided. (D.C. Code § § 29-1024 and 29-1025)
Resignation of member:	• A member may resign from an LLC only at a time or upon the happening of events as are specified in the articles of organization or operating agreement. (D.C. Code § 29-1034)

Transfer of LLC interest:	• A member's LLC interest is assignable in whole or in part, unless otherwise provided. (D.C. Code § 29-1035)
Dissolution:	• An LLC is dissolved: (1) at the time or upon the happening of events specified in the articles of incorporation or the operating agreement; (2) upon the unanimous consent of the members with voting rights; (3) when an event of dissociation occurs to a member, unless the remaining members unanimously consent to continue the LLC or there is compliance with the procedures set forth in the articles of organization or operating agreement for continuing the LLC; or (4) a decree of judicial dissolution is entered. (D.C. Code § § 29-1047 and 29-1048)
Mergers and consolidation:	• Mergers or consolidations are permitted expressly by statute. (D.C. Code § 29-1040)

¶ 1012
Florida

Name of act:	• Florida Limited Liability Company Act, Fla. Stat. ch. 608.401 to Fla. Stat. ch. 608.705.
Federal tax classification:	• The LLC statute is flexible. Any "business entity" not required to be treated as a "corporation" for federal tax purposes under Reg. § 301.7701-2 may choose its classification under Reg. § 301.7701-3.
State tax treatment:	• An LLC that is classified for federal income tax purposes as a partnership, or a single-member LLC that is disregarded as an entity separate from its owner, is not an "artificial entity" subject to Florida corporate income tax. (Fla. Stat. ch. 608.471) An LLC is treated as having the status for Florida tax purposes as its classification for federal income tax purposes (Florida Department of Revenue, Tax Information Publication No. 0460BB-01, January 16, 2004)
Securities treatment:	• The Florida Act does not expressly provide for the treatment of an LLC interest as a security.
Limited liability partnerships:	• The formation of Limited Liability Partnerships is expressly permitted by statute. (Fla. Stat. ch. 620.9001)
Limited liability limited partnerships:	• Limited Liability Limited Partnerships are expressly permitted by statute. (Fla. Stat. ch. 620.187)
Professional LLCs:	• Professional LLCs are expressly permitted by statute, subject to compliance with other state regulatory provisions. (Fla. Stat. ch. 621.051)

Foreign LLCs:	• Foreign LLCs are expressly permitted by statute. Laws of the formation jurisdiction govern organization and internal affairs, except that rights and privileges are limited to those of Florida LLCs. (Fla. Stat. ch. 608.505)
Formation:	• A Florida LLC must be formed by at least one person. The LLC must consist of at least one member. (Fla. Stat. ch. 608.405 and 608.407)
Naming requirements:	• The name of each LLC must contain the words "limited liability company" or "limited company," the abbreviation "L.L.C." or "L.C," or the designation "LLC" or "LC." The word "limited" may be abbreviated as "Ltd." and the word "company" may be abbreviated as "Co." (Fla. Stat. ch. 608.406)
Effective date of organization:	• Unless a delayed effective date is specified, the LLC's existence begins at the date and time when the articles of organization are filed. (Fla. Stat. ch. 608.409)
Filing requirements:	• The articles of organization must include: (1) the LLC's name; (2) the address of the principal office; (3) the name and street address of the initial registered agent for service of process, together with a written statement in which the registered agent accepts appointment as the registered agent; (4) if the LLC is to be managed by one or more managers, a statement indicating that the LLC will be manager-managed; and (5) any other matters that the members elect to include. (Fla. Stat. ch. 608.407)
Fees—Organization and Annual:	• The fee for filing articles of organization is $100 plus a $25 registered agent fee. The fee for filing a foreign LLC registration application is $100 plus a $25 registered agent fee. The filing fee for annual report is $50. (Fla. Stat. ch. 608.452)
Recordkeeping:	• The LLC must compile and maintain at its principal office: (1) a list of the names and addresses of all members and managers; (2) a copy of the articles of organization and all certificates of conversion, together with executed copies of any powers of attorney; (3) federal, state, and local tax returns and information for the last three years; (4) copies of any then-effective LLC operating agreement (if any) and any financial statements for the last three years; and (5) a writing that sets forth the members' capital contributions, agreements to contribute capital and dissolution events. (Fla. Stat. ch. 608.4101)

158   Limited Liability Companies

Annual reporting:	• An annual report is required. This report must be delivered to the Department of State between January 1 and May 1. (Fla. Stat. ch. 608.4511)
Management:	• Management is vested in the members, unless otherwise provided. (Fla. Stat. ch. 608.422)
Membership rights and obligations:	• LLC members and managers are not liable for any debt, obligation, or liability of the LLC, whether under a judgment, decree, or order of a court, or in any other manner, unless otherwise provided. A member is obligated to perform any promised capital contribution, even if the member is unable to perform because of death, disability or other reason, unless otherwise provided. If a member fails to make the promised capital contribution, the member is obligated, at the option of the LLC, to contribute cash equal to that portion of agreed value of the stated contribution that has not been made. A member or manager who assents to a wrongful distribution is liable to the LLC for the amount of the wrongful distribution. (Fla. Stat. ch. 608.4211, 608.4227 and 608.426)
Piercing the corporate veil:	• In any case where a party seeks to hold the members of an LLC personally responsible for the liabilities or alleged improper actions of the LLC, the court shall apply the case law which interprets the conditions and circumstances under which the corporate veil of a corporation may be pierced. (Fla. Stat. ch. 608.701)
Contributions:	• Contributions consist of cash, property, or services, or a promise to contribute the same. (Fla. Stat. ch. 608.4211)
Distributions:	• Profits, losses and distributions are allocated on the basis of the agreed value of the contributions made by each member, unless otherwise provided. (Fla. Stat. ch. 608.426 and 608.4261)
Resignation of member:	• A member may withdraw from an LLC only at the time or upon the occurrence of an event specified in the articles of organization or operating agreement. Otherwise, a member may not resign from an LLC prior to the dissolution or winding up of the LLC. (Fla. Stat. ch. 608.427)
Transfer of LLC interest:	• Unless otherwise provided, an LLC interest is assignable in whole or in part. Unanimous consent of all non-assigning members is required for an assignee to become a member, unless otherwise provided. (Fla. Stat. ch. 608.432 and 608.433)

¶1012

Dissolution:	• An LLC is dissolved: (1) at the time specified in the articles of organization or the operating agreement; (2) upon the occurrence of events specified in the articles of organization or operating agreement; (3) upon written consent of all LLC members, unless otherwise provided; (4) at any time there are no members, unless the personal or legal representative of the last remaining member agrees in writing to continue the LLC; (5) upon judicial dissolution; or (6) upon administrative dissolution. (Fla. Stat. ch. 608.441 and 608.448)
Mergers and consolidations:	• Mergers or consolidations are permitted expressly by statute. (Fla. Stat. ch. 608.438)

¶ 1013

Georgia

Name of act:	• Georgia Limited Liability Company Act, Ga. Code § 14-11-100 to Ga. Code § 14-11-1109.
Federal tax classification:	• The LLC statute is flexible. Any "business entity" not required to be treated as a "corporation" for federal tax purposes under Reg. § 301.7701-2 may choose its classification under Reg. § 301.7701-3.
State tax treatment:	• State tax classification follows federal. Thus, Georgia LLCs and LLCs doing business in Georgia are treated as partnerships or disregarded as entities, unless classified as corporations for federal tax purposes. (Ga. Code § 14-11-1104)
Securities treatment:	• Nothing in the LLC Act shall be construed as establishing that an LLC is not a "security." (Ga. Code § 14-11-1107)
Limited liability partnerships:	• The formation of limited liability partnerships is expressly provided for by statute. (Ga. Code § 14-8-62)
Limited liability limited partnerships:	• Limited Liability Limited Partnerships are expressly provided for by statute. (Ga. Code §§ 14-8-62(g) and 14-8-63(b))
Professional LLCs:	• Professional LLCs are expressly permitted by statute, subject to compliance with other state regulatory statutes. (Ga. Code § 14-11-314)
Foreign LLCs:	• Foreign LLCs are expressly permitted by statute. Laws of the formation jurisdiction govern organization, internal affairs and the liability of members, managers and other owners. (Ga. Code § 14-11-701)
Formation:	• One or more persons may form an LLC. Single-member LLCs are permitted. (Ga. Code § 14-11-203)

Naming requirements:

- A Georgia LLC name must contain the words "limited liability company" or "limited company" or the abbreviations "L.L.C.", "LLC", "L.C." or "LC." The word "limited" may be abbreviated as "ltd." and the word "company" may be abbreviated "co." (Ga. Code § 14-11-207)

Effective date of organization:

- An LLC's existence begins when the articles of organization are filed, or at the delayed effective date specified therein. (Ga. Code § 14-11-206)

Filing requirements:

- The articles of organization shall set forth the name of the LLC and may set forth that management of the LLC is vested in one or more managers and any other provisions not inconsistent with the law. (Ga. Code § 14-11-204)

Fees—Organization and Annual:

- The fee for filing the articles of organization is $100. The fee for filing the application for certificate of authority is $225. The fee for annual registration is $30. (Ga. Code § 14-11-1101)

Recordkeeping:

- Each LLC shall compile and maintain: (1) a current copy of the name and last known address of each member and manager; (2) copies of records that would enable a member to determine the relative voting rights, if any, of the members; (3) a copy of the articles of organization, together with any amendments thereto; (4) copies of the LLC's federal, state, and local tax returns, if any, for the three most recent years; (5) copies of any written operating agreements and all amendments thereto; and (6) copies of financial statements, if any, of the LLC for the three most recent years. (Ga. Code § 14-11-313)

Annual reporting:

- An annual report is required. (Ga. Code § 14-11-1103)

Management:

- Management is vested in the members, unless otherwise provided. (Ga. Code § 14-11-304)

Membership rights and obligations:	• A member or manager is not liable, solely by reason of being a member or manager, under a judgment, decree, or order of a court, or in any other manner, for a debt, obligation, or liability of the LLC, whether arising in contract, tort, or otherwise, or for the acts or omissions of any other member or manager, whether arising in contract, tort or otherwise. A member who fails to make a required contribution is subject to specified penalties for or specified consequences of such failure. A member or manager who assents to a wrongful distribution is personally liable to the LLC for the amount of the distribution that was wrongfully made. Each member or manager held liable is entitled to contribution from each member who knowingly received a wrongful distribution. (Ga. Code § § 14-11-303, 14-11-402 and 14-11-408)
Piercing the corporate veil:	• The failure of an LLC to observe the formalities relating to the exercise of its powers or the management of its business and affairs is not a ground for imposing personal liability on a member, manager, agent or employee of the LLC for liabilities of the LLC. (Ga. Code § 14-11-314)
Contributions:	• Contributions may consist of cash, tangible or intangible property, services rendered, or a promissory note or other obligation to contribute the same. (Ga. Code § 14-11-401)
Distributions:	• Distributions, profits and losses are allocated equally, unless otherwise provided. (Ga. Code § § 14-11-403 and 14-11-404)
Resignation of member:	• *For LLCs formed prior to July 1, 1999,* thirty days' written notice is required prior to resignation, unless otherwise provided. (Ga. Code § 14-11-601) *For LLCs formed on or after July 1, 1999,* a member's right to resign is governed by the articles or organization or written operating agreement. (Ga. Code § 14-11-601.1)
Transfer of LLC interest:	• A member's LLC interest is assignable in whole or in part, unless otherwise provided. Unanimous consent is required for an assignee to become a member, unless otherwise provided. (Ga. Code § § 14-11-502 and 14-11-503)

Dissolution:	• *For LLCs formed prior to July 1, 1999,* an LLC is dissolved: (1) at the time or upon the happening of events specified in the articles of organization or a written operating agreement; (2) at a time approved by all the members; (3) subject to contrary provision in the articles of organization or a written operating agreement, 90 days after any event of dissociation (other than voluntary withdrawal) that occurs to a member, unless the business of the LLC is continued by the written consent of all other members or as otherwise provided in the articles of organization or a written operating agreement; or (4) upon the entry of a judicial dissolution. *For LLCs formed on or after July 1, 1999,* an LLC is dissolved: (1) at the time or upon the happening of events specified in the articles of organization or written operating agreement; (2) at a time approved by all members; (3) subject to contrary provision in the articles of organization or written operating agreement, 90 days after an event of dissociation with respect to the last remaining member, unless otherwise provided; or (4) upon the entry of a judicial dissolution. (Ga. Code §§ 14-11-602 and 14-11-603)
Mergers and consolidations:	• Mergers are permitted expressly by statute. (Ga. Code § 14-11-901)

¶ 1014

Hawaii

Name of act:	• Hawaii Uniform Limited Liability Company Act, Haw. Rev. Stat. § 428-101 to Haw. Rev. Stat. § 428-1302.
Federal tax classification:	• The LLC statute is flexible. Any "business entity" not required to be treated as a "corporation" for federal tax purposes under Reg. § 301.7701-2 may choose its classification under Reg. § 301.7701-3.
State tax treatment:	• State tax classification follows federal classification. Thus, Hawaii LLCs and foreign LLCs doing business in Hawaii are treated as partnerships or disregarded as entities, unless classified as corporations for federal tax purposes.
Securities treatment:	• The Hawaii Act does not expressly provide for the treatment of an LLC interest as a security.
Limited liability partnerships:	• The formation of limited liability partnerships is expressly permitted by statute. (Haw. Rev. Stat. § 425-151)
Limited liability limited partnerships:	• The formation of limited liability limited partnerships is expressly permitted by statute. (Haw. Rev. Stat. § 425E-102)

Professional LLCs:	• An LLC may be organized for any lawful purpose. (Haw. Rev. Stat. § 428-111)
Foreign LLCs:	• Foreign LLCs are expressly permitted by statute. Laws of the formation jurisdiction govern the LLC's organization and internal affairs, as well as the liability of its members and managers. (Haw. Rev. Stat. § 428-1001)
Formation:	• A Hawaii LLC may be formed by one or more persons and may consist of one or more members. (Haw. Rev. Stat. § 428-202)
Naming requirements:	• The name of a LLC must contain "limited liability company" or the abbreviation "L.L.C." or "LLC". "Limited" may be abbreviated as "Ltd.", and "company" may be abbreviated as "Co." The letters in the name of a LLC must be letters of the English alphabet. (Haw. Rev. Stat. § 428-105)
Effective date of organization:	• The existence of a LLC begins when the articles of organization are filed. (Haw. Rev. Stat. § 428-202)
Filing requirements:	• The articles of organization must include: (1) the LLC's name; (2) the address of the designated office; (3) the name and address of the agent for service of process; (4) the name and address of each organizer; (5) whether the company is a term LLC, and, if so, the duration of the term; (6) whether the company is to be manager-managed, and, if so, the name and address of each manager, or if not, the name and address of each initial member; and (7) whether the members of the company are to be liable for its debts and obligations. (Haw. Rev. Stat. § 428-203)
Fees—Organization and Annual:	• The fee for filing articles of organization is $50. The fee for filing an application for a certificate of authority is $50. The annual report fee is $15. (Haw. Rev. Stat. § 428-1301)
Recordkeeping:	• The Hawaii statute is silent as to records and information required to be kept by LLCs. However, it might be prudent for the LLC to compile and maintain: (1) a current list of the name and address of each member and manager; (2) copies of federal, state and local income tax returns and company information; (3) copies of the articles of organization, including any amendments; (4) copies of any effective written operating agreement; (5) financial statements; (6) information regarding members' capital contributions, agreements to contribute capital and the date each became a member; and (7) any other information regarding LLC affairs that is just and reasonable to maintain.

164   Limited Liability Companies

Annual reporting:	• An annual report must be filed according to the following schedule. LLCs whose date of organization was: (1) between January 1 and March 31 must file on or before March 31 and reflect the LLC's affairs as of January 1 of the year when filed; (2) between April 1 and June 30 must file on or before June 30 and reflect the LLC's affairs as of April 1 of the year when filed; (3) between July 1 and September 30 must file on or before September 30 and reflect the LLC's affairs as of July 1 of the year when filed; and (4) between October 1 and December 31 must file on or before December 31 and reflect the LLC's affairs as of October 1 of the year when filed. Information required includes: (1) the name of the company and the state or country under whose law it is organized; (2) the address of its designated office and the name of its designated agent at that office in this state; (3) the address of its principal office; and (4) whether the LLC is manager-managed, and if so, the names and addresses of each manager, or if not, the names and addresses of each member. (Haw. Rev. Stat. § 428-210)
Management:	• Management of a Hawaii LLC may be by member or manager, as provided in the operating agreement. (Haw. Rev. Stat. § 428-404)
Membership rights and obligations:	• The Hawaii statute does not excuse members from their contribution obligation to the LLC, even in cases of death, disability or inability to perform personally. If a member does not make the required contribution, he is obligated, at the option of the LLC, to contribute money equal to the value of that portion of the contribution that has not been made. If a member has received a wrongful distribution, then the member is liable to the company to the extent that the distribution received exceeded the amount that could properly have been paid. (Haw. Rev. Stat. §§ 428-402 and 428-407)
Piercing the corporate veil:	• The Act has no express provision that concerns piercing the corporate veil.
Contributions:	• Contributions may consist of tangible or intangible property or other benefit to the company, including money, promissory notes, services performed or other obligations to contribute cash or property or contracts for services to be performed. (Haw. Rev. Stat. § 428-401)
Distributions:	• Any distributions made by a LLC, prior to dissolution and winding up, must be in equal shares. (Haw. Rev. Stat. § 428-405)

¶1014

Resignation of member:	• A member may resign at any time, unless otherwise provided. A member who wrongfully dissociates from a LLC is liable to the company and to the other members for damages caused by the dissociation. (Haw. Rev. Stat. § 428-602)
Transfer of LLC interest:	• A member's LLC interest is transferable and assignable. A transferee of a distributional interest may become a member in accordance with the operating agreement or if all other members consent. (Haw. Rev. Stat. § § 428-501 and § 428-503)
Dissolution:	• A LLC is dissolved upon the occurrence of any of the following events: (1) an event specified in the operating agreement; (2) consent of the number or percentage of members specified in the operating agreement; (3) dissociation of a member-manager or, if none, a member of an at-will company, unless the business of the LLC is continued by the remaining members; (4) an event that makes it unlawful for all or substantially all of the business of the company to be continued; (5) on application by a member, upon entry of a final judicial decree; or (6) the expiration of a term specified in the company's articles of organization. (Haw. Rev. Stat. § 428-602)
Mergers and consolidations:	• Mergers are permitted, expressly by statute. (Haw. Rev. Stat. § 428-904)

¶ 1015

Idaho

Name of act:	• Idaho Limited Liability Company Act, Idaho Code § 53-601 to Idaho Code § 53-672.
Federal tax classification:	• The LLC statute is flexible. Any "business entity" not required to be treated as a "corporation" for federal tax purposes under Reg. § 301.7701-2 may choose its classification under Reg. § 301.7701-3.
State tax treatment:	• State tax classification follows federal. Thus, Idaho LLCs and foreign LLCs doing business in Idaho are treated as partnerships or disregarded as entities, unless classified as corporations for federal tax purposes. (Idaho Code § 63-3006A)
Securities treatment:	• The Idaho Act does not expressly provide for the treatment of an LLC interest as a security.
Limited liability partnerships:	• The formation of Limited Liability Partnerships is expressly permitted by statute. (Idaho Code § 53-3-1001)
Limited liability limited partnerships:	• The formation of Limited Liability Limited Partnerships is expressly permitted by statute. (Idaho Code § 53-2-108)

Professional LLCs:	• Professional LLCs are expressly permitted by statute, subject to compliance with other state regulatory provisions. (Idaho Code § 53-615)
Foreign LLCs:	• Foreign LLCs are expressly permitted by statute. Laws of the formation jurisdiction govern the LLC's organization, internal affairs, and liability and authority of its members and managers. However, professional corporations rendering services in Idaho are subject to Idaho law. (Idaho Code § 53-650)
Formation:	• One or more persons may form an LLC. The statute gives no indication that two members are required. Thus, it appears that Idaho permits single-member LLCs. (Idaho Code § 53-607)
Naming requirements:	• The name of each LLC must contain the words "Limited Liability Company" or "Limited Company" or the abbreviation "L.L.C.," "L.C.," "LLC" or "LC." The word "Limited" may be abbreviated as "Ltd." and the word "Company" may be abbreviated as "Co." The name of each professional services LLC must end with the words "Professional Company" or either of the abbreviations "P.L.L.C." or "PLLC." (Idaho Code § 53-602)
Effective date of organization:	• An LLC's existence begins when each copy of the articles of organization is stamped "filed" and marked with the filing date. (Idaho Code § 53-612)
Filing requirements:	• The articles of organization must contain: (1) the LLC's name; (2) the address of its registered office, and the name of the registered agent at that address; (3) a statement that the LLC's management is vested in a manager or managers, if applicable; (4) the name and address of one or more of the company's initial members, if the LLC is member-managed, (5) the name and address of one or more of the company's initial managers, if the LLC is manager-managed, and (6) the principal profession for which the members are duly licensed, or otherwise legally authorized to render, if the LLC is a professional services LLC. (Idaho Code § 53-608)

¶1015

Fees—Organization and Annual:	• The fee for filing the original articles of organization is $100 if typed and completely included on the standard form prescribed by the Idaho Secretary of State or $120 if not typed or if attachments are included. The fee for filing a foreign LLC registration application is also $100 if typed and completely included on the standard form prescribed by the Idaho Secretary of State or $120 if not typed or if attachments are included. There is no fee for filing the annual report. (Idaho Code § 53-665)
Recordkeeping:	• Unless otherwise provided in a written operating agreement, the LLC must compile and maintain: (1) a list of current and past members' and managers' names and addresses; (2) a copy of the articles of organization, including all amendments and executed powers of attorney; (3) copies of federal, state and local tax returns and financial statements for the last three years, or if not prepared, copies of the information and statements provided to members to enable them to prepare their returns for the period; (4) copies of any effective written operating agreements, including all amendments, and copies of any written operating agreements no longer in effect; and (5) any writing that sets forth members' capital contributions, agreements to contribute capital, dissolution events, if not set forth in a written operating agreement, or any other writing required by an operating agreement. (Idaho Code § 53-625)
Annual reporting:	• An LLC's annual report must be delivered each year to the secretary of state before the end of the month in which a domestic LLC was initial organized or a foreign LLC was initially authorized to transact business in the state. (Idaho Code § 53-613)
Management:	• Management is vested in members, unless otherwise provided. (Idaho Code § 53-621)

Membership rights and obligations:	• A member is not liable for a debt, obligation or liability of the LLC, whether arising in contract, tort or otherwise, or for the acts or omissions of any other member, manager, agent or employee of the LLC. A member is obligated to perform any enforceable promise to contribute, even if the member is unable to perform because of death, disability or other reason, unless otherwise provided. If a member fails to make the required contribution, the member is obligated, at the option of the LLC, to contribute cash equal to that portion of value of the stated contribution that has not been made. A member's obligation to make a contribution may be compromised only with the unanimous consent of the members. The statute does not specifically address liability incurred for wrongful distributions. (Idaho Code § § 53-619 and 53-627)
Piercing the corporate veil:	• The Act has no express provision that concerns piercing the corporate veil.
Contributions:	• Contributions may consist of cash, property, services rendered, guarantee of an obligation of the LLC, promissory note or other obligation to contribute the same. (Idaho Code § 53-626)
Distributions:	• Distributions are shared equally, unless otherwise provided. Profits and assets remaining after all liabilities have been satisfied are shared on a per capita basis, unless otherwise provided. The statute is silent as to the allocation of losses. (Idaho Code § § 53-628 and 53-629)
Resignation of member:	• Thirty days' written notice is required prior to resignation. The power of a member to voluntarily withdraw may be limited by an operating agreement. (Idaho Code § 53-641)
Transfer of LLC interest:	• A member's LLC interest is assignable in whole or in part, unless otherwise provided. Unanimous consent is required for an assignee to become a member, unless otherwise provided. (Idaho Code § § 53-636 and 53-638)

Dissolution:	• An LLC is dissolved: (1) at the time or upon the occurrence of events specified in the articles of organization or an operating agreement; (2) upon the written consent of all of the members; (3) upon an event of dissociation of a member, unless the remaining members unanimously consent to continue the LLC within 90 days of the event or the operating agreement provides otherwise; (4) upon the entry of a decree of judicial dissolution; or (5) upon administrative dissolution. (Idaho Code § § 53-642, 53-643 and 53-643A)
Mergers and consolidations:	• Mergers or consolidations are expressly permitted by statute. (Idaho Code § 53-661)

¶ 1016
Illinois

Name of act:	• Limited Liability Company Act, 805 Ill. Comp. Stat.180/1-1 to 805 Ill. Comp. Stat. 180/60-1.
Federal tax classification:	• The LLC statute is flexible. Any "business entity" not required to be treated as a "corporation" for federal tax purposes under Reg. § 301.7701-2 may choose its classification under Reg. § 301.7701-3.
State tax treatment:	• State tax classification follows federal. Thus, Illinois LLCs and foreign LLCs doing business in Illinois are treated as partnerships or disregarded as entities, unless classified as corporations for federal tax purposes. (35 Ill. Comp. Stat. 5/502(f) and 5/1501(a))
Securities treatment:	• The Illinois Act does not expressly provide for the treatment of an LLC interest as a security.
Limited liability partnerships:	• The formation of limited liability partnerships is permitted expressly by statute. (805 Ill. Comp. Stat. 205/8.1)
Limited liability limited partnerships:	• Limited Liability Limited Partnerships are expressly authorized by statute. (805 Ill. Comp. Stat. 215/102)
Professional LLCs:	• Professional LLCs are permitted impliedly by statute. LLCs may carry on any lawful business, except banking, exclusive of fiduciaries organized for the purpose of accepting and executing trusts, or insurance, unless the company meets requirements set forth in the Illinois Insurance Code. Dentists must comply with the Illinois Dental Practice Act and LLCs organized to engage in the practice of medicine must comply with the Medical Practice Act of 1987. (805 Ill. Comp. Stat. 180/1-25)

Foreign LLCs:	• Foreign LLCs are expressly permitted by statute. Laws of formation jurisdiction govern the LLC's organization, internal affairs, and member liability. (805 Ill. Comp. Stat. 180/45-1)
Formation:	• One or more persons may organize an Illinois LLC. One or more members are required. (805 Ill. Comp. Stat. 180/5-1)
Naming requirements:	• The name of each LLC must have the words "limited liability company" or the abbreviation "L.L.C." or "LLC" in its name. The name must not contain any of the following words or abbreviations: "Corporation," "Corp.," "Incorporated," "Inc.," "Ltd.," "Co.," "Limited Partnership," or "L.P." (805 Ill. Comp. Stat. 180/1-10)
Effective date of organization:	• An LLC's existence begins when the articles of organization are filed by the secretary of state. (805 Ill. Comp. Stat. 180/5-40)
Filing requirements:	• The articles of organization must contain: (1) the LLC's name and address of its principal place of business; (2) its business purpose; (3) the name of its registered agent and the address of its registered office; (4) the name and address of the initial manager or managers, if the LLC is manager-managed; (5) the name and address of the company's initial members, if the LLC is member-managed; (6) the LLC's duration, which may be perpetual; (7) the name and address of each organizer; and (8) any other provision the members elect to include. (805 Ill. Comp. Stat. 180/5-5)
Fees—Organization and Annual:	• The fee for filing articles of organization is $500. The filing fee for a foreign LLC application for admission is $500. The filing fee for a Series LLC is $750. The fee for filing the annual report is $250 plus $50 for each series. (805 Ill. Comp. Stat. 180/50-10)
Recordkeeping:	• Records that must be kept include: (1) a list of each member's name, last known address, amount of cash contributed to the LLC, description and statement of the agreed value of other property and services contributed or to be contributed in the future, and the date on which each became a member; (2) copies of the articles of organization, including any amendments and executed powers of attorney; (3) federal, state and local tax returns and information for the last three years; (4) the written operating agreement, if any exists, including any amendments; and (5) financial statements for the last three years. (805 Ill. Comp. Stat. 180/1-40)

¶1016

Annual reporting:	• An annual report is required. The report must be filed within 60 days before the first day of the LLC's anniversary month. (805 Ill. Comp. Stat. 180/50-1)
Management:	• An LLC may be either member-managed or manager-managed. (805 Ill. Comp. Stat. 180/15-1)
Membership rights and obligations:	• Members or managers are not liable for debts, obligations or liabilities of the LLC solely by reason of being a member or manager of the LLC. (805 Ill. Comp. Stat. 180/10-10, 180/20-5 and 180/25-35)
Piercing the corporate veil:	• The failure of an LLC to observe the usual company formalities or requirements relating to the exercise of its company powers or management of its business is not a ground for imposing personal liability on the members or managers for liabilities of the company. (805 Ill. Comp. Stat. 180/10-10)
Contributions:	• Contributions may consist of cash, property, or services, or a promise to contribute the same. (805 Ill. Comp. Stat. 180/20-1)
Distributions:	• Distributions, profits and losses are to be allocated based on relative book values of members' interests, unless otherwise provided. (805 Ill. Comp. Stat. 180/20-10 and 180/20-15)
Resignation of member:	• A member may resign at any time upon written notice. (805 Ill. Comp. Stat. 180/25-5)
Transfer of LLC interest:	• A member's LLC interest is assignable in whole or in part, unless otherwise provided. Unanimous consent is required for an assignee to become a member, unless otherwise provided. (805 Ill. Comp. Stat. 180/30-5)
Dissolution:	• An LLC is dissolved: (1) at the time or upon the happening of events specified in the operating agreement; (2) upon the consent of the number or percentage of members specified in the operating agreement; (3) upon the occurrence of an event that makes it unlawful for all or substantially all of the business of the LLC to be continued; (4) upon the entry of a decree of judicial dissolution; or (5) upon an administrative dissolution. (805 Ill. Comp. Stat. 180/35-1, 180/35-5 and 180/35-25)
Mergers and consolidations:	• Mergers and consolidations are expressly permitted. (805 Ill. Comp. Stat. 180/37-20)

¶ 1017
Indiana

Name of act:	• Indiana Business Flexibility Act, Indiana Code § 23-18-1-1 to Indiana Code § 23-18-13-1.
Federal tax classification:	• The LLC statute is flexible. Any "business entity" not required to be treated as a "corporation" for federal tax purposes under Reg. § 301.7701-2 may choose its classification under Reg. § 301.7701-3.
State tax treatment:	• State tax classification follows federal. Thus, Indiana LLCs and foreign LLCs doing business in Indiana are treated as partnerships or disregarded as entities, unless classified as corporations for federal tax purposes. (Ind. Code § 6-3-1-19(a))
Securities treatment:	• An LLC interest (including any fractional or other interest in an LLC) may be a security, but "security" does not include an interest in an LLC if it can be proven that all of the members of the limited liability company are actively engaged in the management of the limited liability company. (Ind. Code § 23-2-1-1)
Limited liability partnerships:	• The formation of Limited Liability Partnerships is expressly permitted by statute. (Ind. Code § 23-4-1-45)
Professional LLCs:	• Professional LLCs are permitted impliedly by statute. The statute does not alter any law applicable to the relationship between a person rendering professional services and a person receiving professional services, including liability arising out of the professional services. (Ind. Code § § 23-18-2-3 and 23-18-3-4)
Foreign LLCs:	• Foreign LLCs are expressly permitted by statute. Laws of the formation jurisdiction govern organization, internal affairs and the liability of members and managers. (Ind. Code § 23-18-11-1)
Formation:	• An Indiana LLC may be formed by at least one person. Indiana permits an LLC to have a single member. (Ind. Code § 23-18-2-4)
Naming requirements:	• An Indiana LLC's name must contain the words "limited liability company," or either of the abbreviations "L.L.C." or "LLC." (Ind. Code § 23-18-2-8)
Effective date of organization:	• An LLC's existence begins when the articles of organization are on file in the office of the secretary of state. (Ind. Code § 23-18-2-7)

Filing requirements:	• The articles of organization must include: (1) the LLC's name; (2) the street address of the LLC's registered office in Indiana and the name of the LLC's registered agent at that office; (3) the latest date upon which the LLC is to dissolve, or a statement that the duration of the LLC is perpetual until dissolution; (4) if the articles of organization provide for a manager or managers, a statement to that effect; and (5) any other matters that the members agree to include. (Ind. Code § 23-18-2-4)
Fees—Organization and Annual:	• The fee for filing original articles of organization is $90, $75 if filed on-line. The fee for filing an application for certificate of authority is $90, $75 if filed on-line.. A biennial fee of $30 is required along with the biennial report. (Ind. Code § 23-18-12-3)
Recordkeeping:	• The LLC must compile and maintain: (1) a list of the members' and managers' full names and last known mailing address from the date of organization; (2) a copy of the articles of organization and all amendments; (3) copies of federal, state, and local tax returns and financial statements for the three years most recent years, if any, or if the returns and statements were not prepared, copies of the information and statements provided to or that should have been provided to the members to enable them to prepare such returns; (4) copies of any written operating agreements and of all amendments and copies of any operating agreements no longer in effect; and (5) unless contained in a written operating agreement, the following: (a) the amount of cash, if any, and a statement of the agreed value of other property or services contributed by each member and the times at which or events the happening of which any additional contributions agreed to be made by each member are to be made; (b) the events, if any, upon the happening of which the LLC is to be dissolved and its affairs wound up; and (c) other writings, if any, required by the operating agreement. (Ind. Code § 23-18-4-8)
Annual reporting:	• A biennial report must be delivered to the secretary of state in the second year following the calendar year in which a domestic LLC was organized or a foreign LLC was authorized to transact business. (Ind. Code § 23-18-12-11)
Management:	• Management is vested in the members, unless otherwise provided. (Ind. Code § 23-18-4-1)

Membership rights and obligations:	• LLC members, managers, agents and employees are not liable for any debt, obligation, or liability of the LLC, whether arising in contract, tort, or otherwise, or for the acts or omissions of any other member, manager, agent, or employee of the LLC. If a member does not make a promised contribution, the member is obligated, even in the event of death, disability, or any other reason, to contribute cash equal to that portion of the value of the contribution that was not made, unless otherwise provided. A member or manager who assents to a wrongful distribution is personally liable to the LLC for the amount of the distribution wrongfully made. (Ind. Code §§ 23-18-3-3, 23-18-5-1 and 23-18-5-7)
Piercing the corporate veil:	• The Act has no express provision concerning piercing the corporate veil.
Contributions:	• Contributions may consist of any cash, property, services rendered, a promissory note or other binding obligation to contribute the same. (Ind. Code § 23-18-1-5)
Distributions:	• Distributions, profits and losses are allocated on the basis of agreed value of each member's contribution, unless otherwise provided. (Ind. Code §§ 23-18-5-3 and 23-18-5-4)
Resignation of member:	• A member may withdraw from an LLC only as specified in the operating agreement. (Ind. Code §§ 23-18-6-6 and 23-18-6-6.1)
Transfer of LLC interest:	• An assignee of an interest in a single-member LLC may become a member in accordance with terms of an agreement between the assignor and the assignee. (Ind. Code §§ 23-18-6-3, 23-18-6-3.1, 23-18-6-4 and 23-18-6-4.1)
Dissolution:	• An LLC is dissolved: (1) at the time or on the occurrence of events specified in writing in the articles of organization or operating agreement; (2) if there is one class or group of members, upon written consent of 2/3 in interest of the members, or if there is more than one class or group of members, upon written consent of 2/3 in interest of each class or group of members; (3) upon the entry of a decree of judicial dissolution; or (4) if there are no members, unless the business of the LLC is continued, under a provision in the operating agreement, by the personal representative of the last remaining member, and either the personal representative or a nominee of the personal representative is admitted as a member. (Ind. Code §§ 23-18-9-1, 23-18-9-1.1 and 23-18-9-2)
Mergers and consolidations:	• Mergers or consolidations are permitted expressly by statute. (Ind. Code § 23-18-7-1)

¶ 1018

Iowa

Name of act:	• Iowa Limited Liability Company Act, Iowa Code § 490A.100 to Iowa Code § 490A.1601.
Federal tax classification:	• The LLC statute is flexible. Any "business entity" not required to be treated as a "corporation" for federal tax purposes under Reg. § 301.7701-2 may choose its classification under Reg. § 301.7701-3.
State tax treatment:	• Iowa LLCs and LLCs doing business in Iowa that are taxed as corporations for federal tax purposes are taxed as corporations for state income tax purposes. (Iowa Code § 422.32(4))
Securities treatment:	• "Security" includes an interest in an LLC or any class or series of such interest, including any fractional or other interests in such interest. A security, however, does not include an LLC if the person claiming the interest is not a security proves that all of the members of the LLC are actively engaged in management of the LLC, provided specified conditions regarding this management are satisfied. (Iowa Code § 502.102)
Limited liability partnerships:	• Formation of limited liability partnerships is expressly permitted. (Iowa Code § 486A.1001)
Limited liability limited partnerships:	• Limited Liability Limited Partnerships are expressly permitted by statute. (Iowa Code §§ 488.102(13) and 488.108)
Professional LLCs:	• Professional LLCs are expressly permitted by statute. (Iowa Code § 490A.1501)
Foreign LLCs:	• Foreign LLCs are expressly permitted by statute. Laws of the formation jurisdiction govern organization and internal affairs, except that rights and privileges are limited to those of Iowa LLCs. (Iowa Code § 490A.1401)
Formation:	• One or more persons may form an Iowa LLC. One or more members are required. (Iowa Code §§ 490A.102 and 490A.301)
Naming requirements:	• A limited liability name must contain the words "limited company" or "Limited Liability Company" or the abbreviation "L.C." or "L.L.C." or words or abbreviations of like import in another language. (Iowa Code § 490A.401)
Effective date of organization:	• Unless a delayed effective time and date is specified, the LLC's existence begins at the date and time when the articles of organization are filed. (Iowa Code § 490A.122)

Filing requirements:	• The articles of organization must include: (1) the LLC's name; (2) its duration, which may be perpetual; (3) the name and address of the initial registered agent for service of process; and (4) the address of the principal office. Other minimal filing requirements must be satisfied. (Iowa Code § § 490A.120 and 490A.303)
Fees—Organization and Annual:	• The fee for filing articles of organization is $50. The fee for filing the certificate of authority application for foreign LLC registration is $100. There is no annual registration fee. (Iowa Code § 490A.124)
Recordkeeping:	• The LLC must compile and maintain: (1) a list of the members' and managers' names and addresses; (2) copies of federal, state, and local tax returns and reports for the three most recent years; (3) a copy of the articles of organization, including any amendments; (4) copies of any then-effective operating agreement and any financial statements for the three most recent years; and (5) a writing that sets forth the members' capital contributions, agreements to contribute capital, distribution rights and dissolution events, if not set forth in the LLCs's written operating agreement. (Iowa Code § 490A.709)
Annual reporting:	• A biennial report is required.
Management:	• Management is vested in the members, unless otherwise provided. (Iowa Code § 490A.702)
Membership rights and obligations:	• A member or manager of an LLC is not personally liable solely by reason of being a member or manager of the LLC under any judgment, or in any other manner, for any debt, obligation or liability of the LLC, whether that liability or obligation arises in contract, tort or otherwise. If a member does not make a promised contribution, the member is obligated, even in the event of death, disability, or any other reason, to contribute cash equal to that portion of the value of the contribution that was not made. An operating agreement may provided that the interest of any member who fails to make a contribution that the member is obligated to make is subject to specified penalties for, or specified consequences of, such failure. A member who has received a wrongful distribution is liable to the LLC for a period of five years thereafter for the amount of the wrongful distribution. (Iowa Code § § 490A.601, 490A.801 and 490A.808)
Piercing the corporate veil:	• The Act has no express provision that concerns piercing the corporate veil.

¶1018

Contributions:	• Contributions may consist of cash, property, services, promissory notes or other promise to contribute the same. (Iowa Code § 490A.801)
Distributions:	• Profits, losses and distributions are allocated based on the members' relative capital accounts, unless otherwise provided. (Iowa Code § § 490A.802 and 490A.803)
Resignation of member:	• For LLCs whose articles of organization were filed prior to July 1, 1997, six months' written notice is required prior to resignation, unless otherwise provided. The resignation of a member may be prohibited. For LLCs whose articles of organization were filed on or after July 1, 1997, a member may resign only as specified in the operating agreement. However, if not specified, a member may resign if any amendment to the articles of organization or operating agreement, adopted over the member's written dissent, adversely affects certain rights or preferences of the dissenting member's membership interest. (Iowa Code § § 490A.704 and 490A.704A)
Transfer of LLC interest:	• A member's interest is assignable in whole or in part, unless otherwise provided. Unanimous consent is required for an assignee to become a member, unless otherwise provided. (Iowa Code § § 490A.902 and 490A.903)
Dissolution:	• An LLC is dissolved: (1) at the time or happening of an event specified in the articles of organization or operating agreement; (2) upon the unanimous written agreement of the members; or (3) when there is a judicial dissolution. (Iowa Code § § 490A.1301 and 490A.1302)
Mergers and consolidations:	• Mergers or consolidations are expressly permitted by statute. (Iowa Code § 490A.1201)

¶ 1019
Kansas

Name of act:	• Kansas Revised Limited Liability Company Act, Kan. Stat. § 17-7662 to Kan. Stat. § 17-76,142. Provisions governing mergers and consolidations of constituent entities appear at Kan. Stat. § 17-7701 to Kan. Stat. § 17-7709.
Federal tax classification:	• The LLC statute is flexible. Any "business entity" not required to be treated as a "corporation" for federal tax purposes under Reg. § 301.7701-2 may choose its classification under Reg. § 301.7701-3.

State tax treatment:	• State tax classification follows federal. Thus, Kansas LLCs and foreign LLCs doing business in Kansas are treated as partnerships, unless classified as corporations for federal tax purposes. (Kan. Admin. Regs. § 92-12-8)
Securities treatment:	• The Kansas Act does not expressly provide for the treatment of an LLC interest as a security.
Limited liability partnerships:	• The formation of limited liability partnerships is expressly provided for by statute. (Kan. Stat. § 56-345)
Limited liability limited partnerships:	• The formation of limited liability limited partnerships is expressly provided for by statute. (Kan. Stat. § 17-7684)
Professional LLCs:	• Professional LLCs are expressly permitted by statute. An LLC may not engage in the business of granting policies of insurance or assuming insurance risks or banking. (Kan. Stat. § 17-7668)
Foreign LLCs:	• Foreign LLCs are expressly permitted by statute. The laws of the formation jurisdiction govern the LLC's organization, internal affairs, and the liability of its members. (Kan. Stat. § 17-76,120)
Formation:	• Any person may form an LLC. An LLC must have at least one member. (Kan. Stat. § 17-7663)
Naming requirements:	• An LLC's name must contain the words "limited liability company" or "limited company," or the abbreviation "LLC," "LC" or the designation "LLC" or "LC." (Kan. Stat. § 76-7664)
Effective date of organization:	• An LLC existence begins upon the filing of its articles of organization. An LLC may specify a date of formation that is no later than 90 days after the date the initial articles of organization are filed; otherwise existence begins the articles are filed. (Kan. Stat. § 76-7673)
Filing requirements:	• The articles of organization must include: (1) The LLC's name; (2) the address of the registered office and the name and address of the resident agent for service of process; (3) any other matters the members determine to include therein; and (4) if the limited liability company is organized to exercise the powers of a professional association or corporation, each such profession shall be stated. (Kan. Stat. § 17-7673)

¶1019

Fees—Organization and Annual:	• The fee for filing articles of organization is $165. The fee for filing a foreign LLC application is $165. At the time of filing the annual report, a franchise tax is due for businesses with a net worth of more than $100,000. (Kan. Stat. § § 17-76,136 and 17-76,139)
Recordkeeping:	• The Kansas statute is silent as to records and information required to be kept by LLCs. However it might be prudent for the LLC to compile and maintain: (1) a current list of the name and address of each member and manager; (2) copies of federal, state and local income tax returns and company information; (3) copies of the articles of organization, including any amendments; (4) copies of any effective written operating agreement; (5) financial statements; (6) information regarding members' capital contributions, agreements to contribute capital and the date each became a member; and (7) any other information regarding LLC affairs that is just and reasonable to maintain.
Annual reporting:	• An annual report is required. The report must be filed at the time prescribed for filing the LLC's state income tax return. (Kan. Stat. § 17-76,139)
Management:	• Management is vested in members, unless otherwise provided. (Kan. Stat. § 17-7693)
Membership rights and obligations:	• A member who fails to make the a promised contribution of cash, property or services is obligated, at the option of the LLC, to contribute cash equal to that portion of the agreed value of the unmade contribution. A member who receives a wrongful distribution, and who knew at the time of the distribution that it was wrongful, is liable to the LLC for the amount of the distribution. A member who receives a wrongful distribution and does not know that the distribution was wrongful is not liable for the amount of the distribution. (Kan. Stat. § § 76-7688, 17-76,100 and 17-76,110)
Piercing the corporate veil:	• The Act has no express provision that concerns piercing the corporate veil.
Contributions:	• Contributions may consist of cash, property, services rendered or a promissory note or other obligation to contribute the same. (Kan. Stat. § 17-7699)
Distributions:	• Distributions, profits and losses are allocated on the basis of the agreed value of each member's contributions that have not been returned. (Kan. Stat. § § 17-76,101 and 17-76, 102)

Resignation of member:	• A member may resign from a limited liability company only at the time or upon the happening of events specified in agreement and in accordance with the operating agreement. (Kan. Stat. § 17-76,112)
Transfer of LLC interest:	• A member's LLC interest is assignable in whole or in part, unless otherwise provided. Unanimous consent is required for an assignee to become a member. (Kan. Stat. § 17-76,112)
Dissolution:	• An LLC is dissolved: (1) at the time specified in an operating agreement; (2) upon the happening of events specified in an operating agreement; (3) upon the written consent of the members of the limited liability company, unless otherwise provided; (4) at any time there are no members, unless, within 90 days or other specified period, the personal representative of the last remaining member agrees in writing to continue the LLC; or 5) upon the entry of a decree of judicial dissolution. (Kan. Stat. § 17-76,116)
Mergers and consolidations:	• Mergers or consolidations are expressly permitted by statute. (Kan. Stat. § 17-7681)

¶ 1020
Kentucky

Name of act:	• Kentucky Limited Liability Company Act, Ky. Rev. Stat. § 275.001 to Ky. Rev. Stat. § 275.455
Federal tax classification:	• The LLC statute is flexible. Any "business entity" not required to be treated as a "corporation" for federal tax purposes under Reg. § 301.7701-2 may choose its classification under Reg. § 301.7701-3.
State tax treatment:	• LLCs are required to file Kentucky corporate income tax returns regardless of their taxation for federal income tax purposes.
Securities treatment:	• The Kentucky Act does not expressly provide for the treatment of an LLC interest as a security.
Limited liability partnerships:	• The formation of limited liability partnerships is expressly provided for by statute. (Ky. Rev. Stat. § 362.174)
Limited liability limited partnerships:	• The formation of limited liability limited partnerships is expressly provided for by statute. (Ky. H.B. 234, effective July 12, 2006)
Professional LLCs:	• Professional LLCs are expressly permitted by statute. (Ky. Rev. Stat. § 275.010)
Foreign LLCs:	• Foreign LLCs are expressly permitted by statute. Laws of the formation jurisdiction govern the LLC's organization, internal affairs, and liability of its members. (Ky. Rev. Stat. § 275.380)

Formation:	• One or more persons may form a Kentucky LLC. An LLC must have at least one member. (Ky. Rev. Stat. § § 275.015 and 275.020)
Naming requirements:	• A Kentucky LLC's name must contain the words "limited liability company" or "limited company" or the abbreviations "LLC" or "LC." A professional LLC's name must contain the words "professional limited liability company" or "professional limited company" or the abbreviations "PLLC" or "PLC." The word "Limited" may be abbreviated as "Ltd." and the word "Company" may be abbreviated as "Co." (Ky. Rev. Stat. § 275.100)
Effective date of organization:	• A Kentucky LLC's existence begins when the articles of organization are filed, or at the specified delayed effective date as set forth in the document. (Ky. Rev. Stat. § 275.060)
Filing requirements:	• The articles of organization must include: (1) the LLC's name; (2) the address of the initial registered office and the name of its initial registered agent; (3) the mailing address of the initial principal office; and (4) a statement indicating whether the LLC is managed by managers or its members. The term of a limited liability company shall be perpetual unless a period of duration other than perpetual is set forth in the articles of organization. (Ky. Rev. Stat. § 275.025)
Fees—Organization and Annual:	• The fee for filing articles of organization is $40. The filing fee for an application for certificate of authority as a foreign LLC is $90. The fee for filing the annual report is $15. (Ky. Rev. Stat. § 275.055)
Recordkeeping:	• An LLC must compile and maintain: (1) a list of members' and managers' names and addresses; (2) a copy of the articles of organization, including any amendments and any executed powers of attorney; (3) any written operating agreements; (4) copies of the LLC's federal, state, and local income tax returns and financial statements for the last three years; and (5) statements containing information about the members' capital contributions and agreements to contribute capital, events triggering additional contributions, and events causing dissolution. (Ky. Rev. Stat. § 275.185)
Annual reporting:	• An annual report is required and must be filed between January 1 and June 30 of each year. (Ky. Rev. Stat. § 275.190)
Management:	• Management is vested in members, unless otherwise provided. (Ky. Rev. Stat. § 275.165)

Membership rights and obligations:

- A member or manager is not personally liable for a debt, obligation, or liability of the LLC, under a judgment, decree or order of a court, or in any other matter, whether arising in contract, tort or otherwise, solely by reason of being a member or manager of the LLC. However, under a written operating agreement or under another written agreement, a member or manager may agree to be obligated personally for any of the debts, obligations, and liabilities of the LLC. If a member fails to make a required contribution, even in the event of death, disability or other reason, the member is obligated, at the option of the LLC, to contribute cash equal to that portion of the fair market value of the stated contribution that has not been made. A member or manager who assents to a wrongful distribution is personally liable to the LLC for the amount of the distribution that was wrongfully made. Each member or manager held liable is entitled to contribution from each member who received a wrongful distribution. (Ky. Rev. Stat. § § 275.150, 275.200 and 275.230)

Piercing the corporate veil:

- The Act has no express provision that concerns piercing the corporate veil.

Contributions:

- Contributions may consist of cash, property, or services, or a promise to contribute the same. (Ky. Rev. Stat. § 275.195)

Distributions:

- Distributions, profits and losses are allocated on the basis of each member's relative capital accounts, unless otherwise provided. (Ky. Rev. Stat. § § 275.205 and 275.210)

Resignation of member:

- A member may not resign from the LLC without the consent of all other members, unless otherwise provided in the operating agreement. (Ky. Rev. Stat. § 275.280)

Transfer of LLC interest:

- A member's LLC interest is assignable in whole or in part, unless otherwise provided. Consent of a majority-in-interest of the members is required for an assignee to become a member, unless otherwise provided. (Ky. Rev. Stat. § § 275.255 and 275.265)

Dissolution:	• An LLC is dissolved: (1) upon the expiration of the term, if any, set in the operating agreement or upon the occurrence of events specified in the articles of organization or operating agreement; (2) upon the consent of a majority-in-interest of the members, unless otherwise provided; (3) upon a decree of judicial dissolution; or (4) upon an administrative dissolution. (Ky. Rev. Stat. § § 275.285, 275.290 and 275.295)
Mergers and consolidation	• Mergers are expressly provided for by statute. (Ky. Rev. Stat. § 275.345)

¶ 1021
Louisiana

Name of act:	• Limited Liability Company Law, La. Rev. Stat. § 12:1301 to La. Rev. Stat. § 12:1369.
Federal tax classification:	• The LLC statute is flexible. Any "business entity" not required to be treated as a "corporation" for federal tax purposes under Reg. § 301.7701-2 may choose its classification under Reg. § 301.7701-3.
State tax treatment:	• State tax classification follows federal. Thus, Louisiana LLCs and foreign LLCs doing business in Louisiana are treated as partnerships or disregarded as entities, unless classified as corporations for federal tax purposes. However, the federal check-the-box election is irrelevant to a determination of whether an entity is subject to the state franchise tax. (La. Rev. Stat. § 12:1368)
Securities treatment:	• The Louisiana Act does not expressly provide for the treatment of an LLC interest as a security.
Limited liability partnerships:	• The formation of limited liability partnerships is expressly provided by statute. (La. Rev. Stat. § 9:3431)
Professional LLCs:	• Professional LLCs are permitted impliedly. No prohibitions concerning lawful businesses are set forth in the statutory provisions.
Foreign LLCs:	• Foreign LLCs are expressly permitted by statute. Laws of the formation jurisdiction govern organization, internal affairs and the liability of its members and managers that arise solely out of their positions as members and managers. (La. Rev. Stat. § 12:1342)
Formation:	• A Louisiana LLC must be formed by one or more persons capable of contracting. The LLC must have one or more members. (La. Rev. Stat. § § 12:1301 and 12:1304)

Naming requirements:	• The name of each limited liability company must contain the words "limited liability company," or the abbreviations "L.C." or "L.L.C.". (La. Rev. Stat. § 12:1306)
Effective date of organization:	• Unless a delayed effective date is specified, the LLC's existence begins on the date and at the time when the articles of organization are filed. (La. Rev. Stat. § 12:1304)
Filing requirements:	• The articles of organization must set forth: (1) the LLC's name; and (2) its purpose. An initial report is required and must be signed by each person who signed the articles of organization, or by his duly authorized agent. The initial report must set forth: (1) the full name and municipal address of each of its registered agents; (2) the location and municipal address of the LLC's registered office; (3) a notarized affidavit of acknowledgement and acceptance signed by each of its registered agents; and (4) the names and municipal addresses of the managers or members. (La. Rev. Stat. § 12:1305)
Fees—Organization and Annual:	• The fee for filing articles of organization is $75. The fee for filing a foreign LLC certificate of authority is $125. The fee for filing the annual report is $25. (La. Rev. Stat. § 12:1364)
Recordkeeping:	• The LLC must keep at its registered office: (1) the full name and last known business address of each member and manager; (2) copies or records setting forth the relative voting rights of the members; (3) federal and state tax returns for the last three years; (4) a copy of the articles of organization, including any amendments; (5) a copy of any operating agreement which is in writing (if any); and (6) financial statements for the last three years. (La. Rev. Stat. § 12:1319)
Annual reporting:	• An annual report is required. (La. Rev. Stat. § 12:1308.1)
Management:	• Management is vested in the members, unless otherwise provided. (La. Rev. Stat. § 12:1311)

¶1021

Membership rights and obligations:	• LLC members are not liable for any debt, obligation, or liability of the LLC, whether under a judgment, decree, or order of a court, or in any other manner, except in instances when the Act provides otherwise. If a member does not make a required contribution, the member or the member's personal representative is obligated, even in the event of death, disability, or any other reason, to contribute cash equal to that portion of the value of the contribution that was not made or forfeit his entire membership interest. Members or managers are jointly and severally liable to the LLC for the amount of any wrongful distribution. (La. Rev. Stat. §§ 12:1314, 12:1322 and 12:1328)
Piercing the corporate veil:	• The Act has no express provision that concerns piercing the corporate veil.
Contributions:	• Contributions may consist of cash, property, services, a promissory note or other promise to contribute the same. (La. Rev. Stat. § 12:1321)
Distributions:	• Distributions, profits and losses are allocated equally among the members, unless otherwise provided. (La. Rev. Stat. §§ 12:1323 and 12:1324)
Resignation of member:	• If an LLC has been constituted for a term, a member may withdraw without the consent of the other members prior to the expiration of the term, provided he has just cause. A member of an LLC not entered into for a term may withdraw or resign at the time or upon the happening of an event specified in a written operating agreement. If not specified in the operating agreement, thirty days' written notice is required. (La. Rev. Stat. § 12:1325)
Transfer of LLC interest:	• A member's LLC interest is assignable in whole or in part, unless otherwise provided. Unanimous consent is required for an assignee to become a member, unless otherwise provided. (La. Rev. Stat. §§ 12:1330 and 12:1332)
Dissolution:	• An LLC is dissolved: (1) upon the occurrence of events specified in writing in the articles or operating agreement; (2) upon a majority vote of the members; (3) upon a judicial or administrative dissolution; or (4) as otherwise provided in the articles or written operating agreement. (La. Rev. Stat. § 12:1334)
Mergers and consolidations:	• Mergers or consolidations are expressly permitted by statute. (La. Rev. Stat. § 12:1357)

¶ 1022
Maine

Name of act:	• Maine Limited Liability Company Act, Me. Rev. Stat. tit. 31, § 601 to Me. Rev. Stat. ch. 13, § 762.
Federal tax classification:	• The LLC statute is flexible. Any "business entity" not required to be treated as a "corporation" for federal tax purposes under Reg. § 301.7701-2 may choose its classification under Reg. § 301.7701-3.
State tax treatment:	• State tax classification follows federal. Thus, Maine LLCs and foreign LLCs doing business in Maine are treated as partnerships, unless classified as corporations or disregarded as entities for federal tax purposes. (Me. Rev. Stat. tit. 31, § 761)
Securities treatment:	• The sale of interests in LLCs organized under Maine law is exempt from securities registration if the number of security holders does not exceed ten at the time of sale. In some circumstances, an LLC with as many as 25 securities holders may be exempt as a consequence of the sale. (Code Me. R. 02-029-536)
Limited liability partnerships:	• The formation of limited liability partnerships is expressly permitted by statute. (Me. Rev. Stat. tit. 31, § 801)
Limited liability limited partnerships:	• The formation of limited liability limited partnerships is expressly permitted by statute. (Me. Rev. Stat. tit. 31, § 59a, effective July 1, 2007)
Professional LLCs:	• Professional LLCs are expressly permitted by statute. (Me. Rev. Stat. tit. 31, § 611)
Foreign LLCs:	• Foreign LLCs are expressly permitted by statute. Laws of the formation jurisdiction govern the LLC's organization, internal affairs, and the liability of its members. (Me. Rev. Stat. tit. 31, § 711)
Formation:	• One or more persons may form an LLC. An LLC must consist of one or more members. (Me. Rev. Stat. tit. 31, § 621)
Naming requirements:	• The LLC's name must include the words "Limited Liability Company." (Me. Rev. Stat. tit. 31, § 603)
Effective date of organization:	• An LLC is formed when the articles of organization are filed with the secretary of state. (Me. Rev. Stat. tit. 31, § 622)

Filing requirements:	• The articles of organization must include: (1) the LLC's name; (2) the address of its registered office and the name and address of its registered agent; (3) if management of the LLC is vested in a manager or managers, a statement to that effect, including the number of managers permitted and, if the initial managers have been selected, their names and addresses; and (4) any other matters the members decide to include. (Me. Rev. Stat. tit. 31, § 622)
Fees—Organization and Annual:	• The fee for filing articles of organization is $175. The fee for filing a foreign LLC application for a certificate of authority is $250. The fee for filing the annual report for a domestic LLC is $85. The fee for filing the report for a foreign LLC is $150. (Me. Rev. Stat. tit. 31, § 751)
Recordkeeping:	• The LLC must compile and maintain: (1) a list of past and present members' and managers' names and addresses; (2) a copy of the articles of organization, amendments to the articles and related executed powers of attorney; (3) copies of federal, state, and local tax returns and financial statements for the six most recent years; (4) copies of effective operating agreements, amendments and copies of operating agreements no longer in effect; and (5) a writing that sets forth out the amount of cash and the agreed value of property to be contributed by each member, any event which will cause the LLC to dissolve and its business affairs to be wound up and any other writings prepared pursuant to an operating agreement. (Me. Rev. Stat. tit. 31, § 655)
Annual reporting:	• An annual report is required. (Me. Rev. Stat. tit. 31, § 757)
Management:	• Management is vested in members, unless otherwise provided. (Me. Rev. Stat. tit. 31, § 651)

Membership rights and obligations:	• A member is not personally obligated for any debt, obligation or liability of the LLC, whether arising in contract, tort or otherwise, solely by reason of being a member of the LLC. If a member does not make a promised contribution, the member is obligated, even in the event of death, disability, or any other reason, to contribute cash equal to that portion of the value of the contribution that was not made. The option of the LLC is in addition to, and not in lieu of, other rights, including the right to specific performance. A member or manager who assents to a wrongful distribution is liable to the LLC for that portion of the distribution that was wrongful. (Me. Rev. Stat. tit. 31, § § 645, 662 and 676)
Piercing the corporate veil:	• The exceptions under common law applying to the limited liability of business corporation shareholders apply also to members of an LLC. (Me. Rev. Stat. tit. 31, § 645)
Contributions:	• Contributions may consist of cash, tangible or intangible property, services rendered or a promissory note or other obligation to contribute the same. (Me. Rev. Stat. tit. 31, § 661)
Distributions:	• Distributions are allocated equally among the members, unless otherwise provided. Profits and losses are allocated on a per capita basis, unless otherwise provided. (Me. Rev. Stat. tit. 31, § § 663 and § 671)
Resignation of member:	• Thirty days' written notice is required prior to resignation, unless otherwise provided. (Me. Rev. Stat. tit. 31, § 692)
Transfer of LLC interest:	• A member's LLC interest is assignable in whole or in part, unless otherwise provided. Unanimous consent is required for an assignee to become a member, unless otherwise provided. (Me. Rev. Stat. tit. 31, § § 685 and 687)
Dissolution:	• An LLC will be dissolved upon: (1) the happening of events specified in an LLC operating agreement or articles of organization; (2) the written consent of all the LLC members; or (3) entry of a decree of judicial dissolution. (Me. Rev. Stat. tit. 31, § § 701 and 702)
Mergers and consolidations:	• Mergers or consolidations are expressly provided by statute. (Me. Rev. Stat. tit. 31, § 741)

¶ 1023

Maryland

Name of act:	• Maryland Limited Liability Company Act, Md. Code Corps. & Ass'ns § 4A-101 to § 4A-1103.
Federal tax classification:	• The LLC statute is flexible. Any "business entity" not required to be treated as a "corporation" for federal tax purposes under Reg. § 301.7701-2 may choose its classification under Reg. § 301.7701-3.
State tax treatment:	• State tax classification follows federal. Thus, Maryland LLCs and foreign LLCs doing business in Maryland are treated as partnerships or disregarded as entities, unless classified as corporations for federal tax purposes.
Securities treatment:	• The Maryland Act does not expressly provide for the treatment of an LLC interest as a security.
Limited liability partnerships:	• The formation of limited liability partnerships is expressly provided for by statute. (Md. Code Corps. & Ass'ns § § 9-803 and 9-901)
Limited liability limited partnerships:	• Limited Liability Limited Partnerships are expressly provided for by statute. (Md. Code Corps. & Ass'ns § 10-805)
Professional LLCs:	• Professional LLCs are expressly permitted by statute, subject to compliance with other state regulatory provisions. (Md. Code Corps. & Ass'ns § 4A-101 and 4A-203.1)
Foreign LLCs:	• Foreign LLCs are expressly permitted by statute. Laws of the formation jurisdiction govern the LLC's organization, internal affairs, and the liability of its members. (Md. Code Corps. & Ass'ns § 4A-1001)
Formation:	• Any person may form an LLC. Single-member LLCs are permitted. (Md. Code Corps. & Ass'ns § § 4A-101 and 4A-202)
Naming requirements:	• A Maryland LLC must have in its name the words "limited liability company" or the abbreviation "L.L.C.," "LLC," "L.C.," or "LC." (Md. Code Corps. & Ass'ns § 4A-208)
Effective date of organization:	• An LLC is formed when the articles of organization are accepted or recorded, or at a later time specified therein. (Md. Code Corps. & Ass'ns § 4A-202)
Filing requirements:	• The articles of organization must include: (1) the LLC's name; (2) its purpose; (3) the address of its principal office; (4) the name and address of its registered agent; and (5) any other provision the members elect to set forth. (Md. Code Corps. & Ass'ns § 4A-204)

Fees—Organization and Annual:	• The filing fee for the articles of organization is $100. The fee for filing an application for foreign LLC registration is $100. The fee for filing the annual report is $300.
Recordkeeping:	• The LLC must compile and maintain: (1) a list of members' and managers' names and addresses; (2) the LLC's federal, state, and local tax returns; (3) a copy of the certificate of organization, including any amendments; (4) the written operating agreement (if any), including any amendments; (5) information regarding the state of the business and the LLC's financial condition; and (6) and any other information that is reasonable and just. (Md. Code Corps. & Ass'ns § 4A-406)
Annual reporting:	• An annual report is required.
Management:	• Management is vested in the members, unless otherwise provided. (Md. Code Corps. & Ass'ns § 4A-403)
Membership rights and obligations:	• No member will be personally liable for the obligations of the LLC, whether arising in contract, tort, or otherwise, solely by reason of being a member of the LLC. If a member fails to make a required contribution, even in the event of the member's death, disability or other change in circumstances, the member is obligated, at the option of the LLC, to contribute cash equal to that portion of the value of that portion of the contribution that has not been made. An operating agreement may also provide that a member who fails to make a capital contribution or other payment shall be subject to specified remedies or consequences. LLCs are subject to the Maryland Uniform Fraudulent Conveyance Act. Conveyances by an LLC that render it insolvent are fraudulent unless they represent reasonable compensation to the members or are in exchange for fair consideration to the LLC. (Md. Code Corps. & Ass'ns § § 4A-301 and 4A-502)
Piercing the corporate veil:	• The Act has no express provision with respect to piercing the corporate veil.
Contributions:	• Contributions may consist of cash, property, or services, or a promise to contribute the same. (Md. Code Corps. & Ass'ns § 4A-501)
Distributions:	• Distributions are allocated based on members' relative rights to share in LLC profits, unless otherwise provided. Profits and losses are allocated based on members' capital interests, unless otherwise provided. (Md. Code Corps. & Ass'ns § 4A-503)

Resignation of member:	• Six months' written notice is required prior to resignation, unless otherwise provided. (Md. Code Corps. & Ass'ns § 4A-605)
Transfer of LLC interest:	• A member's LLC interest is assignable in whole or in part, unless otherwise provided. Unanimous consent is required for an assignee to become a member, unless otherwise provided. (Md. Code Corps. & Ass'ns § § 4A-603 and 4A-604)
Dissolution:	• An LLC is dissolved: (1) at the time or upon the happening of events specified in the articles of organization or the operating agreement; (2) at the time specified by the unanimous consent of the members; (3) upon judicial dissolution; or (4) unless otherwise provided, at the time the LLC has had no members for a period of 90 consecutive days. (Md. Code Corps. & Ass'ns § § 4A-902 and 4A-903)
Mergers and consolidations:	• Mergers are permitted expressly by statute, unless otherwise provided. (Md. Code Corps. & Ass'ns § 4A-701)

¶ 1024

Massachusetts

Name of act:	• Massachusetts Limited Liability Company Act, Mass. Gen. Laws ch. 156C, § 1 to Mass. Gen. Laws ch. 156C, § 69.
Federal tax classification:	• The LLC statute is flexible. Any "business entity" not required to be treated as a "corporation" for federal tax purposes under Reg. § 301.7701-2 may choose its classification under Reg. § 301.7701-3.
State tax treatment:	• State tax classification follows federal. Thus, Massachusetts LLCs and foreign LLCs doing business in Massachusetts are treated as partnerships, unless classified as corporations for federal tax purposes. Although Massachusetts LLCs must have two or more members, non-Massachusetts single-member LLCs are disregarded as entities, unless classified otherwise for federal tax purposes.
Securities treatment:	• The Massachusetts Act does not expressly provide for the treatment of an LLC interest as a security.
Limited liability partnerships:	• Limited Liability Partnerships are expressly permitted by statute. (Mass. Gen. Laws ch. 108A, § 45)
Professional LLCs:	• Professional LLCs are expressly permitted, subject to compliance with other state regulatory provisions. (Mass. Gen. Laws ch. 156C, § 6)

Foreign LLCs:	• Foreign LLCs are expressly permitted by statute. Laws of the formation jurisdiction govern organization, internal affairs and the liability and authority of members and managers. (Mass. Gen. Laws ch. 156C, § 47)
Formation:	• One or more persons may organize an LLC. Single-member LLCs are permitted. (Mass. Gen. Laws ch. 156C, § § 2 and 12)
Naming requirements:	• The name of an LLC must include the words "limited liability company" or "limited company" or end with the abbreviation "L.L.C.", "L.C.", "LLC" or "LC". (Mass. Gen. Laws ch. 156C, § 3)
Effective date of organization:	• The LLC's existence begins on the date when the initial certificate of organization is filed with the office of the secretary of state, unless a delayed effective date is specified. (Mass. Gen. Laws ch. 156C, § 12)
Filing requirements:	• The certificate of organization must include: (1) the LLC's name; (2) the street address of the registered office and the name of the registered agent at that office; (3) the latest date on which the LLC will dissolve, if a specific date is set; (4) if management of the LLC is vested in one or more managers, a statement to that effect; (5) the name of any person in addition to managers who has the authority to execute and file documents with the secretary of state; (6) the general character of the LLC's business; (7) if desired, the names of one or more persons authorized to execute, acknowledge, deliver and record any recordable instrument purporting to affect an interest in real property; and (8) any other matters the authorized persons determine should be included. (Mass. Gen. Laws ch. 156C, § 12)
Fees—Organization and Annual:	• The fee for filing the certificate of organization is $500. The fee for filing foreign LLC registration application is $500. The fee for filing an annual report is $500. (Mass. Gen. Laws ch. 156C, § § 12 and 48)

Recordkeeping:	• The LLC must compile and maintain: (1) a current list of the full names and last known business or residence address of each member and manager; (2) a copy of the certificate of organization, including any amendments, and executed copies of any powers of attorney; (3) copies of federal, state and local income tax returns for the three most recent tax years; (4) a copy of any written operating agreement and any financial statements of the company for the three most recent years; and (5) unless contained in a written operating agreement, a writing containing information regarding the value of each member's contribution made to the LLC, records of the times at which or the events upon which any additional contributions are agreed to be made, any right of a member to receive or a manager to make distributions to a member, and any events upon which the LLC is to be dissolved and its business wound up. (Mass. Gen. Laws ch. 156C, § 9)
Annual reporting:	• An annual report is required. (Mass. Gen. Laws ch. 156C, § 12)
Management:	• Management is vested in the members, unless otherwise provided. (Mass. Gen. Laws ch. 156C, § 24)
Membership rights and obligations:	• Except as otherwise provided, LLC members and managers are not personally liable for any debt, obligation, or liability of the LLC, whether arising in tort, contract or otherwise. If a member fails to make a required contribution, even in the event of the member's death, disability or other change in circumstances, the member is obligated, at the option of the LLC, to contribute cash equal to that portion of the value, as stated in the LLC records, of the stated contribution that has not been fulfilled. An operating agreement may also provide that a member who fails to make a capital contribution or other payment shall be subject to specified remedies or consequences. A member or manager who votes or assents to a wrongful distribution is personally liable to the LLC for the amount of the distribution that exceeds the amount that could have been rightfully distributed. (Mass. Gen. Laws ch. 156C, § § 22, 28 and 35)
Piercing the corporate veil:	• The Act has no express provision that concerns piercing the corporate veil.
Contributions:	• Contributions may consist of cash, property, services rendered, a promissory note or other obligation to contribute the same. (Mass. Gen. Laws ch. 156C, § 27)

Distributions:	• Distributions, profits and losses are allocated based on the value of the contributions made by each member, unless otherwise provided. (Mass. Gen. Laws ch. 156C, §§ 29 and 30)
Resignation of member:	• A member may withdraw by giving six months' written notice, unless otherwise provided. (Mass. Gen. Laws ch. 156C, § 36)
Transfer of LLC interest:	• A member's LLC interest is assignable in whole or in part, unless otherwise provided. Unanimous consent is required for an assignee to become a member, unless otherwise provided. (Mass. Gen. Laws ch. 156C, §§ 39 and 41)
Dissolution:	• An LLC is dissolved: (1) at the time specified in an operating agreement; (2) upon the happening of events specified in an operating agreement; (3) upon the written consent of all the members; (4) when an event of dissociation occurs to a member, unless the business of the LLC is continued within 90 days by the consent of all the remaining members, or as otherwise provided; or (5) upon a judicial dissolution. (Mass. Gen. Laws ch. 156C, §§ 43 and 44)
Mergers and consolidations:	• Mergers or consolidations are permitted expressly by statute. (Mass. Gen. Laws ch. 156C, § 60)

¶ 1025
Michigan

Name of act:	• Michigan Limited Liability Company Act, Mich. Comp. Laws § 450.4101 to Mich. Comp. Laws § 450.5200.
Federal tax classification:	• The Michigan LLC Act is flexible. Any "business entity" not required to be treated as a "corporation" for federal tax purposes under Reg. § 301.7701-2 may choose its classification under Reg. § 301.7701-3.
State tax treatment:	• State tax classification follows federal. Thus, Michigan LLCs and foreign LLCs doing business in Michigan are treated as partnerships or disregarded as entities, unless classified as corporations for federal tax purposes.
Securities treatment:	• An interest in a limited liability company is a security to the same extent as an interest in a corporation, partnership, or limited partnership is a security. (Mich. Comp. Laws § 450.5103)
Limited liability partnerships:	• The formation of limited liability partnerships is expressly provided for by statute. (Mich. Comp. Laws § 449.44)

Limited liability limited partnerships:	• There are no limited liability limited partnership statutes. A limited partnership may elect to become a limited liability limited partnership by registering in each Michigan county where it intends to do business and registering with the state Corporation and Land Development Bureau as a limited liability partnership.
Professional LLCs:	• Professional LLCs are expressly permitted by statute. (Mich. Comp. Laws § 450.4901)
Foreign LLCs:	• Foreign LLCs are expressly permitted by statute. Laws of the formation jurisdiction govern the LLC's organization and internal affairs subject to the Michigan state constitution. (Mich. Comp. Laws § 450.5001)
Formation:	• A Michigan LLC may be formed by one or more persons. An LLC may have one or more members. (Mich. Comp. Laws §§ 450.4202 and 450.4501)
Naming requirements:	• A Michigan LLC must have in its name the words "limited liability company" or the abbreviation "L.L.C." or "L.C.," with or without periods or other punctuation. (Mich. Comp. Laws § 450.4204)
Effective date of organization:	• A Michigan LLC exists as of the date on which the articles of organization are filed, unless a later effective time is set forth therein that is not later than 90 days after the date of delivery. (Mich. Comp. Laws § 450.4104)
Filing requirements:	• The articles of organization must include: (1) the LLC's name; (2) its purpose; (3) its duration, if other than perpetual; (4) the name of its agent and the address of its registered office; and (5) a statement indicating that the LLC is managed by managers, if applicable. (Mich. Comp. Laws § 450.4203)
Fees—Organization and Annual:	• The fee for filing the articles of organization is $50. The fee for filing a foreign LLC certificate of authority application is $50. The fee for filing articles of organization for a professional LLC is $75. The fee for filing the annual statement is $25. (Mich. Comp. Laws § 450.5101)
Recordkeeping:	• The LLC must compile and maintain: (1) a list of the members' and managers' names and last known addresses; (2) federal, state and local tax returns and information for the last three years; (3) copies of the articles, including any amendments; (4) copies of operating agreements; (5) financial statements for the last three years; and (6) copies of records indicating the members' relative distribution shares and relative voting rights. (Mich. Comp. Laws § 450.4213)

¶1025

Annual reporting:	• An annual report is required and must be filed on or before February 15. (Mich. Comp. Laws § 450.4207)
Management:	• Management is vested in members, unless otherwise provided. (Mich. Comp. Laws § 450.4401)
Membership rights and obligations:	• A member is not liable for the acts, debts or obligations of the LLC. If a member fails to make a required contribution, even in the event of the member's death, disability or other change in circumstances, the member is obligated, at the option of the LLC, to contribute cash equal to that portion of value of the stated contribution that has not been made. A member who knowingly receives a wrongful distribution is jointly and severally liable to the LLC for the amount of the distribution that was wrongful. (Mich. Comp. Laws §§ 450.4302, 450.4308 and 450.4501)
Piercing the corporate veil:	• The Act has no express provision that concerns piercing the corporate veil.
Contributions:	• Contributions may consist of any tangible or intangible property or benefit, including cash, property, or services performed, or a promise to contribute the same. (Mich. Comp. Laws § 450.4301)
Distributions:	• Distributions are allocated based on the relative value of the members' capital contributions, as adjusted for any withdrawals, unless otherwise provided. The Michigan Act contains no express provision that addresses sharing profits and losses. (Mich. Comp. Laws § 450.4303)
Resignation of member:	• A member may withdraw from an LLC only as provided in the operating agreement. (Mich. Comp. Laws § 450.4509)
Transfer of LLC interest:	• A member's LLC interest is assignable in whole or in part, unless otherwise provided. Unanimous consent is required for an assignee to become a member, unless otherwise provided. (Mich. Comp. Laws §§ 450.4505 and 450.4506)
Dissolution:	• An LLC is dissolved: (1) at the time specified in the articles of organization; (2) upon the happening of events specified in the articles of organization or the operating agreement; (3) by the unanimous consent of the members; or (4) upon the entry of a judicial decree. (Mich. Comp. Laws §§ 450.4801 and 450.4802)
Mergers and consolidations:	• Mergers are permitted expressly by statute. (Mich. Comp. Laws § 450.4701)

¶1025

¶ 1026

Minnesota

Name of act:	• Minnesota Limited Liability Company Act, Minn. Stat. § 322B.01 to Minn. Stat. § 322B.960.
Federal tax classification:	• The LLC statute is flexible. Any "business entity" not required to be treated as a "corporation" for federal tax purposes under Reg. § 301.7701-2 may choose its classification under Reg. § 301.7701-3.
State tax treatment:	• State tax classification follows federal. Thus, Minnesota LLCs and foreign LLCs doing business in Minnesota are treated as partnerships or disregarded as entities, unless classified as corporations for federal tax purposes.
Securities treatment:	• The Minnesota Act does not expressly provide for the treatment of an LLC interest as a security.
Limited liability partnerships	• The formation of limited liability partnerships is permitted expressly by statute. (Minn. Stat. § 323A.10-01)
Limited liability limited partnerships	• Limited Liability Limited Partnerships are expressly permitted by statute. (Minn. Stat. § 321.102(9))
Professional LLCs:	• Professional LLCs are expressly permitted by statute, subject to compliance by other state regulatory provisions. (Minn. Stat. § 319B.02)
Foreign LLCs:	• Foreign LLCs are expressly permitted by statute. Laws of the formation jurisdiction govern organization, internal affairs and the liability of its members. (Minn. Stat. § 322B.90)
Formation:	• One or more persons may organize an LLC. One or more members are required to form an LLC. (Minn. Stat. § § 322B.105 and 322B.11)
Naming requirements:	• The name of an LLC must contain the words "limited liability company" or the abbreviation "LLC". It must not contain the word "corporation" or "incorporated" or the abbreviation of either. The name must not contain a word or phrase that indicates or implies that the LLC was organized for a purpose other than a legal business purpose. Subject to certain exceptions, the LLC name must be distinguishable on the records from the name of any other foreign or domestic LLC, any foreign or domestic corporation, or any foreign or domestic limited partnership. (Minn. Stat. § 322B.12)
Effective date of organization:	• The LLC's existence begins when the articles of organization are properly filed with the secretary of state. (Minn. Stat. § 322B.175)

Filing requirements:

- The articles of organization must include: (1) the LLC's name; (2) the address of the registered office of the LLC and the name of its registered agent, if any, at that address; (3) the name and address of each organizer; and (4) the LLC's duration if not perpetual. (Minn. Stat. § 322B.115)

Fees—Organization and Annual:

- The fee for filing articles of organization is $160. The fee for filing foreign LLC registration application is $185. There is no fee for filing the annual registration. (Minn. Stat. § § 322B.175, 322B.91 and 322B.960)

Recordkeeping:

- The LLC must compile and maintain: (1) a current list of the full name and last-known business, residence or mailing address of each member, governor and chief manager; (2) a current list of the full name and last-known business, residence or mailing address of each assignee of financial rights other than a secured party, and a description of the rights assigned; (3) copies of the articles of organization, including any amendments; (4) copies of any effective written operating agreement or bylaws; (5) copies of federal, state and local income tax returns and company reports for the three most recent tax years; (6) financial statements; (7) records of all proceedings of members for the last three years; (8) records of all proceedings of the board of governor for the last three years; (9) reports made to members generally within the last three years; (10) member control agreements; (11) a statement of all contributions accepted; (12) a statement of all contribution allowance agreements made; (13) an explanation of any restatement of value; (14) any written consents obtained from members; and (15) a copy of agreements, contracts or other arrangements. (Minn. Stat. § 322B.373)

Annual reporting:

- Annual registration with the secretary of state is required. (Minn. Stat. § 322B.960)

Management:

- A Minnesota LLC must have a chief manager and a treasurer. Management is by or under the direction of a board of governors. (Minn. Stat. § § 322B.606 and 322B.67)

Membership rights and obligations:	• Members are not personally liable for the acts, debts, obligations or liabilities of the LLC. If a member fails to make a required contribution, the member is obligated to contribute cash equal to that portion of the value of the contribution that has not been made. A member who receives a wrongful distribution is liable to the LLC only to the extent that the distribution exceeds the amount that properly could have been paid. (Minn. Stat. §§ 322B.303, 322B.42 and 322B.55)
Piercing the corporate veil:	• The conditions and circumstances under which the corporate veil of a corporation may be pierced under Minnesota law also apply to LLCs. (Minn. Stat. § 322B.303)
Contributions:	• Contributions may consist of cash, property, services rendered, or a written obligation to contribute the same. (Minn. Stat. § 322B.40)
Distributions:	• Unless otherwise provided, distributions, profits and losses are allocated among the members, and among classes and series of members, in proportion to the value of the contributions of the members reflected in the required records. (Minn. Stat. §§ 322B.326 and 322B.50)
Resignation of member:	• A member may resign at any time. (Minn. Stat. § 322B.306)
Transfer of LLC interest:	• A member has the power to transfer all or part of a member's financial rights, unless otherwise provided, and all or part of the member's governance rights, unless otherwise provided. Unanimous consent is required for an assignee of governance rights to participate in the management and affairs of the LLC. (Minn. Stat. §§ 322B.306, 322B.31 and 322B.313)
Dissolution:	• An LLC is dissolved: (1) at the expiration of the period fixed for duration; (2) upon the action of the organizers; (3) upon the action of the members; (4) unless otherwise provided, when an event of dissociation occurs to a member, unless there is one remaining member or a new member is admitted, and the business of the LLC is continued by the consent of all remaining members within 90 days or as provided in the articles of organization, or if the membership of the last or sole member terminates and the legal representative of that last or sole member causes the LLC to admit at least one new member; (5) upon judicial dissolution or upon administrative termination. (Minn. Stat. §§ 322B.80, 322B.833 and 322B.960)
Mergers and consolidations:	• Mergers are permitted expressly by statute. (Minn. Stat. § 322B.70)

¶1026

¶ 1027
Mississippi

Name of act:	• Mississippi Limited Liability Company Act, Miss. Code § 79-29-101 to Miss. Code § 79-29-1204.
Federal tax classification:	• The LLC statute is flexible. Any "business entity" not required to be treated as a "corporation" for federal tax purposes under Reg. § 301.7701-2 may choose its classification under Reg. § 301.7701-3.
State tax treatment:	• State tax classification follows federal. Thus, Mississippi LLCs and foreign LLCs doing business in Mississippi are treated as partnerships or disregarded as entities, unless classified as corporations for federal tax purposes. (Miss. Code § 79-29-112)
Securities treatment:	• The Mississippi Act does not expressly provide for the treatment of an LLC interest as a security.
Limited liability partnerships:	• The formation of limited liability partnerships is expressly provided for by statute. (Miss. Code § 79-12-87)
Professional LLCs:	• Professional LLCs are expressly permitted by statute, subject to compliance by other state regulatory provisions. (Miss. Code § § 79-29-901 and 79-29-904)
Foreign LLCs:	• Foreign LLCs are expressly permitted by statute. Laws of the formation jurisdiction govern organization, internal affairs and the liability of members and managers. (Miss. Code § 79-29-1001)
Formation:	• A Mississippi LLC may be formed by one or more persons and may have one or more members. (Miss. Code § 79-29-103)
Naming requirements:	• The name of each LLC must contain the words "limited liability company," or the abbreviation "L.L.C." or "LLC" and must be distinguishable from the record name of any domestic or foreign corporation, nonprofit corporation, limited partnership or LLC registered in the state of Mississippi. (Miss. Code § 79-29-104)
Effective date of organization:	• Unless a delayed effective date (no later than 90 days after filing) is specified, the LLC's existence begins at the date and time the certificate of formation is filed. (Miss. Code § 79-29-201)

Filing requirements:	• The certificate of formation must include: (1) the LLC's name; (2) the name and address of the registered agent for service of process; (3) the address of the registered office; (4) whether the LLC is to have a specific date of dissolution, and if so, when that date will be; (5) if full or partial management of the LLC is vested in a manager or managers, a statement to that effect; and (6) any other matters the members decide to include. (Miss. Code § 79-29-201)
Fees—Organization and Annual:	• The fee for filing certificate of formation is $50. The fee for filing foreign LLC registration application is $250. Annual registration is not required. (Miss. Code § 79-29-1203)
Recordkeeping:	• The LLC must compile and maintain: (1) a list of the members' and managers' names and addresses; (2) a copy of the certificate of formation, including any amendments, together with executed copies of any powers of attorney; (3) copies of any then effective limited liability company agreement; and (4) information regarding the amount of cash and a description and statement of the agreed value of any other property or services contributed, or promised to be contributed in the future, by each member, the times or events upon which additional contributions agreed to by each member are to be made, and any events upon the happening of which the LLC is to be dissolved and its affairs wound up. (Miss. Code § 79-29-107)
Annual reporting:	• No annual report is required.
Management:	• Management is vested in the members, unless otherwise provided. (Miss. Code § 79-29-302)
Membership rights and obligations:	• Members are not liable for any debt, obligation, or liability of the LLC, whether under a judgment, decree, or order of a court, or in any other manner. If a member does not make a promised contribution, the member is obligated, even in the event of death, disability, or any other reason, to contribute cash equal to that portion of the value of the contribution that was not made. A certificate of formation or LLC agreement may also provide that a member who fails to make a capital contribution or other payment shall be subject to specified remedies or consequences. A member or manager who assents to a wrongful distribution is liable to the LLC for that portion of the distribution that was wrongful. (Miss. Code § § 79-29-305, 79-29-502 and 79-29-606)
Piercing the corporate veil:	• The Act has no express provision that concerns piercing the corporate veil.

¶1027

Contributions:	• Contributions may consist of cash, property, services rendered, a promissory note or other obligation to contribute the same. (Miss. Code § 79-29-501)
Distributions:	• Distributions, profits and losses are allocated based on the value of the contributions made by each member to the extent they had been received by the LLC and not yet returned, unless otherwise provided. (Miss. Code § § 79-29-503 and 79-29-504)
Resignation of member:	• Members may not withdraw from the company unless the certificate of formation or LLC agreement provides that members have the power of withdrawal. (Miss. Code § 79-29-307)
Transfer of LLC interest:	• A member's interest is assignable in whole or in part, unless otherwise provided. Unanimous consent is required for an assignee to participate in the management and affairs of the LLC, unless otherwise provided. (Miss. Code § § 79-29-702 and 79-29-704)
Dissolution:	• An LLC is dissolved: (1) at the time specified in the certificate of formation; (2) upon the happening of events specified in the operating agreement or certificate of formation; (3) upon the written consent of all members, unless otherwise provided; (4) when an event of dissociation occurs to a member, unless the business of the LLC is continued within 90 days by the remaining members; or (5) upon a judicial dissolution. (Miss. Code § § 79-29-801 and 79-29-802)
Mergers and consolidations:	• Mergers are permitted expressly by statute. (Miss. Code § 79-29-209)

¶ 1028
Missouri

Name of act:	• Missouri Limited Liability Company Act, Mo. Rev. Stat. § 347.010 to Mo. Rev. Stat. § 347.740.
Federal tax classification:	• The LLC statute is flexible. Any "business entity" not required to be treated as a "corporation" for federal tax purposes under Reg. § 301.7701-2 may choose its classification under Reg. § 301.7701-3.
State tax treatment:	• State tax classification follows federal. Thus, Missouri LLCs and foreign LLCs doing business in Missouri are treated as partnerships or disregarded as entities, unless classified as corporations for federal tax purposes. (Mo. Rev. Stat. § 347.187)

Securities treatment:	• The Missouri LLC Acts provides a rebuttable presumption against security status for interests in LLCs where management is not vested in one or more members. (Mo. Rev. Stat. § 347.185)
Limited liability partnerships:	• The formation of limited liability partnerships is expressly provided for by statute. (Mo. Rev. Stat. § 358.440)
Limited liability limited partnerships:	• Limited Liability Limited Partnerships are expressly provided for by statute. (Mo. Rev. Stat. § 359.172)
Professional LLCs:	• Professional LLCs are impliedly permitted. No prohibition exists in the provision concerning lawful business. (Mo. Rev. Stat. § 347.035)
Foreign LLCs:	• Foreign LLCs are expressly permitted by statute. Laws of the formation jurisdiction govern the LLC's organization, internal affairs, and the liability of its members. (Mo. Rev. Stat. § 347.151)
Formation:	• Any person may form a Missouri LLC. A Missouri LLC may have one or more members. (Mo. Rev. Stat. § § 347.017 and 347.037)
Naming requirements:	• A Missouri LLC's name must contain the words "limited company" or "limited liability company" or the abbreviation "LC," "LLC," "L.C." or "L.L.C." (Mo. Rev. Stat. § 347.020)
Effective date of organization:	• An LLC's existence begins when the articles of organization are properly filed or on a later date set forth in the articles of organization, not to exceed ninety days from the filing date. (Mo. Rev. Stat. § 347.037)
Filing requirements:	• The articles of organization must include: (1) the LLC's name; (2) its duration, which may be any number of years or perpetual, if specified; (3) its purpose; (4) the registered agent's name and the address of the registered office; (5) the name and address of each organizer; and (6) a statement indicating that the LLC is managed by managers, if applicable. (Mo. Rev. Stat. § 347.039)
Fees—Organization and Annual:	• The fee for filing articles of organization is $105. The fee for filing a foreign LLC's application for registration is $105. There is no annual registration fee. (Mo. Rev. Stat. § 347.179)

¶1028

Recordkeeping:	• The LLC must compile and maintain: (1) a list of members' and managers' names and addresses; (2) copies of federal, state and local tax returns and information for the last three years, or, if such returns and statements were not prepared for any reason, copies of the information and statements provided to or which should have been provided to the members to enable them to prepare such returns; (3) copies of articles of organization, including any amendments; (4) past and current written operating agreements (if any), including any amendments; (5) financial statements for the last three years; (6) a writing that sets forth the members' capital contributions, relative voting rights of the members, and events that would cause dissociation, if not set forth in a written operating agreement; (7) copies of any written promise by a member to make a contribution; (8) copies of written consents by members to admit new members; (9) copies of written consents by members to continue the LLC's business upon dissociation of a member; and (10) copies of any other writings prepared pursuant to the operating agreement. (Mo. Rev. Stat. § 347.091)
Annual reporting:	• An annual report is not required.
Management:	• Management is vested in members, unless otherwise provided. (Mo. Rev. Stat. § 347.079)

Membership rights and obligations:	• Members are not liable, solely by reason of being a member or manager, or both, under a judgment, decree or order of a court, or in any manner, for a debt, obligation, or liability of the LLC, whether arising in contract, tort, or otherwise, or for the acts or omissions of any other member, manager, agent or employee of the LLC. If a member fails to make a required contribution, even in the event of death, disability or other reason, the member is obligated, at the option of the LLC, to contribute cash equal to that portion of the value of the stated contribution that has not been made. An operating agreement may also provide that a member who fails to make a capital contribution or other payment shall be subject to specified remedies or consequences. A member or manager who knowingly assents to a wrongful distribution is personally liable, for a period of three years following the date of the distribution, to the LLC for the value of the wrongful distribution. Each member or manager held liable is entitled to contribution from each member who knowingly received a wrongful distribution. (Mo. Rev. Stat. § § 347.057, 347.099 and 347.109)
Piercing the corporate veil:	• The Act has no express provision that concerns piercing the corporate veil.
Contributions:	• Contributions may consist of cash, property, the use of property, services, or a promissory note or other binding obligation to contribute the same. (Mo. Rev. Stat. § § 347.015 and 347.097)
Distributions:	• Distributions are allocated first to repay members' capital contributions, as adjusted for any withdrawals, and thereafter shared equally, unless otherwise provided. Profits are allocated among the members in accordance with previous allocations of losses until the losses are offset, then according to the allocations of distributions that exceed repayments of capital, unless otherwise provided. Losses are allocated among the members according to their relative capital contributions, including promises to contribute capital, unless otherwise provided. (Mo. Rev. Stat. § § 347.101 and 347.111)
Resignation of member:	• Ninety days' written notice is required prior to resignation, unless otherwise provided. An LLC may recover damages for resignation in violation of the operating agreement. (Mo. Rev. Stat. § 347.121)

Transfer of LLC interest:	• A member's LLC interest is assignable in whole or in part, unless otherwise provided. Unanimous consent is required for an assignee to become a member, unless otherwise provided. (Mo. Rev. Stat. § § 347.113 and 347.115)
Dissolution:	• An LLC is dissolved: (1) upon the happening of a dissolution event specified in the articles of organization or operating agreement; (2) upon the written consent of all members; (3) when an event of dissociation occurs to a member, if a majority, by number, of the remaining members within 90 days of the withdrawal agree to dissolve the LLC, unless otherwise provided; (4) an event of withdrawal with respect to the sole remaining member; (5) upon entry of a decree of dissolution; or (6) upon a merger or consolidation where the LLC is not the surviving entity. (Mo. Rev. Stat. § § 347.137 and 347.143)
Mergers and consolidations:	• Mergers or consolidations are permitted expressly by statute. (Mo. Rev. Stat. § 347.700)

¶ 1029

Montana

Name of act:	• Montana Limited Liability Company Act, Mont. Code § 35-8-101 to Mont. Code § 35-8-1307.
Federal tax classification:	• The LLC statute is flexible. Any "business entity" not required to be treated as a "corporation" for federal tax purposes under Reg. § 301.7701-2 may choose its classification under Reg. § 301.7701-3.
State tax treatment:	• State tax classification follows federal. Therefore, Montana LLCs and foreign LLCs doing business in Montana are treated as partnerships or disregarded as entities, unless classified as corporations for federal tax purposes.
Securities treatment:	• The Montana Act does not expressly provide for the treatment of an LLC interest as a security.
Limited liability partnerships:	• The formation of limited liability partnerships is expressly permitted by statute. (Mont. Code § 35-10-701)
Professional LLCs:	• Professional LLCs are expressly permitted by statute, subject to compliance with other state regulatory provisions. (Mont. Code § 35-8-1301)
Foreign LLCs:	• Foreign LLCs are expressly permitted by statute. Laws of the formation jurisdiction govern the LLC's organization and internal affairs. (Mont. Code § § 35-8-1001 and 35-8-1008)

Formation:	• One or more persons may form an LLC. Single-member LLCs are permitted. (Mont. Code § 35-8-201)
Naming requirements:	• The name of each LLC must contain the words "limited liability company" or "limited company," or the abbreviations "l.l.c.," "l.c.," "llc," or "lc". The word "limited" may be abbreviated as "ltd.," and the word "company" may be abbreviated as "co." (Mont. Code § 35-8-103)
Effective date of organization:	• An LLC's existence begins when the articles of organization are delivered to the secretary of state for filing. (Mont. Code § 35-8-206)
Filing requirements:	• The articles of organization must include: (1) the LLC's name; (2) whether the LLC is a term company and, if so, the term specified; (3) the name and address of its registered agent and the address of its principal place of business and, if different, its registered office; (4) a statement specifying the form of management and the names and business addresses of initial members, if member-managed, or initial managers, if manager-managed; (5) whether one or more members of the company are to be liable for the LLC's debts and obligations; (6) if the LLC is a professional LLC, a statement to that effect and a statement of the professional service or services it will render; and (7) any other provision the members elect to include. (Mont. Code § 35-8-202)
Fees—Organization and Annual:	• The fee for filing articles of organization is $70. The fee for filing a foreign LLC registration application is $70. The annual registration fee is $15, if filed by April 15 ($30 if filed after April 15). (Mont. Code § § 35-8-211 and 35-8-212)

Recordkeeping:

- The LLC must compile and maintain: (1) an alphabetical current and past list of the names and addresses of each member and manager; (2) a copy of the articles of organization, together with any amendments to the articles and executed copies of any powers of attorney; (3) copies of the LLC's federal, state, and local tax returns and financial statements, if any, for the last three years or, if such returns and statements were not prepared for any reason, copies of the information and statements provided to or which should have been provided to the members to enable them to prepare such returns; (4) copies of any effective written operating agreement, as well as operating agreements no longer in effect; (5) if not contained in the operating agreement, a writing, setting forth the amount of cash, the agreed value of other property or services contributed by each member, the times or events upon which additional contributions agreed to by each member are to be made, and a statement of events the occurrence of which requires the LLC to be dissolved and its affairs wound up; and (6) other writings prepared pursuant to a requirement in an operating agreement. (Mont. Code § 35-8-405)

Annual reporting:

- An annual report is required and is due between January 1 and April 15 of the year following the calendar year in which a domestic LLC is organized or a foreign LLC is authorized to transact business, and between January 1 and April 15 in each year thereafter. (Mont. Code § 35-8-208)

Management:

- An LLC may be member-managed or manager-managed. (Mont. Code § 35-8-307)

Membership rights and obligations:

- Members are not liable for any debt, obligation or liability of the LLC, whether arising in contract, tort or otherwise. A member is also not liable for the acts or omissions of any other member, manager, agent or employee of the LLC. If a member fails to make a required contribution, even in the event of death, disability or other reason, the member is obligated at the option of the LLC to contribute cash equal to that portion of the value of the stated contribution that has not been made. A member or manager who votes for or assents to a wrongful distribution is personally liable to the LLC for the amount of the distribution wrongfully made. Each member or manager held liable is entitled to contribution from each other member or manager who voted or assented to the wrongful distribution and from each member who knowingly received a wrongful distribution. (Mont. Code §§ 35-8-304, 35-8-502 and 35-8-605)

Piercing the corporate veil:

- The failure of an LLC to observe the usual company formalities or requirements relating to the exercise of its company powers or management of its business is not a ground for imposing personal liability on the members or managers of the LLC. (Mont. Code § 35-8-304)

Contributions:

- Contributions may consist of tangible or intangible property or other benefits to the company, including money, promissory notes, services performed or other agreements to contribute the same. (Mont. Code § 35-8-501)

Distributions:

- Distributions are shared equally, unless otherwise provided. Profits are allocated first to repay members' capital contributions and profits and losses are shared equally thereafter, unless otherwise provided. (Mont. Code §§ 35-8-503 and 35-8-601)

Resignation of member:

- A member may withdraw upon giving notice to the LLC, unless the LLC is a term company or if otherwise provided. (Mont. Code §§ 35-8-803 and 35-8-804)

Transfer of LLC interest:

- A member's LLC interest is assignable in whole or in part, unless otherwise provided. Unanimous consent is required for an assignee to become a member, unless otherwise provided. (Mont. Code §§ 35-8-704 and 35-8-706)

Dissolution:	• An LLC is dissolved: (1) at the time or upon the occurrence of events specified in writing in the articles of organization or operating agreement; (2) upon consent of the number or percentage of members specified in the operating agreement; (3) when an event makes it unlawful for all or substantially all of the business of the company to be continued, but any cure of an illegality within 90 days after notice to the company of the event is effective retroactively to the date of the event; (4) upon the expiration of the term specified in the articles of organization; or (5) upon entry of a decree of judicial dissolution. (Mont. Code §§ 35-8-901 and 35-8-902)
Mergers and consolidations:	• Mergers are permitted expressly by statute. (Mont. Code § 35-8-1201)

¶ 1030

Nebraska

Name of act:	• Limited Liability Company Act, Neb. Rev. Stat. § 21-2601 to Neb. Rev. Stat. § 21-2653.
Federal tax classification:	• The LLC statute is flexible. Any "business entity" not required to be treated as a "corporation" for federal tax purposes under Reg. § 301.7701-2 may choose its classification under Reg. § 301.7701-3.
State tax treatment:	• State tax classification follows federal. Thus, Nebraska LLCs and foreign LLCs doing business in Nebraska are treated as partnerships or disregarded as entities, unless classified as corporations for federal tax purposes. (Neb. Rev. Stat. § 21-2633)
Securities treatment:	• "Security" includes any membership interest in an LLC unless a member enters into a written commitment to be engaged actively and directly in the management of the LLC and all members of the LLC are actively engaged in the management of the LLC. (Neb. Rev. Stat. § 8-1101)
Limited liability partnerships:	• The formation of limited liability partnerships is expressly permitted. (Neb. Rev. Stat. § 67-454)
Professional LLCs:	• Professional LLCs are expressly permitted by statute, subject to compliance with other state regulatory provisions. (Neb. Rev. Stat. § 21-2631)
Foreign LLCs:	• Foreign LLCs are expressly permitted by statute. Laws of the formation jurisdiction govern organization, internal affairs and the liability of its members and managers. (Neb. Rev. Stat. § 21-2637)

Formation:	• One or more persons may form an LLC. (Neb. Rev. Stat. § 21-2605)
Naming requirements:	• The words "limited liability company," "ltd. liability company" or "ltd. liability co." or the abbreviations "L.L.C." or "LLC" must be the last words of the name of every LLC. (Neb. Rev. Stat. § 21-2604)
Effective date of organization:	• The LLC is considered organized upon the issuance of the certificate of organization, unless a delayed effective date is stated in the articles of organization. (Neb. Rev. Stat. § 21-2608)
Filing requirements:	• The articles of organization must include: (1) the LLC's name; (2) the LLC's purpose; (3) the address of its principal place of business in the state and the name and address of its registered agent in the state; (4) the total amount of cash contributed to stated capital and a description and agreed value of property other than cash contributed; (5) the amounts and times of future contributions agreed to be made by all members; (6) the right, if given, of members to admit additional members; (7) if the LLC is to be managed by managers, the names and addresses of such managers and, if the management is reserved to the members, the names and addresses of the members; and (8) any other provisions the members elect to include. (Neb. Rev. Stat. § 21-2606)
Fees—Organization and Annual:	• The fee for filing articles of organization is $110 plus recording fees. The fee for filing foreign LLC registration application is $120 plus recording fees. As of January 1, 2007, a biennial report is required; however, there is no recording fee. (Neb. Rev. Stat. § 21-2634)
Recordkeeping:	• The Nebraska statute is silent as to records and information required to be kept by LLCs. However it might be prudent for the LLC to compile and maintain: (1) a current list of the names and addresses of the members and managers; (2) copies of federal, state and local income tax returns and company information; (3) copies of the articles of organization, including any amendments; (4) copies of any effective written operating agreement; (5) financial statements; (6) information regarding members' capital contributions, agreements to contribute capital and the date each became a member; and (7) any other information regarding LLC affairs that is just and reasonable to maintain.
Annual reporting:	• An biennial report is required.

Management:	• Management is vested in the members, unless otherwise provided. (Neb. Rev. Stat. § 21-2615)
Membership rights and obligations:	• LLC members and managers are not liable, and not personally liable, for any debt, obligation, or liability of the LLC, whether under a judgment, decree or order of a court. The members, however, shall be liable for any unpaid taxes of the LLC when the management is reserved to the members. If management is reserved to managers, the managers are liable for taxes in the same manner as a corporate officer is liable for taxes. Members are liable to the LLC for the difference between contributions actually made and those stated as actually having been made. Members are also liable for any unpaid contribution that was agreed to be made by the member in the future. Members hold as trustees for the LLC any money or property wrongfully paid to such member. (Neb. Rev. Stat. § § 21-2612 and 21-2620)
Piercing the corporate veil:	• The Nebraska Act has no express provision that concerns piercing the corporate veil.
Contributions:	• Contributions may consist of any tangible or intangible property or benefit to the company. (Neb. Rev. Stat. § 21-2614)
Distributions:	• Profits are allocated as provided by the operating agreement, so long as the aggregate fair market value of the LLC's assets exceed liabilities after the distribution is made. The Nebraska Act is silent as to the allocation of distributions and losses. (Neb. Rev. Stat. § 21-2618)
Resignation of member:	• The Nebraska Act is silent as to the resignation of member, implying that members are free to resign at any time without prior written notice, unless otherwise provided.
Transfer of LLC interest:	• A member's interest in the LLC is assignable or transferable as provided in the operating agreement. Consent by a majority in interest is required for an assignee of a member's interest to become a member or to participate in the management of the business and affairs of the LLC, unless otherwise provided. (Neb. Rev. Stat. § 21-2621)

Dissolution:	• An LLC is dissolved: (1) at the expiration of the period, if any, fixed for duration; (2) upon the unanimous written agreement of all of the members; (3) upon the occurrence of any other event described in the articles of organization; or (4) upon a decree of judicial dissolution. (Neb. Rev. Stat. § 21-2622)
Mergers and consolidations:	• Mergers or consolidations are expressly permitted by statute. (Neb. Rev. Stat. § 21-2647)

¶ 1031
Nevada

Name of act:	• Nevada Limited Liability Company Act, Nev. Rev. Stat. § 86.011 to Nev. Rev. Stat. § 86.590.
Federal tax classification:	• The Nevada LLC Act is flexible. Any "business entity" not required to be treated as a "corporation" for federal tax purposes under Reg. § 301.7701-2 may choose its classification under Reg. § 301.7701-3.
State tax treatment:	• Nevada does not impose personal or corporate income tax.
Securities treatment:	• A limited liability company interest is defined as a security in the Nevada Securities Act. (Nev. Rev. Stat. § 90.295)
Limited liability partnerships:	• The formation of Limited Liability Partnerships is expressly permitted by statute. (Nev. Rev. Stat. § 87.440).
Limited liability limited partnerships:	• The formation of Limited Liability Limited Partnerships is expressly permitted by statute. (Nev. Rev. Stat. § 86.606).
Professional LLCs:	• Professional LLCs are expressly permitted by statute. An LLC may be organized for any lawful purpose, except insurance. (Nev. Rev. Stat. § 86.555)
Foreign LLCs:	• Foreign LLCs are expressly permitted by statute. (Nev. Rev. Stat. § 86.551)
Formation:	• A Nevada LLC may be formed by one or more persons. Single-member LLCs are permitted. (Nev. Rev. Stat. § 86.151)
Naming requirements:	• The name of each LLC must contain the words "Limited-Liability Company," "Limited Company" or "Limited" or the abbreviations "Ltd.," "L.L.C.," "L.C.," "LLC" or "LC." The word "Company" may be abbreviated as "Co." (Nev. Rev. Stat. § 86.171)
Effective date of organization:	• An LLC's existence begins when the articles of organization and the certificate of acceptance of the resident agent are filed and the filing fees are paid. (Nev. Rev. Stat. § 86.201)

Filing requirements:	• The articles of organization must include: (1) the LLC's name; (2) the name and complete street address of the LLC's resident agent and the resident agent's mailing address if different from the street address; (3) the name and post office or street address, either residence or business, of each of the organizers executing the articles; (4) the name and address of each manager, if the LLC is manager-managed; (5) the name and address of each member, if the LLC is member-managed; and (6) any other provision, not inconsistent with the law, which the members elect to set out. (Nev. Rev. Stat. § 86.161)
Fees—Organization and Annual:	• The fee for filing the original articles of organization is $75. The fee for registration of a foreign LLC is $75. The annual registration fee is $125. (Nev. Rev. Stat. §§ 86.263 and 86.561)
Recordkeeping:	• The LLC must compile and maintain: (1) a current, alphabetical list of the members' and managers' full names and last known business addresses, separately identifying the members and managers, if any; (2) a copy of the filed articles of organization, and all amendments thereto, together with executed copies of any powers of attorney; and (3) copies of any then effective operating agreement. Each LLC must continuously maintain in Nevada an office at which it shall keeps these records. This office may, but need not be, a place of the LLC's business in Nevada. (Nev. Rev. Stat. § 86.241)
Annual reporting:	• An annual filing is required and is due on or before the last day of the month in which the anniversary date of formation occurs in each year. (Nev. Rev. Stat. § 86.263)
Management:	• Management of an LLC is vested in its members, unless otherwise provided. (Nev. Rev. Stat. § 86.291)
Membership rights and obligations:	• Members and managers are not liable for any debts or liabilities of the LLC. Members are liable for the difference between the amount of the member's contributions which have actually been made and the amount which is stated as in the operating agreement as having been made and for any unpaid contributions that such member agreed to make in the future. A member holds as trustee for the LLC any money or property that has been wrongfully distributed to the member. (Nev. Rev. Stat. §§ 86.371 and 86.391)
Piercing the corporate veil:	• The Act has no express provision for piercing the corporate veil.

¶1031

Contributions:	• Contributions may consist of cash, property, services rendered, a promissory note or other binding obligation to contribute the same. (Nev. Rev. Stat. § 86.321)
Distributions:	• An LLC may allocate profits and losses to its members in proportion to the value of their contributions. (Nev. Rev. Stat. § 86.341)
Resignation of member:	• A member may not resign from an LLC, except as provided in the articles of organization or operating agreement. (Nev. Rev. Stat. § 86.331)
Transfer of LLC interest:	• A member's LLC interest is transferable or assignable, unless otherwise provided. Consent by a majority in interest of the other LLC members is required for an assignee or a transferee to become a member. (Nev. Rev. Stat. § 86.351)
Dissolution:	• An LLC is dissolved: (1) when the period, if any, fixed for the duration of the LLC expires; (2) upon the occurrence of an event specified in the operating agreement; (3) upon the unanimous written agreement of all members. (Nev. Rev. Stat. § 86.491)
Mergers and consolidations:	• Mergers of LLCs are not expressly provided for by statute. However, the Nevada secretary of state lists a $325 filing fee for LLC mergers.

¶ 1032
New Hampshire

Name of act:	• N.H. Rev. Stat. § 304-C:1 to N.H. Rev. Stat. § 304-C:85.
Federal tax classification:	• The LLC statute is flexible. Any "business entity" not required to be treated as a "corporation" for federal tax purposes under Reg. § 301.7701-2 may choose its classification under Reg. § 301.7701-3.
State tax treatment:	• State tax classification follows federal. Thus, New Hampshire LLCs and foreign LLCs doing business in New Hampshire are treated as partnerships or disregarded as entities, unless classified as corporations for federal tax purposes. New Hampshire LLCs are subject to both the New Hampshire business profits tax and income tax.

Securities treatment:	• "Security" includes a membership interest in an LLC unless the secretary of state, by rule or order, determines that it is not a security or the LLC is a professional limited liability company. Along with a $50 filing fee, a statement shall be filed with the secretary of state that the capital stock of the LLC have been registered or will be registered when offered, are exempted or are not securities. (N.H. Rev. Stat. §§ 421-B:2 and 421-B:11)
Limited liability partnerships:	• The formation of limited liability partnerships is expressly permitted by statute. (N.H. Rev. Stat. § 304-A:44)
Professional LLCs:	• Professional LLCs are permitted expressly by statute. (N.H. Rev. Stat. § 304-D:1)
Foreign LLCs:	• Foreign LLCs are expressly permitted by statute. Laws of the formation jurisdiction govern organization, internal affairs and the liability of members and managers. (N.H. Rev. Stat. §§ 304-C:62 and 304-C:64)
Formation:	• An New Hampshire LLC may be formed by one or more authorized persons. One or more members are required. (N.H. Rev. Stat. §§ 304-C:1 and 304-C:12)
Naming requirements:	• A New Hampshire LLC shall contain the words "limited liability company" or the abbreviation "L.L.C." or similar abbreviation. (N.H. Rev. Stat. § 304-C:3)
Effective date of organization:	• A New Hampshire LLC exists as of the close of business on the date on which a certificate of formation is filed, or at the delayed effective date specified in the document. (N.H. Rev. Stat. § 304-C:11)
Filing requirements:	• The certificate of formation shall include: (1) the LLC's name; (2) its purposes; (3) the address of the registered office and the name and address of the registered agent for service of process; (4) the latest date upon which the LLC is to dissolve, if the LLC is to have a specific date of dissolution; (5) if management of the LLC is vested in a manager or managers, a statement to that effect; and (6) any other matters the members decide to include. (N.H. Rev. Stat. § 304-C:12)
Fees—Organization and Annual:	• The fee for filing the certificate of formation is $100. The fee for filing an application for registration as a foreign LLC is $100. The fee for filing an annual report of domestic LLC is $100. (N.H. Rev. Stat. § 304-C:81)

¶1032

Recordkeeping:	• Every LLC must compile and maintain: (1) true and full information regarding the status of the business and financial condition of the LLC; (2) a current list of the members' and managers' names and addresses; (3) a copy of the LLC agreement and certificate of formation and all amendments, together with executed copies of any powers of attorney, if any; (4) a copy of the LLC's federal, state, and local tax returns for each year; (5) true and full information regarding the amount of cash and a description and statement of the agreed value of any other property or services contributed, or promised to be contributed in the future, and the date on which each became a member; and (6) other information regarding the affairs of the LLC as is just and reasonable. (N.H. Rev. Stat. § 304-C:28)
Annual reporting:	• An annual report is required and is due between January 1 and April 1. (N.H. Rev. Stat. § 304-C:80)
Management:	• Management is vested in the members, unless otherwise provided. (N.H. Rev. Stat. § 304-C:31)
Membership rights and obligations:	• A member or manager of an LLC is not personally liable for any debt, obligation, or liability of the LLC, solely by reason of being a member or acting as a manager of the LLC. If a member does not make the required contribution because of death, disability or any other reason, he is obligated, at the option of the LLC, to contribute cash equal to that portion of the agreed value of the contribution that has not been made. An LLC agreement may also provide that a member who fails to make a capital contribution or other payment shall be subject to specified remedies or consequences. A member who knowingly receives a wrongful distribution is liable to the LLC for the amount of the distribution. A member who receives a wrongful distribution, but did not know that the distribution was wrongful when he received it, is not liable for the amount of the distribution. (N.H. Rev. Stat. §§ 304-C:25, 304-C:37 and 304-C:44)
Piercing the corporate veil:	• The Act has no express provision that concerns piercing the corporate veil.
Contributions:	• Contributions may consist of cash, property, services rendered, a promissory note or other obligation to contribute the same. (N.H. Rev. Stat. § 304-C:36)

Distributions:	• Distributions, profits and losses are allocated on the basis of the value, as of the date of the contribution, of the contributions made by each member to the extent they have been received by the LLC and have not been returned, unless otherwise provided. (N.H. Rev. Stat. §§ 304-C:38 and 304-C:39)
Resignation of member:	• 30 days' written notice is required prior to resignation, unless otherwise provided. (N.H. Rev. Stat. § 304-C:27)
Transfer of LLC interest:	• A member's LLC interest is assignable in whole or in part, unless otherwise provided. Unanimous consent is required for an assignee to become a member of the LLC, unless otherwise provided. (N.H. Rev. Stat. §§ 304-C:46 and 304-C:48)
Dissolution:	• An LLC is dissolved: (1) upon the happening of events specified in the LLC agreement; (2) upon the written consent of all members; or (3) upon the entry of a judicial dissolution. (N.H. Rev. Stat. §§ 304-C:50 and 304-C:51)
Mergers and consolidations:	• Mergers are permitted expressly by statute. (N.H. Rev. Stat. § 304-C:18)

¶ 1033
New Jersey

Name of act:	• New Jersey Limited Liability Company Act, N.J. Rev. Stat. § 42:2B-1 to N.J. Rev. Stat. § 42:2B-70.
Federal tax classification:	• The LLC statute is flexible. Any "business entity" not required to be treated as a "corporation" for federal tax purposes under Reg. § 301.7701-2 may choose its classification under Reg. § 301.7701-3.
State tax treatment:	• State tax classification follows federal. Thus, New Jersey LLCs and foreign LLCs doing business in New Jersey are treated as partnerships or disregarded as entities, unless classified as corporations for federal tax purposes. (N.J. Rev. Stat. § 42:2B-69)
Securities treatment:	• The New Jersey Act does not expressly provide for the treatment of an LLC interest as a security.
Limited liability partnerships:	• The formation of limited liability partnerships is expressly provided for by statute. (N.J. Rev. Stat. § 42:1A-47)
Professional LLCs:	• Professional LLCs are permitted impliedly. No prohibition exists in the statutory provisions concerning lawful business. (N.J. Rev. Stat. § 42:2B-8)

Foreign LLCs:	• Foreign LLCs are expressly permitted by statute. Laws of the formation jurisdiction govern organization, internal affairs and the liability of members and managers. (N.J. Rev. Stat. § 42:2B-52)
Formation:	• One or more authorized persons may form an LLC. The LLC must have one or more members. (N.J. Rev. Stat. § § 42:2B-2 and 42:2B-11)
Naming requirements:	• The name of each LLC must contain the words "limited liability company" or the abbreviation "L.L.C." and must be distinguishable from the record name of any corporation, limited partnership, business trust or LLC, foreign or domestic, registered in the state of New Jersey. (N.J. Rev. Stat. § 42:2B-3)
Effective date of organization:	• An LLC's existence begins on the date and at the time when the certificate of formation is filed, unless a delayed effective date is specified. (N.J. Rev. Stat. § 42:2B-17)
Filing requirements:	• The certificate of formation must include: (1) the LLC's name; (2) the name and address of the registered agent for service of process; (3) the address of the registered office; (4) whether the LLC is to have a specific date of dissolution or, if the LLC is to have perpetual duration, a statement to that effect; and (5) any other matters the members decide to include. (N.J. Rev. Stat. § 42:2B-11)
Fees—Organization and Annual:	• The fee for filing a certificate of formation is $100. The fee for filing a foreign LLC registration application is $100. The fee for filing an annual report is $50. (N.J. Rev. Stat. § 42:2B-65)
Recordkeeping:	• The LLC must compile and maintain: (1) a list of the members' names and addresses; (2) federal, state, and local tax returns and information for each year; (3) a copy of any operating agreement and the certificate of formation, including any amendments; (4) information regarding the amount of cash and a description and statement of the agreed value of any other property or services contributed, or promised to be contributed in the future, by each member; (5) information regarding the status of the business and financial condition of the LLC; and (6) other information regarding LLC affairs that is just and reasonable to maintain. (N.J. Rev. Stat. § 42:2B-25)
Annual reporting:	• An annual report is required. (N.J. Rev. Stat. § 42:2B-8.1)
Management:	• Management is vested in the members, unless otherwise provided. (N.J. Rev. Stat. § 42:2B-27)

Membership rights and obligations:

- A member is not obligated personally for the debts, obligations and liabilities of the LLC or of any other member, manager, employee or agent of the LLC. If a member does not make the required contribution because of death, disability or any other reason, he is obligated, at the option of the LLC, to contribute cash equal to that portion of the agreed value of the contribution that has not been made. A member who knowingly receives a wrongful distribution shall be liable to the LLC for the amount of the distribution for three years after receipt of the distribution. A member who received a wrongful distribution, but did not know the distribution was wrongful, shall not be liable for the amount of the distribution. (N.J. Rev. Stat. §§ 42:2B-23, 42:2B-33 and 42:2B-42)

Piercing the corporate veil:

- The New Jersey Act has no express provision that concerns piercing the corporate veil.

Contributions:

- Contributions may consist of cash, property, services rendered, a promissory note or other obligation to contribute the same. (N.J. Rev. Stat. § 42:2B-32)

Distributions:

- Profits, losses and distributions are allocated based on the agreed value of the contributions made by each member to the extent they had been received by the LLC and not yet returned, unless otherwise provided. (N.J. Rev. Stat. §§ 42:2B-34 and 42:2B-35)

Resignation of member:

- Six months' written notice is required prior to resignation, unless otherwise provided. (N.J. Rev. Stat. § 42:2B-38)

Transfer of LLC interest:

- A member's LLC interest is assignable in whole or in part, unless otherwise provided. Unanimous consent is required for an assignee to participate in the management and affairs of the LLC, unless otherwise provided. (N.J. Rev. Stat. § 42:2B-44)

Dissolution:

- An LLC is dissolved: (1) unless the certificate of formation specifies that the LLC is perpetual, at the time specified in an operating agreement, or 30 years from the date of formation; (2) upon the happening of events specified in the operating agreement; (3) upon the written consent of all members, which includes written consent of the sole member of a single-member LLC; (4) 90 days after the date on which the LLC no longer has at least one member, unless at least one member is admitted within 90 days; or (5) upon a judicial dissolution. (N.J. Rev. Stat. §§ 42:2B-48 and 42:2B-49)

Mergers and consolidations:

- Mergers or consolidations are permitted expressly by statute. (N.J. Rev. Stat. § 42:2B-20)

¶ 1034
New Mexico

Name of act:	• Limited Liability Company Act, N.M. Stat. § 53-19-1 to N.M. Stat. § 53-19-75.
Federal tax classification:	• The LLC statute is flexible. Any "business entity" not required to be treated as a "corporation" for federal tax purposes under Reg. § 301.7701-2 may choose its classification under Reg. § 301.7701-3.
State tax treatment:	• State tax classification follows federal. Thus, New Mexico LLCs and foreign LLCs doing business in New Mexico are treated as partnerships or disregarded as entities, unless classified as corporations for federal tax purposes.
Securities treatment:	• The New Mexico Securities Act includes "any interest in a limited liability company" in the definition of "security." (N.M. Stat. 58-13B-2)
Limited liability partnerships:	• The formation of Limited Liability Partnerships is expressly permitted by statute. (N.M. Stat. § 54-1A-1001).
Professional LLCs:	• Professional LLCs are permitted impliedly by statute, subject to compliance with other state regulatory provisions. No prohibition is set forth in the provision concerning lawful business. (N.M. Stat. § 53-19-6)
Foreign LLCs:	• Foreign LLCs are expressly permitted by statute. Laws of the formation jurisdiction govern organization, internal affairs and the liability of members and managers. (N.M. Stat. § § 53-19-47 to 53-19-56)
Formation:	• A New Mexico LLC may be formed by one or more persons. An LLC may consist of one or more members. (N.M. Stat. § 53-19-7)
Naming requirements:	• A New Mexico LLC must contain the words "limited liability company," or "limited company" or the abbreviations "L.L.C.," "LLC," "L.C." or "LC" in its name. The word "limited" may be abbreviated "ltd." and the word "company" may be abbreviated "co." (N.M. Stat. § 53-19-3)
Effective date of organization:	• An LLC is formed when the articles of organization are filed with the Commission, unless a delayed effective date is specified. (N.M. Stat. § 53-19-10)

Filing requirements:
- The articles of organization shall set forth: (1) the LLC's name; (2) the street address of the registered office and the name of the registered agent and the street address of the LLC's current principal place of business, if different from the registered office; (3) the latest date upon which the LLC is to dissolve, unless the LLC's duration is perpetual; (4) if management is vested to any extent in a manager or managers, a statement to that effect and of the extent to which management is so vested; (5) if the LLC is a single-member entity; and (6) any other provision that the persons signing the articles choose to include in the articles, including provisions for the regulation of the internal affairs of the LLC. (N.M. Stat. § 53-19-8)

Fees—Organization and Annual:
- The fee for filing the original articles of organization is $50. The fee for the issuance of a foreign company registration is $100. No annual fee is required. (N.M. Stat. § 53-19-63)

Recordkeeping:
- The LLC must compile and maintain: (1) a list containing the full name and last known mailing address of all current and former members and managers; (2) a copy of the articles of organization, including any amendments and any executed copies of any powers of attorney; (3) copies of federal, state, and local tax returns and financial statements for the three most recent years or, if such returns and statements were not prepared for any reason, copies of the information and statements necessary to enable the members to prepare such returns; (4) a copy of every current and prior operating agreement, including any amendments; (5) unless contained in the articles of organization or a written operating agreement, a writing containing information regarding the value of each member's contribution made to the LLC, information regarding future contributions promised to the LLC, and records of the times at which or the events upon which any additional contributions are agreed to be made; and (6) documents or any other writings required to be made available to members by the articles of organization or operating agreements. (N.M. Stat. § 53-19-19)

Annual reporting:
- An annual report is not required.

Management:
- Management of an LLC is vested in the members, unless otherwise provided. (N.M. Stat. § 53-19-15)

¶1034

Membership rights and obligations:	• A member is not personally liable for the debts, obligations, and liabilities of the LLC, whether arising in contract, tort, or otherwise. If a member fails to make a required contribution, even in the event of the member's death, disability or other change in circumstances, the member is obligated, at the option of the LLC, to contribute cash equal to that portion of the value of the stated contribution that has not been fulfilled. An operating agreement may also provide that a member who fails to make a capital contribution or other payment shall be subject to specified remedies or consequences. A member or manager who votes or assents to a wrongful distribution is jointly but not severally liable for the amount of the distribution that exceeds the amount that could have been rightfully distributed. (N.M. Stat. § § 53-19-13, 53-19-21 and 53-19-27)
Piercing the corporate veil:	• The Act has no express provision for piercing the corporate veil.
Contributions:	• Contributions may consist of cash, property received by or services rendered to an LLC. (N.M. Stat. § 53-19-20)
Distributions:	• Distributions are allocated on the basis of the value of contributions made by each member, unless otherwise provided. Profits and losses are allocated to the members in proportion to the value of the respective contributions to capital, unless otherwise provided. (N.M. Stat. § § 53-19-22 and 53-19-23)
Resignation of member:	• Thirty days' written notice is required prior to resignation, unless otherwise provided. (N.M. Stat. § 53-19-37)
Transfer of LLC interest:	• A member's LLC interest is assignable in whole or in part, unless otherwise provided. Unanimous consent is required for assignee to become a member. (N.M. Stat. § § 53-19-32 and 53-19-33)
Dissolution:	• An LLC is dissolved: (1) upon the happening of an event specified in the articles of organization or operating agreement; (2) upon the written consent of members, unless otherwise provided; (3) when an event of dissociation occurs to a member unless the business of the LLC is continued by consent of the remaining members; or (4) upon the entry of a decree of judicial dissolution. (N.M. Stat. § § 53-19-39 and 53-19-40)
Mergers and consolidations:	• Mergers are permitted expressly by statute. (N.M. Stat. § 53-19-62)

¶ 1035
New York

Name of act:	• New York Limited Liability Company Law, N.Y. LLC Law § 101 to N.Y. LLC Law § 1403.
Federal tax classification:	• The LLC statute is flexible. Any "business entity" not required to be treated as a "corporation" for federal tax purposes under Reg. § 301.7701-2 may choose its classification under Reg. § 301.7701-3.
State tax treatment:	• State tax classification follows federal. Thus, New York LLCs and foreign LLCs doing business in New York are treated as partnerships or disregarded as entities, unless classified as corporations for federal tax purposes.
Securities treatment:	• The New York Act does not expressly provide for the treatment of an LLC interest as a security.
Limited liability partnerships:	• The Act expressly permits the formation of professional limited liability partnerships. (N.Y. Partnership Law § 121-1500)
Professional LLCs:	• Professional LLCs are expressly permitted by statute, subject to compliance with other state regulatory provisions. (N.Y. LLC Law § 1202)
Foreign LLCs:	• Foreign LLCs are expressly permitted by statute. The laws of the formation jurisdiction govern the LLC's organization, internal affairs, and the liability of its members and managers. (N.Y. LLC Law § 801)
Formation:	• A New York LLC may be formed by one or more persons. At least one member is required. (N.Y. LLC Law § 203)
Naming requirements:	• The name of an LLC must contain the words "Limited Liability Company" or the abbreviation "L.L.C." or "LLC." (N.Y. LLC Law § 204)
Effective date of organization:	• An LLC's existence begins when the executed articles of organization are filed. (N.Y. LLC Law § 209)

Filing requirements:	• The articles of organization must include: (1) the LLC's name; (2) the county in which the LLC's office is to be located or, if more than one office, the county in which the principal office is to be located; (3) the latest date on which the LLC is to dissolve, if specified; (4) a designation of the secretary of state as agent of the LLC upon who process may be served and a post office address to which the secretary of state shall mail a copy of any process against the LLC served upon him or her; (5) the name and address of the registered agent, if one is designated; (6) a statement that all or specified members are liable in their capacity as members for the LLC's debts, obligations, or other liabilities, if that is the case; and (7) any other provision the members elect to include. An LLC is required to publish, within 120 days after the articles of organization become effective, a copy of the articles of organization or a notice containing such information in two newspapers in the county in which the LLC was organized, once a week, for six successive weeks. (N.Y. LLC Law § 203)
Fees—Organization and Annual:	• The fee for filing the articles of organization is $200. The fee for filing an application for foreign LLC registration is $250. The annual fee is $100 per member ($500 minimum; $25,000 maximum). There is a minimum filing fee of $100 for single-member LLCs. The filing fee for a biennial statement is $9. (N.Y. LLC Law § 1101)
Recordkeeping:	• LLCs must compile and maintain: (1) a list of members' and managers' names and addresses; (2) a copy of articles of organization, including any amendments and executed powers of attorney, if any; (3) a copy of any operating agreements including any amendments; and (4) copies of the LLC's federal, state and local tax returns and financial statements for the last three years of operation. (N.Y. LLC Law § 1102)
Annual reporting:	• A biennial statement is required to be filed with the Department of State, Division of Corporations.
Management:	• Management is vested in members, unless otherwise provided. (N.Y. LLC Law § 401)

Membership rights and obligations:	• No member conducting business for the LLC will be liable for any debts, obligations, or liabilities of the LLC or each other arising therefrom, solely by virtue of being a member of the LLC. If a member fails to make a required contribution, even in the event of death, disability or other reason, the member is obligated at the option of the LLC to contribute cash equal to that portion of the value of the stated contribution that has not been made. A member who knowingly receives a wrongful distribution is liable to the LLC for the amount of the distribution wrongfully made, for a period of three years after such distribution has been made. A member who unknowingly receives a wrongful distribution is not liable for the amount of the distribution. (N.Y. LLC Law § § 502, 508 and 609)
Piercing the corporate veil:	• The Act has no express provision that concerns piercing the corporate veil.
Contributions:	• Contributions may consist of cash, property, or services, or a promise to contribute the same. (N.Y. LLC Law § 501)
Distributions:	• Distributions, profits and losses are allocated based on the value of each member's contribution, unless otherwise provided. (N.Y. LLC Law § § 503 and 504)
Resignation of member:	• A member may withdraw as a member of an LLC only at the time and upon the happening of events specified in the operating agreement and in accordance with the operating agreement. A member may not withdraw from an LLC prior to dissolution, unless otherwise provided. (N.Y. LLC Law § 606)
Transfer of LLC interest:	• A member's LLC interest is assignable in whole or in part, unless otherwise provided. Consent from a majority in interest is required for an assignee to become a member, unless otherwise provided. (N.Y. LLC Law § § 603 and 604)

Dissolution:	• An LLC is dissolved: (1) upon the latest date on which the LLC is to dissolve, as provided in the articles of organization (if applicable); (2) at the time or upon the happening of events specified in the operating agreement; (3) upon the vote or written consent of at least a majority in interest of the members, unless otherwise provided; (4) at any time there are no members, unless the legal representative of the last remaining member agrees in writing within 180 days to continue the LLC; or (5) upon the entry of a decree of judicial dissolution. (N.Y. LLC Law § § 701 and 702)
Mergers and consolidations:	• Mergers or consolidations are permitted expressly by statute. (N.Y. LLC Law § 1001)

¶ 1036

North Carolina

Name of act:	• North Carolina Limited Liability Company Act, N.C. Gen. Stat. § 57C-1-01 to N.C. Gen. Stat. § 57C-10-07.
Federal tax classification:	• The LLC statute is flexible. Any "business entity" not required to be treated as a "corporation" for federal tax purposes under Reg. § 301.7701-2 may choose its classification under Reg. § 301.7701-3.
State tax treatment:	• State tax classification follows federal. Thus, North Carolina LLCs and foreign LLCs doing business in North Carolina are treated as partnerships or disregarded as entities, unless classified as corporations for federal tax purposes. (N.C. Gen. Stat. § 57C-10-06)
Securities treatment:	• Membership interests in an LLC will be presumed to be securities within the North Carolina Securities Act where (1) the articles of organization of the LLC provide that all members are not necessarily managers by virtue of their status as members; or (2) where all members by virtue of their status as members are managers of the LLC and the number of members is greater than 15. (N.C. Admin. Code, tit. 18, 6.1510)
Limited liability partnerships:	• The formation of limited liability partnerships is expressly provided for by statute. (N.C. Gen. Stat. § 59-84.2)
Limited liability limited partnerships:	• Limited Liability Limited Partnerships are expressly permitted by statute. (N.C. Gen. Stat. § 59-210)
Professional LLCs:	• Professional LLCs are expressly permitted by statute, subject to compliance with other state regulatory provisions. (N.C. Gen. Stat. § 57C-2-01)

Foreign LLCs:
- Foreign LLCs are expressly permitted by statute. Laws of the formation jurisdiction govern the LLC's organization, internal affairs, and liability of its members and managers. (N.C. Gen. Stat. § 57C-7-01)

Formation:
- A North Carolina LLC may be formed by one or more persons. One or more members are required. (N.C. Gen. Stat. § 57C-2-20)

Naming requirements:
- The name of the LLC must contain the words "limited liability company" or the abbreviation "L.L.C." or "LLC," or the combination "ltd. liability co.," "limited liability co.," or "ltd. liability company." (N.C. Gen. Stat. § § 57C-2-30)

Effective date of organization:
- The articles of organization are effective when filed, unless a delayed effective date is specified. (N.C. Gen. Stat. § 55D-13)

Filing requirements:
- The articles of organization must include: (1) the LLC's name; (2) its duration, if specified; (3) the name and the address of each person executing the articles of organization and whether the person is executing the articles of organization in the capacity of a member or an organizer; and (4) the address of the LLC's initial registered office, the county in which the initial registered office is located and the name of the LLC's initial registered agent at that address. (N.C. Gen. Stat. § 57D-10)

Fees—Organization and Annual:
- The fee for filing articles of organization is $125. The filing fee for an application for a certificate of authority is $250. The fee for filing the annual report is $200. (N.C. Gen. Stat. § 57C-1-22)

Recordkeeping:
- A North Carolina LLC must compile and maintain: (1) a list of the members' names and addresses; (2) a copy of the LLC's federal, state and local tax returns and information for each year; (3) copies of articles, including any amendments; (4) the written operating agreement, including amendments, if one exists; (5) information regarding the status of the LLC's business and its financial condition; (6) information concerning the members' capital contributions and agreements to contribute capital; and (7) any other information about the affairs of the LLC that is just and reasonable. (N.C. Gen. Stat. § 57C-3-04)

Annual reporting:
- An annual report is required. This report must be filed by the fifteenth day of the fourth month following the close of the LLC's fiscal year. (N.C. Gen. Stat. § 57C-2-23)

Management:	• Management is vested in the members, unless otherwise provided. (N.C. Gen. Stat. § 57C-3-20)
Membership rights and obligations:	• Members and managers are not liable for the obligations of the LLC. However, a member or manager may become personally liable by reason of his own acts or conduct. If a member fails to make a required contribution, even in the event of the member's death, disability or other change in circumstances, the member is obligated, at the option of the LLC, to contribute cash equal to that portion of the value of the stated contribution that has not been made. A manager who assents to a wrongful distribution is liable to the LLC for the amount of the distribution that was wrongful. Each manager who is liable is entitled to reimbursement from each member who knowingly received a wrongful distribution. (N.C. Gen. Stat. § § 57C-3-30, 57C-4-02 and 57C-4-07)
Piercing the corporate veil:	• The Act has no express provision that concerns piercing the corporate veil.
Contributions:	• Contributions may consist of cash, property, services rendered, promissory notes or a promise to contribute the same. (N.C. Gen. Stat. § 57C-4-01)
Distributions:	• Distributions, profits and losses are allocated and allocations of income, gain, loss, deduction or credit are based on the agreed value of the contributions made by each member, unless otherwise provided. (N.C. Gen. Stat. § § 57C-4-03 and 57C-4-04)
Resignation of member:	• A member may withdraw only at the time or upon the happening of the events specified in the articles or organization or a written operating agreement. (N.C. Gen. Stat. § 57C-5-06)
Transfer of LLC interest:	• A member's LLC interest is assignable in whole or in part, unless otherwise provided. Unanimous consent is required for an assignee to become a member, unless otherwise provided. (N.C. Gen. Stat. § § 57C-5-02 and 57C-5-04)

Dissolution:	• An LLC is dissolved: (1) at the time or upon the occurrence of events specified in the articles of organization or the operating agreement; (2) upon the written consent of all of the members; (3) whenever the LLC no longer has any members, unless otherwise provided, or if, within 90 days after the withdrawal of the last remaining member, the assignee or fiduciary of the estate of the last remaining member agrees in writing to continue the business of the LLC until the admission of a new member; or (4) upon a judicial or administrative dissolution. (N.C. Gen. Stat. § § 57C-6-01 and 57C-6-02)
Mergers and consolidations:	• Mergers are permitted expressly by statute. (N.C. Gen. Stat. § § 57C-9A-01 and 57C-9A-05)

¶ 1037

North Dakota

Name of act:	• North Dakota Limited Liability Act, N.D. Cent. Code, § 10-32-01 to N.D. Cent. Code § 10-32-156.
Federal tax classification:	• The LLC statute is flexible. Any "business entity" not required to be treated as a "corporation" for federal tax purposes under Reg. § 301.7701-2 may choose its classification under Reg. § 301.7701-3.
State tax treatment:	• State tax classification follows federal. Thus, North Dakota LLCs and foreign LLCs doing business in North Dakota are treated as partnerships or disregarded as entities, unless classified as corporations for federal tax purposes.
Securities treatment:	• The North Dakota Act does not expressly provide for the treatment of an LLC interest as a security.
Limited liability partnerships:	• The formation of limited liability partnerships is expressly permitted by statute. (N.D. Cent. Code § 45-22-01)
Limited liability limited partnerships:	• Limited Liability Limited Partnerships are expressly permitted by statute. (N.D. Cent. Code § 45-23-04)
Professional LLCs:	• Professional LLCs are expressly permitted by statute. (N.D. Cent. Code § 10-31-01)
Foreign LLCs:	• Foreign LLCs are expressly permitted by statute. Laws of the formation jurisdiction govern organization, internal affairs and the liability of members. (N.D. Cent. Code § 10-32-135)
Formation:	• An North Dakota LLC may be organized by one or more individuals. One or more members are required. (N.D. Cent. Code § § 10-32-05 and 10-32-06)

Naming requirements:	• An LLC's name must contain the words "limited liability company" or the abbreviation "L.L.C." or "LLC." (N.D. Cent. Code § 10-32-10)
Effective date of organization:	• A North Dakota LLC's existence begins upon the issuance of a certificate of organization, unless a later date (no more than 90 days after issuance of the certificate of organization) is specified. (N.D. Cent. Code § 10-32-09)
Filing requirements:	• The articles of organization must contain: (1) the LLC's name; (2) the address of the registered office and the name of the registered agent at that address; (3) the name and address of each organizer; (4) the date the LLC's existence will begin, if later than (but not more than 90 days after) the date upon which the certificate of organization is issued; (5) if the articles or organization are filed with the secretary of state; and (6) the duration of the LLC, if other than perpetual. (N.D. Cent. Code § 10-32-07)
Fees—Organization and Annual:	• The fee for filing articles of organization and issuing a certificate of organization is $125 plus a $10 registered agent fee. The fee for filing a foreign LLC's application for a certificate of authority is $125 plus a $10 registered agent fee. The fee for filing an annual report is $50. (N.D. Cent. Code § 10-32-150)

Recordkeeping:	• An LLC shall compile and maintain: (1) a current list of the full name and last-known address of each member, each governor, and the president; (2) a current list of the full name and last-known address of each assignee of financial rights and a description of the rights assigned; (3) a copy of the articles of organization and all amendments to the articles; (4) copies of any currently effective written operating agreement; (5) copies of the LLC's federal, state and local income tax returns and reports, if any, for the three most recent years; (6) financial statements; (7) records of all proceedings of members for the last three years; (8) records of all proceedings of the board of governors for the last three years; (9) reports made to members generally within the last three years; (10) member-control agreements; (11) a statement of all contributions accepted; (12) a statement of all contribution agreements; (13) a statement of all contribution allowance agreements; (14) an explanation of any restatement of value; (15) any written consents obtained from members; and (16) a copy of agreements, contracts, or other agreements or portions of them incorporated by reference. (N.D. Cent. Code § 10-32-51)
Annual reporting:	• An annual report is required. The report must be delivered to the secretary of state on or before November 15th of each year. (N.D. Cent. Code § 10-32-149) An LLC engaged in ranching or farming activities is required to file an annual report on April 15th of each year.
Management:	• Management is vested in the managers and agents of the LLC. The managers of an LLC must consist of a president and a treasurer and may contain one or more vice presidents and a secretary, as may be prescribed in the operating agreement. (N.D. Cent. Code § § 10-32-88 and 10-32-89)

¶1037

Membership rights and obligations:	• A member, governor, manager or other agent of an LLC is not personally liable for the acts, debts, liabilities, or obligations of the LLC. If a member fails to make a required contribution, the member is obligated, at the option of the LLC, to contribute cash equal to that portion of the value, as stated in the LLC records, of the contribution that the member has not made. Upon forfeiture of a contribution agreement, the LLC may sell the member's interest that was subject to such contribution agreement. A member who receives a wrongful distribution is liable to the LLC only for the amount of the distribution wrongfully made. (N.D. Cent. Code § § 10-32-29, 10-32-58 and 10-32-65)
Piercing the corporate veil:	• Case law that states the conditions and circumstances under which the corporate veil of a corporation may be pierced also applies to LLCs. (N.D. Cent. Code § 10-32-29)
Contributions:	• Contributions may consist of money or property. (N.D. Cent. Code § 10-32-56)
Distributions:	• Distributions, profits and losses are allocated in proportion to the value of the contributions of the members reflected in the required records, unless otherwise provided. (N.D. Cent. Code § § 10-32-36 and 10-32-60)
Resignation of member:	• A member always has the power, though not necessarily the right, to terminate his membership by resigning or retiring at any time. (N.D. Cent. Code § 10-32-30)
Transfer of LLC interest:	• A member's financial and governance rights are assignable in whole or in part, subject to certain restrictions. (N.D. Cent. Code § § 10-32-31 and 10-32-32)

Dissolution:	• An LLC is dissolved: (1) when its duration expires; (2) by order of a court; (3) by action of the organizers; (4) by action of the members; (5) *for LLCs with articles of organization filed with the secretary of state before July 1, 1999,* upon an event of dissociation of a member unless the business of the LLC is continued by consent of all remaining members, or *for LLCs with articles of organization filed with the secretary of state after June 30, 1999,* upon the occurrence of an event terminating the continued membership of a member as specified in the articles of organization or member control agreement; (6) *for LLCs with articles of organization filed with the secretary of state after June 30, 1999,* if the membership of the last member terminates and another member is not admitted within 180 days; or (7) *for LLCs with articles of organization filed with the secretary of state after June 30, 1999,* a merger in which the LLC is not the surviving organization. (N.D. Cent. Code § 10-32-109)
Mergers and consolidations:	• Mergers are expressly permitted by statute. (N.D. Cent. Code § 10-32-100)

¶ 1038

Ohio

Name of act:	• Ohio Limited Liability Company Act, Ohio Rev. Code § 1705.01 to Ohio Rev. Code § 1705.58.
Federal tax classification:	• The LLC statute is flexible. Any "business entity" not required to be treated as a "corporation" for federal tax purposes under Reg. § 301.7701-2 may choose its classification under Reg. § 301.7701-3.
State tax treatment:	• State tax classification follows federal. Thus, Ohio LLCs and LLCs doing business in Ohio are treated as partnerships or disregarded as entities, unless classified as corporations for federal tax purposes.
Securities treatment:	• A limited liability company interest is defined as a security in the Ohio Securities Act. (Ohio Rev. Code § 1707.01)
Limited liability partnerships:	• The formation of limited liability partnerships is expressly provided for by statute. (Ohio Rev. Code § 1775.61)
Limited liability limited partnerships:	• There are no statutes that mention a limited liability limited partnership by that name. Limited partnerships may register as registered limited partnerships and be treated as a limited liability limited partnership. (Ohio Rev. Code § 1775.61 *et seq.*)

Professional LLCs:	• Professional LLCs are expressly permitted by statute. (Ohio Rev. Code § 1705.04)
Foreign LLCs:	• Foreign LLCs are expressly permitted by statute. Laws of the formation jurisdiction govern organization, internal affairs and the liability of its members and managers. (Ohio Rev. Code § 1705.53)
Formation:	• One or more persons may form an LLC, and one or more members are required. (Ohio Rev. Code § § 1705.04 and 1705.43)
Naming requirements:	• The name of an LLC must include the words "limited liability company" without abbreviation or it must include one of the following abbreviations: "limited," "ltd." or "ltd". The name must be distinguishable on the records of the Secretary of State from the name of any other foreign or domestic LLC or any foreign or domestic corporation. (Ohio Rev. Code § 1705.05)
Effective date of organization:	• An LLC's existence begins when the articles of organization have been signed and filed with the Secretary of State. (Ohio Rev. Code § 1705.04)
Filing requirements:	• The articles of organization must include: (1) the LLC's name; (2) the period of its duration, which may be perpetual; (3) the address to which interested persons may direct requests for copies of any operating agreement and any bylaws of the LLC; and (4) any other matters the members decide to include. (Ohio Rev. Code § 1705.04)
Fees—Organization and Annual:	• The fee for filing and recording articles of organization is $125. The fee for registering a foreign LLC is $125. Annual registration is not required. (Ohio Rev. Code § 111.16)

Recordkeeping:	• The LLC must compile and maintain: (1) a current list of the full names, in alphabetical order, and last known business or residence address of each member; (2) a copy of the articles of organization, including any amendments, and executed copies of any powers of attorney; (3) a copy of any written operating agreement, including any amendments and any executed powers of attorney; (4) copies of any federal, state and local income tax returns and LLC reports for the three most recent tax years; (5) copies of any financial statements of the LLC for the three most recent years; and (6) unless contained in a written operating agreement, information regarding the amount of cash and a description and statement of the agreed value of any other property or services contributed or promised to be contributed in the future by each member, when any additional contribution is to be made by each member, any right of the LLC to make to a member, or of a member to receive, any distribution that includes a return of all or any part of his contribution, and each event upon the happening of which the LLC is to be dissolved and its affairs wound up. (Ohio Rev. Code § 1705.28)
Annual reporting:	• An annual report is not required.
Management:	• Management is vested in the members, unless otherwise provided. (Ohio Rev. Code § 1705.24)
Membership rights and obligations:	• Except as otherwise provided, LLC members and managers are not liable for any debt, obligation, or liability of the LLC, whether arising in tort, contract or otherwise, or under a judgment, decree or order of a court. If a member fails to make a required contribution, even in the event of the member's death, disability or other change in circumstances, the LLC may require the member to contribute cash equal to the portion of the value as stated in the LLC records of the stated contribution that the member has failed to make. A member who knowingly receives any wrongful distribution or payment is liable to the LLC for a period of two years thereafter for the amount received that is in excess of the amount of the rightful distribution or payment. (Ohio Rev. Code §§ 1705.09, 1705.23 and 1705.48)
Piercing the corporate veil:	• The Act has no express provision that concerns piercing the corporate veil.

Contributions:	• Contributions may consist of cash, property, services rendered, a promissory note or other binding obligation to contribute the same. (Ohio Rev. Code § 1705.09)
Distributions:	• Distributions, profits and losses are allocated based on the value of the contributions made by each member to the extent they have been received by the LLC and have not been returned, unless otherwise provided. (Ohio Rev. Code § § 1705.10 and 1705.11)
Resignation of member:	• If management is reserved to the members, a member may withdraw at any time by giving written notice. If the management is reserved to the managers, six months' written notice is required prior to resignation, unless otherwise provided. *If the LLC is formed after November 21, 1997,* or if so specified in the articles of organization or operating agreement, a member may withdraw only at the time or upon the occurrence of an event specified in the articles of organization or operating agreement. (Ohio Rev. Code § 1705.16)
Transfer of LLC interest:	• A member's LLC interest is assignable in whole or in part, unless otherwise provided. An assignee may become a member if the assignor is given the authority by the operating agreement or the members unanimously consent. (Ohio Rev. Code § § 1705.18 and 1705.20)
Dissolution:	• An LLC is dissolved: (1) at the expiration of the period fixed in the operating agreement or articles of organization for duration; (2) upon the happening of events specified in the operating agreement; (3) upon the unanimous written agreement of all the members; (4) when a member withdraws, unless the business of the LLC is continued by the consent of all the remaining members, or as otherwise provided; or (5) upon the entry of a decree of judicial dissolution. For LLCs formed on or after December 3, 1999, or for any LLC existing prior to that date that specifically amends its articles of incorporation or operating agreement to incorporate this provision, the withdrawal of a member will not cause dissolution of the LLC. (Ohio Rev. Code § § 1705.43 and 1705.47)
Mergers and consolidations:	• Mergers or consolidations are expressly permitted by statute. (Ohio Rev. Code § 1705.36)

¶ 1039
Oklahoma

Name of act:	• Oklahoma Limited Liability Company Act, Okla. Stat. tit. 18, § 2000 to Okla. Stat. tit. 18, § 2060.
Federal tax classification:	• The LLC statute is flexible. Any "business entity" not required to be treated as a "corporation" for federal tax purposes under Reg. § 301.7701-2 may choose its classification under Reg. § 301.7701-3.
State tax treatment:	• State tax classification follows federal. Thus, Oklahoma LLCs and LLCs doing business in Oklahoma are treated as partnerships or disregarded as entities, unless classified as corporations for federal tax purposes. (Okla. Stat. tit. 68, § 202)
Securities treatment:	• The Oklahoma Act does not expressly provide for the treatment of an LLC interest as a security.
Limited liability partnerships:	• The formation of limited liability partnerships is expressly permitted. (Okla. Stat. tit. 54, §§ 1-1001 and 1-1101)
Professional LLCs:	• Professional LLCs are permitted impliedly by statute. An LLC may be formed for any lawful purpose, except an LLC may not conduct business as a bank or domestic insurer. (Okla. Stat. tit. 18, § 2002)
Foreign LLCs:	• Foreign LLCs are expressly permitted by statute. Laws of the formation jurisdiction govern organization, internal affairs and the liability of members and managers. (Okla. Stat. tit. 18, § 2042)
Formation:	• One or more persons may form an Oklahoma LLC, and one or more members are required. (Okla. Stat. tit. 18, §§ 2001 and 2004)
Naming requirements:	• An Oklahoma LLC's name shall contain either the words "limited liability company" or "limited company" or the abbreviations "L.L.C." or "L.C.". The word "limited" may be abbreviated as "LTD." and the word "Company" may be abbreviated "Co." The abbreviations "LLC" and "LC" may also be used. (Okla. Stat. tit. 18, § 2008)
Effective date of organization:	• An LLC's existence begins when the articles of organization are filed. (Okla. Stat. tit. 18, § 2004)

Filing requirements:	• The articles of organization shall set forth: (1) the LLC's name; (2) the LLC's duration, which may be perpetual; (3) the street address of its principal place of business, wherever located; and (4) the name and street address of the resident agent, which must be identical to the address of the registered office. (Okla. Stat. tit. 18, § 2005)
Fees—Organization and Annual:	• The fee for filing the articles of organization is $100. The fee for filing the application for registration as a foreign LLC is $300. There is no annual registration fee. (Okla. Stat. tit. 18, § 2055)
Recordkeeping:	• An LLC must compile and maintain: (1) a current and a past list of the full name and last known mailing address of each member and manager; (2) copies of records that would enable a member to determine the relative voting rights of the members; (3) a copy of the articles of organization, together with any amendments thereto; (4) a copy of the LLC's federal, state, and local tax returns and financial statements, if any, for the three most recent years or, if such returns and statements were not prepared for any reason, copies of the information and statements provided to or which should have been provided to the members to enable them to prepare such returns; (5) copies of any effective written operating agreements and all amendments thereto, and copies of any written operating agreements no longer in effect; and (6) unless provided in writing in an operating agreement, a writing setting out the amount of cash and a statement of the agreed value of any other property or services contributed by each member and the times at which or events the happening of which any additional contributions agreed to be made by each member are to be made, the events upon the happening of which the LLC is to be dissolved and its affairs wound up, and any other information prepared pursuant to a requirement in an operating agreement. (Okla. Stat. tit. 18, § 2021)
Annual reporting:	• Every LLC must file an annual report due on the anniversary date of filing the certificate (Okla. Stat. tit. 18, § 2055.2)
Management:	• Management is vested in the members, unless otherwise provided. (Okla. Stat. tit. 18, § 2013)

Membership rights and obligations:	• A member or manager is not liable for the obligations of the LLC. If a member fails to make a required contribution, even in the event of death, disability or other reason, the member is obligated at the option of the LLC to contribute cash equal to that portion of the value of the stated contribution that has not been made. A member who receives a wrongful distribution is liable to the LLC for the amount of the distribution wrongfully made. An action for the recovery of any wrongful distribution must be brought within three years from the date of the distribution. (Okla. Stat. tit. 18, §§ 2022, 2024 and 2031)
Piercing the corporate veil:	• The Act has no express provision that concerns piercing the corporate veil.
Contributions:	• Contributions may consist of cash, property, services rendered, a promissory note or other binding obligation to contribute the same. (Okla. Stat. tit. 18, § 2023)
Distributions:	• Distributions shall be made to the members in proportion to their right to share in the profits of the LLC, unless otherwise provided. Profits and losses are allocated among the members in proportion to their respective capital interests, unless otherwise provided. (Okla. Stat. tit. 18, § 2025)
Resignation of member:	• A member may not withdraw at any time unless the operating agreement specifically permits voluntary withdrawal. A member in a member-managed LLC may resign in accordance with the operating agreement or articles of organization. If there are no resignation provisions in the operating agreement or the articles of organization, a member may resign upon written notice to the LLC. (Okla. Stat. tit. 18, §§ 2015 and 2036)
Transfer of LLC interest:	• A member's LLC interest is assignable in whole or in part, unless otherwise provided. Majority consent is required for assignee to become a member, unless otherwise provided. (Okla. Stat. tit. 18, §§ 2033 and 2035)
Dissolution:	• An LLC is dissolved upon the earlier of: (1) the occurrence of the latest date on which the LLC is to dissolve set forth in the articles of organization; (2) the occurrence of events specified in writing in the operating agreement; (3) upon the written consent of all members; or (4) upon the entry of a judicial dissolution. (Okla. Stat. tit. 18, §§ 2037 and 2038)
Mergers and consolidations:	• Mergers or consolidations are permitted expressly by statute. (Okla. Stat. tit. 18, § 2054)

¶1039

¶ 1040
Oregon

Name of act:	• Oregon Limited Liability Company Act, Or. Rev. Stat. § 63.001 to Or. Rev. Stat. § 63.990.
Federal tax classification:	• The LLC statute is flexible. Any "business entity" not required to be treated as a "corporation" for federal tax purposes under Reg. § 301.7701-2 may choose its classification under Reg. § 301.7701-3.
State tax treatment:	• State tax classification follows federal. Thus, Oregon LLCs and LLCs doing business in Oregon are treated as partnerships or disregarded as entities, unless classified as corporations for federal tax purposes. (Or. Rev. Stat. § 63.810)
Securities treatment:	• The Oregon Act does not expressly provide for the treatment of an LLC interest as a security.
Limited liability partnerships:	• Limited liability partnerships are expressly authorized by statute. (Or. Rev. Stat. § § 67.500 and 67.700)
Professional LLCs:	• Professional LLCs are expressly permitted by statute. (Or. Rev. Stat. § 63.074)
Foreign LLCs:	• Foreign LLCs are expressly permitted by statute. Laws of the formation jurisdiction govern organization, internal affairs and the liability of members and managers. (Or. Rev. Stat. § 63.701)
Formation:	• An Oregon LLC may be formed by one or more individuals 18 years of age or older or by other entities. At least one member is required. (Or. Rev. Stat. § 63.001 and Or. Rev. Stat. § 63.044)
Naming requirements:	• An Oregon LLC's name shall contain the words "limited liability company" or the abbreviation "L.L.C." or "LLC". (Or. Rev. Stat. § 63.094)
Effective date of organization:	• An Oregon LLC's existence begins when a certificate of existence for a domestic LLC or a certificate of authorization for a foreign LLC is issued. (Or. Rev. Stat. § 63.027)

Filing requirements:	• The articles of organization shall include: (1) the LLC's name; (2) the name and address of the initial registered agent for mailing of required notices; (3) the address of the initial registered office, if different than the address of the initial registered agent; (4) a mailing address to which notices may be mailed; (5) whether the LLC is to be member-managed or manager-managed; (6) the name and address of each organizer; (7) the latest date upon which the LLC is to dissolve or a statement that its existence is perpetual; and (8) if the LLC is to render professional services, a statement as to what professional services will be rendered. (Or. Rev. Stat. § 63.047)
Fees—Organization and Annual:	• The fee for filing articles of organization is $50. The fee for filing an application for registration of a foreign LLC is $50. The fee for filing a domestic LLC's annual report is $50. The fee for filing a foreign LLC's annual report is $50.
Recordkeeping:	• The LLC must compile and maintain: (1) a current list of the members' and managers' names and addresses, both past and present; (2) a copy of the articles of organization, all amendments thereto, together with executed copies of any powers of attorney; (3) copies of the LLC's federal, state, and local tax returns and reports for the three most recent years; (4) copies of any currently effective written operating agreements and all amendments thereto and copies of any writings permitted or required by statute; and (5) information regarding the amount of cash and a description and statement of the agreed value of any other property or services contributed, or promised to be contributed in the future by each member, any events upon the happening of which any additional contributions agreed to be made by each member are to be made and the time at which or the events on the occurrence of which the LLC is to be dissolved and its affairs wound up. (Or. Rev. Stat. § 63.771)
Annual reporting:	• An annual report is required of each domestic and foreign LLC. The annual report is due by the LLC's anniversary date. (Or. Rev. Stat. § 63.787)
Management:	• Management is vested in the members, unless otherwise provided. (Or. Rev. Stat. § 63.130)

¶1040

Membership rights and obligations:	• A member or manager of an LLC is not personally liable for any debt, obligation, or liability of the LLC, solely by reason of being or acting as a member or manager. If a member fails to make a required contribution, even in the event of death, disability or other reason, the member is obligated at the option of the LLC to contribute cash equal to that portion of the value of the stated contribution that has not been made. A member of a member-managed LLC or a member or manager of a manager-managed LLC who votes for or assents to a wrongful distribution is personally liable to the LLC for the amount of the distribution that is improper. A member of a manager-managed LLC who receives a distribution knowing that it was wrongful is personally liable to the LLC, but only to the extent that the distribution exceeded the proper amount. (Or. Rev. Stat. § § 63.165, 63.180 and 63.235)
Piercing the corporate veil:	• The Act has no express provision that concerns piercing the corporate veil.
Contributions:	• Contributions may consist of cash, property, services rendered, a promissory note or other obligation to contribute the same. (Or. Rev. Stat. § 63.175)
Distributions:	• Distributions shall be allocated among the members in proportion to their right to share in the profits of the LLC, unless otherwise provided. Profits and losses shall be allocated among all the members equally, unless otherwise provided. (Or. Rev. Stat. § § 63.185 and 63.195)
Resignation of member:	• Six months' written notice is required prior to resignation, unless otherwise provided. (Or. Rev. Stat. § 63.205)
Transfer of LLC interest:	• A member's LLC interest is assignable in whole or in part, unless otherwise provided. Consent of all members other than the assignor is required for an assignee to become a member, unless otherwise provided. (Or. Rev. Stat. § § 63.249 and 63.255)
Dissolution:	• An LLC is dissolved: (1) at the time or upon the happening of events specified in the articles of organization or an operating agreement; (2) upon the written consent of all members; (3) when the LLC has no members; (4) upon the entry of a judicial dissolution; or (5) upon an administrative or judicial dissolution. (Or. Rev. Stat. § § 63.621, 63.647 and 63.661)
Mergers and consolidations:	• Mergers are permitted expressly by statute. (Or. Rev. Stat. § 63.481)

¶ 1041
Pennsylvania

Name of act:	• Limited Liability Company Law of 1994, 15 Pa. Cons. Stat. § 8901 to 15 Pa. Cons. Stat. § 8998.
Federal tax classification:	• The LLC statute is flexible. Any "business entity" not required to be treated as a "corporation" for federal tax purposes under Reg. § 301.7701-2 may choose its classification under Reg. § 301.7701-3.
State tax treatment:	• LLCs will be taxed as corporations only if they are taxed as corporations for federal income tax purposes. (15 Pa. Cons. Stat. § § 8925 and 8997)
Securities treatment:	• "Security" includes an interest in an LLC and any class or series of such interests (including any fractional or other interest in such interest), except a membership interest in an LLC in which the person claiming this exception can prove that all of the members are actively engaged in the management of the LLC; provided that evidence that members vote or have the right to vote, or the right to information concerning the business and affairs of the LLC, or the right to participate in management, shall not establish, without more, that all members are actively engaged in the management of the LLC. (70 Pa. Cons. Stat. § 1-102(t))
Limited liability partnerships:	• The formation of limited liability partnerships is expressly permitted by statute. (15 Pa. Cons. Stat. § 8201)
Limited liability limited partnerships:	• Limited liability limited partnerships are authorized by statute. (15 Pa. Cons. Stat. § 8201 (committee comment (a))
Professional LLCs:	• Professional LLCs are permitted impliedly by statute. No prohibition exists in the provision concerning lawful business, except banking and insurance. However, an LLC providing services that are considered restricted professional services must register as a Restricted Professional Service Company and will be deemed limited partnerships for tax purposes. (15 Pa. Cons. Stat. § § 8903 and 8995)
Foreign LLCs:	• Foreign LLCs are expressly permitted by statute. A qualified foreign LLC enjoys the same rights and privileges as a domestic LLC. (15 Pa. Cons. Stat. § 8981)
Formation:	• One or more persons may organize an LLC. One or more members are required. (15 Pa. Cons. Stat. § § 8912 and 8944(a))

Naming requirements:	• A Pennsylvania LLC must contain the term "company," "limited" or "limited liability company" or an abbreviation of one of those terms. (15 Pa. Cons. Stat. § 8905)
Effective date of organization:	• An LLC is organized upon the filing of the certificate of organization with the Department of State, or at any later effective time specified in the certificate of organization. (15 Pa. Cons. Stat. § 8914)
Filing requirements:	• The certificate of organization must include: (1) the LLC's name; (2) the address of its initial registered office in the Commonwealth; (3) the name and address of each organizer; (4) if a member's interest in the LLC is to be evidenced by a certificate of membership interest, a statement to that effect; (5) if management is vested in a manager or managers, a statement to that effect; (6) if the certificate of organization is to be effective on a specified date, the hour, if any, and the month, day and year of the effective date; (7) if the LLC is a restricted professional company, a statement to that effect, including a brief description of the restricted professional service or services to be rendered by the company; and (8) any other provision the members elect to include. (15 Pa. Cons. Stat. § 8913)
Fees—Organization and Annual:	• The filing fee for a certificate of organization is $125. The fee for filing an application for registration of a foreign LLC is $250. The annual registration fee for restricted professional companies is $380 or more, depending upon the number of company members, and is subject to change every third year. (15 Pa. Cons. Stat. § 8998)
Recordkeeping:	• The Pennsylvania statute is silent as to records and information required to be kept by LLCs. However, it might be prudent for the LLC to compile and maintain: (1) a current list of the name and address of each member and manager; (2) copies of federal, state and local income tax returns and company information; (3) copies of the articles of organization, including any amendments; (4) copies of any effective written operating agreement; (5) financial statements; (6) information regarding members' capital contributions, agreements to contribute capital and the date each became a member; and (7) any other information regarding LLC affairs that is just and reasonable to maintain.

Annual reporting:	• An annual report is required for restricted professional companies. (15 Pa. Cons. Stat. § 8998)
Management:	• Management is vested in the members, unless otherwise provided. (15 Pa. Cons. Stat. § 8941)
Membership rights and obligations:	• Members and managers are not liable, solely by reason of being a member or manager, for any debt, obligation or liability of the LLC or for the acts or omissions of any other member, manager, agent or employee of the LLC. A member is obligated to the LLC to perform any enforceable promise to contribute cash or property or to perform services, unless otherwise provided. If a member fails to make a required contribution, even in the event of death, disability or other reason, the member is obligated, at the option of the LLC, to contribute cash equal to that portion of the value of the stated contribution that has not been made. The Pennsylvania statute is silent as to liability for wrongful distributions. (15 Pa. Cons. Stat. § § 8922 and 8931)
Piercing the corporate veil:	• The Act has no express provision that concerns piercing the corporate veil.
Contributions:	• Contributions consist of cash, tangible or intangible property, or services, or a promise to contribute the same. (15 Pa. Cons. Stat. § 8931)
Distributions:	• Distributions, profits and losses are allocated on a per capita basis, unless otherwise provided in the operating agreement. (15 Pa. Cons. Stat. § 8932)
Resignation of member:	• A member may or may not voluntarily withdraw from an LLC as provided in the operating agreement. (15 Pa. Cons. Stat. § 8948)
Transfer of LLC interest:	• A member's LLC interest is assignable as provided in the operating agreement. Unanimous consent is required for assignee to become a member, unless otherwise provided. (15 Pa. Cons. Stat. § 8924)

¶1041

Dissolution:	• An LLC is dissolved: (1) at the time or upon the happening of events specified in the certificate of organization; (2) at the time or upon the happening of events specified in writing in the operating agreement; (3) by unanimous written consent of all of the members; (4) when an event of dissociation occurs to a member, unless the business of the LLC is continued by unanimous consent of the remaining members given within 90 days of the dissociation event, or under a right to do so stated in the operating agreement; or (5) upon entry of an order of judicial dissolution. (15 Pa. Cons. Stat. §§ 8971 and 8972)
Mergers and consolidations:	• Mergers or consolidations are expressly permitted by statute. (15 Pa. Cons. Stat. § 8956)

¶ 1042

Rhode Island

Name of act:	• Rhode Island Limited Liability Company Act, R.I. Gen. Laws § 7-16-1 to R.I. Gen. Laws § 7-16-75.
Federal tax classification:	• The LLC statute is flexible. Any "business entity" not required to be treated as a "corporation" for federal tax purposes under Reg. § 301.7701-2 may choose its classification under Reg. § 301.7701-3.
State tax treatment:	• State tax classification follows federal. Thus, Rhode Island LLCs and foreign LLCs doing business in Rhode Island are treated as partnerships or disregarded as entities, unless classified as corporations for federal tax purposes. (R.I. Gen. Laws § 7-16-73).
Securities treatment:	• The Rhode Island Securities Act does not expressly provide for the treatment of an LLC interest as a security.
Limited liability partnerships:	• The registration of limited liability partnerships is expressly permitted by statute. (R.I. Gen. Laws § 7-12-56)
Limited liability limited partnerships:	• The registration of limited liability limited partnerships is expressly permitted by statute. (R.I. Gen. Laws § 7-12-56)
Professional LLCs:	• Professional LLCs are expressly permitted by statute. (R.I. Gen. Laws § 7-16-3.1)
Foreign LLCs:	• Foreign LLCs are expressly permitted by statute. Laws of the formation jurisdiction govern the LLC's organization, internal affairs, and liability of its members. (R.I. Gen. Laws § 7-16-48)
Formation:	• One or more persons may form an LLC in Rhode Island. One or more members are required. (R.I. Gen. Laws §§ 7-16-2 and 7-16-5)

Naming requirements:	• An LLC's name must end with either the words "limited liability company" or the upper or lower case letters "l.l.c." with or without punctuation. (R.I. Gen. Laws § 7-16-9)
Effective date of organization:	• An LLC's existence begins when the articles of organization are accepted for filing and the certificate of organization is issued. (R.I. Gen. Laws § 7-16-5)
Filing requirements:	• The articles of organization must include: (1) the LLC's name; (2) the name and address of the resident agent; (3) a statement indicating whether the LLC is intended to be treated as a corporation, a partnership or disregarded as an entity separate from its member for federal tax purposes; (4) the address of the principal office; (5) any other provisions the members elect to include; and (6) a statement as to whether the LLC is to be member-managed or manager-managed. (R.I. Gen. Laws § 7-16-6)
Fees—Organization and Annual:	• The fee for filing articles of organization is $150. The fee for filing a foreign LLC registration application is $150. The filing fee for the annual report is $50. (R.I. Gen. Laws § 7-16-65)
Recordkeeping:	• An LLC must compile and maintain: (1) a list of the members' and managers' names and addresses; (2) copies of records that indicate the members' relative voting rights and the capital value of their interests; (3) a copy of the articles of organization, including any amendments and restatements; (4) executed copies of any powers of attorney pursuant to which any certificate has been issued; (5) copies of the LLC's federal, state and local tax returns and information for the last five years; (6) a copy of the written operating agreement; (7) any written records of proceedings of members or managers; and (8) financial statements for the last five years. (R.I. Gen. Laws § 7-16-22)
Annual reporting:	• An annual report is required and is due between September 1 and November 1 of each year following the calendar year in which the LLC was organized. (R.I. Gen. Laws § 7-16-66)
Management:	• Management is vested in the members, unless otherwise provided. (R.I. Gen. Laws § 7-16-14)

¶1042

Membership rights and obligations:	• Members and managers are not liable for the LLC's obligations solely by reason of being a member or manager. If a member fails to make a required contribution, even in the event of death, disability or other reason, unless otherwise provided, the member is obligated, at the option of the LLC, to contribute cash equal to that portion of the value of the stated contribution that has not been made. A member or manager who assents to a wrongful distribution is personally liable to the LLC for the amount of the distribution wrongfully made. Each member or manager held liable is entitled to contribution from each member who received a wrongful distribution. (R.I. Gen. Laws § § 7-16-23, 7-16-25 and 7-16-32)
Piercing the corporate veil:	• The Act has no express provision that concerns piercing the corporate veil.
Contributions:	• Contributions may consist of cash, property, or services, or a written promise to contribute the same. (R.I. Gen. Laws § § 7-16-2 and 7-16-24)
Distributions:	• Distributions, profits and losses are allocated on the basis of each member's capital value, unless otherwise provided. (R.I. Gen. Laws § § 7-16-26 and 7-16-27)
Resignation of member:	• The Rhode Island act is silent as to the resignation of a member, implying that members are free to resign at any time without prior written notice, unless otherwise provided.
Transfer of LLC interest:	• A member's LLC interest is assignable in whole or in part, unless otherwise provided. Unanimous consent is required for an assignee to become a member, unless otherwise provided. (R.I. Gen. Laws § § 7-16-35 and 7-16-36)

Dissolution:
- An LLC is dissolved: (1) at the time, if any, specified in the articles of organization; (2) upon an event specified in the articles of organization or a written operating agreement to cause dissolution; (3) upon a vote to dissolve by a majority of capital values of all membership interests, unless otherwise provided; (4) upon the written consent of a majority of the capital values of the remaining members, when an event of dissociation occurs to a member, unless otherwise provided; (5) when an event of dissociation occurs to the last remaining member, unless, within 90 days, the successors-in-interest agree to admit at least one member to continue the business of the LLC, or (6) upon the entry of a decree of judicial dissolution. (R.I. Gen. Laws §§ 7-16-39 and 7-16-40)

Mergers and consolidations:
- Mergers or consolidations are permitted expressly by statute. (R.I. Gen. Laws § 7-16-59)

¶ 1043

South Carolina

Name of act:
- Uniform Limited Liability Company Act, S.C. Code § 33-44-101 to S.C. Code § 33-44-1208.

Federal tax classification:
- Any "business entity" not required to be treated as a "corporation" for federal tax purposes under Reg. § 301.7701-2 may choose its classification under Reg. § 301.7701-3.

State tax treatment:
- State tax classification follows federal. Thus, South Carolina LLCs and LLCs doing business in South Carolina are treated as partnerships or disregarded as entities, unless classified as corporations for federal tax purposes.

Securities treatment:
- The South Carolina Act does not expressly provide for the treatment of an LLC interest as a security.

Limited liability partnerships:
- The formation of limited liability partnerships is expressly provided for by statute. (S.C. Code § 33-41-1110)

Professional LLCs:
- The Uniform Limited Liability Company Act does not make express provisions for Professional LLCs.

Foreign LLCs:
- Foreign LLCs are expressly permitted by statute. Laws of the formation jurisdiction govern organization, internal affairs and the liability of members and managers. (S.C. Code § 33-44-1001)

Formation:
- One person may form an LLC, and an LLC may have one or more members. (S.C. Code § 33-44-202)

Naming requirements:	• A South Carolina LLC must have the words "limited liability company" or "limited company" or the abbreviations "L.L.C.", "L.C.", "LLC" or "LC" in its name. The word "Limited" may be abbreviated as "Ltd" and the word "Company" may be abbreviated as "Co." (S.C. Code § 33-44-105)
Effective date of organization:	• A South Carolina LLC's existence begins on the date the articles of organization are filed. A delayed effective date may be specified. (S.C. Code § 33-44-202(b))
Filing requirements:	• The articles of organization must set forth: (1) the company's name; (2) the initial designated office's address; (3) the initial agent's name and street address for service of process; (4) the name and address of each organizer; (5) whether the company is to be a term company, and, if so, the term specified; (6) whether the company is to be manager-managed, and if so, the name and address of each initial manager; and (7) whether one or more of the members of the company are to be liable for its debts and obligations under S.C. Code § 33-44-303(c). (S.C. Code § 33-44-203)
Fees—Organization and Annual:	• The fee for filing the articles of organization is $110. The fee for filing an application for a certificate of authority is $110. Annual registration (or renewal) of a foreign LLC name is $10. (S.C. Code § 33-44-1204)
Recordkeeping:	• The South Carolina statute is silent as to records and information required to be kept by LLCs. However, it might be prudent for the LLC to compile and maintain: (1) a current list of the name and address of each member and manager; (2) copies of federal, state and local income tax returns and company information; (3) copies of the articles of organization, including any amendments; (4) copies of any effective written operating agreement; (5) financial statements; (6) information regarding members' capital contributions, agreements to contribute capital and the date each became a member; and (7) any other information regarding LLC affairs that is just and reasonable to maintain.
Annual reporting:	• As of 2005, an LLC is no longer required to file an annual report.

Management:	• An LLC may be member-managed or manager-managed. In a member-managed company, each member has equal management rights and, except as provided, any matter relating to the business of the company may be decided by a majority of members. In a manager-managed company, each manager has equal management rights, and except as provided, any matter relating to the business of the company may be decided by the manager or by a majority of managers. (S.C. Code § 33-44-404)
Membership rights and obligations:	• Members are not liable for any debt, obligation, or liability of the LLC, whether under a judgment, decree, or order of a court, or in any other manner. If a member fails to make a required contribution, even in the event of death, disability or other reason, the member is obligated, at the option of the LLC, to contribute cash equal to that portion of the value of the stated contribution that has not been made. A member or manager who votes for or assents to a wrongful distribution is personally liable to the LLC for the amount of the distribution wrongfully made. Each member or manager held liable is entitled to contribution from each member who received a wrongful distribution. (S.C. Code § § 33-44-402 and 33-44-407)
Piercing the corporate veil:	• The failure of an LLC to observe the usual company formalities or requirements relating to the exercise of its company powers or management of its business is not a ground for imposing personal liability on the members or managers for liabilities of the company. (S.C. Code § 33-44-303)
Contributions:	• Contributions may consist of tangible or intangible property or other benefit to the company, including money, promissory notes, services performed or other agreements to contribute cash or property, or contracts for services to be performed. (S.C. Code § 33-44-401)
Distributions:	• Distributions made by an LLC before its dissolution and winding up shall be in equal shares. Distributions may not be made if the LLC would not be able to pay its debts or if the LLC's total assets would be less than its total liabilities plus the amount needed to satisfy preferential rights upon dissolution. (S.C. Code § § 33-44-405 and 33-44-406)

¶1043

Resignation of member:	• A member is dissociated from an LLC upon the LLC's having notice of the member's express will to withdraw upon date of notice or on a later date specified by the member. (S.C. Code § 33-44-601)
Transfer of LLC interest:	• A member may transfer, in whole or in part, a distributional interest in an LLC, but has no transferable interest in LLC property. Unanimous consent is required for a transferee to become a member of the LLC. (S.C. Code § 33-44-501)
Dissolution:	• An LLC is dissolved by the occurrence of any of the following events: (1) an event specified in the operating agreement; (2) consent of the number or percentage of members specified in the operating agreement; (3) an event that makes it unlawful for the business of the company to be continued, unless the defect is cured within 90 days; (4) on application by a member or dissociated member, upon entry of judicial decree; or (5) on application by a transferee of a member's interest, a judicial determination that it is equitable to wind up the company's business. (S.C. Code § 33-44-801(b))
Mergers and consolidations:	• Mergers are expressly permitted. (S.C. Code § 33-44-904)

¶ 1044
South Dakota

Name of act:	• South Dakota Limited Liability Company Act, S.D. Codified Laws § 47-34A-101 to S.D. Codified Laws § 47-34A-1207.
Federal tax classification:	• The South Dakota LLC Act is flexible. Any "business entity" not required to be treated as a "corporation" for federal tax purposes under Reg. § 301.7701-2 may choose its classification under Reg. § 301.7701-3.
State tax treatment:	• State tax classification follows federal. Thus, South Dakota LLCs doing business in South Dakota are classified as partnerships or disregarded as entities, unless classified as corporations for federal income tax purposes. South Dakota does not impose a corporate income tax.
Securities treatment:	• The South Dakota Act does not expressly provide for the treatment of an LLC interest as a security.
Limited liability partnerships:	• The formation of limited liability partnerships is expressly provided for by statute. (S.D. Codified Laws § 48-7A-1001)

Limited liability limited partnerships:	• Limited Liability Limited Partnerships are expressly authorized by statute. (S.D. Codified Laws § 48-7-1106)
Professional LLCs:	• An LLC may be organized for any lawful purpose, subject to any law governing or regulating business, including regulation of professional service firms. (S.D. Codified Laws § 47-34A-112)
Foreign LLCs:	• Foreign LLCs are expressly permitted by statute. The laws of the formation jurisdiction govern the LLC's organization, internal affairs, and liability of its members. (S.D. Codified Laws § 47-34A-1001)
Formation:	• South Dakota LLCs may be formed by one or more persons and may consist of one or more members. (S.D. Codified Laws § 47-34A-202A)
Naming requirements:	• Each LLC must have the words "limited liability company" or "limited company" in its name or the abbreviations "L.L.C.," "LLC," "L.C.," or "LC." The word "Limited" may be abbreviated as "Ltd." and the word "Company" may be abbreviated as "Co." (S.D. Codified Laws § 47-34A-105)
Effective date of organization:	• The existence of the LLC begins when the articles of organization and the first annual report are filed. (S.D. Codified Laws § 47-34A-202A)
Filing requirements:	• An LLC's articles of organization must set forth: (1) the LLC's name; (2) the address of the initial designated office; (3) the name and street address of the initial agent for service of process; (4) the name and address of each organizer; (5) the LLC's duration, if other than perpetual; (6) whether the company is to be manager-managed, and if so the name and address of each initial manager; and (7) whether one or more of the members of the company are to be liable for its debts and obligations. (S.D. Codified Laws § 47-34A-203)
Fees—Organization and Annual:	• The fee for filing the articles of organization is $125. The fee for filing a foreign LLC registration application is $550. The filing fee for the annual report is $50. (S.D. Codified Laws §§ 47-34A-212)
Recordkeeping:	• The LLC Act is silent as to records and information required to be kept by LLCs.
Annual reporting:	• LLCs are required to submit annual reports to the secretary of state before the second month of the year following the year in which the LLC was organized. (S.D. Codified Laws § 47-34A-211)
Management:	• An LLC may be member-managed or manager-managed. (S.D. Codified Laws § 47-34A-301)

¶1044

Membership rights and obligations:	• Any member or manager that improperly votes for or assents to a wrongful distribution is personally liable to the company for the amount of the distribution that exceeds the permissible amount. (S.D. Codified Laws § § 47-34A-303, 47-34A-402 and 47-34A-407)
Piercing the corporate veil:	• The failure of an LLC to observe the usual company formalities or requirements relating to the exercise of its company powers or management of its business is not a ground for imposing personal liability on the members or managers for liabilities of the company. (S.D. Codified Laws § 47-34A-303)
Contributions:	• Contributions may consist of money, promissory notes, services performed or other obligation to contribute the same. (S.D. Codified Laws § 47-34A-401)
Distributions:	• Any distributions made by an LLC before its dissolution and winding up must be in equal shares. (S.D. Codified Laws § 47-34A-405)
Resignation of member:	• A member of an LLC may resign at any time, unless otherwise provided. (S.D. Codified Laws § 47-34A-602)
Transfer of LLC interest:	• A member's LLC interest may be transferred or assigned as provided in the operating agreement. Unanimous consent is required for an assignee to become a member. (S.D. Codified Laws § § 47-34A-501 and 47-34A-503)
Dissolution:	• An LLC is dissolved upon the occurrence of any of the following events: (1) an event specified in the operating agreement; (2) consent of the number or percentage of members specified in the operating agreement; (3) an event that makes it unlawful for all or substantially all of the business of the company to be continued, unless cured within ninety days after notice to the company of the event; (4) entry of judicial decree upon the application by a member or a dissociated member; or (5) entry of a judicial determination upon the application by a transferee of a member's interest. (S.D. Codified Laws § 47-34A-801)
Mergers and consolidations:	• Mergers or consolidations are permitted expressly by statute. (S.D. Codified Laws § 47-34A-904)

¶ 1045
Tennessee

Name of act:	• Tennessee Limited Liability Company Act, Tenn. Code § 48-201-101 to Tenn. Code § 48-248-606. *Effective January 1, 2006*, Tennessee Revised Limited Liability Company Act, Tenn. Code § 48-286-101 to Tenn. Code § 48-286-1133. The Tennessee Revised Limited Liability Act will apply to every domestic LLC formed on or after January 1, 2006, and to any domestic LLC that was formed prior to January 1, 2006, that has elected to be governed by the Revised Act. The Act also governs every foreign LLC that first files a certificate of authority on or after January 1, 2006. The Prior Act will apply to foreign LLCs until the due date of their first annual report required to be filed after January 1, 2006. At that time, the Revised Act will apply to foreign LLCs. (Tenn. Code § 48-286-1002)
Federal tax classification:	• The LLC statute is flexible. Any "business entity" not required to be treated as a "corporation" for federal tax purposes under Reg. § 301.7701-2 may choose its classification under Reg. § 301.7701-3.
State tax treatment:	• State tax classification follows federal. Thus, Tennessee LLCs and LLCs doing business in Tennessee are classified as partnerships, unless classified as corporations for federal income tax purposes. (Tenn. Code § 48-211-101 and Tenn. Code § 48-286-1003)
Securities treatment:	• The Tennessee Securities Act does not expressly provide for the treatment of an LLC interest as a security.
Limited liability partnerships:	• The formation of limited liability partnerships is expressly permitted. (Tenn. Code § 61-1-1001)
Limited liability limited partnerships:	• A limited partnership may become a registered limited liability partnership. The statutes do not refer to "limited liability limited partnerships." (Tenn. Code § 61-1-1001(b))
Professional LLCs:	• Professional LLCs are expressly permitted by statute. (Tenn. Code § 48-248-101 and Tenn. Code § 48-286-1101)

Foreign LLCs:

- Foreign LLCs are expressly permitted by statute. Laws of the formation jurisdiction govern formation, organization, internal affairs and the liability of members and managers. (Tenn. Code § 48-246-101 and Tenn. Code § 48-286-901)

Formation:

- One or more individuals may form an LLC. One or more members are required. (Tenn. Code § 48-203-102 and Tenn. Code § 48-286-201)

Naming requirements:

- An Tennessee LLC name shall contain the either the words "limited liability company" or the abbreviation "L.L.C." or "LLC," or words or abbreviations of like import in another language. (Tenn. Code § 48-207-101 and Tenn. Code § 48-286-106)

Effective date of organization:

- An LLC's existence begins when the articles of organization are filed, or on the delayed date specified therein. (Tenn. Code § 48-203-102 and Tenn. Code § 48-286-201(c))

Filing requirements:

- The articles of organization must set forth: (1) the LLC's name; (2) the street address and zip code of the initial registered office of the LLC, the county in which the office is located and the name of its initial registered agent at that office; (3) the street address and zip code of the principal executive office of the LLC and the county in which the office is located; (4) a statement as to whether the LLC will be member-managed, manager-managed, or director-managed; (5) if the LLC will have more than six members at the date of filing the articles, a statement of the number of members at the date of filing the articles; (6) if one or more members are personally liable for all the debts, obligations and liabilities of the LLC; (7) if the existence of the LLC is to begin upon a certain date or the occurrence of a specific event, the future date or a description of the specific event except that in no event may the future date or the actual occurrence of the specific event be more than 90 days after the filing of the articles of organization; (8) if the LLC, while being formed under Tennessee law, is not to engage in business in Tennessee, a statement that the LLC is prohibited from engaging in business in Tennessee; and (9) if the duration of the LLC is to be limited to a specified period of time. (Tenn. Code § 48-286-202)

Fees—Organization and Annual:	• The fee for filing articles of organization, for filing the application for certificate of authority and the annual fee is equal to $50 per LLC member on the date of filing, with a minimum fee of $300 and a maximum fee of $3,000. (Tenn. Code § 48-247-103 and Tenn. Code § 48-286-1107(d))
Recordkeeping:	• An LLC must compile and maintain (1) a current list of the full name and last-known business, residence, or mailing address of each member, each member or director, as applicable, and each officer, if any, of the LLC, together with the taxpayer identification number of each member of the LLC; (2) a current list of the full name and last-known business, residence, or mailing address of each holder of financial rights and a description of the financial rights held, together with the taxpayer identification number of each holder of financial rights of the LLC; (3) a copy of the articles, and all amendments to the articles; (4) a copy of the currently effective operating agreement; (5) copies of the LLC's federal, state, and local income tax returns and reports, if any, for the three most recent years; (6) financial information sufficient to provide true and full information regarding the status of the business and financial condition of the LLC for the three most recent fiscal years; (7) records of all proceedings of members and of the holders, if any; (8) any written consents obtained from members of the LLC or from the holders, if any; (9) records of all proceedings of the managers or board of directors for the last three years; (10) a statement of all contributions accepted, the identity of the contributors and agreed value of the contributions; (11) a copy of all contribution agreements to which the LLC is bound; and (12) a copy of the LLC's most recent annual report. (Tenn. Code § 48-286-406)
Annual reporting:	• An annual report is required. (Tenn. Code § 48-228-203 and Tenn. Code. § 48-286-1011)
Management:	• An LLC may be member-managed, manager-managed or director-managed. (Tenn. Code § 48-286-401)

Membership rights and obligations:	• A member, holder, director, manager, officer, employee or other agent of the LLC is not personally liable for the acts, debts, liabilities, or obligations of the LLC whether such arise in contract, tort or otherwise, except for sales tax liability or as otherwise provided. (Tenn. Code § 48-286-114) In addition, a member, manager or director who votes for or receives a wrongful distribution is personally liable. (Tenn. Code § 48-286-307)
Piercing the corporate veil:	• The failure of a domestic or foreign LLC to observe the usual entity formalities or requirements relating to the exercise of its powers or management of its business is not a ground for imposing personal liability of members, holders, managers, directors, officers, employees or other agents of the LLC. (Tenn. Code § 48-286-114(e))
Contributions:	• Contributions may consist of tangible or intangible property or other benefit to the LLC, including money, a promissory note, services performed or an obligation or agreement to contribute money or property or to perform services. (Tenn. Code § 48-286-301)
Distributions:	• The LLC documents control the allocation of profits and losses. If the LLC documents are silent, then profits and losses shall be allocated among members and holders of financial rights in equal shares. (Tenn. Code § 48-286-304)
Resignation of member:	• A member always has the power, though not necessarily the right, to withdraw at any time. (Tenn. Code § 48-216-101 and Tenn. Code §§ 48-286-503 and 48-286-504)
Transfer of LLC interest:	• A member's LLC financial interest is transferable in whole or in part, unless otherwise provided. A member may transfer ownership of the member's full membership interest only by transferring all of the member's governance rights coupled with a transfer to the same transferee of all of the member's financial rights. (Tenn. Code §§ 48-286-507 and 48-286-508)
Dissolution:	• An LLC is dissolved upon the first of the following to occur: (1) when the LLC's duration, if fixed, expires; (2) the occurrence of an event specified in the LLC documents; (3) when the members or organizers agree to dissolve the LLC; (by order of a court or action of the secretary of state; (7) at any time there are no members if the LLC files a notice of dissolution. (Tenn. Code § 48-286-601)
Mergers and consolidations:	• Mergers, conversions and transfer of assets are permitted expressly by statute. (Tenn. Code §§ 48-268-702, 48-268-703 and 48-268-705)

260   Limited Liability Companies

¶ 1046

Texas

Name of act:	• Texas Limited Liability Company Act, Texas Rev. Civ. Stat., art. 1528n, §§ 1.01 to 11.07.
Federal tax classification:	• The LLC statute is flexible. Any "business entity" not required to be treated as a "corporation" for federal tax purposes under Reg. § 301.7701-2 may choose its classification under Reg. § 301.7701-3.
State tax treatment:	• LLCs are subject to the corporate franchise tax. (Texas Tax Code § 171.001)
Securities treatment:	• The Texas Act expressly exempts a professional LLC interest from treatment under the securities laws. (Texas Rev. Civ. Stat. art. 1528n, § 11.06)
Limited liability partnerships:	• The formation of limited liability partnerships is expressly provided for by Texas Rev. Civ. Stat., art. 6132b § 3.08.
Limited liability limited partnerships:	• Limited Liability Limited Partnerships are expressly authorized by statute. (Texas Rev. Civ. Stat., art. 6132a-1, § 2.14)
Professional LLCs:	• Professional LLCs are permitted expressly by statute, subject to compliance with other state regulatory provisions. (Texas Rev. Civ. Stat. art.1528n, § 11.01)
Foreign LLCs:	• Foreign LLCs are expressly permitted by statute. Laws of the formation jurisdiction govern organization, internal affairs and the liability of its members and managers. (Texas Rev. Civ. Stat. art. 1528n, §§ 7.01 and 7.02)
Formation:	• A Texas LLC may be formed by one or more persons. At least one member is required. (Texas Rev. Civ. Stat. art. 1528n, § 4.01)
Naming requirements:	• The name of each LLC must contain the words "limited liability company," or "limited company" or the abbreviations "L.L.C.," "LLC," "L.C." or "LC" and must be distinguishable from the record name of any domestic or foreign LLC, corporation or limited partnership registered in the state of Texas. The word "limited" may be abbreviated as "Ltd." or "LTD" and the word "company" may be abbreviated as "Co." *An LLC formed before September 1, 1993,* that complied with naming requirements at the time of formation, is not required to change its name to comply with revised requirements. (Texas Rev. Civ. Stat. art. 1528n, § 2.03)
Effective date of organization:	• The LLC's existence begins when the certificate of organization is issued. (Texas Rev. Civ. Stat. art. 1528n, § 3.04)

Filing requirements:

- The articles of organization must include: (1) the LLC's name; (2) the period of duration, which may be perpetual; (3) the address of its initial registered office and the name of its initial registered agent at that address; (4) the LLC's purpose; (5) if management of the LLC is vested in a manager or managers, a statement to that effect and the names and addresses of the initial manager or managers, or if the LLC will not have managers, a statement to that effect and the names and addresses of the initial members; (6) the name and address of each organizer; (7) a statement whether the LLC is a professional LLC, and, if so, any provision required by the sections governing professional LLCs; (8) if the LLC is organized pursuant to a plan of conversion or merger, a statement to that effect, and in the case of a plan of conversion, the name, address, prior form of organization, date of incorporation, formation or organization and jurisdiction of the converting entity; and (9) any other matters the members decide to include. (Texas Rev. Civ. Stat. art. 1528n, § 3.02)

Fees—Organization and Annual:

- The fee for filing articles of organization is $300. The fee for filing a foreign LLC registration application is $750. Annual registration is not required. (Texas Rev. Civ. Stat. art. 1528n, § 9.01)

Recordkeeping:

- The LLC must compile and maintain: (1) a list of the members' and managers' names and addresses; (2) the percentage or other interest in the LLC owned by each member; (3) the names of the members who are members of each specified group or class, if one or more groups or classes are otherwise established; (4) copies of federal, state and local information or income tax returns of the six most recent tax years; (5) a copy of the articles of organization and regulations, including any amendments, together with copies of any executed powers of attorney and any documents that create groups or classes of members; (6) unless contained in the articles of organization, information regarding the amount of cash and a description and statement of the agreed value of any other property or services contributed, or promised to be contributed in the future, by each member, the times at which additional contributions will be made, any events upon the happening of which the LLC is to be dissolved and its affairs wound up and the date on which each member became a member; and (7) correct and complete books and records of account. (Texas Rev. Civ. Stat. art. 1528n, § 2.22)

Annual reporting:

- When the annual franchise taxes are paid, a Texas Franchise Tax Public Information Report must be filed with the Comptroller of Public Accounts.

Management:

- Management is vested in the managers, unless otherwise provided. (Texas Rev. Civ. Stat. art. 1528n, § 2.12)

Membership rights and obligations:

- Members and managers are not liable for any debt, obligation, or liability of the LLC, whether under a judgment decree or order of a court, unless otherwise provided. If a member fails to make a required contribution, notwithstanding the member's death, disability or other change in circumstances, the member or the member's legal representative is obligated, at the option of the LLC, to contribute cash equal to that portion of the value of the stated contribution represented by the amount of cash that has not been paid or the value of the property that has not been transferred. The regulations of an LLC may also provide that a member who fails to make a capital contribution or other payment shall be subject to specified consequences. A member who receives a wrongful distribution is under no obligation to return the distribution unless such member knew that the distribution was wrongful. (Texas Rev. Civ. Stat. art. 1528n, § § 4.03, 5.02 and 5.09)

Piercing the corporate veil:

- The Act has no express provision that concerns piercing the corporate veil.

Contributions:

- Contributions may consist of any tangible or intangible benefit to the LLC or other property of any kind or nature, including cash, services rendered, a promissory note, other obligation to contribute the same or other interests in or securities or other obligations of any other LLC or other entity. (Texas Rev. Civ. Stat. art. 1528n, § 5.01)

Distributions:

- Distributions are based on the agreed value, as stated in the LLC records, of the contributions made by each member, unless otherwise provided. Profits and losses are allocated in accordance with the then current percentage or other interest in the LLC of the members as stated in the LLC records, unless otherwise provided. (Texas Rev. Civ. Stat. art. 1528n, § § 5.02-1 and 5.03)

Resignation of member:

- A member may withdraw as specified in the LLC's regulations. (Texas Rev. Civ. Stat. art. 1528n, § 5.05)

Transfer of LLC interest:

- A member's LLC interest is assignable in whole or in part, unless otherwise provided. Unanimous consent required for an assignee to become a member of the LLC, unless otherwise provided. (Texas Rev. Civ. Stat. art. 1528n, § § 4.05 and 4.07)

Dissolution:	• An LLC is dissolved: (1) at the expiration of the period fixed for duration, if any; (2) upon the happening of events specified in the articles or organization or regulations; (3) upon the action of the members to dissolve the LLC; (4) upon the action of a majority of the managers or members to dissolve the LLC, if no capital has been paid into the LLC; (5) when an event of dissolution occurs to a member, unless the business of the LLC is continued by the vote of the remaining members, or as otherwise provided; or (6) upon a judicial dissolution. (Texas Rev. Civ. Stat. art. 1528n, § § 6.01 and 6.02)
Mergers and consolidations:	• Mergers are permitted expressly by statute. (Texas Rev. Civ. Stat. art. 1528n, § 10.01)

¶ 1047
Utah

Name of act:	• Utah Revised Limited Liability Company Act, Utah Code § 48-2c-101 to Utah Code § 48-2c-1902.
Federal tax classification:	• The LLC statute is flexible. Any "business entity" not required to be treated as a "corporation" for federal tax purposes under Reg. § 301.7701-2 may choose its classification under Reg. § 301.7701-3.
State tax treatment:	• State tax classification follows federal. Utah LLCs and LLCs doing business in Utah are treated as partnerships or disregarded as entities, unless classified as corporations for federal tax purposes. (Utah Code § 59-10-801)
Securities treatment:	• The Utah Securities Act expressly provides for the treatment of an LLC interest as a security. However, excluded from this definition is an interest in an LLC in which the LLC is formed as part of an estate plan where all of the members are related by blood or marriage, there are five or fewer members or the person claiming this exception can prove that all of the members are actively engaged in the management of the LLC. Evidence that members have a right to vote, the right to information concerning the business and affairs of the LLC or the right to participate in management shall not establish, without more, that all members are actively engaged in the management of the LLC. (Utah Code § 61-1-13)
Limited liability partnerships:	• The formation of limited liability partnerships is expressly provided for by statute. (Utah Code § § 48-1-41 to 48-1-48)
Professional LLCs:	• Professional LLCs are expressly permitted by statute. (Utah Code § 48-2c-1501)

Foreign LLCs:	• Foreign LLCs are expressly permitted by statute. Laws of formation jurisdiction govern organization and internal affairs. (Utah Code § 48-2c-1601)
Formation:	• A Utah LLC may be formed by one or more individuals 18 years of age or over. One or more members are required. (Utah Code §§ 48-2c-401(1) and 48-2c-401(2))
Naming requirements:	• A Utah LLC must contain the words "limited liability company" or "limited company" or the abbreviations "L.L.C."or "L.C." (Utah Code § 48-2c-106)
Effective date of organization:	• A Utah LLC exists when a stamp or seal is placed on the articles of organization. (Utah Code § 48-2c-402(3))
Filing requirements:	• The articles of organization must set forth: (1) the LLC's name; (2) its duration, not to exceed 99 years; (3) its purpose; (4) the street address of its registered office in Utah and the name, street address and signature of its initial registered agent in Utah; (5) if the LLC is to be managed by a manager or managers, a statement to that effect; (6) a statement that the director of the Division of Corporations and Commercial Code is appointed agent of the LLC is the agent has resigned, the agent's authority has been revoked, or the agent cannot be found or served with the exercise of due diligence; (7) if the management of an LLC is reserved to the members, the names and street addresses of the members; and (8) any other provision that the members choose to include. If an LLC is to be managed by one or more managers, the articles of organization do not need to state the name or address of any member. If the articles of organization do not specify the LLC's period of duration, as required, the period of duration shall be 99 years. (Utah Code § 48-2c-403)
Fees—Organization and Annual:	• The fee for filing articles of organization is $52. The fee for filing foreign LLC registration application is $52. Annual registration is $12.

Recordkeeping:	• The LLC must compile and maintain: (1) a current list, in alphabetical order, of the members' and managers' full names and last known addresses; (2) a copy of the stamped articles of organization, and all amendments thereto, together with copies of any powers of attorney; (3) copies of the LLC's federal, state, and local income tax returns and reports, if any, for the three most recent years; (4) copies of any financial statements of the LLC, if any, for the three most recent years; (5) copies of the LLC's operating agreement, if any; and (6) unless contained in its certificate of formation or an LLC agreement, a written statement of the amount of cash, and a description of contributions and future contributions by each member, when any additional contributions agreed to be made by each member are to be made, any right of any member to receive distributions which include a return of all or any part of the member's contribution, and any event upon the happening of which the LLC is to be dissolved. (Utah Code § 48-2c-112)
Annual reporting:	• A domestic LLC's annual report is required and is due during the month of the LLC's anniversary date of formation. (Utah Code § 48-2c-203(1)(a)(i)) A foreign LLC's annual report is due during the month of the anniversary in which it was granted authority to transact business. (Utah Code § 48-2c-203(1)(a)(ii))
Management:	• Management shall be vested in the members, unless otherwise provided. (Utah Code § 48-2c-801(1))
Membership rights and obligations:	• LLC members are not personally liable for any debt, obligation, or liability of the LLC under a judgment, decree, or order of a court, or in any other manner, unless otherwise provided. However, members are liable for the difference between the amount of the member's contributions which have actually been made and the amount which is stated in the operating agreement as having been made and for any unpaid contributions that such member agreed to make in the future. A member holds as trustee for the LLC any money or property that has been wrongfully distributed. (Utah Code §§ 48-2c-601 and 602)
Piercing the corporate veil:	• The Utah Act has no express provision that concerns piercing the corporate veil.
Contributions:	• Contributions may consist of cash, property, services rendered, a promissory note or other binding obligation to contribute the same. (Utah Code § 48-2c-901)

¶1047

Distributions:	• Distributions of profits and losses are allocated among members in proportion to the members' capital account balances as of the beginning of the LLC's current fiscal year, unless otherwise provided. (Utah Code §§ 48-2c-906 and 48 2c 1001)
Resignation of member:	• A member's right to resign from the LLC is determined by the operating agreement. If the operating agreement does not specify the time or events upon the happening of which a member may withdraw, a member may not withdraw prior to the dissolution and winding up of the LLC, without the written consent of all LLC members. (Utah Code § 48-2c-709)
Transfer of LLC interest:	• A member's LLC interest is assignable, in whole or in part, unless otherwise provided in the operating agreement. Unanimous consent is required for an assignee to participate in the management and affairs of the LLC, unless otherwise provided. (Utah Code §§ 48-2c-1101 and 1104)
Dissolution:	• An LLC is dissolved: (1) when its duration expires; (2) when the LLC fails to meet the requirement to maintain at least one member; (3) upon written consent of the members entitled to receive a majority of the profits of the LLC, unless otherwise provided; (4) when the LLC is not the successor LLC in the merger or consolidation of two or more LLCs; or (5) upon the occurrence of an event specified in the articles of organization or operating agreement as an event resulting in dissolution. (Utah Code § 48-2c-1201)
Mergers and consolidations:	• Mergers and consolidations are expressly permitted by statute. (Utah Code § 48-2c-1401)

¶ 1048

Vermont

Name of act:	• Vermont Limited Liability Company Act, Vt. Stat. Ann., tit. 11, § 3001 to Vt. Stat. Ann., tit. 11, § 3162.
Federal tax classification:	• The LLC statute is flexible. Any "business entity" not required to be treated as a "corporation" for federal tax purposes under Reg. § 301.7701-2 may choose its classification under Reg. § 301.7701-3.
State tax treatment:	• State tax classification follows federal classification. Thus, Vermont LLCs and LLCs doing business in Vermont are classified as partnerships or disregarded as entities, unless classified as corporations for federal income tax purposes. (Vt. Stat. Ann., tit. 32, § 5921)

Securities treatment:
- The term "security" includes a membership interest in an LLC (Vt. Stat. Ann., tit. 9, § 4202(a))

Limited liability partnerships:
- The formation of limited liability partnerships is expressly permitted. (Vt. Stat. Ann., tit.11, § 03291)

Professional LLCs:
- Professional LLCs are expressly permitted by statute, subject to compliance with other state regulatory statutes. (Vt. Stat. Ann., tit. 11, § 3012(c))

Foreign LLCs:
- Foreign LLCs are expressly permitted by statute. Laws of the formation jurisdiction govern the LLC's organization and internal affairs, as well as the liability of its members and managers. (Vt. Stat. Ann., tit. 11, § 3131)

Formation:
- A Vermont LLC may be formed by one or more persons and may consist of one or more members. (Vt. Stat. Ann., tit. 11, § 3022(b))

Naming requirements:
- The name of an LLC must contain the words "limited liability company" or "limited company" or the abbreviation "L.L.C.", "LLC", "L.C." or "LC". The word "limited" may be abbreviated as "Ltd." and "company" may be abbreviated as "Co." (Vt. Stat. Ann., tit. 11, § 3005)

Effective date of organization:
- The existence of an LLC begins when the articles of organization are filed, unless a delayed effective date is specified. (Vt. Stat. Ann., tit. 11, § 3022)

Filing requirements:
- The articles of organization must include: (1) the LLC's name; (2) the address of the designated office; (3) the name and address of the agent for service of process; (4) the name and address of each organizer; (5) whether the company is a term LLC, and, if so, the duration of the term; (6) whether the company is to be manager-managed, and, if so, the name and address of each manager; and (7) whether the members of the company are to be liable for its debts and obligations. (Vt. Stat. Ann., tit. 11, § 3023)

Fees—Organization and Annual:
- The fee for filing articles of organization is $75. The fee for filing an application for a certificate of authority is $100. The annual report fee for a domestic LLC is $20, and the annual report fee of a foreign LLC is $100. (Vt. Stat. Ann., tit. 11, § 3013)

¶1048

Recordkeeping:	• The Vermont statute is silent as to records and information required to be kept by LLCs. However, it might be prudent for the LLC to compile and maintain (1) a current list of the name and address of each member and manager; (2) copies of federal, state and local income tax returns and company information; (3) copies of the articles of organization, including any amendments; (4) copies of any effective written operating agreement; (5) financial statements; (6) information regarding members' capital contributions, agreements to contribute capital and the date each became a member; and (7) any other information regarding LLC affairs that is just and reasonable to maintain.
Annual reporting:	• An annual report must be filed within two and one-half months after the expiration of the company's fiscal year. Information required includes: (1) the name of the company and the state or country under whose law it is organized; (2) the address of its designated office and the name of its designated agent at that office in this state; (3) the address of its principal office; and (4) the names and business addresses of any managers. (Vt. Stat. Ann., tit. 11, § 3161)
Management:	• Management of a Vermont LLC may be by member or manager, as provided in the operating agreement. (Vt. Stat. Ann., tit. 11, § § 3023 and 3054)
Membership rights and obligations:	• The Vermont statute does not excuse members from their contribution obligation to the LLC, even in cases of death, disability or inability to perform personally. If a member does not make the required contribution, he is obligated, at the option of the LLC, to contribute money equal to the value of that portion of the contribution that has not been made. If a member has received a wrongful distribution, then the member is liable to the company to the extent that the distribution received exceeded the amount that could properly have been paid. (Vt. Stat. Ann., tit. 11, § § 3052 and 3057)
Piercing the corporate veil:	• The Act has no express provision that concerns piercing the corporate veil.
Contributions:	• Contributions may consist of tangible or intangible property or other benefit to the company, including money, promissory notes, services performed or other obligations to contribute cash or property or contracts for services to be performed. (Vt. Stat. Ann., tit. 11, § 3051)

Distributions:	• An LLC may distribute profits and losses among the members or the holders of distributional interests in proportion to the agreed value of the contributions made by each member. (Vt. Stat. Ann., tit. 11, § 3055)
Resignation of member:	• A member may resign at any time by giving 90 days' advance written notice, unless otherwise provided. A member who wrongfully dissociates from a limited liability company is liable to the company and to the other members for damages caused by the dissociation. (Vt. Stat. Ann., tit. 11, § 3082)
Transfer of LLC interest:	• A member's LLC interest is transferable and assignable. A transferee of a distributional interest may become a member in accordance with the operating agreement or if all other members consent. (Vt. Stat. Ann., tit. 11, § § 3071 and 3073)
Dissolution:	• An LLC is dissolved upon the occurrence of any of the following events: (1) an event specified in the operating agreement; (2) consent of the number or percentage of members specified in the operating agreement; (3) dissociation of a member-manager or, if none, a member of an at-will company, unless the business of the LLC is continued by the remaining members; (4) an event that makes it unlawful for all or substantially all of the business of the company to be continued; (5) on application by a member, upon entry of a final judicial decree; or (6) the expiration of a term specified in the company's articles of organization. (Vt. Stat. Ann., Tit. 11, § 3101)
Mergers and consolidations:	• Mergers are permitted, expressly by statute. (Vt. Stat. Ann., tit. 11, § 3124)

¶ 1049
Virginia

Name of act:
• Virginia Limited Liability Company Act, Va. Code § 13.1-1000 to Va. Code § 13.1-1073, and Virginia Professional Limited Liability Company Act, Va. Code § 13.1-1100 to Va. Code § 13.1-1123.

Federal tax classification:
• The LLC statute is flexible. Any "business entity" not required to be treated as a "corporation" for federal tax purposes under Reg. § 301.7701-2 may choose its classification under Reg. § 301.7701-3.

State tax treatment:
• State tax classification follows federal. Thus, Virginia LLCs and LLCs doing business in Virginia are classified as partnerships or disregarded as entities, unless classified as corporations for federal income tax purposes. (Va. Code § 58.1-391)

Securities treatment:
• The Virginia Securities Act does not expressly provide for the treatment of an LLC interest as a security.

Limited liability partnerships:
• The formation of limited liability partnerships is expressly provided by statute. (Va. Code § 50-73.132)

Limited liability limited partnerships:
• Limited Liability Limited Partnerships are expressly authorized by statute. (Va. Code § 50-73.78)

Professional LLCs:
• Professional LLCs are expressly permitted by statute. (Va. Code §§ 13.1-1100 to 13.1-1123)

Foreign LLCs:
• Foreign LLCs are expressly permitted by statute. Laws of the formation jurisdiction govern organization, internal affairs and the liability of its members and managers. (Va. Code § 13.1-1051)

Formation:
• One or more persons may form an LLC. Single-member LLCs are permitted. No members are required. (Va. Code § 13.1-1010)

Naming requirements:
• The name of an LLC must include the words "limited company" or "limited liability company" or their abbreviations "L.C.," "LC," "L.L.C." or "LLC." (Va. Code § 13.1-1012)

Effective date of organization:
• The LLC's existence begins upon the issuance of the certificate of organization, unless a later date and time are specified. (Va. Code § 13.1-1004)

Filing requirements:
- The articles of organization must include: (1) the LLC's name; (2) the post office address, including street and number, if any, of the LLC's initial registered office, the name of the city or county in which it is located, the name of its initial registered agent at that office and that the agent meets certain requirements set forth in Va. Code § 13.1-1011; (3) the address of the principal office of the LLC; and (4) any other matters permitted to be set forth. (Va. Code § 13.1-1011)

Fees—Organization and Annual:
- The fee for filing articles of organization is $100. The fee for filing foreign LLC registration application is $100. The fee for annual registration is $50. (Va. Code §§ 13.1-1005 and 13.1-1062)

Recordkeeping:
- The LLC must compile and maintain: (1) a current list of the full names, in alphabetical order, and last known business or residence address of each member; (2) a copy of the articles of organization and the certificate of organization, including any amendments, (3) copies of federal, state and local income tax returns and company reports for the three most recent tax years; (4) copies of any then-effective written operating agreement and of any financial statements of the LLC for the three most recent years; and (5) unless contained in the articles of organization, information regarding the amount of cash and a description and statement of the agreed value of any other property or services contributed or promised to be contributed in the future by each member, when any additional contribution is to be made by each member, any right of the LLC to make to a member or of a member to receive any distribution that includes a return of all or any part of his contribution, and each event upon the happening of which the LLC is to be dissolved and its affairs wound up. (Va. Code § 13.1-1028)

Annual reporting:
- An annual report is not required.

Management:
- Management is vested in the members, unless otherwise provided. (Va. Code § 13.1-1022)

Membership rights and obligations:	• Members and managers shall not have any personal obligation for any liabilities of the LLC, whether such liabilities arise in contract, tort or otherwise, unless otherwise provided. If a member fails to make a required contribution, thc mcmbcr is subjcct to penalties specified in Va. Code § 13.1-1027(D). If a member receives a wrongful distribution, the member is liable to the LLC for a period of six years thereafter for the amount of the distribution wrongfully made. (Va. Code §§ 13.1-1019, 13.1-1027 and 13.1036)
Piercing the corporate veil:	• The Act has no express provision that concerns piercing the corporate veil.
Contributions:	• Contributions may consist of cash, property, services rendered, a promissory note or other obligation to contribute the same. (Va. Code § 13.1-1027)
Distributions:	• Distributions, profits and losses are based on the value of the contributions made by each member, unless otherwise provided. (Va. Code §§ 13.1-1029 and 13.1-1030)
Resignation of member:	• A member may resign only to the extent provided for in the articles of organization or an operating agreement. (Va. Code § 13.1-1032)
Transfer of LLC interest:	• A member's LLC interest is assignable in whole or in part, unless otherwise provided. Consent of a majority in interest of remaining members is required for an assignee to become a member. (Va. Code §§ 13.1-1039 and 13.1-1040)
Dissolution:	• An LLC is dissolved: (1) upon the happening of any events specified in the articles or organization or operating agreement; (2) upon the unanimous written agreement of the members; (3) at any time there are no members, unless otherwise provided; however, the LLC will not be dissolved if, within six months, the personal representative of the last member agrees in writing to continue the business; (4) upon a judicial dissolution; or (5) upon automatic cancellation of certification for failure to pay annual registration fees. (Va. Code §§ 13.1-1046 and 13.1-1047)
Mergers and consolidations:	• Mergers are permitted expressly by statute. (Va. Code § 13.1-1070)

¶ 1050

Washington

Name of act:	• Washington Limited Liability Company Act, Wash. Rev. Code § 25.15.005 to Wash. Rev. Code § 25.15.902.
Federal tax classification:	• The LLC statute is flexible. Any "business entity" not required to be treated as a "corporation" for federal tax purposes under Reg. § 301.7701-2 may choose its classification under Reg. § 301.7701-3.
State tax treatment:	• Washington imposes no state personal income tax.
Securities treatment:	• The Washington Act does not expressly provide for the treatment of an LLC interest as a security.
Limited liability partnerships:	• The formation of Limited Liability Partnerships is expressly permitted by statute. (Wash. Rev. Code § 25.05.500)
Professional LLCs:	• Professional LLCs are expressly permitted by statute, subject to compliance with other state regulatory provisions. (Wash. Rev. Code § 25.15.045)
Foreign LLCs:	• Foreign LLCs are expressly permitted by statute. Laws of the formation jurisdiction govern organization, internal affairs and the liability of members and managers. (Wash. Rev. Code § 25.15.310)
Formation:	• A Washington LLC may be formed by one or more persons. One or more members are required. (Wash. Rev. Code § 25.15.070)
Naming requirements:	• A Washington LLC name must contain the words "Limited Liability Company," the words "Limited Liability" and abbreviation "Co.," or the abbreviations "L.L.C." or "LLC." (Wash. Rev. Code § 25.15.010)
Effective date of organization:	• An LLC is formed when the certificate of formation is filed, unless a delayed effective date is specified. (Wash. Rev. Code § 25.15.070)
Filing requirements:	• The certificate of formation shall set forth: (1) the name of the LLC; (2) the address of the registered office and the name and address of the registered agent; (3) the address of the principal place of business of the LLC; (4) if the LLC is to have a specific date of dissolution, the latest date on which the LLC is to dissolve; (5) if management is vested in a manager or managers, a statement to that effect; (6) any other matters the members decide to include therein; and (7) the name and address of each person executing the certificate of formation. (Wash. Rev. Code § 25.15.070)

Fees—Organization and Annual:

- The fee for filing articles of organization is $175 plus $10 for the initial report. The fee for filing foreign LLC registration application is $175 plus $10 for the initial report. The annual registration fee, for all years after initial registration, is $59. (Wash. Rev. Code § 25.15.805)

Recordkeeping:

- The LLC must compile and maintain: (1) a current and past list setting forth the full name and last known mailing address of each member and manager; (2) a copy of the certificate of formation and all amendments thereto; (3) a copy of its current LLC agreement and all amendments thereto and a copy of any prior agreements no longer in effect; (4) unless contained in its certificate of formation or an LLC agreement, a written statement of the amount of cash, and a description of contributions and future contributions by each member, when any additional contributions agreed to be made by each member are to be made, and any right of any member to receive distributions which include a return of all or any part of the member's contribution; (5) a copy of the LLC's federal, state, and local tax returns and reports, if any, for the three most recent years; and (6) a copy of any financial statements of the LLC for the three most recent years. (Wash. Rev. Code § 25.15.135)

Annual reporting:

- An annual report is required. (Wash. Rev. Code § 25.15.105)

Management:

- Management of the LLC is vested in the members, unless otherwise provided. (Wash. Rev. Code § 25.15.150)

Membership rights and obligations:

- A member or manager is not personally liable for any debt, obligation, or liability of the LLC solely by reason of being a member or manager of the LLC. If a member fails to make a required contribution, even in the event of the member's death, disability or other change in circumstances, the member is obligated at the option of the LLC to contribute cash equal to that portion of the value, as stated in the LLC records, of the stated contribution that has not been made. A member who knowingly receives any wrongful distribution is liable to the LLC for the amount of the distribution. A member who did not know at the time of the distribution that the distribution was wrongful is not liable for the amount of the distribution. (Wash. Rev. Code § § 25.15.125, 25.15.195 and 25.15.235)

Piercing the corporate veil:
- Members of an LLC shall be personally liable for any act, debt, obligation, or liability of the LLC to the extent that shareholders of a Washington business corporation would be liable in analogous circumstances. (Wash. Rev. Code § 25.15.060)

Contributions:
- Contributions may consist of cash, property or services, or a promissory note or other obligation to contribute cash or property or to perform services. (Wash. Rev. Code § 25.15.190)

Distributions:
- Distributions, profits and losses are allocated in proportion to the agreed value of the contributions made, or required to be made, by each member, unless otherwise provided. (Wash. Rev. Code § § 25.15.200 and 25.15.205)

Resignation of member:
- A member may withdraw at the time specified in the agreement. If the agreement does not specify, a member may not withdraw prior to dissolution without the written consent of all other members at the time. (Wash. Rev. Code § 25.15.130)

Transfer of LLC interest:
- An LLC interest is assignable in whole or in part, unless otherwise provided. Unanimous consent is required for an assignee to become a member, unless otherwise provided. (Wash. Rev. Code § § 25.15.250 and 25.15.260)

Dissolution:
- An LLC is dissolved: (1) on the date, if any, specified in an LLC agreement; (2) upon the happening of events specified in an LLC agreement; (3) upon the written consent of all members; (4) when an event of dissociation occurs to a member, unless the business of the LLC is continued either by the consent of all the remaining members within ninety (90) days following the occurrence of any such event or pursuant to a right to continue stated in the LLC agreement; (5) upon the entry of a decree of judicial dissolution; or (6) two years after the effective date of an administrative dissolution. (Wash. Rev. Code § § 25.15.270 and 25.15.275)

Mergers and consolidations:
- Mergers of LLCs are expressly provided for by statute. (Wash. Rev. Code § 25.15.395)

¶ 1051
West Virginia

Name of act:	• West Virginia Uniform Limited Liability Company Act, W.Va. Code § 31B-1-101 to W.Va. Code § 31B-13-1306.
Federal tax classification:	• Any "business entity" not required to be treated as a "corporation" for federal tax purposes under Reg. § 301.7701-2 may choose its classification under Reg. § 301.7701-3.
State tax treatment:	• The state tax classification follows federal. Thus, West Virginia LLCs and foreign LLCs doing business in West Virginia are treated as partnerships or disregarded as entities, unless classified as corporations for federal tax purposes.
Securities treatment:	• The West Virginia Act does not expressly provide for the treatment of an LLC interest as a security.
Limited liability partnerships:	• The formation of limited liability partnerships is expressly permitted. (W.Va. Code § 47B-10-1)
Professional LLCs:	• Professional LLCs are expressly permitted by statute. (W.Va. Code § 31B-13-1301)
Foreign LLCs:	• Foreign LLCs are expressly permitted by statute. Laws of the formation jurisdiction govern organization, internal affairs and the liability of members and managers. (W.Va. Code § 31B-10-1001)
Formation:	• One or more persons may form an LLC, and an LLC may have one or more members. (W.Va. Code § 31B-2-202)
Naming requirements:	• The name of each LLC must contain the words "limited liability company," "limited company" or "L.C.," "LLC," "L.C." or "LC." "Limited" may be abbreviated as "Ltd." and "company" may be abbreviated as "Co." (W.Va. Code § 31B-1-105)
Effective date of organization:	• The LLC's existence begins when the articles of organization are filed, unless a delayed effective date is specified. (W.Va. Code § 31B-2-202(b))

Filing requirements:

- The articles of organization must set forth: (1) the company's name; (2) the initial designated office's address; (3) the initial agent's name and street address for service of process; (4) the name and address of each organizer and of each member having authority to execute instruments on behalf of the LLC; (5) whether the company is to be a term company and, if so, the term specified; (6) whether the company is to be manager-managed, and if so, the name and address of each initial manager; (7) whether one or more of the members of the company are to be liable for its debts and obligations under W.Va. Code § 31B-3-303(c); and (8) the purpose or purposes for which the LLC is formed. (W.Va. Code § 31B-2-203)

Fees—Organization and Annual:

- The fee for filing a certificate of formation is $100 (prorated) plus a $25 attorney-in-fact fee. The fee for filing a foreign LLC registration application is $150 (prorated) plus a $25 attorney-in-fact fee. The fee for the annual registration is $25. (W.Va. Code §§ 31-1A-17 and 59-1-2)

Recordkeeping:

- The West Virginia statute is silent as to records and information required to be kept by LLCs. However it might be prudent for the LLC to compile and maintain: (1) a current list of the name and address of each member and manager; (2) copies of federal, state and local income tax returns and company information; (3) copies of the articles of organization, including any amendments; (4) copies of any effective written operating agreement; (5) financial statements; (6) information regarding members' capital contributions, agreements to contribute capital and the date each became a member; and (7) any other information regarding LLC affairs that is just and reasonable to maintain.

Annual reporting:

- An annual report must be filed between January 1 and April 1 each year following the year the LLC was organized. Information required includes: (1) the company name and the state or country under whose law it is organized; (2) the designated office address and the name and address of its agent for service of process; (3) the address of the principal office; and (4) the names and business addresses of any managers. (W.Va. Code § 31B-2-211)

Management:	• An LLC may be member-managed or manager-managed. In a member-managed company, each member has equal management rights and, except as provided, any matter relating to the business of the company may be decided by a majority of members. In a manager-managed company, each manager has equal management rights, and except as provided, any matter relating to the business of the company may be decided by the manager or by a majority of managers. (W.Va. Code § 31B-4-404)
Membership rights and obligations:	• Members are not excused from their contribution obligation to the LLC, even in cases of death, disability or inability to perform personally. If a member does not make the required contribution, he is obligated, at the option of the LLC, to contribute money equal to the value of that portion of the contribution that has not been made. If a member has received a wrongful distribution, then the member is liable to the company to the extent that the distribution received exceeded the amount that could properly have been paid. (W.Va. Code §§ 31B-4-402 and 31B-4-407)
Piercing the corporate veil:	• The failure of an LLC to observe the usual company formalities or requirements relating to the exercise of its company powers or management of its business is not a ground for imposing personal liability on the members or managers for liabilities of the company. (W.Va. Code § 31B-3-303)
Contributions:	• Contributions may consist of tangible or intangible property or other benefit to the company, including money, promissory notes, services performed or other agreements to contribute cash or property, or contracts for services to be performed. (W.Va. Code § 31B-4-401)
Distributions:	• Distributions made by an LLC before its dissolution and winding up shall be in equal shares. Distributions may not be made if the LLC would not be able to pay its debts or if the LLC's total assets would be less than its total liabilities plus the amount needed to satisfy preferential rights upon dissolution. (W.Va. Code §§ 31B-4-405 and 31B-4-406)
Resignation of member:	• A member is dissociated from an LLC upon the LLC's having notice of the member's express will to withdraw upon date of notice or on a later date specified by the member. (W.Va. Code § 31B-6-601)

Transfer of LLC interest:	• A member may transfer, in whole or in part, a distributional interest in an LLC, but has no transferable interest in LLC property. Unanimous consent is required for a transferee to become a member. (W.Va. Code §§ 31B-5-501 and 31B-5-503(a))
Dissolution:	• An LLC is dissolved by the occurrence of any of the following events: (1) an event specified in the operating agreement; (2) consent of the number or percentage of members specified in the operating agreement; (3) dissociation of a member who is a manager, unless the business of the LLC is continued by the remaining members; (4) an event that makes it unlawful for the business of the company to be continued; (5) on application by a member or dissociated member, upon entry of judicial decree; or (6) on application by a transferee of a member's interest, a judicial determination that it is equitable to wind up the company's business. (W.Va. Code § 31B-8-801(b))
Mergers and consolidations:	• Mergers are permitted expressly by statute. (W.Va. Code § 31B-9-904)

¶ 1052
Wisconsin

Name of act:	• Wisconsin Limited Liability Company Act, Wis. Stat. § 183.0102 to Wis. Stat. § 183.1305.
Federal tax classification:	• The LLC statute is flexible. Any "business entity" not required to be treated as a "corporation" for federal tax purposes under Reg. § 301.7701-2 may choose its classification under Reg. § 301.7701-3.
State tax treatment:	• State tax classification follows federal. Thus, Wisconsin LLCs and foreign LLCs doing business in Wisconsin are treated as partnerships or disregarded as entities, unless classified as corporations for federal tax purposes.

Securities treatment:	• The term "security" does not include any interest in an LLC organized under the Wisconsin LLC Act if there are 15 or fewer members of the LLC after the interest is transferred and the right to manage the LLC is vested in its members. However, "security" is presumed to include an interest in a Wisconsin LLC if management of the LLC is vested in one or more members or if there are more than 35 members after the interest is sold. This presumption is rebuttable and may potentially allow interests in some manager-managed LLCs to avoid securities status. If the aggregate number of members is more than 15, but less than 36, and the right to manage the LLC is vested in the members, the LLC interests are presumed not to be securities. This negative presumption is also rebuttable, allowing the LLCs interests to be characterized as securities if the requisite degree of dependence can be shown. (Wis. Stat. § 551.02(13))
Limited liability partnerships:	• Registration of limited liability partnerships is expressly permitted. (Wis. Stat. § 178.40)
Professional LLCs:	• Professional LLCs are permitted impliedly. No prohibition exists in the statutory provision concerning lawful business. (Wis. Stat. § 183.0106)
Foreign LLCs:	• Foreign LLCs are expressly permitted by statute. Laws of the formation jurisdiction govern organization, internal affairs and the liability and authority of members and managers. Foreign LLCs may only carry on businesses that may be carried on by Wisconsin LLCs. (Wis. Stat. § 183.1001)
Formation:	• A Wisconsin LLC may be formed by one or more persons. (Wis. Stat. § 183.0201)
Naming requirements:	• The name of an LLC must include the words "limited liability company" or "limited liability co." or end with the abbreviation "L.L.C." or "LLC." (Wis. Stat. § 183.0103)
Effective date of organization:	• The LLC's existence begins on the date when the document is received by the office of the secretary of state for filing, unless a delayed effective date is specified. (Wis. Stat. § 183.0111)

Filing requirements:
- The articles of organization must include: (1) a statement that the LLC is organized under Wis. Stat. Ch. 183; (2) the LLC's name; (3) the street address of the registered office and the name of the registered agent at that office; (4) if management of the LLC is vested in one or more managers, a statement to that effect; (5) the name and address of each person organizing the LLC; and (6) if applicable, the delayed effective date and time of the articles of organization. (Wis. Stat. § 183.0202)

Fees—Organization and Annual:
- The fee for filing articles of organization is $130, if filed electronically and $170, if filed on paper. The fee for a foreign LLC's application for certificate of registration is $100. The fee for filing the annual report of a domestic LLC is $25. The fee for filing the annual report of foreign LLC is $80. (Wis. Stat. § 183.0114)

Recordkeeping:
- The LLC must compile and maintain: (1) a current list of the full names, in alphabetical order, and last known business or residence address of each past and present member or manager, the date on which the person became member or manager and the date, if applicable, on which the person ceased to be a member or manager; (2) a copy of the articles of organization, including any amendments; (3) copies of federal, state and local income tax returns and financial statements for the four most recent tax years or, if such returns and statements are not prepared, information and statements provided to members to enable them to prepare their federal, state and local income tax returns for the four most recent years; (4) a copy of any written operating agreement, including any amendments and any operating agreements no longer in effect; and (5) unless contained in the articles of organization, a writing containing information regarding the value of each member's contribution made to the LLC, records of the times at which or the events upon which any additional contributions are agreed to be made, any events upon which the LLC is to be dissolved and its business wound up, and any other writings prepared under a requirement, if any, in an operating agreement. (Wis. Stat. § 183.0405)

Annual reporting:
- An annual report is required. (Wis. Stat. § 183.0120)

Management:
- Management is vested in the members, unless otherwise provided. (Wis. Stat. § 183.0401)

Membership rights and obligations:	• Except as otherwise provided, LLC members and managers are not personally liable for any debt, obligation, or liability of the LLC, whether arising in tort, contract or otherwise. If a member fails to make a required contribution, even in the event of the member's death, disability or other change in circumstances, the member is obligated, at the option of the LLC, to contribute cash equal to that portion of the value, as stated in the LLC records, of the stated contribution that has not been fulfilled. A member or manager who votes or assents to a wrongful distribution is personally liable to the LLC for the amount of the distribution that exceeds the amount that could have been rightfully distributed. (Wis. Stat. § § 183.0304, 183.0502 and 183.0608)
Piercing the corporate veil:	• In regard to personal liability, a court is not precluded from ignoring the LLC entity under principles of common law that are similar to those applicable to business corporations and shareholders. (Wis. Stat. § 183.0304)
Contributions:	• Contributions may consist of cash, property, services rendered, a promissory note or other obligation to contribute the same. (Wis. Stat. § 183.0501)
Distributions:	• Distributions, profits and losses are allocated based on the value of the contributions made by each member, unless otherwise provided. (Wis. Stat. § § 183.0503 and 183.0602)
Resignation of member:	• A member may withdraw at any time by giving written notice, unless otherwise provided. For an LLC organized for a definite term or particular undertaking, a member may not withdraw before the expiration of the term or completion of the undertaking, unless otherwise provided in the operating agreement. (Wis. Stat. § 183.0802)
Transfer of LLC interest:	• A member's LLC interest is assignable in whole or in part, unless otherwise provided. Unanimous consent is required for an assignee to become an LLC member, unless otherwise provided. (Wis. Stat. § § 183.0704 and 183.0706)
Dissolution:	• An LLC is dissolved: (1) upon the happening of events specified in an operating agreement; (2) upon the written consent of all the members; (3) when an event of dissociation occurs to a member, unless the business of the LLC is continued within 90 days by the consent of all the remaining members, or as otherwise provided; or (4) upon a judicial dissolution. (Wis. Stat. § § 183.0901 and 183.0902)
Mergers and consolidations:	• Mergers or consolidations are permitted expressly by statute. (Wis. Stat. § 183.1201)

¶ 1053
Wyoming

Name of act:	• Wyoming Limited Liability Act, Wyo. Stat. § 17-15-101 to § 17-15-144 and the Wyoming Close Limited Liability Company Supplement, Wyo. Stat. § 17-25-101 to § 17-25-109.
Federal tax classification:	• The LLC statute is flexible. Any "business entity" not required to be treated as a "corporation" for federal tax purposes under Reg. § 301.7701-2 may choose its classification under Reg. § 301.7701-3. (Wyo. Stat. § 17-15-144)
State tax treatment:	• Wyoming has no individual or corporate income taxes.
Securities treatment:	• The Wyoming Securities Act does not expressly provide for the treatment of an LLC interest as a security.
Limited liability partnerships:	• The formation of limited liability partnerships is expressly permitted. (Wyo. Stat. § § 17-21-1101 to 17-21-1105)
Limited liability limited partnerships:	• The formation of limited liability limited partnerships is expressly permitted. (Wyo. Stat. § 17-14-202)
Professional LLCs:	• Professional LLCs are expressly permitted by statute. (Wyo. Stat. § 17-15-103)
Foreign LLCs:	• Foreign LLCs are expressly permitted by statute. To the extent not inconsistent with the LLC Act, an LLC organized in another jurisdiction may do business in Wyoming by complying with statutes applicable to foreign corporations. The statute is silent as to governing law. (Wyo. Stat. § § 17-15-143 and 17-16-1533)
Formation:	• Any person may form an LLC. A flexible LLC may have one or more members. (Wyo. Stat. § § 17-15-106, 17-15-144 and 17-25-104)
Naming requirements:	• The words "limited liability company," "limited company," "limited liability co.," "ltd. liability company" or "ltd. liability co." or the abbreviations "LLC," "L.L.C.," "LC" or "L.C." must be contained in the LLC's name. (Wyo. Stat. § 17-15-105)
Effective date of organization:	• The LLC's existence begins upon the issuance of the certificate of organization. (Wyo. Stat. § 17-15-109)

Filing requirements:
- The articles of organization must include: (1) the LLC's name; (2) the LLC's duration, which is 30 years if not otherwise specified; (3) the LLC's purpose; (4) the name and address of its registered agent in the state; (5) the total amount of cash and a description and agreed value of property other than cash contributed; (6) the total additional contributions, if any, agreed to be made by all members and the times at which or events upon the happening of which they shall be made; (7) the right, if given, of the members to admit additional members, and the terns and conditions of the admission; (8) the right, if given, of the members to continue the business of the LLC upon the termination of the continued membership of a member; (9) if the LLC is managed by managers, a statement as to such, including the names and addresses of such managers and if the LLC is managed by members, the names and addresses of the members; (10) if the LLC is flexible, a statement to that effect; and (11) any other provisions which to members elect to include. (Wyo. Stat. § 17-15-107)

Fees—Organization and Annual:
- The fee for filing articles of organization is $100. The fee for filing a foreign LLC registration application is $100. The annual report license tax is assessed based on the greater of $50 or two-tenths of one mill on the dollar ($.0002) based on the company's assets located and employed in the state of Wyoming. (Wyo. Stat. § 17-15-132)

Recordkeeping:
- The Wyoming statute is silent as to records and information required to be kept by LLCs. However, it might be prudent for the LLC to compile and maintain: (1) a current list of the name and address of each member and manager; (2) copies of federal, state and local income tax returns and company information; (3) copies of the articles of organization, including any amendments; (4) copies of any effective written operating agreement; (5) financial statements; (6) information regarding members' capital contributions, agreements to contribute capital and the date each became a member; and (7) any other information regarding LLC affairs that is just and reasonable to maintain.

Annual reporting:	• The Wyoming LLC statute does not set forth an annual report requirement. However, the secretary of state administrative rules provide that an annual report form will be mailed to existing LLCs approximately two months prior to the due date.
Management:	• Management is vested in the members, unless otherwise provided. (Wyo. Stat. § 17-15-116)
Membership rights and obligations:	• Members and managers shall not be liable under a judgment, decree or order of a court, or in any other manner, for a debt, obligation or liability of the LLC, unless otherwise provided. A member is liable to the LLC for the difference between the contributions actually made and that stated in the articles of organization as having been made by the member and for any unpaid contribution which the member agreed to make. The member holds as trustee for the LLC any wrongful distribution paid or conveyed to such member on account of the member's contribution. (Wyo. Stat. § § 17-15-113 and 17-15-121)
Piercing the corporate veil:	• The Act has no express provision that concerns piercing the corporate veil.
Contributions:	• Contributions may consist of cash, property, services rendered, a promissory note or other obligation to contribute the same. (Wyo. Stat. § 17-15-115)
Distributions:	• Unless otherwise provided, distributions, profits and losses are allocated based on the value of the contributions made by each member to the extent they have been received by the LLC and have not been returned. (Wyo. Stat. § 17-15-119)
Resignation of member:	• Six months' written notice is required prior to resignation, unless otherwise provided. (Wyo. Stat. § 17-15-120)
Transfer of LLC interest:	• A member's LLC interest is assignable in whole or in part, unless otherwise provided. (Wyo. Stat. § 17-15-144)
Dissolution:	• An LLC is dissolved: (1) when the period fixed for duration of LLC expires; (2) upon the unanimous written agreement of the members; or (3) when an event of dissociation occurs to a member, unless the business of the LLC is continued by the consent of all the remaining members. (Wyo. Stat. § § 17-15-123 and 17-15-144)
Mergers and consolidations:	• Mergers or consolidations are permitted expressly by statute. (Wyo. Stat. 17-15-139)

¶1053

Appendix A
Model LLC Operating Agreement

Introductory Comments

This Model Agreement is a relatively simple operating agreement for an LLC with two or more members that is to be managed by designated managers. Many of the provisions in this agreement also can be used for single-member LLCs. An operating agreement for an LLC is equivalent to a partnership agreement for a partnership. All 50 states and the District of Columbia have adopted LLC statutes. In addition, the National Conference of Commissioners on Uniform State Laws has created a Uniform Limited Liability Company Act (ULLCA), similar in style to those for general and limited partnerships. However, only a handful of states have adopted the ULLCA. The states that have adopted the ULLCA have also adopted provisions that vary from the ULLCA. Therefore, when utilizing this Model Agreement, it is also important to consult the statutes of the state of the LLC's organization and operation.

Under the default provisions of the federal "check-the-box" regulations, an LLC with two or more members is a limited liability vehicle that is taxed as a partnership for federal tax purposes or disregarded as a separate entity if it has only one member. In late 2002, the IRS issued Rev. Proc. 2002-69, 2002-2 CB 831, that provided guidance on the classification, for federal tax purposes, of an entity that is solely owned by a husband and wife as community property. If the husband and wife treat the entity as a disregarded entity for federal tax purposes, the IRS will accept that position. This Rev. Proc. did not offer guidance regarding the treatment for federal income tax purposes of a similarly situated husband and wife in a noncommunity property state, such as a husband and wife who own the LLC as tenants by the entirety. However, the IRS has indicated that its ruling is limited to community property states. Many partnership agreement provisions relating to allocations of profits and losses and the sharing of liabilities are equally relevant to two-or-more-member LLCs.

This agreement does not contain many of the complex tax-related provisions that are often contained in a limited partnership agreement relating to the allocation of profits and losses (for such information, see the sample agreement at ¶ 200 of CCH's PARTNERSHIP TAX PLANNING AND PRACTICE Guide). This LLC agreement contemplates that at all times during the life of the LLC, the members' interests in all items of LLC income and loss and all distributions of LLC cash and property will be allocated and distributed in the same proportion as the members' respective capital contributions. Consequently, the various safe harbor provisions provided by the Code Sec. 704(b) regulations, which necessitate qualified income offset, minimum gain chargeback and adjusted capital account deficit language, are not necessary because an allocation according to the "partner's interest in the partnership" (the fallback test under Code Sec. 704(b)) should produce the same allocation as is contained in the agreement.

However, to the extent that it is desired to allocate losses or deductions to the members in an amount in excess of their capital commitment to the LLC (*i.e.,* capital contributed to the LLC plus the members' obligations to contribute additional capital), tax-related provisions similar to those contained in the limited partnership agreement mentioned above should be considered.

Outline for LLC Agreement

Article I—Organization
    .01 Formation of Limited Liability Company
    .02 Name
    .03 Principal Office, Registered Office, and Registered Agent
    .04 Purpose
    .05 Fiscal Years
Article II—General Definitions
    .01 Act
    .02 Affiliate of a Member
    .03 Agreement
    .04 Bankrupt
    .05 Bankruptcy Code
    .06 Cash Flow
    .07 Code
    .08 Company
    .09 Managers
    .10 Members
    .11 Membership Interest
    .12 Property
Article III—Capital Contributions and Capital Accounts
    .01 Capital Contributions
    .02 Capital Accounts
    .03 Limited Liability
    .04 No Interest on or Right to Withdraw Capital Contributions
Article IV—Company Funds
Article V—Allocations and Distributions
    .01 Distributions
    .02 Allocation of Profits and Losses
Article VI—Management: Rights, Powers, and Obligations of the Manager(s)
    .01 Management and Control in General
    .02 Number and Appointment of Manager(s)
    .03 Employment of Others, Including Affiliates

Model LLC Agreement

OPERATING AGREEMENT
AMONG THE MEMBERS OF
_____, L.L.C.

OPERATING AGREEMENT, made and entered into as of _____, 20___, by and between those persons who have executed this Operating Agreement or a counterpart hereof.

The parties, intending to be legally bound, agree as follows:

ARTICLE I
Organization

.01 FORMATION OF LIMITED LIABILITY COMPANY

On _____, 20___, [name] and [name] organized a [name of state] limited liability company (the "Company") pursuant to the Act, as hereinafter defined. The Articles of Organization as filed by [name] and [name] are hereby adopted and ratified by the Members. In the event of a conflict between the terms of this Operating Agreement and the terms of the Articles of Organization, the terms of the Articles of Organization shall prevail.

.02 NAME

The business of the Company shall be conducted under the name of [name] or such other name as the Manager(s) may designate in writing to the Members.

.03 PRINCIPAL OFFICE, REGISTERED OFFICE, AND REGISTERED AGENT

The principal business office of the Company shall be located at [location], the Company's registered office shall be located at [location] and its initial registered agent shall be [name]. The Manager(s) may, within their sole and unrestricted discretion, change the principal office, registered office or registered agent of the Company, in such event, shall give written notice thereof to all Members, and the Manager(s) may establish additional offices of the Company.

.04 PURPOSE

The purpose of the Company is to [purpose], and to pursue other business and investment opportunities as the Manager(s) shall determine may be beneficial for the Company.

.05 FISCAL YEARS

The fiscal year of the Company shall be the calendar year or other fiscal year as the Manager(s) shall determine pursuant to the provisions of Code Sec. 706(b).

ARTICLE II
General Definitions

As used in this Agreement, the following terms shall each have the meaning set forth in this Article (unless the context otherwise requires). For purposes of this Agreement, the term "person" includes individuals, corporations, associations, partnerships, limited liability companies, trusts, estates and other entities.

.01 ACT

Act shall mean the [name of state] Liability Company Act, as now in effect or as hereafter amended or revised.

.02 AFFILIATE OF A MEMBER

Affiliate of a Member shall mean any person directly or indirectly controlling, controlled by or under common control with a Member or Members.

.03 AGREEMENT

Agreement shall mean this Operating Agreement, and it may be amended or supplemented from time to time in accordance with the provisions hereof.

.04 BANKRUPT

Bankrupt shall mean, with respect to any Member, the occurrence of any one or more of the following: (i) the making by the Member of an assignment for the benefit of creditors; (ii) the filing of an involuntary petition seeking an adjudication of bankruptcy under Chapter 7 of the Bankruptcy Code, which filing is not dismissed within sixty (60) days of the filing; (iii) the filing of a voluntary petition by the Member under Chapter 7 of the Bankruptcy Code; (iv) the filing of a voluntary or involuntary petition under Chapters 11 or 13 of the Bankruptcy Code which is not dismissed within sixty (60) days of the filing, but only if the Member is not the debtor-in-possession of his or her assets; (v) the entry of an order, judgment or decree by a court of competent jurisdiction providing for the liquidation of the assets of the Member or appointing a receiver, trustee or other administrator of the Member's assets which continues in effect and unstayed for a period of sixty (60) days; (vi) the confirmation of any plan of reorganization under either Chapter 11 or 13 of the Bankruptcy Code providing for the liquidation of substantially all of the Member's assets. For purposes of (iv) above, a Member shall not be considered a debtor-in-possession of his or her assets if a trustee, receiver or other person or entity is appointed to, or in fact does, control or operate the assets of the Member.

.05 BANKRUPTCY CODE

Bankruptcy Code shall mean Title 11 of the United States Code, as now in effect or as hereafter amended.

.06 CASH FLOW

Cash Flow shall mean all cash received by the Company from all sources (including capital contributions and borrowings), less cash expended or reserved in the discretion of the Manager(s) for liabilities (contingent or otherwise), expenses, capital expenditures, and obligations of the Company or obligations secured by the assets of the Company.

.07 CODE

Code shall mean the Internal Revenue Code of 1986, as now in effect or as later amended.

.08 COMPANY

Company shall mean [name of company], the limited liability company formed by the filing of the Articles of Organization, as constituted from time to time.

.09 MANAGERS

Managers shall mean [name(s) of Manager(s)], and any successor or additional Manager elected in accordance with Article VII, in such person's capacity as a Manager.

.10 MEMBERS

Members shall mean the persons set forth on the attached Schedule A, and any person admitted as an additional or substitute Member in accordance with Article VIII, in such person's capacity as a Member.

.11 MEMBERSHIP INTEREST

Membership Interest shall mean, with respect to a Member, the percentage of ownership interest in the Company of such Member, as set forth on Schedule A. Each Member's percentage of Membership Interest in the Company shall be based on his or her relative capital contributions to the Company.

.12 PROPERTY

Property shall mean, at any time, all property, whether real or personal, interests, assets or rights owned or held by or on behalf of the Company at such time.

ARTICLE III
Capital Contributions and Capital Accounts

.01 CAPITAL CONTRIBUTIONS

Upon execution of this Agreement, each Member shall contribute to the Company cash, securities and/or other assets in the amount set forth opposite his or her respective name on the attached Schedule A.

.02 CAPITAL ACCOUNTS

Separate capital accounts shall be maintained by the Company for each Member. The capital account of each Member shall be credited with his or her capital contributions (at net fair market value with respect to contributed property) and shall be appropriately adjusted to reflect each Member's allocations of profits, gains, losses, deductions, the net fair market value of distributions made to the Member, and other adjustments as shall be required by Code Sec. 704(b) and the regulations promulgated thereunder.

.03 LIMITED LIABILITY

The Members shall not have any personal liability for liabilities or obligations of the Company except to the extent of their capital contribution set forth in Section 3.01, and the Members shall not be required to make any further or additional contribution to the Company or to lend or advance funds to the Company for any purpose. Notwithstanding the foregoing, (i) if any court of competent jurisdiction holds that distributions (or any part thereof) received by a Member pursuant to the provisions hereof constitute a return of capital and directs that a Member pay such amount (with or without interest thereon) to or for the account of the Company or any creditor thereof, the obligation shall be the obligation of said Member and not of any other Member or the Company, and (ii) a Member shall indemnify and hold harmless the Company and each Member from any liability or loss incurred by virtue of the assessment of any tax with respect to the Member's allocable share of the profits or gain of the Company.

.04 NO INTEREST ON OR RIGHT TO WITHDRAW CAPITAL CONTRIBUTIONS

No interest shall be paid by the Company on capital contributions or on the balance in any capital account and no Member shall have the right to withdraw his or her capital contribution or to demand or receive a return of his or her capital contribution.

ARTICLE IV
Company Funds

All funds received by the Company shall be utilized for Company purposes as determined by the Manager(s) in the best interests of the Company. Until required for the Company's business, all Company funds shall be deposited and maintained in such accounts in banks or other financial institutions as shall be selected by the Manager(s) or shall be invested in securities of the United States government, certificates of deposit or money market funds designated by the Manager(s). The Manager(s) or their designee shall have the right to draw checks payable in such funds and make, deliver, accept and endorse negotiable instruments in connection with the Company's business. Company funds shall not be commingled with the funds of any other person.

ARTICLE V
Allocations and Distributions

.01 DISTRIBUTIONS

Cash Flow shall be distributed to the Members in amounts and at intervals as the Manager(s) shall determine, and among the Members in proportion to their respective Membership Interests.

PLANNING TIP: _____

Many LLCs' operating agreements contain a provision requiring a mandatory distribution of cash flow to the parties so that they can pay their income taxes attributable to their allocable share of the LLC income. Such a provision could read as follows:

"Notwithstanding the foregoing, within ninety (90) days of the end of each fiscal year of the Company, Cash Flow shall be distributed to the Members in an amount ('Tax Distribution') equal to (i) % [or a percentage equal to the highest combined marginal federal and (name of state) income tax rates]of the aggregate net income of the Company allocated to the Members through the end of the Company fiscal year for which such allocation is being made, reduced by (ii) the aggregate amount of Tax Distributions previously made to the Members."

.02 ALLOCATION OF PROFITS AND LOSSES

All profits and losses of the Company shall be allocated among the Members in proportion to their respective Membership Interests; provided, however, that for federal income tax purposes, income, gain, loss and deduction, with respect to property contributed to the Company, shall be shared by the Members so as to take account of the variation between the federal income tax basis of the property to the Company and its fair market value at the time of its contribution to the Company utilizing any such method as is selected by the Manager(s) that is authorized pursuant to Code Sec. 704(c) and regulations relating thereto.

ARTICLE VI
Management: Rights, Powers, and Obligations of the Manager(s)

.01 MANAGEMENT AND CONTROL IN GENERAL

(a) Except as set forth in Paragraph 6.01(b), the Manager(s) shall have the full and exclusive power to manage and control the business and affairs of the Company, and the Members shall have no right to act on behalf of or bind the Company. The Manager(s) shall have all the rights, powers and obligations of a manager as provided in the Act and as otherwise provided by law, and any action taken by the Manager(s) shall constitute the act of and serve to bind the Company. In dealing with the Manager(s), no persons shall be required to inquire into, and all persons are entitled to rely conclusively on, the authority of the Manager(s) to bind the Company.

(b) Notwithstanding the provisions of Paragraph 6.01(a), the Manager(s) shall not (i) confess a judgment against the Company or execute or deliver any assignment for the benefit of creditors of the Company, or (ii) sell or assign substantially all the Property in bulk, without the written consent of the Members holding a majority of the Membership Interests.

PLANNING TIP: _____

Some operating agreements expand the scope of company decisions that require a membership consent process, such as expenditures in excess of $____, incurring debt on behalf of the company, or entering into contracts that are not cancelable or have a duration in excess of one year.

.02 NUMBER AND APPOINTMENT OF MANAGER(S)

(a) The initial number of Managers of the Company shall be [insert number]. The number may be changed from time to time upon the affirmative vote of Members holding [insert fraction] of the Membership Interests who are present at a meeting called for such purpose, and a Manager may be removed at a meeting called for such purpose upon the same vote.

(b) A Manager may resign at any time upon prior written notice to the Company. In the event of a vacancy in the position of Manager by reason of resignation, removal, death, or Bankruptcy, a successor shall be appointed by the affirmative vote of the Members holding a majority of the Membership Interests who are present at a meeting called for such purpose.

(c) A Manager shall not be required to be a Member of the Company or a resident of [state of organization].

PLANNING TIP: _____

This Agreement appoints managers for the term of the Agreement, subject to removal, resignation, death, or bankruptcy. It is not uncommon, however, to have an annual election of managers, much like the election of a board of directors of a corporation. If such were the case, the Agreement might contain the following provision:

(b) The Managers shall serve for a __-year term or, if later, until their successors shall have been elected. On or about the anniversary date of this Agreement, the Company shall hold a meeting for the appointment of new Managers (who may or may not be one or more of the former Managers).

.03 EMPLOYMENT OF OTHERS, INCLUDING AFFILIATES

The Manager(s) shall not be required to devote full time to the affairs of the Company and shall devote time to Company affairs as they in their sole and unrestricted discretion deem necessary to manage and supervise the operations and business of the Company. Nothing contained in this Agreement shall preclude the employment by the Manager(s), on behalf of and at the expense of the Company, of themselves or any agent or third party to operate and manage all or any portion of the Property or to provide any service relating to the business, subject to the control of the Manager(s). The Manager(s) may, on behalf of the Company, engage one or more Affiliates of any of the Manager(s) to render services to the Company, provided that any such engagement shall be upon terms and conditions no less favorable to the Company than could be obtained from an independent third party. Neither the Company nor any of the Members shall have, as a consequence of the relationship created hereby, any right in or to any income or profits derived by the Manager(s) or an Affiliate of any of the Manager(s) from any business arrangements with the Company which are consistent with this Section.

.04 COMPENSATION TO MANAGER(S)

The compensation of the Manager(s) shall be established from time to time by the affirmative vote of the Member(s) holding a majority of the Membership Interests who are present at a meeting called for such purpose.

.05 EXPENSES

The Company shall pay all costs and expenses arising from or relating to the organization of the Company, the acquisition of Property and the commencement and continuation of Company operations. The Company shall not be required to reimburse the Manager(s) or their Affiliates for overhead expenses incurred by them in providing services to the Company, but shall be required to reimburse such parties for reasonable out-of-pocket expenses so incurred by them.

.06 OTHER ACTIVITIES

The Manager(s), an Affiliate of any of the Manager(s) and any Member may engage in or possess an interest in other business ventures or investments of any kind, independently or with others, including but not limited to ventures engaged in owning, operating, or managing businesses or properties similar to those businesses or properties owned or operated by the Company. The fact that a Manager, any Affiliate of a Manager, or any Member may avail itself of such opportunities, either by itself or with other persons, including persons in which it has an interest, and not offer the opportunities to the Company or to a Member, shall not subject the Manager, the Member or the Affiliate to liability to the Company or to any other Member on account of lost opportunity. Neither the Company nor any Member shall have any right by virtue of this Agreement or the relationship created hereby in or to such opportunities, or to the income or profits derived therefrom, and the pursuit of such opportunities, even though competitive with the business of the Company, shall not be deemed wrongful or improper or in violation of this Agreement.

PLANNING TIP: _____

This liberal provision is relevant to businesses where competition between members and/or managers is not particularly relevant, such as certain rental real estate ventures. Other types of businesses may desire to restrict the ability of a member to own an interest in a business that is competitive with the company's business, either while the person is a member in the company or for some period of time thereafter.

Similarly, it may be wise for an operating agreement to address fiduciary duties, liabilities, and defenses with respect to such fiduciary issues as care, loyalty, candor and confidentiality.

.07 TITLE TO PROPERTY

Title to Property shall be taken in the name of the Company or in the name or names of a nominee or nominees designated by the Manager(s).

.08 LIABILITY OF A MANAGER

Each Manager and any Affiliate of a Manager, and their respective officers, shareholders, controlling persons, directors, agents and employees, shall not be liable, responsible, or accountable in damages or otherwise to the Company or to any of the Members, their successors or permitted assigns, except by reason of acts or omissions due to gross negligence or willful misconduct. Any action taken in good faith in reliance upon and in accordance with the advice or opinion of counsel shall be conclusively deemed not to constitute gross negligence or willful misconduct.

.09 INDEMNIFICATION

The Company shall indemnify, defend, and hold harmless any person (the "Indemnified Party") who was or is a party or is threatened to be made a party to any threatened, pending or completed action, suit or proceeding, whether civil, criminal, administrative or investigative, against losses, damages, claims or expenses actually and reasonably incurred by it for which the Indemnified Party has not otherwise been reimbursed (including reasonable attorneys' fees, judgments, fines and amounts paid in settlement) in connection with such action, suit or proceeding, by reason of any acts, omissions or alleged acts or omissions arising out of the Indemnified Party's activities as a Member, or as an officer, shareholder, director, agent or employee of a Member, on behalf of the Company or in furtherance of the interests of the Company, so long as the Indemnified Party did not act in a manner constituting gross negligence or willful misconduct. The termination of any action, suit or proceeding by judgment, order, settlement, or upon a plea of *nolo contendere* or its equivalent, shall not of itself create a presumption that the Indemnified Party's conduct constituted gross negligence or willful misconduct.

.10 TAX MATTERS PARTNER

[Name of Manager] shall be the "tax matters partner" for purposes of Subchapter C of Chapter 63 of Subtitle F of the Internal Revenue Code (Code Secs. 6221–6234) and shall have the authority to exercise all functions provided for in said Act, or in regulations promulgated thereunder by Treasury, including, to the extent permitted by such regulations, the authority to delegate the function of "tax matters partner" to any other person. [Name of Manager] shall be reimbursed for all reasonable expenses incurred as a result of his or her duties as tax matters partner. If [name of Manager]resigns as tax matters partner or as a Manager, or his entire Membership Interest is disposed of or terminated, [name of Manager] shall become the tax matters partner. In order for such a resignation to be effective, the resignation must be in writing and specify the taxpayer to which the resignation relates.

ARTICLE VII
Meetings and Voting

.01 MEETINGS

Meetings of the Members may be called by any Manager or by Members holding at least 10 percent of the Membership Interests upon [number] days' prior written notice to each Member of the Company. The notice shall set forth the time and place of the meeting. If no place for the meeting is designated, the place of meeting shall be the principal office of the Company. Members holding at least [insert fraction] of all Membership Interests shall constitute a quorum at any meeting of Members, whether present in person or by proxy.

.02 MANNER OF ACTING

If a quorum is present at a meeting, the affirmative vote of Members holding at least [insert fraction] of all Membership Interests shall be the act of the Members, unless the vote of a greater or lesser proportion or number is otherwise required by the Act, by the Articles of Organization or by this Agreement.

.03 ACTION BY MEMBERS

Any action required or permitted to be taken at a meeting of Members may be taken without a meeting if the action is evidenced by a written consent describing the action taken, executed by each Member and delivered to the Manager(s) for inclusion in the Company records. Any action taken pursuant to this Section 7.03 shall be effective when all Members have executed the consent, unless the consent specifies a different effective date.

.04 WAIVER OF NOTICE

When any notice is required to be given to any Members, a waiver thereof in writing executed by the person entitled to such notice, whether before, at or after the time stated therein, shall be equivalent to the giving of such notice.

ARTICLE VIII
Transfers of Membership Interests; Admission of New Members

.01 RESTRICTIONS ON TRANSFER

A Member may not sell or transfer all or any part of his or her Membership Interest except with the prior written consent of Members holding [insert fraction] of the Membership Interests, which consent may be withheld by a Member in his or her sole and unrestricted discretion. Any sale or transfer without said consent shall be null and void and confer no rights on the transferee as against the Company or as against the Members. In addition, before a permitted transferee shall be admitted to the Company as a substitute or additional Member, the conditions set forth in Section 8.04 must be satisfied.

PLANNING TIP: _____

Under the federal "check-the-box" regulations, it is currently unnecessary to restrict the free transferability of membership interests in order to be classified as a partnership for federal tax purposes (see Chapter 9). Regardless of this rule, members may want to continue such restrictions in order to retain control in the LLC and to ensure that the value of such interests are reduced for estate, gift and generation-skipping transfer tax purposes.

It is important to review the LLC statute of the state in which the LLC is organized insofar as state partnership classification matters are concerned. State statutes may not necessarily coordinate with federal partnership classification standards, and it may be necessary to insert various provisions in an operating agreement relative to the transferability of interests (and possibly continuity of life) to ensure partnership classification for state income tax purposes.

.02 ADMISSION OF ADDITIONAL OR SUBSTITUTE MEMBERS

No person may be admitted as an additional or substitute Member without the unanimous written consent of all Members.

.03 TERMINATION OF MEMBER'S INTEREST IN COMPANY

Upon a Member's death, a Member becoming bankrupt or the termination of a Member's interest in the Company (by withdrawal or otherwise), such Member's legal representative shall have all the rights of the Member for the purpose of settling the Member's estate and such power as the Member possessed to transfer his or her Membership Interest and to join with the transferee thereof in satisfying the conditions precedent to such transferee becoming a substitute Member that are set forth in this Article VIII.

PLANNING TIP: _____

It is not uncommon in many LLCs for Members to waive their right to an accounting upon death. If such a provision is desired, the following sentence may be added at the end of the Section:

"Each Member expressly agrees that in the event of his (or her) death he waives on behalf of himself and his estate, and he directs the legal representative of his estate and any person interested therein, to waive the furnishing of any inventory, accounting or appraisal of the assets of the Company and any right to any audit or examination of the books of the Company."

.04 SUBSTITUTE OR ADDITIONAL MEMBER

(a) A person shall only be admitted as a substitute or additional Member under this Agreement in compliance with the following:

(i) a transfer contemplated by Section 8.01 shall be made only by written document, signed by the transferor Member and accepted in writing by the transferee, and a duplicate original of the document shall be delivered to the Company and consented to by all Members (which consent may be withheld in the sole and unrestricted discretion of any Member);

(ii) the transferee shall execute and deliver to the Company a written agreement, in form reasonably satisfactory to the Manager(s), pursuant to which said person agrees to be bound by this Agreement and grants the power of attorney contained in this Agreement; and

(b) If a transfer is made in accordance with the terms of this Article, unless otherwise required by the Code:

(i) the effective date of the transfer shall be the date the written documents described in Subparagraphs 8.04(a)(i) and (ii) are approved by all Members; and

(ii) the Company shall be entitled to treat the transferor Member as the absolute owner of the transferred Membership Interest in all respects and shall incur no liability for distributions or allocations made pursuant to Article V in good faith to such transferor until the written documents described in Subparagraphs 8.04(a)(i) and (ii) are approved by all Members.

(c) The costs incurred by the Company associated with the admission of a substitute or additional Member contemplated by this Article (including reasonable attorneys' fees) shall be borne by the transferee.

ARTICLE IX
Reports and Tax Matters

.01 BOOKS, RECORDS, AND REPORTS

(a) Accurate books, records and reports shall be maintained by the Company showing its assets, liabilities, operations, transactions, and financial condition, as well as the names and addresses of the Members. The Company books and records may be kept under such permissible method of accounting as the Manager(s) may determine. The Company books shall be maintained at the principal office of the Company, and each Member shall have the right upon reasonable notice given to the Company to inspect, extract and copy the books during regular business hours of the Company.

(b) The Manager(s) shall cause income tax returns for the Company to be prepared and filed with the appropriate authorities. Within [number] days after the close of each fiscal year of the Company, the Manager(s) shall send to each person who was a Member at any time during the fiscal year the information as will be sufficient to prepare documents that may be required to be filed under relevant federal and state income tax laws.

(c) Within [number] days after the close of the Company's fiscal year, the Manager(s) shall use their best efforts to cause each Member to receive financial statements of the Company for the fiscal year then ended (including a balance sheet and statement of income).

.02 SECTION 754 ELECTION

If a distribution of property is made in the manner provided in Section 734 of the Code, or if a transfer of any Membership Interest permitted by this Agreement is made in the manner provided in Section 743 of the Code, the Manager(s), on behalf of the Company, may, but shall not be required to, file an election under Section 754 of the Code in accordance with the procedures set forth in the applicable regulations promulgated thereunder.

ARTICLE X
Dissolution and Termination

.01 DISSOLUTION OF THE COMPANY

The Company shall dissolve and be terminated upon the earlier happening of any one of the following:

(a) upon written agreement of Members holding [insert fraction] of the Membership Interests;

(b) upon the sale of substantially all of the Property or other conversion of substantially all the Company's assets to cash; or

(c) upon the occurrence of any other event other than one specified in this Section 10.01 which, under the Act or as otherwise provided by law, causes a dissolution and termination of the Company.

.02 LIQUIDATOR

(a) Upon dissolution of the Company, the Manager(s), or if there is no Manager, such person as the Members holding a majority of the Membership Interests may designate, shall act as liquidator of the Company (in either case, the "Liquidator"). The Liquidator shall, with reasonable speed, wind up the affairs of the Company and liquidate the Property. The Liquidator shall have unlimited discretion to determine the time, manner and terms of any sale of Property having due regard to the activity and condition of the relevant market and general financial and economic conditions. The Liquidator shall distribute any proceeds received from the disposition of the Property and any other assets of the Company in accordance with the provisions of Article V.

(b) If any Member shall be indebted to the Company, then until payment of such amount by him, the Liquidator shall retain the Member's distributive share of Property and apply the same to the liquidation of the indebtedness.

(c) The Liquidator shall comply with all requirements of the Act and other applicable law pertaining to the winding up of a limited liability company, following which the Company shall stand liquidated and terminated.

.03 SOURCE OF DISTRIBUTIONS

Each Member shall look solely to the assets of the Company for all distributions with respect to the Company, the return of his or her capital contribution thereto and his or her share of profits or losses thereof, and shall have no recourse (upon dissolution or otherwise) against any other Member or Manager.

ARTICLE XI
Power of Attorney

.01 POWER OF ATTORNEY

Each Member, by executing this Agreement or a counterpart hereof, does hereby irrevocably constitute and appoint each Manager, and any successor Manager of the Company, with full power of substitution, as such Member's true and lawful attorney-in-fact (the "Attorney-in-Fact"), in his or her name, place and stead, to execute, acknowledge, swear to, deliver, file, and record such documents that are now or may hereafter be required by law to be filed on behalf of the Company or are deemed necessary or desirable by the Manager(s) to carry out fully the provisions of this Agreement in accordance with its terms.

.02 NATURE OF POWER OF ATTORNEY

The grant of authority in Section 11.01 by each Member (i) is a special power of attorney coupled with an interest in favor of the Attorney-in-Fact and shall be irrevocable and shall survive the death or legal incapacity of the Member; (ii) may be exercised for the Member by a facsimile signature of the Attorney-in-Fact; and (iii) shall survive the assignment by the Member of all or any portion of his or her Membership Interest, except that if the assignee of the entire Membership Interest of the Member has furnished a power of attorney and has been approved by the Company for admission to the Company as a substitute Member pursuant to Article VIII, the power of attorney granted in Section 11.01 shall survive the assignment for the sole purpose of enabling the Attorney-in-Fact to execute, acknowledge and file any instrument necessary to effect such substitution and shall thereafter terminate.

ARTICLE XII
Miscellaneous Provisions

.01 NOTICES

All notices or other communications required or permitted to be given pursuant to this Agreement shall be in writing and shall be considered as properly given: (i) in the case of a report to be given to a Member, if personally delivered or if mailed by United States first-class mail, postage prepaid, addressed to such Member at his or her address on the records of the Company; and (ii) in the case of notices or communications to be given to any Member, if personally delivered or if mailed by United States first-class certified or registered mail, return receipt requested, postage prepaid, or if sent by prepaid telegram or telex, addressed to the Member at his or her address on the records of the Company. A Member may change his or her address for notices by giving notice in like manner. Any notice or other communication shall be deemed to have been given to, or received by, the appropriate party as of the date on which it is personally delivered or, if mailed, on the third business day after the date on which it is deposited in the United States mail, or if telegraphed or telexed, on the business day after it is transmitted.

.02 GOVERNING LAW

This Agreement shall be governed by and construed in accordance with the laws of the State of [name of state].

.03 SUCCESSORS AND ASSIGNS

This Agreement and all the terms and provisions hereof shall be binding upon and shall inure to the benefit of the Members and their respective heirs, executors, administrators, successors, and permitted assigns. Any person acquiring or claiming an interest in the Company, in any manner whatsoever, shall be subject to and bound by all the terms, conditions and obligations of this Agreement to which his or her predecessor in interest was subject or bound, without regard to whether such person has executed this Agreement or a counterpart hereof or any other document contemplated hereby. No person shall have any rights or obligations relating to the Company greater than those set forth in this Agreement, and no person shall acquire an interest in the Company or become a Member thereof except as permitted by the terms of this Agreement.

.04 COUNTERPARTS

This Agreement may be executed in any number of identical counterparts, each of which, for all purposes, shall be deemed an original, and all of which constitute, collectively, one and the same Agreement. In addition, this Agreement may contain more than one counterpart signature page and may be executed by the affixing of the signature of each of the Members to one of the counterpart signature pages, and all such counterpart signature pages shall be read as one and shall have the same force and effect as though all the signers had signed the same signature page.

.05 ADDITIONAL ASSURANCES

Upon the request of a Manager, each Member agrees to perform all further acts and execute, acknowledge, and deliver any documents that the Manager deems reasonably necessary to effectuate the provisions of this Agreement.

.06 MODIFICATION TO BE IN WRITING

This Agreement constitutes the entire understanding of the parties hereto with respect to the subject matter and supersedes any and all prior negotiations, understandings and agreements. No amendment, modification or alteration of the terms hereof shall be binding unless the same is in writing and is effected in accordance with this Agreement.

.07 PARTITION

Each of the parties hereto irrevocably waives during the term of the Company any right that he or she may have to maintain any action for partition with respect to Company Property.

.08 NO WAIVER

Failure or delay of any party in exercising any right or remedy under this Agreement, or any other agreement between the parties, or otherwise, will not operate as a waiver. The express waiver by any party of a breach of any provision of this Agreement by any other party shall not operate or be construed as a waiver of any subsequent breach by said party. No waiver will be effective unless and until it is in written form and signed by the waiving party.

.09 GENDER AND NUMBER

Wherever from the context it appears appropriate, each term stated in either the singular or plural shall include the singular and plural, and pronouns stated in either the masculine, the feminine or the neuter gender shall include the masculine, feminine and neuter.

.10 HEADINGS

The captions in this Agreement are inserted for convenience of reference only and shall not affect the construction of this Agreement. References in this Agreement to any Article, Section, Paragraph, Sub-paragraph or Schedule are to the same contained in this Agreement.

.11 VALIDITY AND SEVERABILITY

If any provision of this Agreement contravenes any law and such contravention would thereby invalidate this Agreement, or if the operation of any provision hereof is determined by law, administrative regulation, or otherwise to result in classification of the Company as an association taxable as a corporation for federal income tax purposes, or to make a Member generally liable for the obligations of the Company, then the provision is declared to be invalid and subject to severance from the remaining portion of this Agreement, and this Agreement shall be read and construed as though it did not contain such provision in a manner to give effect to the intention of the parties to the fullest extent possible.

.12 NO THIRD-PARTY RIGHTS

This Agreement and the covenants and agreements contained herein are solely for the benefit of the parties hereto and their Affiliates. No other person shall be entitled to enforce or make any claims, or have any right pursuant to the provisions of this Agreement.

IN WITNESS WHEREOF, the Members have caused this Agreement to be executed as of the date first set forth above.

STATE OF _____)
)   SS:
COUNTY OF _____)

I, [insert name], a Notary Public for the said County and State, do hereby certify that [insert name], personally known to me to be the President of [insert name], a corporation, and personally known to me to be the same person whose name is subscribed to the foregoing instrument, appeared before me this day in person and acknowledged and swore that the statements set forth in the foregoing instrument are true and correct and that he (or she) signed and delivered the said instrument as President of said corporation, pursuant to authority given by the Board of Directors of said corporation and as his (or her) free and voluntary act, and as the free and voluntary act and deed of said corporation, for the uses and purposes therein set forth.

Given under my hand and official seal, this ___ day of ___, 20__.

                                _____

                                   Notary Public

(SEAL)
My Commission Expires: _____

STATE OF   )

)   SS:

COUNTY OF   )

I, [insert name], a Notary Public in and for said County and State, do hereby certify that [insert name], personally known to me to be the same person whose name is subscribed to the foregoing instrument, appeared before me this day in person and acknowledged and swore that the statements set forth in the foregoing instrument are true and correct and that he (or she) signed and delivered the said instrument as his free and voluntary act for the uses and purposes therein set forth.

Given under my hand and official seal, this ___ day of ___, 20 ___.

_____

                                 Notary Public

(SEAL)

My Commission Expires: _____

SCHEDULE A
Operating Agreement of [Company Name]
Limited Liability Company

Name and
Address   *Capital*
of Member   *Contribution Interest*

Appendix B
Model LLC Articles of Organization

Introductory Comments

The following is a simple example of the articles of organization for a limited liability company (LLC). An LLC begins its formal existence when the articles of organization are signed and filed by the organizer with the Secretary of State's office, or other appropriate official, along with the prescribed fee. Enabling statutes vary greatly from state to state in their requirements for the content of the articles of organization. However, each LLC act requires certain information and leaves the inclusion of any additional information to the discretion of the organizers. It should be noted that any information included in the articles of organization will be accessible to anyone wishing to see it, as this is a public document. As such, discretion should be exercised, especially in the case of someone who wishes to maintain a certain level of financial privacy. It is therefore important to consult the local state statute before filing the articles of organization, in order to determine exactly what is required, and what is optional.

Outline for Articles of Organization

Article I—Name of the Limited Liability Company

Article II—Registered Office and Registered Agent

Article III—Principal Office

Article IV—Period of Duration

Article V—Written Operating Agreement

Article VI—Management

Model Articles of Organization

ARTICLES OF ORGANIZATION
OF
_____, L.L.C.

The undersigned Organizer(s) of a limited liability company organized under the _____ [name of state] Limited Liability Company Act do(es) hereby adopt the following Articles of Organization for such limited liability company.

ARTICLE I
NAME OF THE LIMITED LIABILITY COMPANY

The name of the limited liability company shall be _____, L.L.C.

ARTICLE II
REGISTERED OFFICE AND REGISTERED AGENT

The address of the initial registered office of the limited liability company is _____. The initial registered agent at such address is _____.

ARTICLE III
PRINCIPAL OFFICE

The address of the principal office of the limited liability company is _____.

ARTICLE IV
PERIOD OF DURATION

The limited liability company's existence shall commence upon the acceptance of these Articles of Organization by the Secretary of State of _____ [name of state] for filing and shall continue for a period of _____ years, unless sooner dissolved pursuant to the terms of its operating agreement, or as otherwise provided by law.

ARTICLE V
WRITTEN OPERATING AGREEMENT

Any operating agreement entered into by the members of the limited liability company, and any amendments or restatements thereof, shall be in writing. No oral agreement among any of the members or managers of the limited liability company shall be deemed or construed to constitute any portion of, or otherwise affect the interpretation of, any written operating agreement of the limited liability company in existence and as amended from time to time.

ARTICLE VI
MANAGEMENT

The business and affairs of the limited liability company shall be governed by managers in the manner and subject to the limitations set forth in an operating agreement. The actions of a member, manager, or any other person acting in any capacity other than as a manager of the limited liability company in accordance with the terms of its operating agreement shall not bind the limited liability company.

IN WITNESS WHEREOF, the aforesaid organizer has caused the execution of the foregoing Articles of Organization on this _____ day of _____, 20_____.

_____

Organizer of _____, L.L.C.

Appendix C

Delaware

Delaware Synopsis

Name of Act

Delaware Limited Liability Company Act, Del. Code tit. 6, §§ 18-101 to 18-1109.

Federal Tax Classification

The LLC statute is flexible. Any "business entity" not required to be treated as a "corporation" for federal tax purposes under Treas. Reg. § 301.7701-2 may choose its classification under Treas. Reg. § 301.7701-3.

State Tax Treatment

LLCs are classified as partnerships for state and local purposes, unless classified otherwise for federal income tax purposes. (Del. Code tit. 6, § 18-1107)

Securities Treatment

The Delaware Act does not expressly provide for the treatment of an LLC interest as a security.

Limited Liability Partnerships

Limited liability partnerships are expressly authorized by statute. (Del. Code tit. 6, § 15-1001 [not reproduced])

Limited Liability Limited Partnerships

Limited liability limited partnerships are expressly authorized by statute. (Del. Code tit. 6, § 17-214 [not reproduced])

Professional LLCs

Professional LLCs are permitted impliedly, subject to compliance with other state regulatory provisions. Banking LLCs are expressly prohibited. (Del. Code tit. 6, § 18-106)

Foreign LLCs

Foreign LLCs are expressly permitted by statute. Laws of the formation jurisdiction govern the organization, internal affairs and the liability of the members and managers. (Del. Code tit. 6, § 18-901)

Formation

A Delaware LLC may be formed by one or more authorized persons. At least one member is required. (Del. Code tit. 6, §§ 18-101 and 18-201)

Naming Requirements

The name of each LLC must contain the words "limited liability company", the abbreviation "L.L.C." or the designation "LLC". (Del. Code tit. 6, § 18-102)

Effective Date of Organization

A Delaware LLC is formed when the initial certificate of formation is filed with the office of the Secretary of State, unless a delayed effective date is stated. (Del. Code tit. 6, § 18-201)

Filing Requirements

The certificate of formation must include: (1) the LLC's name; (2) the address of the registered office and the name and address of the registered agent for service of process required to be maintained by § 18-104; and (3) any other matters that the members decide to include. (Del. Code tit. 6, § 18-201)

Fees—Organization and Annual

The fee for filing the certificate of formation is $70 plus a $20 courthouse municipality fee. The fee for filing the application for registration as a foreign LLC is $100. An annual tax of $200 is imposed. (Del. Code tit. 6, §§ 18-1105 and 18-1107)

Recordkeeping

The LLC must compile and maintain: (1) true and full information regarding the status of the business and financial condition of the LLC; (2) a copy of the LLC's federal, state and local income tax returns for each year; (3) a current list of the members' and managers' names and addresses; (4) a copy of any written LLC agreement and certificate of formation, including all amendments and any powers of attorney; (5) true and full information regarding the amount of cash and a description and statement of the agreed value of any other property or services contributed, or promised to be contributed in the future, and the date on which each member became a member; and (6) other information regarding the affairs of the LLC as is just and reasonable. (Del. Code tit. 6, § 18-305)

Annual Reporting

Annual reporting is not required. However, the state does impose a $200 annual tax on LLCs.

Management

Management is vested in the members, unless otherwise provided. An LLC may have more than one manager. (Del. Code tit. 6, § 18-402)

Membership Rights and Obligations

A member is not liable for a debt, obligation or liability of the LLC whether arising in contract, tort or otherwise, unless otherwise provided. A member is obligated to perform any promised capital contribution, even if the member is unable to perform because of death, disability or other reason, unless otherwise provided. If a member fails to make the promised capital contribution, the member is obligated, at the option of the LLC, to contribute cash equal to that portion of value of the stated contribution that has not been made. If a member knowingly receives a wrongful distribution, that member is liable to the LLC for the amount of the wrongful distribution. If a member unknowingly receives a wrongful distribution, that member is not liable to the LLC for the amount of the wrongful distribution. (Del. Code tit. 6, §§ 18-303, 18-502 and 18-607)

Piercing the Corporate Veil

The Act has no express provision that concerns piercing the corporate veil.

Contributions

Contributions may consist of anything of value including cash, property, services rendered, a promissory note or other obligation to contribute cash, property or services. (Del. Code tit. 6, § 18-501)

Distributions

Profits, losses and distributions are allocated on the basis of the agreed value of each member's contribution, unless otherwise provided. (Del. Code tit. 6, §§ 18-503 and 18-504)

Resignation of Member

A member may not resign from an LLC prior to the dissolution and winding up of the LLC, unless otherwise provided. (Del. Code tit. 6, § 18-603)

Transfer of LLC Interest

A member's LLC interest is assignable in whole or in part, unless otherwise provided. Unanimous consent is required for the assignee to become a member, unless otherwise provided. (Del. Code tit. 6, § 18-702)

Dissolution

An LLC will be dissolved: (1) at the time specified in the LLC agreement, but if not specified, the duration is perpetual; (2) upon the happening of events specified in the LLC agreement; (3) upon the written consent of the members, unless otherwise provided; (4) at any time there are no members, unless, within 90 days, the personal representative of the last remaining member agrees in writing to continue the LLC and to the admission of the personal representative or its nominee or designee to the LLC as a member, unless otherwise provided; or (5) upon the entry of a judicial dissolution. An event of dissociation shall not cause the LLC to be dissolved, unless within 90 days following the occurrence of such event, the LLC members agree in writing to dissolve the LLC. An LLC's certificate of formation may be canceled upon a continuing failure to pay the annual state tax. (Del. Code tit. 6, § § 18-801, 18-802 and 18-1108)

Mergers and Consolidations

Mergers and consolidations are permitted expressly by statute. (Del. Code tit. 6, § 18-209)

DELAWARE

TITLE 6
CHAPTER 18
Delaware Limited Liability Company Act

SUBCHAPTER I. GENERAL PROVISIONS

§ 18-101. Definitions.

As used in this chapter unless the context otherwise requires:

(1) "Bankruptcy" means an event that causes a person to cease to be a member as provided in § 18-304 of this title.

(2) "Certificate of formation" means the certificate referred to in § 18-201 of this title, and the certificate as amended.

(3) "Contribution" means any cash, property, services rendered or a promissory note or other obligation to contribute cash or property or to perform services, which a person contributes to a limited liability company in his capacity as a member.

(4) "Foreign limited liability company" means a limited liability company formed under the laws of any state or under the laws of any foreign country or other foreign jurisdiction and denominated as such under the laws of such state or foreign country or other foreign jurisdiction.

(5) "Knowledge" means a person's actual knowledge of a fact, rather than the person's constructive knowledge of the fact.

(6) "Limited liability company" and "domestic limited liability company" means a limited liability company formed under the laws of the State of Delaware and having 1 or more members.

(7) "Limited liability company agreement" means any agreement (whether referred to as a limited liability company agreement, operating agreement or otherwise), written, oral or implied, of the member or members as to the affairs of a limited liability company and the conduct of its business. A limited liability company is not required to execute its limited liability company agreement. A limited liability company is bound by its limited liability company agreement whether or not the limited liability company executes the limited liability company agreement. A limited liability company agreement of a limited liability company having only one member shall not be unenforceable by reason of there being only one person who is a party to the limited liability company agreement. A limited liability company agreement may provide rights to any person, including a person who is not a party to the limited liability company agreement, to the extent set forth therein. A written limited liability company agreement or another written agreement or writing:

a. May provide that a person shall be admitted as a member of a limited liability company, or shall become an assignee of a limited liability company interest or other rights or powers of a member to the extent assigned. A member or manager of a limited liability company or an assignee of a limited liability company interest is bound by the limited liability company agreement whether or not the member or manager or assignee executes the limited liability company agreement.

1. If such person (or a representative authorized by such person orally, in writing or by other action such as payment for a limited liability company interest) executes the limited

liability company agreement or any other writing evidencing the intent of such person to become a member or assignee; or

2. Without such execution, if such person (or a representative authorized by such person orally, in writing or by other action such as payment for a limited liability company interest) complies with the conditions for becoming a member or assignee as set forth in the limited liability company agreement or any other writing; and

b. Shall not be unenforceable by reason of its not having been signed by a person being admitted as a member or becoming an assignee as provided in subparagraph a. of this paragraph, or by reason of its having been signed by a representative as provided in this chapter.

(8) "Limited liability company interest" means a member's share of the profits and losses of a limited liability company and a member's right to receive distributions of the limited liability company's assets.

(9) "Liquidating trustee" means a person carrying out the winding up of a limited liability company.

(10) "Manager" means a person who is named as a manager of a limited liability company in, or designated as a manager of a limited liability company pursuant to, a limited liability company agreement or similar instrument under which the limited liability company is formed.

(11) "Member" means a person who is admitted to a limited liability company as a member as provided in § 18-301 of this title or, in the case of a foreign limited liability company, in accordance with the laws of the state or foreign country or other foreign jurisdiction under which the foreign limited liability company is formed.

(12) "Person" means a natural person, partnership (whether general or limited), limited liability company, trust, estate, association (including any group, organization, co-tenancy, plan, board, council or committee), corporation, government (including a country, state, county or any other governmental subdivision, agency or instrumentality), custodian, nominee or any other individual or entity (or series thereof) in its own or any representative capacity, in each case, whether domestic or foreign.

(13) "Personal representative" means, as to a natural person, the executor, administrator, guardian, conservator or other legal representative thereof and, as to a person other than a natural person, the legal representative or successor thereof.

(14) "State" means the District of Columbia or the Commonwealth of Puerto Rico or any state, territory, possession or other jurisdiction of the United States other than the State of Delaware.

[As last amended by S 414, effective August 1, 2007]

§ 18-102. Name set forth in certificate.

The name of each limited liability company as set forth in its certificate of formation:

(1) Shall contain the words "Limited Liability Company" or the abbreviation "L.L.C." or the designation "LLC";

(2) May contain the name of a member or manager;

(3) Must be such as to distinguish it upon the records in the office of the secretary of state from the name on such records of any corporation, partnership, limited partnership, statutory trust, or limited liability company reserved, registered, formed or organized under the laws of the State of Delaware or qualified to do business or registered as a foreign corporation, foreign limited partnership, foreign statutory trust, foreign partnership or foreign limited liability company in the State of Delaware; provided however, that a limited liability company may register under any name which is not such as to distinguish it upon the records in the office of the secretary of state from the name on such records of any domestic or foreign corporation, partnership, limited partnership, statutory trust, or limited liability company reserved, registered, formed or organized under the laws of the State of Delaware with the written consent of the other corporation, partnership, limited partnership, statutory trust,

or limited liability company, which written consent shall be filed with the secretary of state; and

(4) May contain the following words: "Company," "Association," "Club," "Foundation," "Fund," "Institute," "Society," "Union," "Syndicate," "Limited" or "Trust" (or abbreviations of like import).

§ 18-103. Reservation of name.

(a) The exclusive right to the use of a name may be reserved by:

(1) Any person intending to organize a limited liability company under this chapter and to adopt that name;

(2) Any domestic limited liability company or any foreign limited liability company registered in the State of Delaware which, in either case, proposes to change its name;

(3) Any foreign limited liability company intending to register in the State of Delaware and adopt that name; and

(4) Any person intending to organize a foreign limited liability company and intending to have it register in the State of Delaware and adopt that name.

(b) The reservation of a specified name shall be made by filing with the secretary of state an application, executed by the applicant, specifying the name to be reserved and the name and address of the applicant. If the secretary of state finds that the name is available for use by a domestic or foreign limited liability company, he shall reserve the name for the exclusive use of the applicant for a period of 120 days. Once having so reserved a name, the same applicant may again reserve the same name for successive 120-day periods. The right to the exclusive use of a reserved name may be transferred to any other person by filing in the office of the secretary of state a notice of the transfer, executed by the applicant for whom the name was reserved, specifying the name to be transferred and the name and address of the transferee. The reservation of a specified name may be canceled by filing with the secretary of state a notice of cancellation, executed by the applicant or transferee, specifying the name reservation to be canceled and the name and address of the applicant or transferee. Unless the secretary of state finds that any application, notice of transfer, or notice of cancellation filed with the secretary of state as required by this subsection does not conform to law, upon receipt of all filing fees required by law he shall prepare and return to the person who filed such instrument a copy of the filed instrument with a notation thereon of the action taken by the secretary of state.

(c) A fee as set forth in § 18-1105(a)(1) of this title shall be paid at the time of the initial reservation of any name, at the time of the renewal of any such reservation and at the time of the filing of a notice of the transfer or cancellation of any such reservation.

§ 18-104. Registered office; registered agent.

(a) Each limited liability company shall have and maintain in the State of Delaware:

(1) A registered office, which may but need not be a place of its business in the State of Delaware; and

(2) A registered agent for service of process on the limited liability company, having a business office identical with such registered office which agent may be any of

a. the limited liability company itself,

b. an individual resident in the State of Delaware,

c. a domestic limited liability company (other than the limited liability company itself), a domestic corporation, a domestic partnership (whether general (including a limited liability partnership) or limited (including a limited liability limited partnership)), or a domestic statutory trust, or

d. a foreign corporation, a foreign partnership (whether general (including a limited liability partnership) or limited (including a limited liability limited partnership)), a foreign limited liability company, or a foreign statutory trust.

(b) A registered agent may change the address of the registered office of the limited liability copany(ies) for which it is registered agent to another address in the State of Delaware by paying a fee as set forth in § 18-1105(a)(2) of this title and filing with the Secretary of State a certificate, executed by such registered agent, setting forth the address at which such registered agent has maintained the registered office for each of the limited liability companies for which it is a registered agent, and further certifying to the new address to which each such registered office will be changed on a given day, and at which new address such registered agent will thereafter maintain the registered office for each of the limited liability companies for which it is a registered agent. Upon the filing of such certificate, the Secretary of State shall furnish to the registered agent a certified copy of the same under the Secretary's hand and seal of office, and thereafter, or until further change of address, as authorized by law, the registered office in the State of Delaware of each of the limited liability companies for which the agent is a registered agent shall be located at the new address of the registered agent thereof as given in the certificate. In the event of a change of name of any person acting as a registered agent of a limited liability company, such registered agent shall file with the Secretary of State a certificate executed by such registered agent setting forth the new name of such registered agent, the name of such registered agent before it was changed, and the address at which such registered agent has maintained the registered office for each other limited liability companies for which it is a registered agent, and shall pay a fee as set forth in § 18-1105(a)(2) of this title. Upon the filing of such certificate, the Secretary of State shall furnish to the registered agent a certified copy of the certificate under the Secretary of State's own hand and seal of office. A change of name of any person acting as a registered agent of a limited liability company as a result of a merger or consolidation of the registered agent with or into another person which succeeds to its assets and liabilities by operation of law this section shall be deemed to be an amendment of the certificate of formation of each limited liability company affected thereby, and each such limited liability company shall not be required to take any further action with respect thereto to amend its certificate of formation under § 18-202 of this title. Any registered agent filing a certificate under this section shall promptly, upon such filing, deliver a copy of any such certificate to each limited liability company affected thereby.

The registered agent to 1 or more limited liability companies may resign and appoint a successor registered agent by paying a fee as set forth in § 18-1105(a)(2) of this title and filing a certificate with the Secretary of State stating that it resigns and the name and address of the successor registered agent. There shall be attached to such certificate a statement of each affected limited liability company ratifying and approving such change of registered agent. Upon such filing, the successor registered agent shall become the registered agent of such limited liability companies as have ratified and approved such substitution, and the successor registered agent's address, as stated in such certificate, shall become the address of each such limited liability company's registered office in the State of Delaware. The Secretary of State shall than issue a certificate that the successor registered agent has become the registered agent of the limited liability companies so ratifying and approving such change and setting out the names of such limited liability companies. Filing of such certificate of resignation shall be deemed to be an amendment of the certification of formation of each limited liability company affected thereby, and each such limited liability company shall not be required to take any further action with respect thereto amend its certificate of formation under § 18-202 of this title.

The registered agent of 1 or more limited liability companies may resign without appointing a successor registered agent by paying a fee as set forth in § 18-1105(a)(2) of this title and filing a certificate of resignation with the Secretary of State, but such resignation shall not become effective until 30 days after the certificate is filing. The certificate shall contain a statement that written notice of resignation was given to each affected limited liability company at least 30 days prior to the filing of the certificate by mailing or delivering such notice to the limited liability company at its address last known to the registered agent and shall set forth the date of such notice. After receipt of the notice of the resignation of its registered agent, the limited liability company for which such registered agent was acting shall obtain and designate a new registered agent, to take the place of the registered agent so resigning. If such limited liability company fails to obtain and designate a new registered agent as aforesaid prior to the expiration of the period of 20 days after the filing by the registered agent of the certificate of resignation, the certificate of formation of such limited liability company shall be canceled. After the resignation of the registered agent shall have become effective as provided in this section and if no new registered agent shall have been obtained and designated in the time and manner aforesaid, service of legal process against each limited liability company for which the resigned registered agent has been acting shall thereafter be upon the Secretary of State in accordance with § 18-105 of this title.

(e) Every registered agent shall:

(1) If an entity, maintain a business office in the State of Delaware which is generally open, or if an individual, be generally present at a designated location in the State of Delaware, at sufficiently frequent times to accept service of process and otherwise perform the functions of a registered agent;

(2) If a foreign entity, be authorized to transact business in the State of Delaware;

(3) Accept service of process and other communications directed to the limited liability companies and foreign limited liability companies for which it serves as registered agent and forward same to the limited liability company or foreign limited liability company to which the service or communication is directed; and

(4) Forward to the limited liability companies and foreign limited liability company for which it serves as registered agent the statement for the annual tax described in § 18-1107 of this title or an electronic notification of same in a form satisfactory to the Secretary of State.

(f) Any registered agent who at any time serves as registered agent for more than fifty entities (a "Commercial Registered Agent"), whether domestic or foreign, shall satisfy and comply with the following qualifications:

(1) A natural person serving as a Commercial Registered Agent shall:

a. Maintain a principal residence or a principal place of business in the State of Delaware;

b. Maintain a Delaware business license;

c. Be generally present at a designated location within the State of Delaware during normal business hours to accept service of process and otherwise perform the functions of a registered agent as specified in subsection (e); and

d. Provide the Secretary of State upon request with such information identifying and enabling communication with such Commercial Registered Agent as the Secretary of State shall require.

(2) A domestic or foreign corporation, a domestic or foreign partnership (whether general (including a limited liability partnership) or limited (including a limited liability limited partnership)), a domestic or foreign limited liability company, or a domestic or foreign statutory trust serving as a Commercial Registered Agent shall:

a. Have a business office within the State of Delaware which is generally open during normal business hours to accept service of process and otherwise perform the functions of a registered agent as specified in subsection (e);

b. Maintain a Delaware business license;

c. Have generally present at such office during normal business hours an officer, director or managing agent who is a natural person; and

d. Provide the Secretary of State upon request with such information identifying and enabling communication with such Commercial Registered Agent as the Secretary of State shall require.

(3) For purposes of this subsection and subsection (i)(2)a., a Commercial Registered Agent shall also include any registered agent which has an officer, director or managing agent in common with any other registered agent or agents if such registered agents at any time during such common service as officer, director or managing agent collectively served as registered agents for more than fifty entities, whether domestic or foreign.

(g) Every limited liability company formed under the laws of the State of Delaware or qualified to do business in the State of Delaware shall provide to its registered agent and update from time to time as necessary the name, business address and business telephone number of a natural person who is a member, manager, officer, employee or designated agent of the limited liability company, who is then authorized to receive communications from the registered agent. Such person shall be deemed the communications contact for the limited liability company. Every registered agent shall retain (in paper or electronic form) the above information concerning the current communications contact for each limited liability company for which he, she, or it serves as registered agent. If the limited liability company fails to provide the registered agent with a current communications contact, the registered agent may resign as the registered agent for such limited liability company pursuant to this section.

(h) The Secretary of State is authorized to issue such rules and regulations as may be necessary or appropriate to carry out the enforcement of subsections (e), (f) and (g) of this Section, and to take actions reasonable and necessary to assure registered agents' compliance with subsections (e), (f) and (g). Such actions may include refusal to file documents submitted by a registered agent.

(i) Upon application of the Secretary of State, the Court of Chancery may enjoin any person or entity from serving as a registered agent or as an officer, director or managing agent of a registered agent.

(1) Upon the filing of a complaint by the Secretary of State pursuant to this Section, the Court may make such orders respecting such proceeding as it deems appropriate, and may enter such orders granting interim or final relief as it deems proper under the circumstances.

(2) Any one (1) or more of the following grounds shall be a sufficient basis to grant an injunction pursuant to this Section:

a. With respect to any registered agent who at any time within one (1) year immediately prior to the filing of the Secretary of State's complaint is a Commercial Registered Agent, failure after notice and warning to comply with the qualifications set forth in subsection (e) and/or the requirements of subsections (f) or (g) above;

b. The person serving as a registered agent, or any person who is an officer, director or managing agent of an entity registered agent, has been convicted of a felony or any crime which includes an element of dishonesty or fraud or involves moral turpitude; or

c. The registered agent has engaged in conduct in connection with acting as a registered agent that is intended to or likely to deceive or defraud the public.

(3) With respect to any order the Court enters pursuant to this Section with respect to an entity that has acted as a registered agent, the Court may also direct such order to any person who has served as an officer, director or managing agent of such registered agent. Any person who, on or after January 1, 2007, serves as an officer, director or managing agent of an entity acting as a registered agent in the State of Delaware shall be deemed thereby to have consented to the appointment of such registered agent as agent upon whom service of process may be made in any action brought pursuant to this Section, and service as an officer, director or managing agent of an entity acting as a registered agent in the State of Delaware shall be a signification of the consent of such person that any process when so served shall be of the same legal force and validity as if served upon such person within the State of Delaware, and such appointment of the registered agent shall be irrevocable.

(4) Upon the entry of an order by the Court enjoining any person or entity from acting as a registered agent, the Secretary of State shall mail or deliver notice of such order to each affected limited liability company

a. that has specified the address of a place of business in a record of the Secretary of State, to the address specified, or

b. an address of which the Secretary of State has obtained from the limited liability company's former registered agent, to the address obtained.

If such a limited liability company is a domestic limited liability company and fails to obtain and designate a new registered agent within thirty (30) days after such notice is given, the certificate of formation of such limited liability company shall be cancelled. If such a limited liability company is a foreign limited liability company and fails to obtain and designate a new registered agent within thirty (30) days after such notice is given, such foreign limited liability company shall not be permitted to do business in the State of Delaware and its registration shall be cancelled. If any other affected limited liability company is a domestic limited liability company and fails to obtain and designate a new registered agent within sixty (60) days after entry of an order by the Court enjoining such limited liability company's registered agent from acting as a registered agent, the certificate of formation of such limited liability company shall be cancelled. If any other affected limited liability company is a foreign limited liability company and fails to obtain and designate a new registered agent within sixty (60) days after entry of an order by Court enjoining such limited liability company's registered agent from acting as a registered agent, such foreign limited liability company shall not be permitted to do business in the State of Delaware and its registration shall be cancelled. If the Court enjoins a person or entity from acting as a registered agent as provided in this Section and no new registered agent shall have been obtained and designated in the time and manner aforesaid, service of legal process against the limited liability company for which the registered agent had been acting shall thereafter be upon the Secretary of State in accordance with Section 18-105 or Section 18-911 of this Title. The Court of Chancery may, upon application of the Secretary of State on notice to the former registered agent, enter such orders as it deems appropriate to give the Secretary of State access to information in the former registered agent's possession in order to facilitate communication with the limited liability companies the former registered agent served.

(j) The Secretary of State is authorized to make a list of registered agents available to the public, and to establish such qualifications and issue such rules and regulations with respect to such listing as the Secretary of State deems necessary or appropriate.

[As last amended by S 96, effective August 1, 2007]

§ 18-105. Service of process on domestic limited liability companies.

(a) Service of legal process upon any domestic limited liability company shall be made by delivering a copy personally to any manager of the limited liability company in the State of Delaware or the registered agent of the limited liability company in the State of Delaware, or by leaving it at the dwelling house or usual place of abode in the State of Delaware of any such manager or registered agent (if the registered agent be an individual), or at the registered office or other place of business of the limited liability company in the State of Delaware. If the registered agent be a corporation, service of process upon it as such may be made by serving, in the State of Delaware. a copy thereof on the president, vice-president, secretary, assistant secretary or any director of the corporate registered agent. Service by copy left at the dwelling house or usual place of abode of a manager or registered agent, or at the registered office or other place of business of the limited liability company in the State of Delaware, to be effective, must be delivered thereat at least 6 days before the return date of the process, and in the presence of an adult person, and the officer serving the process shall distinctly state the manner of service in his return thereto. Process returnable forthwith must be delivered personally to the manager or registered agent.

(b) In case the officer whose duty it is to serve legal process cannot by due diligence serve the process in any manner provided for by subsection (a) of this section, it shall be lawful to serve the process against the limited liability company upon the secretary of state, and such service shall be as effectual for all intents and purposes as if made in any of the ways provided for in subsection (a) of this section. In the event that service is effected through the secretary of state in accordance with this subsection, the secretary of state shall forthwith notify the limited liability company by letter, certified mail, return receipt requested, directed to the limited liability company at its address as it appears on the records relating to such limited liability company on file with the secretary of state or, if no such address appears, at its last registered office. Such letter shall enclose a copy of the process and any other papers served on the secretary of state pursuant to this subsection. It shall be the duty of the plaintiff in the event of such service to serve process and any other papers in duplicate, to notify the secretary of state that service is being effected pursuant to this subsection, and to pay the secretary of state the sum of $50 for the use of the State of Delaware, which sum shall be taxed as part of the costs in the proceeding if the plaintiff shall prevail therein. The secretary of state shall maintain an alphabetical record of any such service setting forth the name of the plaintiff and defendant, the title, docket number and nature of the proceeding in which process has been served upon him, the fact that service has been effected pursuant to this subsection, the return date thereof, and the day and hour when the service was made. The secretary of state shall not be required to retain such information for a period longer than 5 years from his receipt of the service of process.

§ 18-106. Nature of business permitted; powers.

(a) A limited liability company may carry on any lawful business, purpose or activity, whether or not for profit, with the exception of the business of banking as defined in § 126 of title 8.

(b) A limited liability company shall possess and may exercise all the powers and privileges granted by this chapter or by any other law or by its limited liability company agreement, together with any powers incidental thereto, including such powers and privileges as are necessary or convenient to the conduct, promotion or attainment of the business, purposes or activities of the limited liability company.

(c) Notwithstanding any provision of this chapter to the contrary, without limiting the general powers enumerated in subsection (b) above, a limited liability company shall, subject to such standards and restrictions, if any, as are set forth in its limited liability company agreement, have the power and authority to make contracts of guaranty and suretyship, and enter into interest rate, basis, currency, hedge or other swap agreements, or cap, floor, put, call, option, exchange or collar agreements, derivative agreements or other agreements similar to any of the foregoing.

§ 18-107. Business transactions of member or manager with the limited liability company.

Except as provided in a limited liability company agreement, a member or manager may lend money to, borrow money from, act as a surety, guarantor or endorser for, guarantee or assume 1 or more obligations of, provide collateral for, and transact other business with, a limited liability company and, subject to other applicable law, has the same rights and obligations with respect to any such matter as a person who is not a member or manager.

§ 18-108. Indemnification.

Subject to such standards and restrictions, if any, as are set forth in its limited liability company agreement, a limited liability company may, and shall have the power to, indemnify and hold harmless any member or manager or other person from and against any and all claims and demands whatsoever.

§ 18-109. Service of process on managers and liquidating trustees.

(a) A manager or a liquidating trustee of a limited liability company may be served with process in the manner prescribed in this section in all civil actions or proceedings brought in the State of Delaware involving or relating to the business of the limited liability company or a violation by the manager or the liquidating trustee of a duty to the limited liability company, or any member of the limited liability company, whether or not the manager or the liquidating trustee is a manager or a liquidating trustee at the time suit is commenced. A manager's or a liquidating trustee's serving as such constitutes such person's consent to the appointment of the registered agent of the limited liability company (or, if there is none, the secretary of state) as such person's agent upon whom service of process may be made as provided in this section. Such service as a manager or a liquidating trustee shall signify the consent of such manager or liquidating trustee that any process when so served shall be of the same legal force and validity as if served upon such manager or liquidating trustee within the State of Delaware and such appointment of the registered agent (or, if there is none, the secretary of state) shall be irrevocable. As used in this subsection (a) and in subsections (b), (c) and (d) of this §18-109, the term 'manager' refers (i) to a person who is a manager as defined in §18-101(10) of this title and (ii) to a person, whether or not a member of a limited liability company, who, although not a manager as defined in §18-101(10) of this title, participates materially in the management of the limited liability company, provided, however, that the power to elect or otherwise select or to participate in the election or selection of a person to be a manager as defined in §18-101(10) of this title shall not, by itself, constitute participation in the management of the limited liability company.

(b) Service of process shall be effected by serving the registered agent (or, if there is none, the secretary of state) with 1 copy of such process in the manner provided by law for service of writs of summons. In the event service is made under this subsection upon the secretary of state, the plaintiff shall pay to the secretary of state the sum of $50 for the use of the State of Delaware, which sum shall be taxed as part of the costs of the proceeding if the plaintiff shall prevail therein. In addition, the Prothonotary or the Register in Chancery of the court in which the civil action or proceeding is pending shall, within 7 days of such service, deposit in the United States mails, by registered mail, postage prepaid, true and attested copies of the process, together with a statement that service is being made pursuant to this section, addressed to such manager or liquidating trustee at the registered office of the limited liability company and at his address last known to the party desiring to make such service.

(c) In any action in which any such manager or liquidating trustee has been served with process as hereinabove provided, the time in which a defendant shall be required to appear and file a responsive pleading shall be computed from the date of mailing by the Prothonotary or the Register in Chancery as provided in subsection (b) of this section; however, the court in which such action has been commenced may order such continuance or continuances as may be necessary to afford such manager or liquidating trustee reasonable opportunity to defend the action.

(d) In a written limited liability company agreement or other writing, a manager or member may consent to be subject to the nonexclusive jurisdiction of the courts of, or arbitration in, a specified jurisdiction, or the exclusive jurisdiction of the courts of the State of Delaware, or the exclusivity of arbitration in a specified jurisdiction or the State of Delaware, and to be served with legal process in the manner prescribed in such limited liability company agreement or other writing. Except by agreeing to arbitrate any arbitrable matter in a specified jurisdiction or in the State of Delaware, a member who is not a manager may not waive its right to maintain a legal action or proceeding in the courts of the State of Delaware with respect to matters relating to the organization or internal affairs of a limited liability company.

(e) Nothing herein contained limits or affects the right to serve process in any other manner now or hereafter provided by law. This section is an extension of and not a limitation upon the right otherwise existing of service of legal process upon nonresidents.

(f) The Court of Chancery and the Superior Court may make all necessary rules respecting the form of process, the manner of issuance and return thereof and such other rules which may be necessary to implement this section and are not inconsistent with this section.

§18-110. Contested matters relating to managers; contested votes.

(a) Upon application of any member or manager, the Court of Chancery may hear and determine the validity of any admission, election, appointment, removal or resignation of a manager of a limited liability company, and the right of any person to become or to continue to be a manager of a limited liability company, and, in case the right to serve as a manager is claimed by more than 1 person, may determine the person or persons entitled to serve as managers; and to that end make such order or decree in any such case as may be just and proper, with power to enforce the production of any books, papers and records of the limited liability company relating to the issue. In any such application, the limited liability company shall be named as a party, and service of copies of the application upon the registered agent of the limited liability company shall be deemed to be service upon the limited liability company and upon the person or persons whose right to serve as a manager is contested and upon the person or persons, if any, claiming to be a manager or claiming the right to be a manager; and the registered agent shall forward immediately a copy of the application to the limited liability company and to the person or persons whose right to serve as a manager is contested and to the person or persons, if any, claiming to be a manager or the right to be a manager, in a postpaid, sealed, registered letter addressed to such limited liability company and such person or persons at their post-office addresses last known to the registered agent or furnished to the registered agent by the applicant member or manager. The Court may make such order respecting further or other notice of such application as it deems proper under these circumstances.

(b) Upon application of any member or manager, the Court of Chancery may hear and determine the result of any vote of members or managers upon matters as to which the members or managers of the limited liability company, or any class or group of members or managers, have the right to vote pursuant to the limited liability company agreement or other agreement or this chapter (other than the admission, election, appointment, removal or resignation of managers). In any such application, the limited liability company shall be named as a party, and service of the application upon the registered agent of the limited liability company shall be deemed to be service upon the limited liability company, and no other party need be joined in order for the Court to adjudicate the result of the vote. The Court may make such order respecting further or other notice of such application as it deems proper under these circumstances.

(c) Nothing herein contained limits or affects the right to serve process in any other manner now or hereafter provided by law. This section is an extension of and not a limitation upon the right otherwise existing of service of legal process upon nonresidents.

§ 18-111. Interpretation and enforcement of limited liability company agreement.

Any action to interpret, apply or enforce the provisions of a limited liability company agreement, or the duties, obligations or liabilities of a limited liability company to the members or managers of the limited liability company, or the duties, obligations or liabilities among members or managers and of members or managers to the limited liability company, or the rights or powers of, or restrictions on, the limited liability company, members or managers, may be brought in the Court of Chancery.

SUBCHAPTER II. FORMATION; CERTIFICATE OF FORMATION

§ 18-201. Certificate of formation.

(a) In order to form a limited liability company, 1 or more authorized persons must execute a certificate of formation. The certificate of formation shall be filed in the office of the secretary of state and set forth:

(1) The name of the limited liability company;

(2) The address of the registered office and the name and address of the registered agent for service of process required to be maintained by § 18-104 of this title; and

(3) Any other matters the members determine to include therein.

(b) A limited liability company is formed at the time of the filing of the initial certificate of formation in the office of the secretary of state or at any later date or time specified in the certificate of formation if, in either case, there has been substantial compliance with the requirements of this section. A limited liability company formed under this chapter shall be a separate legal entity, the existence of which as a separate legal entity shall continue until cancellation of the limited liability company's certificate of formation.

(c) The filing of the certificate of formation in the office of the secretary of state shall make it unnecessary to file any other documents under Chapter 31 of this title.

(d) A limited liability company agreement shall be entered into or otherwise existing either before, after or at the time of the filing of a certificate of formation and, whether entered into or otherwise existing before, after or at the time of such filing, may be made effective as of the formation of the limited liability company or at such other time or date as provided in or reflected by the limited liability company agreement.

[As last amended by S 96, effective August 1, 2007]

§ 18-202. Amendment to certificate of formation.

(a) A certificate of formation is amended by filing a certificate of amendment thereto in the office of the secretary of state. The certificate of amendment shall set forth:

(1) The name of the limited liability company; and

(2) The amendment to the certificate of formation.

(b) A manager or, if there is no manager, then any member who becomes aware that any statement in a certificate of formation was false when made, or that any matter described has changed making the certificate of formation false in any material respect, shall promptly amend the certificate of formation.

(c) A certificate of formation may be amended at any time for any other proper purpose.

(d) Unless otherwise provided in this chapter or unless a later effective date or time (which shall be a date or time certain) is provided for in the certificate of amendment, a certificate of amendment shall be effective at the time of its filing with the secretary of state.

§ 18-203. Cancellation of certificate.

A certificate of formation shall be canceled upon the dissolution and the completion of winding up of a limited liability company, or as provided in § 18-104(d) or § 18-104(i)(4) or § 18-1108 of this title, or upon future effective date or time of a certificate of merger or consolidation if the limited liability company is not the surviving or resulting entity in a merger or consolidation, or upon the filing of a certificate of merger or consolidation if the limited liability company is not the surviving or resulting entity in a merger or consolidation, or upon the filing of a certificate of transfer, or upon the future effective date or time of a certificate or transfer or upon the filing of a certificate of conversion to non-Delaware entity or upon the future effective fate or time of a certificate of conversion to non-Delaware entity. A certificate of cancellation shall be filed in the office of the secretary of state to accomplish the cancellation of a certificate of formation upon the dissolution and the completion of winding up of a limited liability company and shall set forth:

(1) The name of the limited liability company;

(2) The date of filing of its certificate of formation;

(3) The future effective date or time (which shall be a date or time certain) of cancellation if it is not to be effective upon the filing of the certificate; and

(4) Any other information the person filing the certificate of cancellation determines.

The Secretary of State shall not issue a certificate of good standing with respoect to a limited liability company if its certificate of formation is cancelled.

[As last amended by S 96, effective August 1, 2007]

§ 18-204. Execution.

(a) Each certificate required by this subchapter to be filed in the office of the secretary of state shall be executed by 1 or more authorized persons.

(b) Unless otherwise provided in a limited liability company agreement, any person may sign any certificate or amendment thereof or enter into a limited liability company agreement or amendment thereof by an agent, including an attorney-in-fact. An authorization, including a power of attorney to sign any certificate or amendment thereof or to enter into a limited liability company agreement or amendment thereof need not be in writing, need not be sworn to, verified or acknowledged, and need not be filed in the office of the secretary of state, but if in writing, must be retained by the limited liability company.

(c) The execution of a certificate by an authorized person constitutes an oath or affirmation, under the penalties of perjury in the third degree, that, to the best of the authorized person's knowledge and belief, the facts stated therein are true.

§ 18-205. Execution, amendment or cancellation by judicial order.

(a) If a person required to execute a certificate required by this subchapter fails or refuses to do so, any other person who is adversely affected by the failure or refusal may petition the Court of Chancery to direct the execution of the certificate. If the Court finds that the execution of the certificate is proper and that any person so designated has failed or refused to execute the certificate, it shall order the secretary of state to record an appropriate certificate.

(b) If a person required to execute a limited liability company agreement or amendment thereof fails or refuses to do so, any other person who is adversely affected by the failure or refusal may petition the Court of Chancery to direct the execution of the limited liability company agreement or amendment thereof. If the Court finds that the limited liability company agreement or amendment thereof should be executed and that any person required to execute the limited liability company agreement or amendment thereof has failed or refused to do so, it shall enter an order granting appropriate relief.

§ 18-206. Filing.

(a) The signed copy of the certificate of formation and of any certificates of amendment, correction, amendment of a certificate with a future effective date or time, termination of a certificate with a future effective date or time or cancellation (or of any judicial decree of amendment or cancellation), and of any certificate of merger or consolidation, any restated certificate, any corrected certificate, any certificate of conversion to limited liability company, any certificate of conversion to a non-Delaware entity, any certificate of transfer, any certificate of transfer and domestic continuance, any certificate of limited liability company domestication, and of any certificate of revival shall be delivered to the secretary of state. A person who executes a certificate as an agent or fiduciary need not exhibit evidence of his authority as a prerequisite to filing. Any signature on any certificate authorized to be filed with the secretary of state under any provision of this chapter may be a facsimile, a conformed signature or an electronically transmitted signature. Upon delivery of any certificate, the Secretary of State shall record the date and time of its delivery. Unless the secretary of state finds that any certificate does not conform to law, upon receipt of all filing fees required by law he shall:

(1) Certify that the certificate of formation, the certificate of amendment, the certificate of correction, the certificate of amendment of a certificate with a future effective date or time, the certificate of termination of a certificate with a future effective date or time, the certificate of cancellation (or of any judicial decree of amendment or cancellation), the certificate of merger or consolidation, the restated certificate, the corrected certificate, the certificate of conversion to limited liability company, the certificate of conversion to a non-Delaware entity, the certificate of transfer, the certificate of transfer and domestic continuance, the certificate of limited liability company domestication or the certificate of revival has been filed in his office by endorsing upon the original certificate the word "Filed," and the date and time of the filing. This endorsement is conclusive of the date and time of its filing in the absence of actual fraud. Except as provided in subsection (a)(5) or (a)(6) of this section, such date and time of filing of a certificate shall be the date and time of delivery of the certificate;

(2) File and index the endorsed certificate;

(3) Prepare and return to the person who filed it or his representative a copy of the signed certificate, similarly endorsed, and shall certify such copy as a true copy of the signed certificate; and

(4) Cause to be entered such information from the certificate as the Secretary of State deems appropriate into the Delaware Corporation Information System or any system which is a successor thereto in the office of the Secretary of State, and such information and a copy of such certificate shall be permanently maintained as a public record on a suitable medium. The Secretary of State is authorized to grant direct access to such system to registered agents subject to the execution of an operating agreement between the Secretary of State and such registered agent. Any registered agent granted such access shall demonstrate the existence of policies to ensure that information entered into the system accurately reflects the content of certificates in the possession of the registered agent at the time of entry.

(5) Upon request made upon or prior to delivery, the Secretary of State may, to the extent deemed practicable, establish as the date and time of filing of a certificate a date and time after its delivery. If the Secretary of State refuses to file any certificate due to an error, omission or other imperfection, the Secretary of State may hold such certificate in suspension, and in such event, upon delivery of a replacement certificate in proper form for filing and tender of the required fees within five business days after notice of such suspension is given to the filer, the Secretary of State shall establish as the date and time of filing of such certificate the date and time that would have been the date and time of filing of the rejected certificate had it been accepted for filing. The Secretary of State shall not issue a certificate of good standing with respect to any limited liability company with a certificate held in suspension pursuant to this subsection. The Secretary of State may establish as the date and time of filing of a certificate the date and time at which information from such certificate is entered pursuant to subsection (a) (4) of this section if such certificate is delivered on the same date and within four hours after such information is entered.

(6) If:

(A) together with the actual delivery of a certificate and tender of the required fees, there is delivered to the Secretary of State a separate affidavit (which in its heading shall be designated as an affidavit of extraordinary condition) attesting, on the basis of personal knowledge of the affiant or a reliable source of knowledge identified in the affidavit, that an earlier effort to deliver such certificate and tender such fees was made in good faith, specifying the nature, date and time of such good faith effort and requesting that the Secretary of State establish such date and time as the date and time of filing of such certificate; or

(B) upon the actual delivery of a certificate and tender of the required fees, the Secretary of State in his or her discretion provides a written waiver of the requirement for such an affidavit stating that it appears to the Secretary of State that an earlier effort to deliver such certificate and tender such fees was made in good faith and specifying the date and time of such effort; and

(C) the Secretary of State determines that an extraordinary condition existed at such date and time, that such earlier effort was unsuccessful as a result of the existence of such extraordinary condition, and that such actual delivery and tender were made within a reasonable period (not to exceed two business days) after the cessation of such extraordinary condition, then the Secretary of State may establish such date and time as the date and time of filing of such certificate. No fee shall be paid to the Secretary of State for receiving an affidavit of extraordinary condition. For purposes of this subsection, an extraordinary condition means: any emergency resulting from an attack on, invasion or occupation by foreign military forces of, or disaster, catastrophe, war or other armed conflict, revolution or insurrection, or rioting or civil commotion in, the United States or a locality in which the Secretary of State conducts its business or in which the good faith effort to deliver the certificate and tender the required fees is made, or the immediate threat of any of the foregoing; or any malfunction or outage of the electrical or telephone service to the Secretary of State's office, or weather or other condition in or about a locality in which the Secretary of State conducts its business, as a result of which the Secretary of State's office is not open for the purpose of the filing of certificates under this chapter or such filing cannot be effected without extraordinary effort. The Secretary of State may require such proof as it deems necessary to make the determination required under clause (C) of this subsection, and any such determination shall be conclusive in the absence of actual fraud. If the Secretary of State establishes the date and time of filing of a certificate pursuant to this subsection, the date and time of delivery of the affidavit of extraordinary condition or the date and time of the Secretary of State's written waiver of such affidavit shall be endorsed on such affidavit or waiver and such affidavit or waiver, so endorsed, shall be attached to the filed certificate to which it relates. Such filed certificate shall be effective as of the date and time established as the date and time of filing by the Secretary of State pursuant to this subsection, except as to those persons who are substantially and adversely affected by such establishment and, as to those persons, the certificate shall be effective from the date and time endorsed on the affidavit of extraordinary condition or written waiver attached thereto.

(b) Upon the filing of a certificate of amendment (or judicial decree of amendment), certificate of correction, corrected certificate or restated certificate in the office of the secretary of state, or upon the future effective date or time of a certificate of amendment (or judicial decree thereof) or restated certificate, as provided for therein, the certificate of formation shall be amended corrected or restated as set forth therein. Upon the filing of a certificate of cancellation (or a judicial decree thereof), or a certificate of merger or consolidation which acts as a certificate of cancellation, or a certificate of transfer, or a certificate of conversion to a non-Delaware entity, or upon the future effective date or time of a certificate of cancellation (or a judicial decree thereof) or of a certificate of merger or consolidation which acts as a certificate of cancellation, or a certificate of transfer, or a certificate of conversion to a non-Delaware entity, as provided for therein, or as specified in § 18-104(d) or § 18-1108(a) of this title, the certificate of formation is canceled. Upon the filing of a certificate of limited liability company domestication, or upon the future effective date or time of a certificate of limited liability company domestication, the entity filing the certificate of limited liability company domestication is domesticated as a limited liability company with the effect provided in § 18-212 of this title. Upon the filing of a certificate of conversion to limited liability company, or upon the future effective date or time of a certificate of conversion to limited liability company, the entity filing the certificate of conversion to limited liability company is converted to a limited liability company with the effect provided in § 18-214 of this title. Upon the filing of a certificate of amendment of a certificate of merger or consolidation, the certificate of merger or consolidation identified in the certificate of amendment of a certificate of merger or consolidation is amended. Upon the filing of a certificate of termination of a merger or consolidation, the certificate of merger or consolidation identified in the certificate of termination of a merger or consolidation is terminated. Upon the filing of a certificate of revival, the limited liability company is revived with the effect provided in § 18-1109 of this title. Upon the filing of a certificate of transfer and domestic continuance, or upon the future effective date or time of a certificate of transfer and domestic continuance, as provided for therein, the limited liability company filing the certificate of transfer and domestic continuance shall continue to exist as a limited liability company of the State of Delaware with the effect provided in § 18-213 of this title.

(c) If any certificate filed in accordance with this chapter provides for a future effective date or time and if, prior to such future effective date or time set forth in such certificate, the transaction is terminated or its terms are amended to change the future effective date or time or any other matter described in such certificate so as to make such certificate false or inaccurate in any respect, such certificate shall, prior to the future effective date or time set forth in such certificate, be terminated or amended by the filing of a certificate of termination or certificate of amendment of such certificate, executed in accordance with Section 18-204 of this chapter, which shall identify the certificate which has been terminated or amended and shall state that the certificate has been terminated or the manner in which it has been amended. Upon the filing of a certificate of amendment of a certificate with a future effective date or time, the certificate identified in such certificate of amendment is amended. Upon the filing of a certificate of termination of a certificate with a future effective date or time, the certificate identified in such certificate of termination is terminated.

(d) A fee as set forth in § 18-1105(a)(3) of this title shall be paid at the time of the filing of a certificate of formation, a certificate of amendment, a certificate of correction, a certificate of amendment of a certificate with a future effective date or time, a certificate of termination of a certificate with a future effective date or time, a certificate of cancellation, a certificate of merger or consolidation, a restated certificate, a corrected certificate, a certificate of conversion to limited liability company, a certificate of conversion to a non-Delaware entity, a certificate of transfer, a certificate of transfer of transfer and domestic continuance, a certificate of limited liability company domestication or a certificate of revival.

(e) The Secretary of State, acting as agent, shall collect and deposit in a separate account established exclusively for that purpose, a courthouse municipality fee with respect to each filed instrument and shall thereafter monthly remit funds from such account to the treasuries of the municipalities designated in Title 10, Section 301. Said fees shall be for the purposes of defraying certain costs incurred by such municipalities in hosting the primary locations for the Delaware Courts. The fee to such municipalities shall be $20 for each instrument filed with the Secretary of State in accordance with this Section. The municipality to receive the fee shall be the municipality designated in Title 10, Section 301 in the county in which the limited liability company's registered office in this State is, or is to be, located, except that a fee shall not be charged for a document filed in accordance with Subchapter IX of this Chapter.

(f) A fee as set forth in § 18-1105(a)(4) of this title shall be paid for a certified copy of any paper on file as provided for by this chapter, and a fee as set forth in § 18-1105(a)(5) of this title shall be paid for each page copied.

[As last amended by S 96, effective August 1, 2007]

§ 18-207. Notice.

The fact that a certificate of formation is on file in the office of the secretary of state is notice that the entity formed in connection with the filing of the certificate of formation is a limited liability company formed under the laws of the State of Delaware and is notice of all other facts set forth therein which are required to be set forth in a certificate of formation by § 18-201(a)(1) and (2) of this chapter and which are permitted to be set forth in a certificate of formation by § 18-215(b) of this title.

§ 18-208. Restated certificate.

(a) A limited liability company may, whenever desired, integrate into a single instrument all of the provisions of its certificate of formation which are then in effect and operative as a result of there having theretofore been filed with the secretary of state 1 or more certificates or other instruments pursuant to any of the sections referred to in this subchapter, and it may at the same time also further amend its certificate of formation by adopting a restated certificate of formation.

(b) If a restated certificate of formation merely restates and integrates but does not further amend the initial certificate of formation, as theretofore amended or supplemented by any instrument that was executed and filed pursuant to any of the sections in this subchapter, it shall be specifically designated in its heading as a "Restated Certificate of Formation" together with such other words as the limited liability company may deem appropriate and shall be executed by an authorized person and filed as provided in § 18-206 of this title in the office of the secretary of state. If a restated certificate restates and integrates and also further amends in any respect the certificate of formation, as theretofore amended or supplemented, it shall be specifically designated in its heading as an "Amended and Restated Certificate of Formation" together with such other words as the limited liability company may deem appropriate and shall be executed by at least 1 authorized person, and filed as provided in § 18-206 of this title in the office of the secretary of state.

(c) A restated certificate of formation shall state, either in its heading or in an introductory paragraph, the limited liability company's present name, and, if it has been changed, the name under which it was originally filed, and the date of filing of its original certificate of formation with the secretary of state, and the future effective date or time (which shall be a date or time certain) of the restated certificate if it is not to be effective upon the filing of the restated certificate. A restated certificate shall also state that it was duly executed and is being filed in accordance with this section. If a restated certificate only restates and integrates and does not further amend a limited liability company's certificate of formation as theretofore amended or supplemented and there is no discrepancy between those provisions and the restated certificate, it shall state that fact as well.

(d) Upon the filing of a restated certificate formation with the secretary of state, or upon the future effective date or time of a restated certificate of formation as provided for therein, the initial certificate of formation, as theretofore amended or supplemented, shall be superseded; thenceforth, the restated certificate of formation, including any further amendment or changes made thereby, shall be the certificate of information of the limited liability company, but the original effective date of formation shall remain unchanged

(e) Any amendment or change effected in connection with the restatement and integration of the certificate of formation shall be subject to any other provision of this chapter, not inconsistent with. this section, which would apply if a separate certificate of amendment were filed to effect such amendment or change.

§ 18-209. Merger and consolidation.

(a) As used in this section, "other business entity" means a corporation, a statutory trust, a business trust, an association, a real estate investment trust, a common-law trust, or any other unincorporated business or entity, including a partnership (whether general (including a limited liability partnership) or limited (including a limited liability limited partnership)), and a foreign limited liability company, but excluding a domestic limited liability company.

(b) Pursuant to an agreement of merger or consolidation, 1 or more domestic limited liability company may merge or consolidate with or into 1 or more domestic limited liability companies or 1 or more other business entities formed or organized under the laws of the State of Delaware or any other state or the United States or any foreign country or other foreign jurisdiction, or any combination thereof, with such domestic limited liability companies or other business entity as the agreement shall provide being the surviving or resulting domestic limited liability companies or other business entity. Unless otherwise provided in the limited liability company agreement, a merger or consolidation shall be approved by each domestic limited liability company which is to merge or consolidate by the members or, if there is more than one class or group of members, then by each class or group of members, in either case, by members who own more than 50 percent of the then current percentage or other interest in the profits of the domestic limited liability company owned by all of the members or by the members in each class or group, as appropriate. In connection with a merger or consolidation hereunder, rights or securities of, or interests in, a domestic limited liability company or other business entity which is a constituent party to the merger or consolidation may be exchanged for or converted into cash, property, rights or securities of, or interests in, the surviving or resulting domestic limited liability company or other business entity or, in addition to or in lieu thereof, may be exchanged for or converted into cash, property, rights or securities of, or interests in, a domestic limited liability company or other business entity which is not the surviving or resulting limited liability company or other business entity in the merger or consolidation or may be cancelled. Notwithstanding prior approval, an agreement of merger or consolidation may be terminated or amended pursuant to a provision for such termination or amendment contained in the agreement of merger or consolidation.

(c) If a domestic limited liability company is merging or consolidating under this section, the domestic limited liability company or other business entity surviving or resulting in or from the merger or consolidation shall file a certificate of merger or consolidation executed by one or more authorized persons on behalf of the domestic limited liability company when it is the surviving or resulting entity in the office of the secretary of state. The certificate of merger or consolidation shall state:

(1) The name and jurisdiction of formation or organization of each of the domestic limited liability companies and other business entities which is to merge or consolidate;

(2) That an agreement of merger or consolidation has been approved and executed by each of the domestic limited liability companies and other business entities which is to merge or consolidate;

(3) The name of the surviving or resulting domestic limited liability company or other business entity;

(4) In the case of a merger in which a domestic limited liability company is the surviving entity, such amendments, if any, to the certificate of formation of the surviving domestic limited liability company to change its name as are desired to be effected by the merger;

(5) The future effective date or time (which shall be a date or time certain) of the merger or consolidation if it is not to be effective upon the filing of the certificate of merger or consolidation;

(6) That the agreement of merger or consolidation is on file at a place of business of the surviving or resulting domestic limited liability company or other business entity, and shall state the address thereof;

(7) That a copy of the agreement of merger or consolidation will be furnished by the surviving or resulting domestic limited liability company or other business entity, on request and without cost, to any member of any domestic limited liability company or any person holding an interest in any other business entity which is to merge or consolidate; and

(8) If the surviving or resulting entity is not a domestic limited liability company, or a corporation, partnership whether general (including a limited liability liability partnership) or limited (including a limited liability limited partnership)) or statutory trust organized under the laws of the State of Delaware, a statement that such surviving or resulting other business entity agrees that it may be served with process in the State of Delaware in any action, suit or proceeding for the enforcement of any obligation of any domestic limited liability company which is to merge or consolidate, irrevocably appointing the secretary of state as its agent to accept service of process in any such action, suit or proceeding and specifying the address to which a copy of such process shall be mailed to it by the secretary of state. In the event of service hereunder upon the secretary of state, the procedures set forth in § 18-911(c) of this title shall be applicable, except that the plaintiff in any such action, suit or proceeding shall furnish the secretary of state with the address specified in the certificate of merger or consolidation provided for in this section and any other address which the plaintiff may elect to furnish, together with copies of such process as required by the secretary of state, and the secretary of state shall notify such surviving or resulting other business entity at all such addresses furnished by the plaintiff in accordance with the procedures set forth in § 18-911(c) of this title.

(d) Unless a future effective date or time is provided in a certificate of merger or consolidation, in which event a merger or consolidation shall be effective at any such future effective date or time, a merger or consolidation shall be effective upon the filing in the office of the secretary of state of a certificate of merger or consolidation.

(e) A certificate of merger or consolidation shall act as a certificate of cancellation for a domestic limited liability company which is not the surviving or resulting entity in the merger or consolidation. A certificate of merger that sets forth any amendment in accordance with Subsection (c)(4) of this Section shall be deemed to be an amendment to the certificate of formation of the limited liability company, and the limited liability company shall not be required to take any further action to amend its certificate of formation under Section 18-202 of this title with respect to such amendments set forth in the cerificate of merger. Whenever this section requires the filing of a certificate of merger or consolidation, such requirement shall be deemed satisfied by the filing of an agreement of merger or consolidation containing the information required by this section to be set forth in the certificate of merger or consolidation.

(f) An agreement of merger or consolidation approved in accordance with subsection (b) of this section may:

(1) Effect any amendment to the limited liability company agreement; or

(2) Effect the adoption of a new limited liability company agreement, for a limited liability company if it is the surviving or resulting limited liability company in the merger or consolidation.

Any amendment to a limited liability company agreement or adoption of a new limited liability company agreement made pursuant to the foregoing sentence shall be effective at the effective time or date of the merger or consolidation. The provisions of this subsection shall not be construed to limit the accomplishment of a merger or of any of the matters referred to herein by any other means provided for in a limited liability company agreement or other agreement or as otherwise permitted by law, including that the limited liability company agreement of any constituent limited liability company to the merger or consolidation (including a limited liability company formed for the purpose of consummating a merger or consolidation) shall be the limited liability company agreement of the surviving or resulting limited liability company.

(g) When any merger or consolidation shall have become effective under this section, for all purposes of the laws of the State of Delaware, all of the rights, privileges and powers of each of the domestic limited liability companies and other business entities that have merged or consolidated, and all property, real, personal and mixed, and all debts due to any of said domestic limited liability companies and other business entities, as well as all other things and causes of action belonging to each of such domestic limited liability companies and other business entities, shall be vested in the surviving or resulting domestic limited liability company or other business entity, and shall thereafter be the property of the surviving or resulting domestic limited liability company or other business entity as they were of each of the domestic limited liability companies and other business entities that have merged or consolidated, and the title to any real property vested by deed or otherwise, under the laws of the State of Delaware, in any of such domestic limited liability companies and other business entities, shall not revert or be in any way impaired by reason of this chapter; but all rights of creditors and all liens upon any property of any of said domestic limited liability companies and other business entities shall be preserved unimpaired, and all debts, liabilities and duties of each of the said domestic limited liability companies and other business entities that have merged or consolidated shall thenceforth attach to the surviving or resulting domestic limited liability company or other business entity, and may be enforced against it to the same extent as if said debts, liabilities and duties had been incurred or contracted by it. Unless otherwise agreed, a merger or consolidation of a domestic limited liability company, including a domestic limited liability company which is not the surviving or resulting entity in the merger or consolidation, shall not require such domestic limited liability company to wind up its affairs under § 18-803 of this chapter or pay its liabilities and distribute its assets under § 18-804 of this chapter and the merger or consolidation shall not constitute a dissolution of such limited liability company.

(h) A limited liability company agreement may provide that a domestic limited liability copany shall not have the power to merge or consolidate as set forth in the section.

[As last amended by S 96, effective August 1, 2007]

§ 18-210. Contractual appraisal rights.

A limited liability company agreement or an agreement of merger or consolidation may provide that contractual appraisal rights with respect to a limited liability company interest or another interest in a limited liability company shall be available for any class or group or series of members or limited liability company interests in connection with any amendment of a limited liability company agreement, any merger or consolidation in which the limited liability company is a constituent party to the merger or consolidation, any conversion of the limited liability company to another business form, any transfer to or domestication or continuance in any jurisdiction by the limited liability company, or the sale of all or substantially all of the limited liability company's assets. The Court of Chancery shall have jurisdiction to hear and determine any matter relating to any such appraisal rights.

[As last amended by S 96, effective August 1, 2007]

§ 18-211. Certificate of correction.

(a) Whenever any certificate authorized to be filed with the office of the secretary of state under any provision of this chapter has been so filed and is an inaccurate record of the action therein referred to, or was defectively or erroneously executed, such certificate may be corrected by filing with the office of the secretary of state a certificate of correction of such certificate. The certificate of correction shall specify the inaccuracy or defect to be corrected, shall set forth the portion of the certificate in corrected form and shall be executed and filed as required by this chapter. The certificate of correction shall be effective as of the date the original certificate was filed, except as to those persons who are substantially and adversely affected by the correction, and as to those persons the certificate of correction shall be effective from the filing date.

(b) In lieu of filing a certificate of correction, a certificate may be corrected by filing with the secretary of state a corrected certificate which shall be executed and filed as if the corrected certificate were the certificate being corrected, and a fee equal to the fee payable to the secretary of state if the certificate being corrected were then being filed shall be paid and collected by the secretary of state for the use of the State of Delaware in connection with the filing of the corrected certificate. The corrected certificate shall be specifically designated as such in its heading, shall specify the inaccuracy or defect to be corrected, and shall set forth the entire certificate in corrected form. A certificate corrected in accordance with this section shall be effective as of the date the original certificate was filed, except as to those persons who are substantially and adversely affected by the correction and as to those persons the certificate as corrected shall be effective from the filing date.

§ 18-212. Domestication of non-United States entities.

(a) As used in this section, "non-United States entity" means a foreign limited liability company (other than one formed under the laws of a state), or a corporation, a statutory trust, a business trust, an association, a real estate investment trust, a common-law trust, or any other unincorporated business or entity, including a partnership (whether general (including a limited liability partnership) or limited (including a limited liability limited partnership)), formed, incorporated, created or that otherwise came into being under the laws of any foreign country or other foreign jurisdiction (other than any state).

(b) Any non-United States entity may become domesticated as a limited liability company in the State of Delaware by complying with subsection (g) of this section and filing in the Office of the secretary of state in accordance with § 18-206 of this title:

(1) A certificate of limited liability company domestication that has been executed by 1 or more authorized persons in accordance with § 18-204 of this title; and

(2) A certificate of formation that complies with § 18-201 of this title and has been executed by 1 or more authorized persons in accordance with § 18-204 of this title.

(c) The certificate of limited liability company domestication shall state:

(1) The date on which and jurisdiction where the non-United States entity was first formed, incorporated, created or otherwise came into being;

(2) The name of the non-United States entity immediately prior to the filing of the certificate of limited liability company domestication;

(3) The name of the limited liability company as set forth in the certificate of formation filed in accordance with subsection (b) of this section;

(4) The future effective date or time (which shall be a date or time certain) of the domestication as a limited liability company if it is not to be effective upon the filing of the certificate of limited liability company domestication and the certificate of formation;

(5) The jurisdiction that constituted the seat, siege social, or principal place of business or central administration of the non-United States entity, or any other equivalent thereto under applicable law, immediately prior to the filing of the certificate of limited liability company domestication; and

(6) That the domestication has been approved in the manner provided for in the document, instrument, agreement or other writing, as the case may be, governing the internal affairs of a non-United States entity and the conduct of its business or by applicable non-Delaware law, as appropriate.

(d) Upon the filing in the office of the secretary of state of the certificate of limited liability company domestication and the certificate of formation or upon the future effective date or time of the certificate of limited liability company domestication and the certificate of formation, the non-United States entity shall be domesticated as a limited liability company in the State of Delaware and the limited liability company shall thereafter be subject to all of the provisions of this chapter, except that notwithstanding § 18-201 of this title, the existence of the limited liability company shall be deemed to have commenced on the date the non-United States entity commenced its existence in the jurisdiction in which the non-United States entity was first formed, incorporated, created or otherwise came into being.

(e) The domestication of any non-United States entity as a limited liability company in the State of Delaware shall not be deemed to affect any obligations or liabilities of the non-United States entity incurred prior to its domestication as a limited liability company in the State of Delaware, or the personal liability of any person therefor.

(f) The filing of a certificate of limited liability company domestication shall not affect the choice of law applicable to the non-United States entity, except that from the effective date or time of the domestication, the law of the State of Delaware, including the provisions of this chapter, shall apply to the non-United States entity to the same extent as if the non-United States entity had been formed as a limited liability company on that date.

(g) Prior to the filing of a certificate of limited liability company domestication with tie Office of the secretary of state, the domestication shall be approved in the manner provided for by the document, instrument, agreement or other writing, as the case may be, governing the internal affairs of the non-United States entity and the conduct of its business or by applicable non-Delaware law, as appropriate, and a limited liability company agreement shall be approved by the same authorization required to approve the domestication.

(h) When any domestication shall have become effective under this section, for all purposes of the laws of the State of Delaware, all of the rights, privileges and powers of the non-United States entity that has been domesticated (and also in the non-United States entity, if and for so long as the non-United States entity continues its existence in the foreign jurisdiction in which it was existing immediately prior to the domestication), and all property, real, personal and mixed, and all debts due to such non-United States entity, as well as all other things and causes of action belonging to such non-United States entity, shall remain vested in the domestic limited liability company to which such non-United States entity has been domesticated and shall be the property of such domestic limited liability company (and also of the non-United States entity, if and for so long as the non-United States entity continues its existence in the foreign jurisdiction in which it was existing immediately prior to the domestication), and the title to any real property vested by deed or otherwise in such non-United States entity shall not revert or be in any way impaired by reason of this chapter; but all rights of creditors and all liens upon any property of such non-United States entity shall be preserved unimpaired, and all debts, liabilities and duties of the non-United States entity that has been domesticated shall remain attached to the domestic limited liability company to which such non-United States entity has been domesticated (and also to the non-United States entity, if and for so long as the non-United States entity continues its existence in the foreign jurisdiction in which it was existing immediately prior to the domestication), and may be enforced against it to the same extent as if said debts, liabilities and duties had originally been incurred or contracted by it in its capacity as a domestic limited liability company. The rights, privileges, powers and interests in property of the non-United States entity, as well as the debts, liabilities and duties of the non-United States entity, shall not be deemed, as a consequence of the domestication, to have been transferred to the domestic limited liability company to which such non-United States entity has domesticated for any purpose of the laws of the State of Delaware.

(i) When a non-United States entity has become domesticated as a limited liability company pursuant to this section for all purposes of the laws of the State of Delaware, the limited liability company shall, be deemed to be the same entity as the domesticating non-United States entity and the domestication shall constitute a continuation of the existence of the domesticating non-United States entity in the form of a domestic limited liability company. Unless otherwise agreed, for all purposes of the laws of the State of Delaware, the domesticating non-United States entity shall not be required to wind up its affairs or pay its liabilities and distribute its assets, and the domestication shall not be deemed to constitute a dissolution of such non-United States entity. If, following domestication, a non-United States entity that has become domesticated as a limited liability company continues its existence in the foreign country or other foreign jurisdiction in which it was existing immediately prior to domestication, the limited liability company and such non-United States entity shall, for all purposes of the laws of the State of Delaware, constitute a single entity formed, incorporated, created or otherwise having come into being, as applicable, and existing under the laws of the State of Delaware and the laws of such foreign country or other foreign jurisdiction.

(j) In connection with a domestication hereunder, rights or securities of, or interests in, the non-United States entity that is to be domesticated as a domestic limited liability company may be exchanged for or converted into cash, property, rights or securities of, or interests in, such domesticlimited liability company or, in addition to or in lieu thereof, may be exchanged for or converted into cash, property, rights or securities of, or interests in, another domestic limited liability company or other entity or may be cancelled.

[As amended by H 414, effective August 1, 2006.]

§ 18-213. Transfer or continuance of domestic limited liability companies.

(a) Upon compliance with the provisions of this section, any limited liability company may transfer to or domesticate or continue in any jurisdiction, other than any state and, in connection therewith, may elect to continue its existence as a limited liability company in the State of Delaware.

(b) If the limited liability company agreement specifies the manner of authorizing a transfer or domestication or continuance described in subsection (a) of this section, the transfer or domestication or continuance shall be authorized as specified in the limited liability company agreement. If the limited liability company agreement does not specify the manner of authorizing a transfer or domestication or continuance described in subsection (a) of this section and does not prohibit such a transfer or domestication or continuance, the transfer or domestication or continuance shall be authorized in the same manner as is specified in the limited liability company agreement for authorizing a merger or consolidation that involves the limited liability company as a constituent party to the merger or consolidation. If the limited liability company agreement does not specify the manner of authorizing a transfer or domestication or continuancedescribed in subsection (a) of this section or a merger or consolidation that involves the limited liability company as a constituent party and does not prohibit such a transfer or domestication or continuance, the transfer or domestication or continuance shall be authorized by the approval by the members or, if there is more than one class or group of members, then by each class or group of members, in either case, by the members who own more than 50% of the then current percentage or other interest in the profits of the domestic limited liability company owned by all of the members or by the members in each class or group, as appropriate. If a transfer or domestication or continuance described in subsection (a) of this section shall be authorized as provided in this subsection (b), a certificate of transfer if the limited liability company's existence as a limited liability company of the State of Delaware is to cease, or a certificate of transfer and domestic continuance if the limited liability company's existence as a limited liability company in the State of Delaware is to continue, executed in accordance with § 18-204 of this title, shall be filed in the Office of the secretary of state in accordance with § 18-206 of this title. The certificate of transfer or the certificate of transfer and domestic continuance shall state:

(1) The name of the limited liability company and, if it has been changed, the name under which its certificate of formation was originally filed;

(2) The date of the filing of its original certificate of formation with the secretary of state;

(3) The jurisdiction to which the limited liability company shall be transferred or in which it shall be domesticated or continued and the name of the entity or business form formed, incorporated, created or that otherwise comes into being as a consequence of the transfer of the limited liability company to, or its domestication or continuance in, such foreign jurisdiction;

(4) The future effective date or time (which shall be a date or time certain) of the transfer to or domestication or continuance in the jurisdiction specified in subsection (b)(3) of this section if it is not to be effective upon the filing of the certificate of transfer or the certificate of transfer and domestic continuance;

(5) That the transfer or domestication or continuance of the limited liability company has been approved in accordance with the provisions of this section;

(6) In the case of a certificate of transfer, (i) that the existence of the limited liability company as a limited liability company of the State of Delaware shall cease when the certificate of transfer becomes effective, and (ii) the agreement of the limited liability company that it may be seed with process in the State of Delaware in any action, suit or proceeding for enforcement of any obligation of the limited liability company arising while it was a limited liability company of the State of Delaware, and that it irrevocably appoints the secretary of state as its agent to accept service of process in any such action, suit or proceeding;

(7) The address to which a copy of the process referred to in subsection (b)(6) of this section shall be mailed to it by the secretary of state, in the event of service hereunder upon the secretary of state, the procedures set forth in § 18-911(c) of this title shall be applicable, except that the plaintiff in any such action, suit or proceeding shall furnish the secretary of state with the address specified in this subsection and any other address that the plaintiff may elect to furnish, together with copies of such process as required by the secretary of state, and the secretary of state shall notify the limited liability company that has transferred or domesticated or continued out of the State of Delaware at all such addresses furnished by the plaintiff in accordance with the procedures set forth in § 18-911(c) of this title; and

(8) In the case of a certificate of transfer and domestic continuance, that the limited liability company will continue to exist as a limited liability company of the State of Delaware after the certificate of transfer and domestic continuance becomes effective.

(c) Upon the filing in the Office of the secretary of state of the certificate of transfer or upon the future effective date or time of the certificate of transfer and payment to the secretary of state of all fees prescribed in this chapter, the secretary of state shall certify that the limited liability company has filed all documents and paid all fees required by this chapter, and thereupon the limited liability company shall cease to exist as a limited liability company of the State of Delaware. Such certificate of the secretary of state shall be prima facie evidence of the transfer or domestication or continuance by such limited liability company out of the State of Delaware.

(d) The transfer or domestication or continuance of a limited liability company out of the State of Delaware in accordance with this section and the resulting cessation of its existence as a limited liability company of the State of Delaware pursuant to a certificate of transfer shall not be deemed to affect any obligations or liabilities of the limited liability company incurred prior to such transfer or domestication or continuance or the personal liability of any person incurred prior to such transfer or domestication or continuance, nor shall it be deemed to affect the choice of law applicable to the limited liability company with respect to matters arising prior to such transfer or domestication or continuance. Unless otherwise agreed, the transfer or domestication or continuance of a limited liability company out of the State of Delaware in accordance with this section shall not require such limited liability company to wind up its affairs under § 18-803 of this title or pay its liabilities and distribute its assets under § 18-804 of this title and shall not be deemed to constitute a dissolution of such limited liability company.

(e) If a limited liability company files a certificate of transfer and domestic continuance, after the time the certificate of transfer and domestic continuance becomes effective, the limited liability company shall continue to exist as a limited liability company of the State of Delaware, and the laws of the State of Delaware, including the provisions of this chapter, shall apply to the limited liability company, to the same extent as prior to such time. So long as a limited liability company continues to exist as a limited liability company of the State of Delaware following the filing of a certificate of transfer and domestic continuance, the continuing domestic limited liability company and the entity or business form formed, incorporated, created or that otherwise came into being as a consequence of the transfer of the limited liability company to, or its domestication or continuance in, a foreign country or other foreign jurisdiction shall, for all purposes of the laws of the State of Delaware, constitute a single entity formed, incorporated, created or otherwise having come into being, as applicable, and existing under the laws of the State of Delaware and the laws of such foreign country or other foreign jurisdiction.

(f) In connection with a transfer or domestication or continuation of a domestic limited liability company to or in another jurisdiction pursuant to subsection (a) of this section, rights or securities of, or interests in, such limited liability company may be exchanged for or converted into cash, property, rights or securities of, or interests in, the entity or business form in which the limited liability company will exist in such other jurisdiction as a consequence of the transfer or domestication or continuation or, in addition to or in lieu thereof, may be exchanged for or converted into cash, property, rights or securities of, or interests in, another entity or business form or may be cancelled.

(g) When a limited liability company has transferred or domesticated or continued out of the State of Delaware pursuant to this Section, the transferred or domesticated or continued entity or business for shall, for all purposes of the laws of the State of Delaware, be deemed to be the same entity as the limited liability company and shall constitute a continuation of the existence of such limited liability company in the form of the transferred or domesticated or continued entity or business form. When any transfer or domestication or continuance of a limited liability company out of the State of Delaware shall have become effective under this Section, for all purposes of the laws of the State of Delaware, all of the rights, privileges and powers of the limited liability company that has transferred or domesticated or continued, and all property, real, personal and mixed, and all debts due to such limited liability company, as well as all other things and causes of action belonging to such limited liability company, shall remain vested in the transferred or domesticated or continued entity or business form (and also in the limited liability company that has transferred, domesticated or continued, if and for so long as such limited liability company continues its existence as a domestic limited liability company) and shall be the property of the transferred or domesticated or continued entity or business form (and also in the limited liability company that has transferred, domesticated or continued, if and for so long as such limited liability company continues its existence as a domestic limited liability company), and the title to any real property vested by deed or otherwise in such limited liability company shall not revert or be in any way impaired by reason of this Chapter; but all rights of creditors and all liens upon any property of any such limited liability company shall be preserved unimpaired, and all debts, liabilities and duties of the limited liability company that has transferred or domesticated or continued shall remain attached to the transferred or domesticated or continued entity or business form (and also in the limited liability company that has transferred, domesticated or continued, if and for so long as such limited liability company continues its existence as a domestic limited liability company), and may be enforced against it to the same extent as if said debts, liabilities and duties had been originally incurred or contracted by it in its capacity as the transferred or domesticated or continued entity or business form. The rights, privileges, powers and interests in property of the limited liability company that has transferred or domesticated, as well as the debts, liabilities and duties of such limited liability company, shall not be deemed, as a consequence of the transfer or domestication or continuance out of the State of Delaware, to have been transferred to the transferred or domesticated or continued entity or business form for any purpose of the laws of the State of Delaware.

(h) A limited liability company agreement may provide that a domestic limited liability company shall not have the power to transfer, domesticate or continue as set forth in this section.

[As last amended by S 96, effective August 1, 2007]

§ 18-214. Conversion of certain entities to a limited liability company.

(a) As used in this section, the term "other entity" means a corporation, a statutory trust, a business trust, an association, a real estate investment trust, a common-law trust, or any other unincorporated business or entity, including a partnership (whether general (including a limited liability partnership) or limited (including a limited liability limited partnership)) or a foreign limited liability company.

(b) Any other entity may convert to a domestic limited liability company by complying with subsection (h) of this section and filing in the Office of the secretary of state in accordance with § 18-206 of this title:

(1) A certificate of conversion to limited liability company that has been executed by 1 or more authorized persons in accordance with § 18-204 of this title; and

(2) A certificate of formation that complies with § 18-201 of this title and has been executed by 1 or more authorized persons in accordance with § 18-204 of this title.

(c) The certificate of conversion to limited liability company shall state:

(1) The date on which and jurisdiction where the other entity was first created, incorporated, formed, or otherwise came into being and, if it has changed, its jurisdiction immediately prior to its conversion to a domestic limited liability company;

(2) The name of the other entity immediately prior to the filing of the certificate of conversion to limited liability company;

(3) The name of the limited liability company as set forth in its certificate of formation filed in accordance with subsection (b) of this section; and

(4) The future effective date or time (which shall be a date or time certain) of the conversion to a limited liability company if it is not to be effective upon the filing of the certificate of conversion to limited liability company and the certificate of formation.

(d) Upon the filing in the Office of the secretary of state of the certificate of conversion to limited liability company and the certificate of formation or upon the future effective date or time of the certificate of conversion to limited liability company and the certificate of formation, the other entity shall be converted into a domestic limited liability company and the limited liability company shall thereafter he subject to all of the provisions of this chapter, except that notwithstanding § 18-201 of this title, the existence of the limited liability company shall be deemed to have commenced on the date the other entity commenced its existence in the jurisdiction in which the other entity was first created, formed, incorporated or otherwise came into being.

(e) The conversion of any other entity into a domestic limited liability company shall not be deemed to affect any obligations or liabilities of the other entity incurred prior to its conversion to a domestic limited liability company, or the personal liability of any person incurred prior to such conversion.

(f) When any conversion shall have become effective under this section, for all purposes of the laws of the State of Delaware, all of the rights, privileges and powers of the other entity that has converted, and all property, real, personal and mixed, and all debts due to such other entity, as well as all other things and causes of action belonging to such other entity, shall remain vested in the domestic limited liability company to which such other entity has converted and shall be the property of such domestic limited liability company, and the title to any real property vested by deed or otherwise in such other entity shall not revert or be in any way impaired by reason of this chapter; but all rights of creditors and all liens upon any property of such other entity shall be preserved unimpaired, and all debts, liabilities and duties of the other entity that has converted shall remain attached to the domestic limited liability company to which such other entity has converted, and may be enforced against it to the same extent as if said debts, liabilities and duties had originally been incurred or contracted by it in its capacity as a domestic limited liability company. The rights, privileges, powers and interests in property of the other entity, as well as the debts, liabilities and duties of the other entity, shall not be deemed, as a consequence of the conversion, to have been transferred to the domestic limited liability company to which such other entity has converted for any purpose of the laws of the State of Delaware.

(g) Unless otherwise agreed, for all purposes of the laws of the State of Delaware, the converting other entity shall not be required to wind up its affairs or pay its liabilities and distribute its assets, and the conversion shall not be deemed to constitute a dissolution of such other entity. When another entity has been converted to a limited liability company pursuant to this section, for all purposes of the laws of the State of Delaware the limited liability company shall, be deemed to be the same entity as the converting other entity and the conversion shall constitute a continuation of the existence of the converting other entity in the form of a domestic limited liability company.

(h) Prior to filing a certificate of conversion to limited liability company with the Office of the secretary of state, the conversion shall be approved in the manner provided for by the document, instrument, agreement or other writing, as the case may be, governing the internal affairs of the other entity and the conduct of its business or by applicable law, as appropriate, and a limited liability company agreement shall be approved by the same authorization required to approve the conversion.

(i) In connection with a conversion hereunder, rights or securities of, or interests in, the other entity which is to be converted to a domestic limited liability company may be exchanged for or converted into cash, property, rights or securities of, or interests in, such domestic limited liability company or, in addition to or in lieu thereof, may be exchanged for or converted into cash, property, rights or securities of, or interests in, another domestic limited liability company or other entity or may be cancelled.

(j) The provisions of this section shall not be construed to limit the accomplishment of a change in the law governing, or the domicile of, an other entity to the State of Delaware by any other means provided for in a limited liability company agreement or other agreement or as otherwise permitted by law, including by the amendment of a limited liability company agreement or other agreement.

[As amended by H 414, effective August 1, 2006.]

§ 18-215. Series of members, managers, limited liability company interests or assets.

(a) A limited liability company agreement may establish or provide for the establishment of 1 or more designated series of members, managers, limited liability company interests or assets. Any such series may have separate rights, powers or duties with respect to specified property or obligations of the limited liability company or profits and losses associated with specified property or obligations, and any such series may have a separate business purpose or investment objective.

(b) Notwithstanding anything to the contrary set forth in this chapter or under other applicable law, in the event that a limited liability company agreement establishes or provides for the establishment of one or more series and if the records maintained for any such series account for the assets associated with such series separately from the other assets of the limited liability company, or any other series thereof, and if the limited liability company agreement so provides, and if notice of the limitation on liabilities of a series as referenced in this subsection is set forth in the certificate of formation of the limited liability company, then the debts, liabilities, obligations and expenses incurred, contracted for or otherwise existing with respect to a particular series shall be enforceable against the assets of such series only, and not against the assets of the limited liability company generally or any other series thereof, and, unless otherwise provided in the limited liability company agreement, none of the debts, liabilities, obligations and expenses incurred, contracted for or otherwise existing with respect to the limited liability company generally or any other series thereof shall be enforceable against the assets of such series. Assets associated with a series may be held directly or indirectly, including in the name of such series, in the name of the limited liability company, through a nominee or otherwise. Records maintained for a series that reasonably identify its assets, including by specific listing, category, type, quantity, computational or allocational formula or procedure (including a percentage or share of any asset or assets) or by any other method where the identity of such assets is objectively determinable, will be deemed to account for the assets associated with such series separately from the other assets of the limited liability company, or any other series thereof. Notice in a certificate of formation of the limitation on liabilities of a series as referenced in this subsection shall be sufficient for all purposes of this subsection whether or not the limited liability company has established any series when such notice is included in the certificate of formation, and there shall be no requirement that any specific series of the limited liability company be referenced in such notice. The fact that a certificate of formation that contains the foregoing notice of the limitation on liabilities of a series is on the in the Office of the secretary of state shall constitute notice of such limitation on liabilities of a series.

(c) A series established in accordance with subsection (b) of this section may carry of any lawful business, purpose or activity, whether or not for profit, with the exception of the business of banking as defined in Section 126 of Title 8. Unless otherwise provided in a limited liability company agreement, a series established in accordance with subsection (b) of this section shall have the power and capacity to, in its own name, contract, hold title to assets (including real, personal and intangible property), grant liens and security interests, and sue and be sued.

(d) Notwithstanding § 18-303 (a) of this title, under a limited liability company agreement or under another agreement, a member or manager may agree to be obligated personally for any or all of the debts, obligations and liabilities of one or more series.

(e) A limited liability company agreement may provide for classes or groups of members or managers associated with a series having such relative rights, powers and duties as the limited liability company agreement may provide, and may make provision for the future creation in the manner provided in the limited liability company agreement of additional classes or groups of members or managers associated with the series having such relative rights, powers and duties as may from time to time be established, including rights, powers and duties senior to existing classes and groups of members or managers associated with the series. A limited liability company agreement may provide for the taking of an action, including the amendment of the limited liability company agreement, without the vote or approval of any member or manager or class or group of members or managers, including all action to create under the provisions of the limited liability company agreement a class or group of the series of limited liability company interests that was not previously outstanding. A limited liability company agreement may provide that any member or class or group of members associated with a series shall have no voting rights.

(f) A limited liability company agreement may grant to all or certain identified members or managers or a specified class or group of the members or managers associated with a series the right to vote separately or with all or any class or group of the members or managers associated with the series, on any matter. Voting by members or managers associated with a series may be on a per capita, number, financial interest, class, group or any other basis.

(g) Unless otherwise provided in a limited liability company agreement, the management of a series shall be vested in the members associated with such series in proportion to the then current percentage or other interest of members in the profits of the series owned by all of the members associated with such series, the decision of members owning more than 50 percent of the said percentage or other interest in the profits controlling; provided, however, that if a limited liability company agreement provides for the management of the series, in whole or in part, by a manager, the management of the series, to the extent so provided, shall be vested in the manager who shall be chosen in the manner provided in the limited liability company agreement. The manager of the series shall also hold the offices and have the responsibilities accorded to him as set forth in a limited liability company agreement. A series may have more than 1 manager. Subject to § 18-602 of this title, a manager shall cease to be a manager with respect to a series as provided in a limited liability company agreement. Except as otherwise provided in a limited liability company agreement, any event under this chapter or in a limited liability company agreement that causes a manager to cease to be a manager with respect to a series shall not, in itself, cause such manager to cease to be a manager of the limited liability company or with respect to any other series thereof.

(h) Notwithstanding § 18-606 of this title, but subject to subsections (i) and (l) of this section, and unless otherwise provided in a limited liability company agreement, at the time a member associated with a series that has been established in accordance with subsection (b) of this section becomes entitled to receive a distribution with respect to such series, he has the status of, and is entitled to all remedies available to, a creditor of the series, with respect to the distribution. A limited liability company agreement may provide for the establishment of a record date with respect to allocations and distributions with respect to a series.

(i) Notwithstanding § 18-607 (a) of this title, a limited liability company may make a distribution with respect to a series that has been established in accordance with subsection

(b) of this section; A limited liability company shall not make a distribution with respect to a series that has been established in accordance with subsection (b) of this section to a member to the extent that at the time of the distribution, after giving effect to the distribution, all liabilities of such series, other than liabilities to members on account of their limited liability company interests with respect to such series and liabilities for which the recourse of creditors is limited to specified property of such series, exceed the fair value of the assets associated with such series, except that the fair value of property of the series that is subject to a liability for which the recourse of creditors is limited shall be included in the assets associated with such series only to the extent that the fair value of that property exceeds that liability. For purposes of the immediately preceding sentence, the term "distribution" shall not include amounts constituting reasonable compensation for present or past services or reasonable payments made in the ordinary course of business pursuant to a bona fide retirement plan or other benefits program. A member who receives a distribution in violation of this subsection, and who knew at the time of the distribution that the distribution violated this subsection, shall be liable to a series for the amount of the distribution. A member who receives a distribution in violation of this subsection, and who did not know at the time of the distribution that the distribution violated this subsection, shall not be liable for the amount of the distribution. Subject to § 18-607(c) of this title, which shall apply to any distribution made with respect to a series under this subsection, this subsection shall not affect any obligation or liability of a member under an agreement or other applicable law for the amount of a distribution.

(j) Unless otherwise provided in the limited liability company agreement, a member shall cease to be associated with a series and to have the power to exercise any rights or powers of a member with respect to such series upon the assignment of all of his limited liability company interest with respect to such series. Except as otherwise provided in a limited liability company agreement, any event under this chapter or a limited liability company agreement that causes a member to cease to be associated with a series shall not, in itself, cause such member to cease to be associated with any other series or terminate the continued membership of a member in the limited liability company or cause the termination of the series, regardless of whether such member was the last remaining to be associated with such series.

(k) Subject to § 18-801 of this title, except to the extent otherwise provided in the limited liability company agreement, a series may be terminated and its affairs wound up without causing the dissolution of the limited liability company. The termination of a series established in accordance with subsection (b) of this section shall not affect the limitation on liabilities of such series provided by subsection (b) of this section. A series is terminated and its affairs shall be wound up upon the dissolution of the limited liability company under § 18-801 of this title or otherwise upon the first to occur of the following:

(1) At the time specified in the limited liability company agreement;

(2) Upon the happening of events specified in the limited liability company agreement;

(3) Unless otherwise provided in the limited liability company agreement, upon the affirmative vote or written consent of the members of the limited liability company associated with such series, or if there is more than one class or group of members associated with such series, then by each class or group of members associated with such series, in either case, by members associated with such series who own more than two-thirds of the then-current percentage or other interest in the profits of the series of the limited liability company owned by all of the members associated with such series or by the members in each class or group of such series, as appropriate; or

(4) The termination of such series under subsection (m) of this section.

(l) Notwithstanding § 18-803(a) of this title, unless otherwise provided in the limited liability company agreement, a manager associated with a series who has not wrongfully terminated the series or, if none, the members associated with the series or a person approved by the members associated with the series or, if there is more than one class or group of members associated with the series, then by each class or group of members associated with the series, in either case, by members who own more than 50 percent of the then current percentage or other interest in the profits of the series owned by all of the members associated with the series or by the members in each class or group associated with the series, as appropriate, may wind up the affairs of the series; but, if the series has been established in accordance with subsection (b) of this section, the Court of Chancery, upon cause shown, may wind up the affairs of the series upon application of any member associated with the series his personal representative or assignee, and in connection therewith, may appoint a liquidating trustee. The persons winding up the affairs of a series may, in the name of the limited liability company and for and on behalf of the limited liability company and such series, take all actions with respect to the series as are permitted under § 18-803(b) of this title. The persons winding up the affairs of a series shall provide for the claims and obligations of the series and distribute the assets of the series as provided in § 18-804 of this title, which section shall apply to the winding up and distribution of assets of a series. Actions taken in accordance with this subsection shall not affect the liability of members and shall not impose liability on a liquidating trustee.

(m) On application by or for a member or manager associated with a series established in accordance with subsection (b) of this section, the Court of Chancery may decree termination of such series whenever it is not reasonably practicable to carry on the business of the series in conformity with a limited liability company agreement.

(n) If a foreign limited liability company that is registering to do business in the State of Delaware in accordance with § 18-902 of this title is governed by a limited liability company agreement that establishes or provides for the establishment of designated series of members or managers or limited liability company interests or assets having separate rights, powers or duties with respect to specified property or obligations of the foreign limited liability company or profits and losses associated with specified property or obligations, that fact shall be so stated on the application for registration as a foreign limited liability company. In addition, the foreign limited liability company shall state on such application whether the debts, liabilities and obligations incurred, contracted for or otherwise existing with respect to a particular series, if any, shall be enforceable against the assets of such series only, and not against the assets of the foreign limited liability company generally or any other series thereof, and whether any of the debts, liabilities, obligations and expenses incurred, contracted for or otherwise existing with respect to the foreign limited liability company generally or any other series thereof shall be enforceable against the assets of such series.

[As last amended by S 96, effective August 1, 2007]

§ 18-216. Approval of conversion of a limited liability company.

(a) Upon compliance with this section, a domestic limited liability company may convert to a corporation, a statutory trust, a business trust an association, a real estate investment trust, a common-law trust or any other unincorporated business or entity, including a partnership (whether general (including a limited liability partnership) or limited (including a limited liability limited partnership)) or a foreign limited liability company.

(b) If the limited liability company agreement specifies the manner of authorizing a conversion of the limited liability company, the conversion shall be authorized as specified in the limited liability company agreement. If the limited liability company agreement does not specify the manner of authorizing a conversion of the limited liability company and does not prohibit a conversion of the limited liability company, the conversion shall be authorized in the same manner as is specified in the limited liability company agreement for authorizing a merger or consolidation that involves the limited liability company as a constituent party to the merger or consolidation. If the limited liability company agreement does not specify the manner of authorizing a conversion of the limited liability company or a merger or consolidation that involves the limited liability company as a constituent party and does not prohibit a conversion of the limited liability company, the conversion shall be authorized by the approval by the members or, if there is more than 1 class or group of members, then by each class or group of members, in either case, by members who own more than 50 percent of the then current percentage or other interest in the profits of the domestic limited liability company owned by all of the members or by the members in each class or group, as appropriate.

(c) Unless otherwise agreed, the conversion of a domestic limited liability company to another entity or business form pursuant to this section shall not require such limited liability company to wind up its affairs under § 18-803 of this title or pay its liabilities and distribute its assets under § 18-804 of this title, and the conversion shall not constitute a dissolution of such limited liability company. When a limited liability company has converted to another entity or business form pursuant to this Section, for all purposes of the laws of the State of Delaware, the other entity or business form shall be deemed to be the same entity as the converting limited liability company and the conversion shall constitute a continuation of the existence of the limited liability company in the form of such other entity or business form.

(d) In connection with a conversion of a domestic limited liability company to another entity or business form pursuant to this section, rights or securities of or interests in the domestic limited liability company which is to be converted may be exchanged for or converted into cash, property, rights or securities of or interests in the entity or business form into which the domestic limited liability company is being converted or, in addition to or in lieu thereof, may be exchanged for or converted into cash, property, rights or securities of or interests in another entity or business form or may be cancelled.

(e) If a limited liability company shall convert in accordance with this section to another entity or business form organized, formed or created under the laws of a jurisdiction other than the State of Delaware, a certificate of conversion to non-Delaware entity executed in accordance with § 18-204 of this title, shall be filed in the office of the Secretary of State in accordance with § 18-206 of this title. The certificate of conversion to non-Delaware entity shall state:

(1) The name of the limited liability company and, if it has been changed, the name under which its certificate of formation was originally filed;

(2) The date of filing of its original certificate of formation with the Secretary of State;

(3) The jurisdiction in which the entity or business form, to which the limited liability company shall be converted, is organized, formed or created, and the name of such entity or business form;

(4) The future effective date or time (which shall be a date or time certain) of the conversion if it is not to be effective upon the filing of the certificate of conversion to non-Delaware entity;

(5) That the conversion has been approved in accordance with this section;

(6) The agreement of the limited liability company that it may be served with process in the State of Delaware in any action, suit or proceeding for enforcement of any obligation of the limited liability company arising while it was a limited liability company of the State of Delaware, and that it irrevocably appoints the Secretary of State as its agent to accept service of process in any such action, suit or proceeding;

(7) The address to which a copy of the process referred to in subsection (e)(6) of this section shall be mailed to it by the Secretary of State. In the event of service hereunder upon the Secretary of State, the procedures set forth in § 18-911(c) of this title shall be applicable, except that the plaintiff in any such action, suit or proceeding shall furnish the Secretary of State with the address specified in this subsection (e)(7) and any other address that the plaintiff may elect to furnish, together with copies of such process as required by the Secretary of State, and the Secretary of State shall notify the limited liability company that has converted out of the State of Delaware at all such addresses furnished by the plaintiff in accordance with the procedures set forth in § 18-911(c) of this title.

(f) Upon the filing in the office of the Secretary of State of the certificate of conversion to non-Delaware entity or upon the future effective date or time of the certificate of conversion to non-Delaware entity and payment to the Secretary of State of all fees prescribed in this chapter, the Secretary of State shall certify that the limited liability company has filed all documents and paid all fees required by this chapter, and thereupon the limited liability company shall cease to exist as a limited liability company of the State of Delaware. Such certificate of the Secretary of State shall be prima facie evidence of the conversion by such limited liability company out of the State of Delaware.

(g) The conversion of a limited liability company out of the State of Delaware in accordance with this section and the resulting cessation of its existence as a limited liability company of the State of Delaware pursuant to a certificate of conversion to non-Delaware entity shall not be deemed to affect any obligations or liabilities of the limited liability company incurred prior to such conversion or the personal liability of any person incurred prior to such conversion, nor shall it be deemed to affect the choice of law applicable to the limited liability company with respect to matters arising prior to such conversion.

(h) When any transfer or domestication of a limited liability company out of the State of Delaware shall have become effective under this Section, for all purposes of the laws of the State of Delaware, all of the rights, privileges and powers of the limited liability company that has transferred or domesticated, and all property, real, personal and mixed, and all debts due to such limited liability company, as well as all other things and causes of action belonging to such limited liability company, shall remain vested in the transferred or domesticated entity or business form and shall be the property of the transferred or domesticated entity or business form, and the title to any real property vested by deed or otherwise in such limited liability company shall not revert or be in any way impaired by reason of this Chapter; but all rights of creditors and all liens upon any property of any such limited liability company shall be preserved unimpaired, and all debts, liabilities and duties of the limited liability company that has transferred or domesticated shall remain attached to the transferred or domesticated entity or business form, and may be enforced against it to the same extent as if said debts, liabilities and duties had been originally incurred or contracted by it in its capacity as the transferred or domesticated entity or business form. The rights, privileges, powers and interests in property of the limited liability company that has transferred or domesticated, as well as the debts, liabilities and duties of such limited liability company, shall not be deemed, as a consequence of the transfer or domestication out of the State of Delaware, to have been transferred to the transferred or domesticated entity or business form for any purpose of the laws of the State of Delaware.

(i) A limited liability company agreement may provide that a domestic limited liability company shall not have the power to convert as set in forth in this section.

[As last amended by S 96, effective August 1, 2007]

SUBCHAPTER III. MEMBERS

§ 18-301. Admission of members.

(a) In connection with the formation of a limited liability company, a person is admitted as a member of the limited liability company upon the later to occur of:

(1) The formation of the limited liability company; or

(2) The time provided in and upon compliance with the limited liability company agreement or, if the limited liability company agreement does not so provide, when the person's admission is reflected in the records of the limited liability company.

(b) After the formation of a limited liability company, a person is admitted as a member of the limited liability company:

(1) In the case of a person who is not an assignee of a limited liability company interest, including a person acquiring a limited liability company interest directly from the limited liability company and a person to be admitted as a member of the limited liability company without acquiring a limited liability company interest in the limited liability company at the time provided in and upon compliance with the limited liability company agreement or, if the limited liability company agreement does not so provide, upon the consent of all members and when the person's admission is reflected in the records of the limited liability company;

(2) In the case of an assignee of a limited liability company interest, as provided in § 18-704(a) of this title and at the time provided in and upon compliance with the limited liability company agreement or, if the limited liability company agreement does not so

provide, when any such person's permitted admission is reflected in the records of the limited liability company; or

(3) In the case of a person being admitted as a member of a surviving or resulting limited liability company pursuant to a merger or consolidation approved in accordance with § 18-209(b) of this title, as provided in the limited liability company agreement of the surviving or resulting limited liability company or in the agreement of merger or consolidation, and in the event of any inconsistency, the terms of the agreement of merger or consolidation shall control; and in the case of a person being admitted as a member of a limited liability company pursuant to a merger or consolidation in which such limited liability company is not the surviving or resulting limited liability company in the merger or consolidation, as provided in the limited liability company agreement of such limited liability company.

(c) In connection with the domestication of a non-United States entity (as defined in § 18-212 of this title) as a limited liability company in the State of Delaware in accordance with § 18-212 of this title or the conversion of the entity (as defined in § 18-214 of this title) to a domestic limited liability company, in accordance with § 18-214 of this title, a person is admitted as a member of the limited liability company as provided in the limited liability company agreement.

(d) A person may be admitted to a limited liability company as a member of the limited liability company and may receive a limited liability company interest in the limited liability company without making a contribution or being obligated to make a contribution to the limited liability company. Unless otherwise provided in a limited liability company agreement, a person may be admitted to a limited liability company as a member of the limited liability company without acquiring a limited liability company interest in the limited liability company. Unless otherwise provided in a limited liability company agreement, a person may be admitted as the sole member of a limited liability company without making a contribution or being obligated to make a contribution to the limited liability company or without acquiring a limited liability company interest in the limited liability company.

(e) Unless otherwise provided in a limited liability company agreement or another agreement, a member shall have no preemptive right to subscribe to any additional issue of limited liability company interests or another interest in a limited liability company.

§ 18-302. Classes and voting.

(a) A limited liability company agreement may provide for classes or groups of members having such relative rights, powers and duties as the limited liability company agreement may provide, and may make provision for the future creation in the manner provided in the limited liability company agreement of additional classes or groups of members having such relative rights, powers and duties as may from time to time be established, including rights, powers and duties senior to existing classes and groups of members. A limited liability company agreement may provide for the taking of an action including the amendment of the limited liability company agreement, without the vote or approval of any member or class or group of members, including an action to create under the provisions of the limited liability company agreement a class or group of limited liability company interests that was not previously outstanding. A limited liability company agreement may provide that any member or class or group of members shall have no voting rights.

(b) A limited liability company agreement may grant to all or certain identified members or a specified class or group of the members the right to vote separately or with all or any class or group of the members or managers, on any matter. Voting by members may be on a per capita, number, financial interest, class, group or any other basis.

(c) A limited liability company agreement may set forth provisions relating to notice of the time, place or purpose of any meeting at which any matter is to be voted on by any members, waiver of any such notice, action by consent without a meeting, the establishment of a record date, quorum requirements, voting in person or by proxy, or any other matter with respect to the exercise of any such right to vote.

(d) Unless otherwise provided in a limited liability company agreement, meetings of members may be held by means of conference telephone or other communications equipment by means of which all persons participating in the meeting can hear each other, and participation in a meeting pursuant to this subsection shall constitute presence in person at the meeting. Unless otherwise provided in a limited liability company agreement, on any matter that is to voted on, consented to or approved by members, the members may take such action without a meeting, without prior notice and without a vote, if a consent or consents in writing, setting forth the action so taken, shall be signed by the members having not less than the minimum number of votes that would be necessary to authorize or take such action at a meeting at which all members entitled to vote thereon were present and voted. Unless otherwise provided in a limited liability company agreement, on any matter that is to be voted on by the members, the members may vote in person or by proxy, and such proxy may be granted in writing, by means of electronic transmission or as otherwise permitted by applicable law. Unless otherwise provided in a limited liability company agreement, a consent transmitted by electronic transmission by a member or by a person or persons authorized to act for a member shall be deemed to be written and signed for purposes of this subsection (d). For purposes of this subsection (d), the term "electronic transmission" means any form of communication, not directly involving the physical transmission of paper, that creates a record that may be retained, retrieved, and reviewed by a recipient thereof, and that may be directly reproduced in paper form by such a recipient through an automated process.

(e) If a limited liability company agreement provides for the manner in which it may be amended, including by requiring the approval of a person who is not a party to the limited liability company agreement or the satisfaction of conditions, it may be amended only in that manner or as otherwise permitted by law (provided that the approval of any person may be waived by such person and that any conditions may be waived by all persons for whose benefit such conditions were intended).

[As amended by H 414, effective August 1, 2006.]

§ 18-303. Liability to 3rd parties.

(a) Except as otherwise provided by this chapter, the debts, obligations and liabilities of a limited liability company, whether arising in contract, tort or otherwise, shall be solely the debts, obligations and liabilities of the limited liability company, and no member or manager of a limited liability company shall be obligated personally for any such debt, obligation or liability of the limited liability company solely by reason of being a member or acting as a manager of the limited liability company.

(b) Notwithstanding the provisions of subsection (a) of this section, under a limited liability company agreement or under another agreement, a member or manager may agree to be obligated personally for any or all of the debts, obligations and liabilities of the limited liability company.

§ 18-304. Events of bankruptcy.

A person ceases to be a member of a limited liability company upon the happening of any of the following events:

(1) Unless otherwise provided in a limited liability company agreement, or with the written consent of all members, a member:

a. Makes an assignment for the benefit of creditors;

b. Files a voluntary petition in bankruptcy;

c. Is adjudged a bankrupt or insolvent, or has entered against him an order for relief, in any bankruptcy or insolvency proceeding;

d. Files a petition or answer seeking for himself any reorganization, arrangement, composition, readjustment, liquidation, dissolution or similar relief under any statute, law or regulation;

e. Files an answer or other pleading admitting or failing to contest the material allegations of a petition filed against him in any proceeding of this nature;

f. Seeks, consents to or acquiesces in the appointment of a trustee, receiver or liquidator of the member or of all or any substantial part of his properties; or

(2) Unless otherwise provided in a limited liability company agreement, or with the written consent of all members, 120 days after the commencement of any proceeding against the member seeking reorganization, arrangement, composition, readjustment, liquidation, dissolution or similar relief under any statute, law or regulation, if the proceeding has not been dismissed, or if within 90 days after the appointment without his consent or acquiescence of a trustee, receiver or liquidator of the member or of all or any substantial part of his properties, the appointment is not vacated or stayed, or within 90 days after the expiration of any such stay, the appointment is not vacated.

§ 18-305. Access to and confidentiality of information; records.

(a) Each member of a limited liability company has the right, subject to such reasonable standards (including standards governing what information and documents are to be furnished at what time and location and at whose expense) as may be set forth in a limited liability company agreement or otherwise established by the manager or, if there is no manager, then by the members, to obtain from the limited liability company from time to time upon reasonable demand for any purpose reasonably related to the member's interest as a member of the limited liability company:

(1) True and full information regarding the status of the business and financial condition of the limited liability company;

(2) Promptly after becoming available, a copy of the limited liability company's federal, state and local income tax returns for each year;

(3) A current list of the name and last known business, residence or mailing address of each member and manager;

(4) A copy of any written limited liability company agreement and certificate of formation and all amendments thereto, together with executed copies of any written powers of attorney pursuant to which the limited liability company agreement and any certificate and all amendments thereto have been executed;

(5) True and full information regarding the amount of cash and a description and statement of the agreed value of any other property or services contributed by each member and which each member has agreed to contribute in the future, and the date on which each became a member; and

(6) Other information regarding the affairs of the limited liability company as is just and reasonable.

(b) Each manager shall have the right to examine all of the information described in subsection (a) of this section for a purpose reasonably related to his position as a manager.

(c) The manager of a limited liability company shall have the right to keep confidential from the members, for such period of time as the manager deems reasonable, any information which the manager reasonably believes to be in the nature of trade secrets or other information the disclosure of which the manager in good faith believes is not in the best interest of the limited liability company or could damage the limited liability company or its business or which the limited liability company is required by law or by agreement with a 3rd party to keep confidential.

(d) A limited liability company may maintain its records in other than a written form if such form is capable of conversion into written form within a reasonable time.

(e) Any demand by a member under this section shall be in writing and shall state the purpose of such demand.

(f) Any action to enforce any right arising under this section shall be brought in the Court of Chancery. If the limited liability company refuses to permit a member to obtain or a manager to examine the information described in subsection (a)(3) of this section or does not reply to the demand that has been made within 5 business days after the demand has been made, the demanding member or manager may apply to the Court of Chancery for an order to compel such disclosure. The Court of Chancery is hereby vested with exclusive jurisdiction to determine whether or not the person seeking such information is entitled to the information sought. The Court of Chancery may summarily order the limited liability company to permit the demanding member to obtain or manager to examine the information described in subsection (a)(3) of this section and to make copies or abstracts therefrom; or the Court of Chancery may summarily order the limited liability company to furnish to the demanding member or manager the information described in subsection (a)(3) of this section on the condition that the demanding member or manager first pay to the limited liability company the reasonable cost of obtaining and furnishing such information and on such other conditions as the Court of Chancery deems appropriate. When a demanding member seeks to obtain or a manager seeks to examine the information described in subsection (a)(3) of this section, the demanding member or manager shall first establish (1) that the demanding member or manager has complied with the provisions of this section respecting the form and manner of making demand for obtaining or examining of such information, and (2) that the information the demanding member or manager seeks is reasonably related to the member's interest as a member or the manager's position as a manager, as the case may be. The Court of Chancery may, in its discretion, prescribe any limitations or conditions with reference to the obtaining or examining of information, or award such other or further relief as the Court of Chancery may deem just and proper, the Court of Chancery may order books, documents and records, pertinent extracts therefrom, or duly authenticated copies thereof, to be brought within the State of Delaware and kept in the State of Delaware upon such terms and conditions as the order may prescribe.

(g)The rights of a member or manager to obtain information as provided in this section may be restricted in an original limited liability company agreement or in any subsequent amendment approved or adopted by all of the members and in compliance with any applicable requirements of the limited liability company agreement. The provisions of this subsection shall not be construed to limit the ability to impose restrictions on the rights of a member or manager to obtain information by any other means permitted under this section.

§ 18-306. Remedies for breach of limited liability company agreement by member.

A limited liability company agreement may provide that:

(1) A member who fails to perform in accordance with, or to comply with the terms and conditions of, the limited liability company agreement shall be subject to specified penalties or specified consequences; and

(2) At the time or upon the happening of events specified in the limited liability company agreement, a member shall be subject to specified penalties or specified consequences. Such specified penalties or specified consequences may include and take the form of any penalty or consequence set forth in § 18-502(c) of this title.

SUBCHAPTER IV. MANAGERS

§ 18-401. Admission of managers.

A person may be named or designated as a manager of the limited liability company as provided in § 18-101(10) of this title.

§ 18-402. Management of limited liability company.

Unless otherwise provided in a limited liability company agreement, the management of a limited liability company shall be vested in its members in proportion to the then current percentage or other interest of members in the profits of the limited liability company owned by all of the members, the decision of members owning more than 50 percent of the said percentage or other interest in the profits controlling; provided however, that if a limited liability company agreement provides for the management, in whole or in part, of a limited liability company by a manager, the management of the limited liability company, to the extent so provided, shall be vested in the manager who shall be chosen in the manner provided in the limited liability company agreement. The manager shall also hold the offices and have the responsibilities accorded to the manager by or in the manner provided in a limited liability company agreement. Subject to § 18-602 of this title, a manager shall cease to be a manager as provided in a limited liability company agreement. A limited liability company may have more than 1 manager. Unless otherwise provided in a limited liability company agreement, each member and manager has the authority to bind the limited liability company.

§ 18-403. Contributions by a manager.

A manager of a limited liability company may make contributions to the limited liability company and share in the profits and losses of, and in distributions from, the limited liability company as a member. A person who is both a manager and a member has the rights and powers, and is subject to the restrictions and liabilities, of a manager and, except as provided in a limited liability company agreement, also has the rights and powers, and is subject to the restrictions and liabilities, of a member to the extent of his participation in the limited liability company as a member.

§ 18-404. Classes and voting.

(a) A limited liability company agreement may provide for classes or groups of managers having such relative rights, powers and duties as the limited liability company agreement may provide, and may make provision for the future creation in the manner provided in the limited liability company agreement of additional classes or groups of managers having such relative rights, powers and duties as may from time to time be established, including rights, powers and duties senior to existing classes and groups of managers. A limited liability company agreement may provide for the taking of an action, including the amendment of the limited liability company agreement, without the vote or approval of any manager or class or group of managers, including an action to create under the provisions of the limited liability company agreement a class or group of limited liability company interests that was not previously outstanding.

(b) A limited liability company agreement may grant to all or certain identified managers or a specified class or group of the managers the right to vote, separately or with all or any class or group of managers or members, on any matter. Voting by managers may be on a per capita, number, financial interest, class, group or any other basis.

(c) A limited liability company agreement may set forth provisions relating to notice of the time, place or purpose of any meeting at which any matter is to be voted on by any manager or class or group of managers, waiver of any such notice, action by consent without a meeting, the establishment of a record date, quorum requirements, voting in person or by proxy, or any other matter with respect to the exercise of any such right to vote.

(d) Unless otherwise provided in a limited liability company agreement, meetings of managers may be held by means of conference telephone or other communications equipment by means of which all persons participating in the meeting can hear each other, and participation in a meeting pursuant to this subsection shall constitute presence in person at the meeting. Unless otherwise provided in a limited liability company agreement, on any matter that is to be voted on, consented to or approved by managers, the managers may take such action without a meeting, without prior notice and without a vote, if consent or consents in writing, setting forth the action so taken, shall be signed by the managers having not less than the minimum number of votes that would be necessary to authorize or take such action at a meeting at which all managers entitled to vote thereon were present and voted. Unless otherwise provided in a limited liability company agreement, on any matter that is to be voted on by managers, the managers may vote in person or by proxy, and such proxy may be granted in writing, by means of electronic transmission or as otherwise permitted by applicable law. Unless otherwise provided in a limited liability company agreement, a consent transmitted by electronic transmission by a manager or by a person or persons authorized to act for a manager shall be deemed to be written and signed for purposes of this subsection (d). For purposes of this subsection (d), the term "electronic transmission" means any form of communication, not directly involving the physical transmission of paper, that creates a record that may be retained, retrieved, and reviewed by a recipient thereof, and that may be directly reproduced in paper form by such a recipient through an automated process.

[As amended by H 414, effective August 1, 2006.]

§ 18-405. Remedies for breach of limited liability company agreement by manager.

A limited liability company agreement may provide that:

(1) A manager who fails to perform in accordance with, or to comply with the terms and conditions of, the limited liability company agreement shall be subject to specified penalties or specified consequences; and

(2) At the time or upon the happening of events specified in the limited liability company agreement, a manager shall be subject to specified penalties or specified consequences.

§ 18-406. Reliance on reports and information by member or manager.

A member, manager or liquidating trustee of a limited liability company shall be fully protected in relying in good faith upon the records of the limited liability company and upon information, opinions, reports or statements presented by another manager, member or liquidating trustee, an officer or employee of the limited liability company, or committees of the limited liability company, members or managers, or by any other person as to matters the member, manager or liquidating trustees reasonably believes are within such other person's professional or expert competence, including information, opinions, reports or statements as to the value and amount of the assets, liabilities, profits or losses of the limited liability company, or the value and amount of assets or reserves or contracts, agreements or other undertakings that would be sufficient to pay claims and obligations of the limited liability company or to make reasonable provision to pay such claims and obligations, or any other facts pertinent to the existence and amount of assets from which distributions to members or creditors might properly be paid.

§ 18-407. Delegation of rights and powers to manage.

Unless otherwise provided in the limited liability company agreement, a member or manager of a limited liability company has the power and authority to delegate to 1 or more other persons the member's or manager's, as the case may be, rights and powers to manage and control the business and affairs of the limited liability company, including to delegate to agents, officers and employees of a member or manager or the limited liability company, and to delegate by a management agreement or another agreement with, or otherwise to, other persons. Unless otherwise provided in the limited liability company agreement, such delegation by a member or manager of a limited liability company shall not cause the member or manager to cease to be a member or manager, as the case may be, of the limited liability company or cause the person to whom any such rights and powers have been delegated to be a member or manager, as the case may be, of the limited liability company.

SUBCHAPTER V. FINANCE

§ 18-501. Form of contribution.

The contribution of a member to a limited liability company may be in cash, property or services rendered, or a promissory note or other obligation to contribute cash or property or to perform services.

§ 18-502. Liability for contribution.

(a) Except as provided in a limited-liability company agreement, a member is obligated to a limited liability company to perform any promise to contribute cash or property or to perform services, even if he is unable to perform because of death, disability or any other reason. If a member does not make the required contribution of property or services, he is obligated at the option of the limited liability company to contribute cash equal to that portion of the agreed value (as stated in the records of the limited liability company) of the contribution that has not been made. The foregoing option shall be in addition to, and not in lieu of, any other rights, including the right to specific performance, that the limited liability company may have against such member under the limited liability company agreement or applicable law.

(b) Unless otherwise provided in a limited liability company agreement, the obligation of a member to make a contribution or return money or other property paid or distributed in violation of this chapter may be compromised only by consent of all the members. Notwithstanding the compromise, a creditor of a limited liability company who extends credit, after the entering into of a limited liability company agreement or an amendment thereto which, in either case, reflects the obligation, and before the amendment thereof to reflect the compromise, may enforce the original obligation to the extent that, in extending credit, the creditor reasonably relied on the obligation of a member to make a contribution or return. A conditional obligation of a member to make a contribution or return money or other property to a limited liability company may not be enforced unless the conditions of the obligation have been satisfied or waived as to or by such member. Conditional obligations include contributions payable upon a discretionary call of a limited liability company prior to the time the call occurs.

(c) A limited liability company agreement may provide that the interest of any member who fails to make any contribution that he is obligated to make shall be subject to specified penalties for, or specified consequences of, such failure. Such penalty or consequence may take the form of reducing or eliminating the defaulting member's proportionate interest in a limited liability company, subordinating his limited liability company interest to that of nondefaulting members, a forced sale of his limited liability company interest, forfeiture of his limited liability company interest, the lending by other members of the amount necessary to meet his commitment, a fixing of the value of his limited liability company interest by appraisal or by formula and redemption or sale of his limited liability company interest at such value, or other penalty or consequence.

§ 18-503. Allocation of profits and losses.

The profits and losses of a limited liability company shall be allocated among the members, and among classes or groups of members, in the manner provided in a limited liability company agreement. If the limited liability company agreement does not so provide, profits and losses shall be allocated on the basis of the agreed value (as stated in the records of the limited liability company) of the contributions made by each member to the extent they have been received by the limited liability company and have not been returned.

§ 18-504. Allocation of distributions.

Distributions of cash or other assets of a limited liability company shall be allocated among the members, and among classes or groups of members, in the manner provided in a limited liability company agreement. If the limited liability company agreement does not so provide, distributions shall be made on the basis of the agreed value (as stated in the records of the limited liability company) of the contributions made by each member to the extent they have been received by the limited liability company and have not been returned.

§ 18-505. Defense of usury not available.

No obligation of a member or manager of a limited liability company to the limited liability company arising under the limited liability company agreement or a separate agreement or writing, and no note, instrument or other writing evidencing any such obligation of a member or manager, shall be subject to the defense of usury, and no member or manager shall interpose the defense of usury with respect to any such obligation in any action.

SUBCHAPTER VI. DISTRIBUTIONS AND RESIGNATION

§ 18-601. Interim distributions.

Except as provided in this subchapter, to the extent and at the times or upon the happening of the events specified in a limited liability company agreement, a member is entitled to receive from a limited liability company distributions before his resignation from the limited liability company and before the dissolution and winding up thereof.

§ 18-602. Resignation of manager.

A manager may resign as a manager of a limited liability company at the time or upon the happening of events specified in a limited liability company agreement and in accordance with the limited liability company agreement. A limited liability company agreement may provide that a manager shall not have the right to resign as a manager of a limited liability company. Notwithstanding that a limited liability company agreement provides that a manager does not have the right to resign as a manager of a limited liability company, a manager may resign as a manager of a limited liability company at any time by giving written notice to the members and other managers. If the resignation of a manager violates a limited liability company agreement, in addition to any remedies otherwise available under applicable law, a limited liability company may recover from the resigning manager damages for breach of the limited liability company agreement and offset the damages against the amount otherwise distributable to the resigning manager.

§ 18-603. Resignation of member.

A member may resign from a limited liability company only at the time or upon the happening of events specified in a limited liability company agreement and in accordance with the limited liability company agreement.

Notwithstanding anything to the contrary under applicable law, unless a limited liability company agreement provides otherwise, a member may not resign from a limited liability company prior to the dissolution and winding up of the limited liability company. Notwithstanding anything to the contrary under applicable law, a limited liability company agreement may provide that a limited liability company interest may not be assigned prior to the dissolution and winding up of the limited liability company.

Unless otherwise provided in a limited liability company agreement, a limited liability company whose original certificate of formation was filed with the secretary of state and effective on or prior to July 31, 1996, shall continue to be governed by 6 Del. C. § 18-603 as in effect on July 31, 1996, and shall not be governed by this section.

§ 18-604. Distribution upon resignation.

Except as provided in this subchapter, upon resignation any resigning member is entitled to receive any distribution to which such member is entitled under a limited liability company agreement and, if not otherwise provided in a limited liability company agreement, such member is entitled to receive, within a reasonable time after resignation, the fair value of such member's limited liability company interest as of the date of resignation based upon such member's right to share in distributions from the limited liability company.

§ 18-605. Distribution in kind.

Except as provided in a limited liability company agreement, a member, regardless of the nature of his contribution, has no right to demand and receive any distribution from a limited liability company in any form other than cash. Except as provided in a limited liability company agreement, a member may not be compelled to accept a distribution of any asset in kind from a limited liability company to the extent that the percentage of the asset distributed to him exceeds a percentage of that asset which is equal to the percentage in which he shares in distributions from the limited liability company. Except as provided in the limited liability company agreement, a member may be compelled to accept a distribution of any asset in kind from a limited liability company to the extent that the percentage of the asset distributed to him is equal to a percentage of that asset which is equal to the percentage in which he shares in distributions from the limited liability company.

§ 18-606. Right to distribution.

Subject to § 18-607 and § 18-804 of this title, and unless otherwise provided in a limited liability company agreement, at the time a member becomes entitled to receive a distribution, he has the status of, and is entitled to all remedies available to, a creditor of a limited liability company with respect to the distribution. A limited liability company agreement may provide for the establishment of a record date with respect to allocations and distributions by a limited liability company.

§ 18-607. Limitations on distribution.

(a) A limited liability company shall not make a distribution to a member to the extent that at the time of the distribution, after giving effect to the distribution, all liabilities of the limited liability company, other than liabilities to members on account of their limited liability company interests and liabilities for which the recourse of creditors is limited to specified property of the limited liability company, exceed the fair value of the assets of the limited liability company, except that the fair value of property that is subject to a liability for which the recourse of creditors is limited shall be included in the assets of the limited liability company only to the extent that the fair value of that property exceeds that liability. For purposes of this subsection (a), the term "distribution" shall not include amounts constituting reasonable compensation for present or past services or reasonable payments made in the ordinary course of business pursuant to a bona fide retirement plan or other benefits program.

(b) A member who receives a distribution in violation of subsection (a) of this section, and who knew at the time of the distribution that the distribution violated subsection (a) of this section, shall be liable to a limited liability company for the amount of the distribution. A member who receives a distribution in violation of subsection (a) of this section, and who did not know at the time of the distribution that the distribution violated subsection (a) of this section, shall not be liable for the amount of the distribution. Subject to subsection (c) of this section, this subsection shall not affect any obligation or liability of a member under an agreement or other applicable law for the amount of a distribution.

(c) Unless otherwise agreed, a member who receives a distribution from a limited liability company shall have no liability under this chapter or other applicable law for the amount of the distribution after the expiration of 3 years from the date of the distribution unless an action to recover the distribution from such member is commenced prior to the expiration of the said 3-year period and an adjudication of liability against such member is made in the said action.

SUBCHAPTER VII. ASSIGNMENT OF LIMITED LIABILITY COMPANY INTERESTS

§ 18-701. Nature of limited liability company interest.

A limited liability company interest is personal property. A member has no interest in specific limited liability company property.

§ 18-702. Assignment of limited liability company interest.

(a) A limited liability company interest is assignable in whole or in part except as provided in a limited liability company agreement. The assignee of a member's limited liability company interest shall have no right to participate in the management of the business and affairs of a limited liability company except as provided in a limited liability company agreement and upon:

(1) The approval of all of the members of the limited liability company other than the member assigning his limited liability company interest; or

(2) Compliance with any procedure provided for in the limited liability company agreement.

(b) Unless otherwise provided in a limited liability company agreement:

(1) An assignment of a limited liability company interest does not entitle the assignee to become or to exercise any rights or powers of a member;

(2) An assignment of a limited liability company interest entitles the assignee to share in such profits and losses, to receive such distribution or distributions, and to receive such allocation of income, gain, loss, deduction, or credit or similar item to which the assignor was entitled, to the extent assigned; and

(3) A member ceases to be a member and to have the power to exercise any rights or powers of a member upon assignment of all of his limited liability company interest. Unless otherwise provided in a limited liability company agreement, the pledge of, or granting of a security interest, lien or other encumbrance in or against, any or all of the limited liability

company interest of a member shall not cause the member to cease to be a member or to have the power to exercise any rights or powers of a member.

(c) Unless otherwise provided in a limited liability company agreement may provide that a member's interest in a limited liability company may be evidenced by a certificate of limited liability company interest issued by the limited liability company. A limited liability company agreement may provide for the assignment or transfer of any limited liability company interest represented by such a certificate and make other provisions with respect to such certificates. A limited liability company shall not have the power to issue a certificate of limited liability company interest in bearer form.

(d) Unless otherwise provided in a limited liability company agreement and except to the extent assumed by agreement, until an assignee of a limited liability company interest becomes a member, the assignee shall have no liability as a member solely as a result of the assignment.

(e) Unless otherwise provided in the limited liability company agreement, a limited liability company may acquire, by purchase, redemption or otherwise, any limited liability company interest or other interest of a member or manager in the limited liability company. Unless otherwise provided in the limited liability company agreement, any such interest so acquired by the limited liability company shall be deemed canceled.

[As last amended by S 96, effective August 1, 2007]

§ 18-703. Member's limited liability company interest subject to charging order.

(a) On application by a judgment creditor of a member or of a member's assignee, a court having jurisdiction may charge the limited liability company interest of the judgment debtor to satisfy the judgment. To the extent so charged, the judgment creditor has only the right to receive any distribution or distributions to which the judgment debtor would otherwise have been entitled in respect of such limited liability company interest.

(b) A charging order constitutes a lien on the judgment debtor's limited liability company interest.

(c) This chapter does not deprive a member or member's assignee of a right under exemption laws with respect to the judgment debtor's limited liability company interest.

(d) The entry of a charging order is the exclusive remedy by which a judgment creditor of a member or of a member's assignee may satisfy a judgment out of the judgment debtor's limited liability company interest.

(e) No creditor of a member or of a member's assignee shall have any right to obtain possession of, or otherwise exercise legal or equitable remedies with respect to, the property of the limited liability company.

(f) The Court of Chancery shall have jurisdiction to hear and determine any matter relating to any such charging order.

§ 18-704. Right of assignee to become member.

(a) An assignee of a limited liability company interest may become a member as provided in a limited liability company agreement and upon:

(1) The approval of all of the members of the limited liability company other than the member assigning his limited liability company interest; or

(2) Compliance with any procedure provided for in the limited liability company agreement.

(b) An assignee who has become a member has, to the extent assigned, the rights and powers, and is subject to the restrictions and liabilities, of a member under a limited liability company agreement and this chapter. Notwithstanding the foregoing, unless otherwise provided in a limited liability company agreement, an assignee who becomes a member is liable for the obligations of his assignor to make contributions as provided in § 18-502 of this title, but shall not be liable for the obligations of his assignor under subchapter VI of this chapter. However, the assignee is not obligated for liabilities, including the obligations of his assignor to make contributions as provided in § 18-502 of this title, unknown to the assignee at the time he became a member and which could not be ascertained from a limited liability company agreement.

(c) Whether or not an assignee of a limited liability company interest becomes a member, the assignor is not released from his liability to a limited liability company under subchapters V and VI of this chapter.

§ 18-705. Powers of estate of deceased or incompetent member.

If a member who is an individual dies or a court of competent jurisdiction adjudges him to be incompetent to manage his person or his property, the member's personal representative may exercise all of the member's rights for the purpose of settling his estate or administering his property, including any power under a limited liability company agreement of an assignee to become a member. If a member is a corporation, trust or other entity and is dissolved or terminated, the powers of that member may be exercised by its personal representative.

SUBCHAPTER VIII. DISSOLUTION

§ 18-801. Dissolution.

(a) A limited liability company is dissolved and its affairs shall be wound up upon the first to occur of the following:

(1) At the time specified in a limited liability company agreement, but if no such time is set forth in the limited liability company agreement, then the limited liability company shall have a perpetual existence;

(2) Upon the happening of events specified in a limited liability company agreement;

(3) Unless otherwise provided in a limited liability company agreement, upon the affirmative vote or written consent of the members of the limited liability company or, if there is more than one class or group of members, then by each class or group of members, in either case, by members who own more than two-thirds of the then-current percentage or other interest in the profits of the limited liability company owned by all of the members of by the members in each class or group, as appropriate;

(4) At any time there are no members; provided that the limited liability company is not dissolved and is not required to be wound up if,

(a) unless otherwise provided in a limited liability company agreement, within 90 days or such other period as is provided for in the limited liability company agreement after the occurrence of the event that terminated the continued membership of the last remaining member, the personal representative of the last remaining member agrees in writing to continue the limited liability company and to the admission of the personal representative of such member or its nominee or designee to the limited liability company as a member, effective as of the occurrence of the event that terminated the continued membership of the last remaining member; provided that a limited liability company agreement may provide that the personal representative of the last remaining member shall be obligated to agree in writing to continue the limited liability company and to the admission of the personal representative of such member or its nominee or designee to the limited liability company as a member, effective as of the occurrence of the event that terminated the continued membership of the last remaining member, or,

(b) a member is admitted to the limited liability company in the manner provided for in the limited liability company agreement, effective as of the occurrence of the event that terminated the continued membership of the last remaining member, within 90 days or such other period as is provided for in the limited liability company agreement after the occurrence of the event that terminated the continued membership of the last remaining member, pursuant to a provision of the limited liability company agreement that specifically provides for the admission of a member to the limited liability company after there is no longer a remaining member of the limited liability company.

(5) The entry of a decree of judicial dissolution under § 18-802 of this title.

(b) Unless otherwise provided in a limited liability company agreement, the death, retirement, resignation, expulsion, bankruptcy or dissolution of any member or the occurrence of any other event that terminates the continued membership of any member shall not cause the limited liability company to be dissolved or its affairs to be wound up, and upon the occurrence of any such event, the limited liability company shall be continued without dissolution.

§ 18-802. Judicial dissolution.

On application by or for a member or manager the Court of Chancery may decree dissolution of a limited liability company whenever it is not reasonably practicable to carry on the business in conformity with a limited liability company agreement.

§ 18-803. Winding up.

(a) Unless otherwise provided in a limited liability company agreement, a manager who has not wrongfully dissolved a limited liability company or, if none, the members or a person approved by the members or, if there is more than 1 class or group of members, then by each class or group of members, in either case, by members who own more than 50 percent of the then current percentage or other interest in the profits of the limited liability company owned by all of the members or by the members in each class or group, as appropriate, may wind up the limited liability company's affairs; but the Court of Chancery, upon cause shown, may wind up the limited liability company's affairs upon application of any member or manager, his personal representative or assignee, and in connection therewith, may appoint a liquidating trustee.

(b) Upon dissolution of a limited liability company and until the filing of a certificate of cancellation as provided in § 18-203 of this title, the persons winding up the limited liability company's affairs may, in the name of, and for and on behalf of, the limited liability company, prosecute and defend suits, whether civil, criminal or administrative, gradually settle and close the limited liability company's business, dispose of and convey the limited liability company's property, discharge or make reasonable provision for the limited liability company's liabilities, and distribute to the members any remaining assets of the limited liability company, all without affecting the liability of members and managers and without imposing liability on a liquidating trustee.

§ 18-804. Distribution of assets.

(a) Upon the winding up of a limited liability company, the assets shall be distributed as follows:

(1) To creditors, including members and managers who are creditors, to the extent otherwise permitted by law, in satisfaction of liabilities of the limited liability company (whether by payment or the making of reasonable provision for payment thereof) other than liabilities for which reasonable provision for payment has been made and liabilities for distributions to members and former members under § 18-601 or § 18-604 of this title;

(2) Unless otherwise provided in a limited liability company agreement, to members and former members in satisfaction of liabilities for distributions under § 18-601 or § 18-604 of this title; and

(3) Unless otherwise provided in a limited liability company agreement, to members first for the return of their contributions and second respecting their limited liability company interests, in the proportions in which the members share in distributions.

(b) A limited liability company which has dissolved (1) shall pay or make reasonable provision to pay all claims and obligations, including all contingent, conditional or unmatured contractual claims, known to the limited liability company, (2) shall make such provision as will be reasonably likely to be sufficient to provide compensation for any claim against the limited liability company which is the subject of a pending action, suit or proceeding to which the limited liability company is a party and (3) shall make such provision as will be reasonably likely to be sufficient to provide compensation for claims that have not been made known to the limited liability company or that have not arisen but that, based on facts known to the limited liability company, are likely to arise or to become known to the limited liability company within 10 years after the date of dissolution. If there are sufficient assets, such claims and obligations shall be paid in full and any such provision for payment made shall be made in full. If there are insufficient assets, such claims and obligations shall be paid or provided for according to their priority and, among claims of equal priority, ratably to the extent of assets available therefor. Unless otherwise provided in the limited liability company agreement, any remaining assets shall be distributed as provided in this chapter. Any liquidating trustee winding up a limited liability company's affairs who has complied with this section shall not be personally liable to the claimants of the dissolved limited liability company by reason of such person's actions in winding up the limited liability company.

(c) A member who receives a distribution in violation of subsection (a) of this section, and who knew at the time of the distribution that the distribution violated subsection (a) of this section, shall be liable to the limited liability company for the amount of the distribution. For purposes of the immediately preceding sentence, the term "distribution" shall not include amounts constituting reasonable compensation for present or past services or reasonable payments made in the ordinary course of business pursuant to a bona fide retirement plan or other benefits program. A member who receives a distribution in violation of subsection (a) of this section, and who did not know at the time of the distribution that the distribution violated subsection (a) of this section, shall not be liable for the amount of the distribution. Subject to subsection (d) of this section, this subsection shall not affect any obligation or liability of a member under an agreement or other applicable law for the amount of a distribution.

(d) Unless otherwise agreed, a member who receives a distribution from a limited liability company to which this section applies shall have no liability under this chapter or other applicable law for the amount of the distribution after the expiration of 3 years from the date of the distribution unless an action to recover the distribution from such member is commenced prior to the expiration of the said 3-year period and an adjudication of liability against such member is made in the said action.

(e) § 18-607 of this title shall not apply to a distribution to which this section applies.

§ 18-805. Trustees or receivers for limited liability companies; appointment; powers; duties.

When the certificate of formation of any limited liability company formed under this chapter shall be canceled by the filing of a certificate of cancellation pursuant to § 18-203 of this title, the Court of Chancery, on application of any creditor, member or manager of the limited liability company, or any other person who shows good cause therefor, at any time, may either appoint one or more of the managers of the limited liability company to be trustees, or appoint one or more persons to be receivers, of and for the limited liability company, to take charge of the limited liability company's property, and to collect the debts and property due and belonging to the limited liability company, with the power to prosecute and defend, in the name of the limited liability company, or otherwise, all such suits as may be necessary or proper for the purposes aforesaid, and to appoint an agent or agents under them, and to do all other acts which might be done by the limited liability company, if in being, that may be necessary for the final settlement of the unfinished business of the limited liability company. The powers of the trustees or receivers may be continued as long as the Court of Chancery shall think necessary for the purposes aforesaid.

§ 18-806. Revocation of dissolution.

Notwithstanding the occurrence of an event set forth in § 18-801 (a) (1), (2), (3) or (4) of this title, the limited liability company shall not be dissolved and its affairs shall not be wound up if, prior to the filing of a certificate of cancellation in the office of the Secretary of State, the limited liability company is continued, effective as of the occurrence of such event, pursuant to the affirmative vote or written consent of all remaining members of the limited liability company or the personal representative of the last remaining member of the limited liability company if there is no remaining member (and any other person whose approval is required under the limited liability company agreement to revoke a dissolution pursuant to this section), provided, however, if the dissolution was caused by a vote or written consent, the dissolution shall not be revoked unless each member and other person (or their respective personal representatives) who voted in favor of, or consented to, the dissolution has voted or consented in writing to continue the limited liability company. If there is no remaining member of the limited liability company and the personal representative of the last remaining member votes in favor of or consents to the continuation of the limited liability company, such personal representative shall be required to agree in writing to the admission of the personal representative of such member or its nominee or designee to the limited liability company as a member, effective as of the occurrence of the event that terminated the continued member-ship of the last remaining member.

SUBCHAPTER IX. FOREIGN LIMITED LIABILITY COMPANIES

§ 18-901. Law governing.

(a) Subject to the Constitution of the State of Delaware:

(1) The laws of the state, territory, possession, or other jurisdiction or country under which a foreign limited liability company is organized govern its organization and internal affairs and the liability of its members and managers; and

(2) A foreign limited liability company may not be denied registration by reason of any difference between those laws and the laws of the State of Delaware.

(b) A foreign limited liability company shall be subject to § 18-106 of this title.

§ 18-902. Registration required; application.

Before doing business in the State of Delaware, a foreign limited liability company shall register with the secretary of state. In order to register, a foreign limited liability company shall submit to the secretary of state:

(1) A copy executed by an authorized person of an application for registration as a foreign limited liability company, setting forth:

a. The name of the foreign limited liability company and, if different, the name under which it proposes to register and do business in the State of Delaware;

b. The state, territory, possession or other jurisdiction or country where formed, the date of its formation and a statement from an authorized person that, as of the date of filing, the foreign limited liability company validly exists as a limited liability company under the laws of the jurisdiction of its formation;

c. The nature of the business or purposes to be conducted or promoted in the State of Delaware;

d. The address of the registered office and the name and address of the registered agent for service of process required to be maintained by § 18-904(b) of this title;

e. A statement that the secretary of state is appointed the agent of the foreign limited liability company for service of process under the circumstances set forth in § 18-910(b) of this title; and

f. The date on which the foreign limited liability company first did, or intends to do, business in the State of Delaware.

(2) A fee as set forth in § 18-1105(a)(6) of this title shall be paid.

§ 18-903. Issuance of registration.

(a) If the secretary of state finds that an application for registration conforms to law and all requisite fees have been paid, he shall:

(1) Certify that the application has been filed in his office by endorsing upon the original application the word "Filed", and the date and hour of the filing. This endorsement is conclusive of the date and time of its filing in the absence of actual fraud;

(2) File and index the endorsed application.

(b) The secretary of state shall prepare and return to the person who filed the application or his representative a copy of the original signed application, similarly endorsed, and shall certify such copy as a true copy of the original signed application.

(c) The filing of the application with the secretary of state shall make it unnecessary to file any other documents under Chapter 31 of this title.

§ 18-904. Name; registered office; registered agent.

(a) A foreign limited liability company may register with the secretary of state under any name (whether or not it is the name under which it is registered in the jurisdiction of its formation) that includes the words "Limited Liability Company" or the abbreviation "L.L.C." or the designation "LLC" and that could be registered by a domestic limited liability company; provided however, that a foreign limited liability company may register under any name which is not such as to distinguish it upon the records in the office of the secretary of state from the name on such records of any domestic or foreign corporation, partnership, statutory trust, limited liability company or limited partnership reserved, formed, registered or organized under the laws of the State of Delaware with the written consent of the other corporation, partnership, statutory trust, limited liability company or limited partnership, which written consent shall be filed with the secretary of state.

(b) Each foreign limited liability company shall have and maintain in the State of Delaware:

(1) A registered office which may but need not be a place of its business in the State of Delaware; and

(2) A registered agent for service of process on the foreign limited liability company, having a business office identical with such registered office, which agent may be any of:

a. An individual resident in the State of Delaware,

b. A domestic limited liability company, a domestic corporation, a domestic partnership (whether general (including a limited liability partnership) or limited (including a limited liability limited partnership)), or a domestic statutory trust, or

c. A foreign corporation, a foreign partnership (whether general (including a limited liability partnership) or limited (including a limited liability limited partnership)), a foreign limited liability company (other that the foreign limited liability company itself), or a foreign statutory rust.

(c) A registered agent may change the address of the registered office of the foreign limited liability company(ies) for which the agent is registered agent to another address in the State of Delaware by paying a fee as set forth in § 18-1105(a)(7) of this title and filing with the Secretary of State a certificate, executed by such registered agent, setting forth the address at which such registered agent has maintained the registered office for each of the foreign limited liability companies for which it is a registered agent, and further certifying to the new address to which each such registered office will be changed on a given day, and at which new address such registered agent will thereafter maintain the registered office for each of the foreign limited liability companies for which it is registered agent. Upon the filing of such certificate, the Secretary of State shall furnish to the registered agent a certified copy of the same under the Secretary's hand and seal of office, and thereafter, or until further change of address, as authorized by law, the registered office in the State of Delaware of each of the foreign limited liability companies for which the agent is a registered agent shall be located at the new address of the registered agent thereof as given in the certificate. In the event of a change of name of any person acting as a registered agent of a foreign limited liability company, such registered agent shall file with the Secretary of State a certificate, executed by such registered agent, setting forth the new name of such registered agent, the name of such registered agent before it was changed and the address at which such registered agent has maintained the registered office for each of the foreign limited liability companies for which it is registered agent, and shall pay a fee as set forth in § 18-1105(a)(7) of this title. Upon the filing of such certificate, the Secretary of State shall furnish to the registered agent a certified copy of the same under his or her hand and seal of office. A change of name of any person acting as a registered agent of a foreign limited liability company as a result of the merger or consolidation of the registered agent, with or into another person which succeeds to its assets and liabilities by operation of law, shall be deemed a change of name for purposes of this section. Filing a certificate under this section shall be deemed to be an amendment of the application of each foreign limited liability company affected thereby and each such foreign limited liability company shall not be required to take any further action with respect thereto, to amend its application under § 18-905 of this title. Any registered agent filing a certificate under this section shall promptly, upon such filing, deliver a copy of any such certificate to each foreign limited liability company affected thereby.

(d) The registered agent of 1 or more foreign limited liability companies may resign and appoint a successor registered agent by paying a fee as set forth in § 18-1105(a)(7) of this title and filing a certificate with the Secretary of State, stating that it resigns and the name and address of the successor registered agent. There shall be attached to such certificate a statement of each affected foreign limited liability company ratifying and approving such change of registered agent. Upon such filing, the successor registered agent shall become the registered agent of such foreign limited liability companies as have ratified and approved such substitution and the successor registered agent's address, as stated in such certificate, shall become the address of each such foreign limited liability company's registered office in the State of Delaware. The Secretary of State shall then issue a certificate that the successor registered agent has become the registered agent of the foreign limited liability companies so ratifying and approving such change and setting out the names of such foreign limited liability companies. Filing of such certificate of resignation shall be deemed to be an amendment of the application of each foreign limited liability company affected thereby and each such foreign limited liability company shall not be required to take any further action with respect thereto to amend its application under § 18-905 of this title.

(e) The registered agent of one or more foreign limited liability companies may resign without appointing a successor registered agent by paying a fee as set forth in § 18-1105(a)(7) of this title and filing a certificate of resignation with the Secretary of State, but such resignation shall not become effective until 30 days after the certificate is filed. The certificate shall contain a statement that written notice of resignation was given to each affected foreign limited liability company at least 30 days prior to the filing of the certificate by mailing or delivering such notice to the foreign limited liability company at its address last known to the registered agent and shall set forth the date of such notice. After receipt of the notice of the resignation of its registered agent, the foreign limited liability company for which such registered agent was acting shall obtain and designate a new registered agent to take the place of the registered agent so resigning. If such foreign limited liability company fails to obtain and designate a new registered agent as aforesaid prior to the expiration of the period of 30 days after the filing by the registered agent of the certificate of resignation, such foreign limited liability company shall not be permitted to do business in the State of Delaware and its registration shall be cancelled. After the resignation of the registered agent shall have become effective as provided in this section and if no new registered agent shall have been obtained and designated in the time and manner aforesaid, service of legal process against each foreign limited liability company for which the resigned registered agent had been acting shall thereafter be upon the Secretary of State in accordance with § 18-911 of this title.

[As last amended by S 96, effective August 1, 2007]

§ 18-905. Amendments to application.

If any statement in the application for registration of a foreign limited liability company was false when made or any arrangements or other facts described have changed, making the application false in any respect, the foreign limited liability company shall promptly file in the office of the secretary of state a certificate, executed by an authorized person, correcting such statement, together with a fee as set forth in § 18-1105(a)(6) of this title.

§ 18-906. Cancellation of registration.

A foreign limited liability company may cancel its registration by filing with the secretary of state a certificate of cancellation, executed by an authorized person, together with a fee as set forth in § 18-1105(a)(6) of this title. The registration of a foreign limited liability company shall be cancelled as provided in § 18-104(i)(4), § 18-904(e) and § 18-1107(h) of this ttle. A cancellation does not terminate the authority of the secretary of state to accept service of process on the foreign limited liability company with respect to causes of action arising out of the doing of business in the State of Delaware.

[As last amended by S 96, effective August 1, 2007]

§ 18-907. Doing business without registration.

(a) A foreign limited liability company doing business in the State of Delaware may not maintain any action, suit or proceeding in the State of Delaware until it has registered in the State of Delaware, and has paid to the State of Delaware all fees and penalties for the years or parts thereof, during which it did business in the State of Delaware without having registered.

(b) The failure of a foreign limited liability company to register in the State of Delaware does not impair:

(1) The validity of any contract or act of the foreign limited liability company;

(2) The right of any other party to the contract to maintain any action, suit or proceeding on the contract; or

(3) Prevent the foreign limited liability company from defending any action, suit or proceeding in any court of the State of Delaware.

(c) A member or a manager of a foreign limited liability company is not liable for the obligations of the foreign limited liability company solely by reason of the limited liability company's having done business in the State of Delaware without registration.

(d) Any foreign limited liability company doing business in the State of Delaware without first having registered shall be fined and shall pay to the secretary of state $200 for each year or part thereof during which the foreign limited liability company failed to register in the State of Delaware.

§ 18-908. Foreign limited liability companies doing business without having qualified; injunctions.

The Court of Chancery shall have jurisdiction to enjoin any foreign limited liability company, or any agent thereof, from doing any business in the State of Delaware if such foreign limited liability company has failed to register under this subchapter or if such foreign limited liability company has secured a certificate of the secretary of state under § 18-903 of this title on the basis of false or misleading representations. The Attorney General shall, upon his own motion or upon the relation of proper parties, proceed for this purpose by complaint in any county in which such foreign limited liability company is doing or has done business.

§ 18-909. Execution; liability.

§ 18-204(c) of this title shall be applicable to foreign limited liability companies as if they were domestic limited liability companies.

§ 18-910. Service of process on registered foreign limited liability companies.

(a) Service of legal process upon any foreign limited liability company shall be made by delivering a copy personally to any managing or general agent or manager of the foreign limited liability company in the State of Delaware or the registered agent of the foreign limited liability company in the State of Delaware, or by leaving it at the dwelling house or usual place of abode in the State of Delaware of any such managing or general agent, manager or registered agent (if the registered agent be an individual), or at the registered office or other place of business of the foreign limited liability company in the State of Delaware. If the registered agent be a corporation, service of process upon it as such may be made by serving, in the State of Delaware, a copy thereof on the president, vice-president, secretary, assistant secretary or any director of the corporate registered agent. Service by copy left at the dwelling house or usual place of abode of any managing or general agent, manager or registered agent, or at the registered office or other place of business of the foreign limited liability company in the State of Delaware, to be effective must be delivered thereat at least 6 days before the return date of the process, and in the presence of an adult person, and the officer serving the process shall distinctly state the manner of service in his return thereto. Process returnable forthwith must be delivered personally to the managing or general agent, manager or registered agent.

(b) In case the officer whose duty it is to serve legal process cannot by due diligence serve the process in any manner provided for by subsection (a) of this section, it shall be lawful to serve the process against the foreign limited liability company upon the secretary of state, and such service shall be as effectual for all intents and purposes as if made in any of the ways provided for in subsection (a) of this section. In the event service is effected through the secretary of state in accordance with this subsection, the secretary of state shall forthwith notify the foreign limited liability company by letter, certified mail, return receipt requested, directed to the foreign limited liability company at its last registered office. Such letter shall enclose a copy of the process and any other papers served on the secretary of state pursuant to this subsection. It shall be the duty of the plaintiff in the event of such service to serve process and any other papers in duplicate, to notify the secretary of state that service is being effected pursuant to this subsection, and to pay to the secretary of state the sum of $50 for the use of the State of Delaware, which sum shall be taxed as a part of the costs in the proceeding if the plaintiff shall prevail therein. The secretary of state shall maintain an alphabetical record of any such service setting forth the name of the plaintiff and defendant, the title, docket number and nature of the proceeding in which process has been served upon him, the fact that service has been effected pursuant to this subsection, the return date thereof and the day and hour when the service was made. The secretary of state shall not be required to retain such information for a period longer than 5 years from his receipt of the service of process.

§ 18-911. Service of process on unregistered foreign limited liability companies.

(a) Any foreign limited liability company which shall do business in the State of Delaware without having registered under § 18-902 of this title shall be deemed to have thereby appointed and constituted the secretary of state of the State of Delaware its agent for the acceptance of legal process in any civil action, suit or proceeding against it in any state or federal court in the State of Delaware arising or growing out of any business done by it within the State of Delaware. The doing of business in the State of Delaware by such foreign limited liability company shall be a signification of the agreement of such foreign limited liability company that any such process when so served shall be of the same legal force and validity as if served upon an authorized manager or agent personally within the State of Delaware.

(b) Whenever the words "doing business," "the doing of business" or "business done in this State," by any such foreign limited liability company are used in this section, they shall mean the course or practice of carrying on any business activities in the State of Delaware, including, without limiting the generality of the foregoing, the solicitation of business or orders in the State of Delaware.

(c) In the event of service upon the secretary of state in accordance with subsection (a) of this section, the secretary of state shall forthwith notify the foreign limited liability company thereof by letter, certified mail, return receipt requested, directed to the foreign limited liability company at the address furnished to the secretary of state by the plaintiff in such action, suit or proceeding. Such letter shall enclose a copy of the process and any other papers served upon the secretary of state. It shall be the duty of the plaintiff in the event of such service to serve process and any other papers in duplicate, to notify the secretary of state that service is being made pursuant to this subsection, and to pay to the secretary of state the sum of $50 for the use of the State of Delaware, which sum shall be taxed as part of the costs in the proceeding, if the plaintiff shall prevail therein. The secretary of state shall maintain an alphabetical record of any such process setting forth the name of the plaintiff and defendant, the title, docket number and nature of the proceeding in which process has been served upon him, the return date thereof, and the day and hour when the service was made. The secretary of state shall not be required to retain such information for a period longer than 5 years from his receipt of the service of process.

§ 18-912. Activities not constituting doing business.

(a) Activities of a foreign limited liability company in the State of Delaware that do not constitute doing business for the purpose of this subchapter include:

(1) maintaining, defending or settling an action or proceeding;

(2) holding meetings of its members or managers or carrying on any other activity concerning its internal affairs;

(3) maintaining bank accounts;

(4) maintaining offices or agencies for the transfer, exchange or registration of the limited liability company's own securities or maintaining trustees or depositories with respect to those securities;

(5) selling through independent contractors;

(6) soliciting or obtaining orders, whether by mail or through employees or agents or otherwise, if the orders require acceptance outside the State of Delaware before they become contracts;

(7) selling, by contract consummated outside the State of Delaware, and agreeing, by the contract, to deliver into the State of Delaware, machinery, plants or equipment, the construction, erection or installation of which within the State of Delaware requires the supervision of technical engineers or skilled employees performing services not generally available, and as part of the contract of sale agreeing to furnish such services, and such services only, to the vendee at the time of construction, erection or installation;

(8) creating, as borrower or lender, or acquiring indebtedness with or without a mortgage or other security interest in property;

(9) collecting debts or foreclosing mortgages or other security interests in property securing the debts, and holding, protecting and maintaining property so acquired;

(10) conducting an isolated transaction that is not one in the course of similar transactions;

(11) doing business in interstate commerce; and

(12) doing business in the State of Delaware as an insurance company.

(b) A person shall not be deemed to be doing business in the State of Delaware solely by reason of being a member or manager of a domestic limited liability company or a foreign limited liability company.

(c) This section does not apply in determining whether a foreign limited liability company is subject to service of process, taxation or regulation under any other law of the State of Delaware.

SUBCHAPTER X. DERIVATIVE ACTIONS

§ 18-1001. Right to bring action.

A member or an assignee of a limited liability company interest may bring an action in the Court of Chancery in the right of a limited liability company to recover a judgment in its favor if managers or members with authority to do so have refused to bring the action or if an effort to cause those managers or members to bring the action is not likely to succeed.

§ 18-1002. Proper plaintiff.

In a derivative action, the plaintiff must be a member or an assignee of a limited liability company interest at the time of bringing the action and:

(1) At the time of the transaction of which he complains; or

(2) His status as a member or an assignee of a limited liability company interest had devolved upon him by operation of law or pursuant to the terms of a limited liability company agreement from a person who was a member or an assignee of a limited liability company interest at the time of the transaction.

§ 18-1003. Complaint.

In a derivative action, the complaint shall set forth with particularity the effort, if any, of the plaintiff to secure initiation of the action by a manager or member or the reasons for not making the effort.

§ 18-1004. Expenses.

If a derivative action is successful, in whole or in part, as a result of a judgment, compromise or settlement of any such action, the court may award the plaintiff reasonable expenses, including reasonable attorney's fees, from any recovery in any such action or from a limited liability company.

SUBCHAPTER XI. MISCELLANEOUS

§ 18-1101. Construction and application of chapter and limited liability company agreement.

(a) The rule that statutes in derogation of the common law are to be strictly construed shall have no application to this chapter.

(b) It is the policy of this chapter to give the maximum effect to the principle of freedom of contract and to the enforceability of limited liability company agreements.

(c) To the extent that, at law or in equity, a member or manager or other person has duties (including fiduciary duties) to a limited liability company or to another member or manager or to an other person that is a party to or is otherwise bound by a limited liability company agreement, the member's or manager's or other person's duties may be expanded or restricted or eliminated by provisions in the limited liability company agreement; provided that the limited liability company agreement may not eliminate the implied contractual covenant of good faith and fair dealing.

(d) Unless otherwise provided in the limited liability company agreement, a member or manager or other person shall not be liable to the limited liability company or to another member or manager or to another person that is a party to or is otherwise bound by the limited liability company agreement for breach of fiduciary duty for the member's or manager's or other person's good faith reliance on the provisions of the limited liability company agreement.

(e) A limited liability company agreement may provide for the limitation or elimination of any and all liabilities for breach of contract and breach of duties (including fiduciary duties) of a member, manager or other person to a limited liability company or to another member or manager or other person that is a party to or is otherwise bound by the limited liability company agreement; provided that a limited liability company agreement may not limit or eliminate liability for any act or omission that constitutes a bad faith violation of the implied contractual covenant of good faith and fair dealing.

(f) Unless the context otherwise requires, as used herein, the singular shall include the plural and the plural may refer to only the singular. The use of any gender shall be applicable to all genders. The captions contained herein are for purposes of convenience only and shall not control or affect the construction of this chapter.

(g) § 9-406 and § 9-408 of this title do not apply to any interest in a limited liability company, including all rights, powers and interests arising under a limited liability company agreement or this chapter. This provision prevails over § 9-406 and § 9-408 of this title.

§ 18-1102. Short title.

This chapter may be cited as the "Delaware Limited Liability Company Act."

§ 18-1103. Severability.

If any provision of this chapter or its application to any person or circumstances is held invalid, the invalidity does not affect other provisions or applications of the chapter which can be given effect without the invalid provision or application, and to this end, the provisions of this chapter are severable.

§ 18-1104. Cases not provided for in this chapter.

In any case not provided for in this chapter, the rules of law and equity, including the law merchant, shall govern.

§ 18-1105. Fees.

(a) No document required to be filed under this chapter shall be effective until the applicable fee required by this section is paid. The following fees shall be paid to and collected by the secretary of state for the use of the State of Delaware:

(1) Upon the receipt for filing of an application for reservation of name, an application for renewal of reservation or a notice of transfer or cancellation of reservation pursuant to § 18-103(b) of this title, a fee in the amount of $75.

(2) Upon the receipt for filing of a certificate under § 18-104(b) of this title, a fee in the amount of $50, upon the receipt for filing of a certificate under § 18-104(c) of this title, a fee in the amount of $50 and a further fee of $2 for each limited liability company affected by such certificate, and upon the receipt for filing of a certificate under § 18-104(d) of this title, a fee in the amount of $2.50.

(3) Upon the receipt for filing of a certificate of limited liability company domestication under § 18-212 of this title, a certificate of transfer or a certificate of transfer and domestic continuance under § 18-213 of this title, a certificate of conversion to limited liability company under § 18-214 of this title, a certificate of conversion to a non-Delaware entity under § 18-216 of this title, a certificate of formation under § 18-201 of this title a fee in the amount of $70; and upon the receipt for filing of a certificate of amendment under § 18-202 of this title, a certificate of cancellation under § 18-203 of this title, a certificate of merger or consolidation under § 18-209 of this title, a restated certificate of formation under § 18-208 of this title, a certificate of amendment of a certificate with a future effective date or time under § 18-206(c) of this title, a certificate of termination of a certificate with a future effective date or time under § 18-206(c) of this title, a certificate of correction under § 18-211 of this title, or a certificate of revival under § 18-1109 of this title, a fee in the amount of $80.

(4) For certifying copies of any paper on file as provided for by this chapter, a fee in the amount of $30 for each copy certified.

(5) The secretary of state may issue photocopies or electronic image copies of instruments on file, as well as instruments, documents and other papers not on file, and for all such photocopies or electronic image copies, whether certified or not, a fee of $10 shall be paid for the first page and $2 for each additional page. The secretary of state may also issue microfiche copies of instruments on file as well as instruments, documents and other papers not on file, and for each such microfiche a fee of $2 shall be paid therefore. Notwithstanding the State of Delaware's Freedom of Information Act or other provision of this Code granting access to public records, the secretary of state shall issue only photocopies, microfiche or electronic image copies of records in exchange for the fees described above.

(6) Upon the receipt for filing of an application for registration as a foreign limited liability company under § 18-902 of this title, a certificate under § 18-905 of this title or a certificate of cancellation under § 18-906 of this title, a fee in the amount of $100.

(7) Upon the receipt for filing of a certificate under § 18-904(c) of this title, a fee in the amount of $50, upon the receipt for filing of a certificate under § 18-904(d) of this title, a fee in the amount of $50 and a further fee of $2 for each foreign limited liability company affected by such certificate, and upon the receipt for filing of a certificate under § 18-904(e) of this title, a fee in the amount of $2.50.

(8) For preclearance of any document for filing, a fee in the amount of $250.

(9) For preparing and providing a written report of a record search, a fee in the amount of $30.

(10) For issuing any certificate of the secretary of state, including but not limited to a certificate of good standing, other than a certification of a copy under paragraph (4) of this subsection, a fee in the amount of $30, except that for issuing any certificate of the secretary of state that recites all of a limited liability company's filings with the secretary of state, a fee of $125 shall be paid for each such certificate.

(11) For receiving and filing and/or indexing any certificate, affidavit, agreement or any other paper provided for by this chapter, for which no different fee is specifically prescribed, a fee in the amount of $50.

(12) The secretary of state may in his discretion charge a fee of $60 for each check received for payment of any fee that is returned due to insufficient funds or the result of a stop payment order.

(b) In addition to those fees charged under subsection (a) of this section, there shall be collected by and paid to the secretary of state the following:

(1) For all services described in subsection (a) of this Section that are requested to be completed within one (1) hour on the same day as the day of the request, an additional sum of up to $1000 and for all services described in subsection (a) of this section that are requested to be completed within 2 hours on the same day of the request, an additional sum of up to $500;.

(2) For all services described in subsection (a) of this section that are requested to be completed within the same day as the day of the request, an additional sum of up to $200; and

(3) For all services described in subsection (a) of this section that are requested to be completed within a 24-hour period from the time of the request, an additional sum of up to $100.

The secretary of state shall establish (and may from time to time amend) a schedule of specific fees payable pursuant to this subsection.

(c) The secretary of state may in his discretion permit the extension of credit for the fees required by this section upon such terms as he shall deem to be appropriate.

(d) The secretary of state shall retain from the revenue collected from the fees required by this section a sum sufficient to provide at all times a fund of at least $500, but not more than $1,500, from which he may refund any payment made pursuant to this section to the extent that it exceeds the fees required by this section. The funds shall be deposited in a financial institution which is a legal depository of State of Delaware moneys to the credit of the secretary of state and shall be disbursable on order of the secretary of state.

(e) Except as provided in this section, the fees of the secretary of state shall be as provided in § 2315 of Chapter 29.

[As last amended by S 96, effective August 1, 2007]

§ 18-1106. Reserved power of State of Delaware to alter or repeal chapter.

All provisions of this chapter may be altered from time to time or repealed and all rights of members and managers are subject to this reservation. Unless expressly stated to the contrary in this chapter, all amendments of this chapter shall apply to limited liability companies and members and managers whether or not existing as such at the time of the enactment of any such amendment.

§ 18-1107. Taxation of limited liability companies.

(a) For purposes of any tax imposed by the State of Delaware or any instrumentality, agency or political subdivision of the State of Delaware, a limited liability company formed under this chapter or qualified to do business in the State of Delaware as a foreign limited liability company shall be classified as a partnership unless classified otherwise for federal income tax purposes, in which case the limited liability company shall be classified in the same manner as it is classified for federal income tax purposes. For purposes of any tax imposed by the State of Delaware or any instrumentality, agency or political subdivision of the State of Delaware, a member or an assignee of a member of a limited liability company formed under this chapter or qualified to do business in the State of Delaware as a foreign limited liability company shall be treated as either a resident or nonresident partner unless classified otherwise for federal income tax purposes, in which case the member or assignee of a member shall have the same status as such member or assignee of a member has for federal income tax purposes.

(b) Every domestic limited liability company and every foreign limited liability company registered to do business in the State of Delaware shall pay an annual tax, for the use of the State of Delaware, in the amount of $200.

(c) The annual tax shall be due and payable on the first day of June following the close of the calendar year or upon the cancellation of a certificate of formation. The secretary of state shall receive the annual tax and pay over all taxes collected to the Department of Finance of the State of Delaware. If the annual tax remains unpaid after the due date, the tax shall bear interest at the rate of 1 and one-half percent for each month or portion thereof until fully paid.

(d) The secretary of state shall, at least 60 days prior to the first day of June of each year, cause to be mailed to each domestic limited liability company and each foreign limited liability company required to comply with the provisions of this section in care of its registered agent in the State of Delaware an annual statement for the tax to be paid hereunder.

(e) In the event of neglect, refusal or failure on the part of any domestic limited liability company or foreign limited liability company to pay the annual tax to be paid hereunder on or before the 1st day of June in any year, such domestic limited liability company or foreign limited liability company shall pay the sum of $100 to be recovered by adding that amount to the annual tax and such additional sum shall become a part of the tax and shall be collected in the same manner and subject to the same penalties.

(f) In case any domestic limited liability company or foreign limited liability company shall fail to pay the annual tax due within the time required by this section, and in case the agent in charge of the registered office of any domestic limited liability company or foreign limited liability company upon whom process against such domestic limited liability company or foreign limited liability company may be served shall die, resign, refuse to act as such, remove from the State of Delaware or cannot with due diligence be found, it shall be lawful while default continues to serve process against such domestic limited liability company or foreign limited liability company upon the secretary of state. Such service upon the secretary of state shall be made in the manner and shall have the effect stated in § 18-105 of this title in the case of a domestic limited liability company and § 18-910 of this title in the case of a foreign limited liability company and shall be governed in all respects by said sections.

(g) The annual tax shall be a debt due from a domestic limited liability company or foreign limited liability company to the State of Delaware, for which an action at law may be maintained after the same shall have been in arrears for a period of 1 month. The tax shall also be a preferred debt in the case of insolvency.

(h) A domestic limited liability company or foreign limited liability company that neglects, refuses or fails to pay the annual tax when due shall cease to be in good standing as a domestic limited liability company or registered as a foreign limited liability company in the State of Delaware.

(i) A domestic limited liability company that has ceased to be in good standing or a foreign limited liability company that has ceased to be registered by reason of the failure to pay an annual tax shall be restored to and have the status of a domestic limited liability company in good standing or a foreign limited liability company that is registered in the State of Delaware upon the payment of the annual tax and all penalties and interest thereon for each year for which such domestic limited liability company or foreign limited liability company neglected, refused or failed to pay an annual tax.

(j) The Attorney General, either on his own motion or upon request of the secretary of state, whenever any annual tax due under this chapter from any domestic limited liability company or foreign limited liability company shall have remained in arrears for a period of 3 months after the tax shall have become payable, may apply to the Court of Chancery, by petition in the name of the State of Delaware, on 5 days' notice to such domestic limited liability company or foreign limited liability company, which notice may be served in such manner as the Court may direct, for an injunction to restrain such domestic limited liability company or foreign limited liability company from the transaction of any business within the State of Delaware or elsewhere, until the payment of the annual tax, and all penalties and interest due thereon and the cost of the application which shall be fixed by the Court. The

Court of Chancery may grant the injunction, if a proper case appears, and upon granting and service of the injunction, such domestic limited liability company or foreign limited liability company thereafter shall not transact any business until the injunction shall be dissolved.

(k) A domestic limited liability company that has ceased to be in good standing by reason of its neglect, refusal or failure to pay an annual tax shall remain a domestic limited liability company formed under this chapter. The secretary of state shall not accept for filing any certificate (except a certificate of resignation of a registered agent when a successor registered agent is not being appointed) required or permitted by this chapter to be filed in respect of any domestic limited liability company or foreign limited liability company which has neglected, refused or failed to pay an annual tax, and shall not issue any certificate of good standing with respect to such domestic limited liability company or foreign limited liability company, unless or until such domestic limited liability company or foreign limited liability company shall have been restored to and have the status of a domestic limited liability company in good standing or a foreign limited liability company duly registered in the State of Delaware.

(l) A domestic limited liability company that has ceased to be in good standing or a foreign limited liability company that has ceased to be registered in the State of Delaware by reason of its neglect, refusal or failure to pay an annual tax may not maintain any action, suit or proceeding in any court of the State of Delaware until such domestic limited liability company or foreign limited liability company has been restored to and has the status of a domestic limited liability company or foreign limited liability company in good standing or duly registered in the State of Delaware. An action, suit or proceeding may not be maintained in any court of the State of Delaware by any successor or assignee of such domestic limited liability company or foreign limited liability company on any right, claim or demand arising out the transaction of by such domestic limited liability company after it has ceased to be in good standing or a foreign limited liability company that has ceased to be registered in the State of Delaware until such domestic limited liability company or foreign limited liability company, or any person that has acquired all or substantially all of its assets, has paid any annual tax then due and payable, together with penalties and interest thereon.

(m) The neglect, refusal or failure of a domestic limited liability company or foreign limited liability company to pay an annual tax shall not impair the validity on any contract, deed, mortgage, security interest, lien or act or such domestic limited liability company or foreign limited liability company or prevent such domestic limited liability company or foreign limited liability company from defending any action, suit or proceeding with any court of the State of Delaware.

(n) A member or manager of a domestic limited liability company or foreign limited liability company is not liable for the debts, obligations or liabilities of such domestic limited liability company or foreign limited liability company solely by reason of the neglect, refusal or failure of such domestic limited liability company or foreign limited liability company to pay an annual tax or by reason of such domestic limited liability company or foreign limited liability company ceasing to be in good standing or duly registered.

§ 18-1108. Cancellation of certificate of formation for failure to pay taxes.

(a) The certificate of formation of a domestic limited liability company shall be canceled if the domestic limited liability company shall fail to pay the annual tax due under § 18-1107 of this title for a period of three years from the date it is due, such cancellation to be effective on the third anniversary of such due date.

(b) A list of those domestic limited liability companies whose certificates of formation were canceled on June 1 of such calendar year pursuant to § 18-1108(a) of this title shall be filed in the office of the Secretary of State. On or before October 31 of each calendar year, the Secretary of State shall publish such list on the Internet or on a similar medium for a period of 1 week and shall advertise the website or other address where such list can be accessed in at least 1 newspaper of general circulation in the State of Delaware.

[As last amended by S 96, effective August 1, 2007]

§ 18-1109. Revival of domestic limited liability company.

(a) A domestic limited liability company whose certificate of formation has been canceled pursuant to § 18-104(d) or § 18-104(i)(4) or § 18-1108(a) of this title may be revived by filing in the office of the secretary of state a certificate of revival accompanied by the payment of the fee required by § 18-1105(a)(3) of this title and payment of the annual tax due under § 18-1107 of this chapter and all penalties and interest thereon for each year for which such domestic limited liability company neglected, refused or failed to pay such annual tax, including each year between the cancellation of its certificate of formation and its revival. The certificate of revival shall set forth:

(1) The name of the limited liability company at the time its certificate of formation was canceled and, if such name is not available at the time of revival, the name under which the limited liability company is to be revived;

(2) The date of filing of the original certificate of formation of the limited liability company;

(3) The address of the limited liability company's registered office in the State of Delaware and the name and address of the limited liability company's registered agent in the State of Delaware;

(4) A statement that the certificate of revival is filed by 1 or more persons authorized to execute and file the certificate of revival to revive the limited liability company; and

(5) Any other matters the persons executing the certificate of revival determine to include therein.

(b) The certificate of revival shall be deemed to be an amendment to the certificate of formation of the limited liability company, and the limited liability company shall not be required to take any further action to amend its certificate of formation under § 18-202 of this chapter with respect to the matters set forth in the certificate of revival.

(c) Upon the filing of a certificate of revival, a limited liability company shall be revived with the same force and effect as if its certificate of formation had not been canceled pursuant to § 18-104(d) or § 18-104(i)(4) or § 18-1108(a) of this title. Such revival shall validate all contracts, acts, matters and things made, done and performed by the limited liability company, its members, managers, employees and agents during the time when its certificate of formation was canceled pursuant to § 18-104(d) or § 18-104(i)(4) or § 18-1108(a) of this title, with the same force and effect and to all intents and purposes as if the certificate of formation had remained in full force and effect. All real and personal property, and all rights and interests, which belonged to the limited liability company at the time its certificate of formation was canceled pursuant to § 18-104(d) or § 18-104(i)(4) or § 18-1108(a) of this title or which were acquired by the limited liability company following the cancellation of its certificate of formation pursuant to § 18-104(d) or § 18-104(i)(4) or § 18-1108(a) of this title, and which were not disposed of prior to the time of its revival, shall be vested in the limited liability company after its revival as fully as they were held by the limited liability company at, and after, as the case may be, the time its certificate of formation was canceled pursuant to § 18-104(d) or § 18-104(i)(4) or § 18-1108(a) of this title. After its revival, the limited liability company shall be as exclusively liable for all contracts, acts, matters and things made, done or performed in its name and on its behalf by its members, managers, employees and agents prior to its revival as if its certificate of formation had at all times remained in full force and effect.

[As amended by H 414, effective January 1, 2007.]

Topical Index

References are to paragraph (¶) numbers.

CRE

LIQ

SYN

TAX